Chinese for Foreigners

外国人学汉语

邓少君
张 欣 主编

学汉语

外国人学汉语系列

人民教育出版社

图书在版编目（CIP）数据

外国人学汉语 / 邓少君, 张欣主编 . —北京：人民教育出版社，2007（2019.4 重印）
ISBN 978-7-107-20694-8

Ⅰ. 外… Ⅱ. ①邓… ②张… Ⅲ. 汉语—对外汉语教学—教材 Ⅳ. H195.4

中国版本图书馆 CIP 数据核字（2007）第 149436 号

外国人学汉语

邓少君　张　欣　主编

出　　版	人民教育出版社	
	（北京市海淀区中关村南大街 17 号院 1 号楼　邮编：100081）	
网　　址	http://www.pep.com.cn	
发　　行	上海人教海文图书音像有限公司	
印　　刷	上海龙腾印务有限公司	
版　　次	2007 年 9 月第 1 版	
印　　次	2019 年 4 月第 11 次印刷	
开　　本	787 毫米 ×1 092 毫米　1/16	
印　　张	27.25	
字　　数	545 千字	
印　　数	19 501~21 500 册	
书　　号	ISBN 978-7-107-20694-8	
定　　价	100.00 元	

FOREWORD

This textbook is intended for foreigners and their families who are learning Chinese—especially for those who are living and working in China.

The book is divided into four sections.

Part I Basic Knowledge. This section provides a brief introduction to Chinese phonetics and grammar.

Part II Daily Conversations. This section contains 44 lessons including 44 everyday situations. There are about 20 sentences in each lesson. These sentences are those most frequently used on such occasions, with some offering popular phrases which have appeared in recent years. English translation is offered for each sentence. Learners are expected to read aloud this part as often as possible. Besides these sentences, there are also notes, sentence pattern references, word lists and exercises in this part.

Part III Practical Sentence Patterns. This section contains 225 sentence patterns which are the most basic and practical in the Chinese language. For each sentence pattern, several examples are given and the English translation is provided. It will be a great help for learners to master these commonly used Chinese sentence patterns if they read these example sentences often.

Part IV Reading Column. In this section, 12 short Chinese articles are selected to enable the learners to know more about Chinese culture. These articles include fables, stories from Chinese idioms and mythology, and stories introducing historical figures and traditional Chinese festivals. To enhance the learners' interest, some riddles have been added at the end of this section.

The book emphasizes practicality. It aims to help foreigners master day-to-day Chinese and live more successfully in China.

One CD is included and the texts in part II are read by professional Chinese announcers. The learners are encouraged to use the CD to facilitate their study.

For the errors or infeliticities that may exist in the book, we welcome all comments and suggestions from the users.

The Author
September 2007

前　言

　　本书是为初学汉语的外国人编写的教材。主要适用于来华工作的外国人及他们的家属。

　　全书分四大部分。

　　第一部分基础知识,对汉语语音和语法作简单扼要的说明。

　　第二部分日常会话,有 44 课,设计了 44 个日常生活的情景。每课有大约 20 个句子。这些句子都是该情景中最常用、最实用的句子,其中有近年来出现并流行的词语。每个句子都有英语翻译。希望学习者能多多朗读。此外还有注释、句型提示、词语用法举例、词语和练习。

　　第三部分常用句型,编入了 225 个句型。这些是汉语最基本、最常用的句型。每个句型有几个例句,并有英语翻译。学习者如能反复朗读这些例句,对掌握汉语常用句型一定大有帮助。

　　第四部分阅读专栏,编写了 12 篇短文。有的介绍中国的节日,有的是神话故事、寓言故事、古代人物故事和成语故事,以便学习者了解中国文化。为了增加学习者的学习兴趣,最后还收集了几则谜语。

　　本书注重实用,旨在帮助来华的外国朋友掌握日常口语,顺利地在中国生活。

　　本书配有第二部分课文的朗读 CD 一张。请配合使用。

　　如有疏漏之处,敬请批评指正。

编　者
2007 年 9 月

目　　录

Contents

目录

目录

目录

Chinese for Foreigners

外国人学汉语

Basic Knowledge
基 础 知 识

学汉语

汉语语音（Chinese Phonetics）

音节（Syllable）

一个汉字是一个音节。音节一般由声母、韵母和声调组成。有的音节没有声母。

Each Chinese character has one syllable. A syllable usually consists of an initial, final and tone. Some syllables do not have initials.

音节（Syllable）			
汉字 （Chinese character）	声母 （Initial）	韵母声调 （Tone and final）	
他	t	ā	（he）
爱		ài	（love）
上 海	sh h	àng ǎi	（Shanghai）

声母表（Table of initials）

b 玻	p 坡	m 摸	f 佛
d 得	t 特	n 讷	l 勒
g 哥	k 科	h 喝	
j 基	q 欺	x 希	
zh 知	ch 蚩	sh 诗	r 日
z 资	c 雌	s 思	

韵母表 (Table of finals)

	i 衣	u 乌	ü 迂
a 啊	ia 呀	ua 蛙	
o 喔		uo 窝	
e 鹅	ie 耶		üe 约
ai 哀		uai 歪	
ei 欸		uei 威	
ao 熬	iao 腰		
ou 欧	iou 忧		
an 安	ian 烟	uan 弯	üan 冤
en 恩	in 因	uen 温	ün 晕
ang 昂	iang 央	uang 汪	
eng（亨）	ing 英	ueng 翁	
ong（轰）	iong 雍		

拼写规则 (Spelling rules)

1. i、u、ü 和以 i、u、ü 开头的韵母单独成音节时,应这样拼写:
   When a syllable is formed only by the finals "i", "u", "ü" or by the finals beginning with any of them, the syllable should be written as follows:

i ——→ yi	u ——→ wu	ü ——→ yu
ia ——→ ya	ua ——→ wa	
ie ——→ ye	uo ——→ wo	üe ——→ yue
iao ——→ yao	uai ——→ wai	
iou ——→ you	uei ——→ wei	
ian ——→ yan	uan ——→ wan	üan ——→ yuan
in ——→ yin	uen ——→ wen	ün ——→ yun
iang ——→ yang	uang ——→ wang	
ing ——→ ying	ueng ——→ weng	
iong ——→ yong		

2. ü 在 j、q、x 的后面时，ü 上面的两点省略，写作 ju、qu、xu。

When "ü" is after "j", "q" or "x", the two dots in "ü" should be omitted, and the syllable should be written as "ju", "qu" and "xu".

jü ⟶ ju	qü ⟶ qu	xü ⟶ xu
jüe ⟶ jue	qüe ⟶ que	xüe ⟶ xue
jüan ⟶ juan	qüan ⟶ quan	xüan ⟶ xuan
jün ⟶ jun	qün ⟶ qun	xün ⟶ xun

3. iou、uei、uen 前面加声母成音节时省去 o、e。

When a syllable is formed by "iou", "uei" or "uen" after an initial, the "o" and "e" in the finals should be omitted.

例如：(For example：)

丢 diōu ⟶ diū   对 duèi ⟶ duì   敦 duēn ⟶ dūn

牛 nióu ⟶ niú   归 guēi ⟶ guī   论 luèn ⟶ lùn

声调表 (Table of tones)

名称(Tone)	第一声 (First tone)	第二声 (Second tone)	第三声 (Third tone)	第四声 (Fourth tone)	轻声 (Neutral tone)
符号(Mark)	-	ˊ	ˇ	ˋ	
例字(Example)	妈 mā	麻 má	马 mǎ	骂 mà	吗 ma

轻声发音轻而短，不标声调符号。

The neutral tone is light and short, and has no tone mark.

调值示意图 (Illustration of tones)

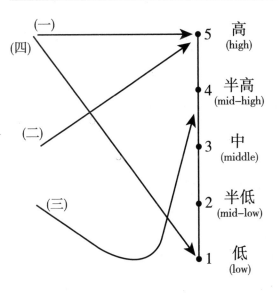

5 高 (high)

4 半高 (mid-high)

3 中 (middle)

2 半低 (mid-low)

1 低 (low)

(一) 第一声(55)　高而平。
1st tone (55)　High and flat.

(二) 第二声(35)　从中(3)升到高(5)。
2nd tone (35)　From middle (3) rises up to high (5).

(三) 第三声(214)　从半低(2)降到低(1)，再升到半高(4)。
3rd tone(214)　From mid - low (2) falls to low (1), and then rises to mid-high (4).

(四) 第四声(51)　从高(5)降到低(1)。
4th tone (51)　From high (5) falls to low (1).

变调规则（Rules of tone changes）

• 第三声变调（Tone change of the third tone）•

1. 两个第三声相连时，前一个第三声变为第二声，但调号不变。
   When a third tone is followed by another third tone, the first tone changes to a second tone, but the tone mark remains unchanged.

$$三声 + 三声 \longrightarrow 二声 + 三声$$

例如：(For example：)

nǐ hǎo ⟶ ní hǎo　　kěyǐ ⟶ kéyǐ　　yǒuhǎo ⟶ yóuhǎo
你　好　　　　　　　　可以　　　　　　友好

2. 第三声在第一声、二声、四声和轻声前面时，变为半三声，就是只读原来第三声的前一半。
   When a third tone follows a tone other than the third tone, the third tone changes to a half-third tone, i.e. only the first half of the third tone is pronounced.

$$三声 + 一声/二声/四声/轻声 \longrightarrow 半三声 + 一声/二声/四声/轻声$$

例如：(For example：)

xiǎodāo　　gǎigé　　bǐjiào　　yǐzi
小刀　　　　改革　　　比较　　　椅子

• "一 yī" 的变调（Tone change of "一 yī"）•

"一"在单用、在词尾和表示序数的时候，念原调 yī。
When "一" is used alone or at the end of a sentence, or used as an ordinal number, it shall be read in its original tone "yī".

1. "一"在第一声、二声、三声前面时，变为第四声。
   When "一" is followed by a first, second or third tone, it changes to the fourth tone.

$$\overset{yī}{一} + 一声/二声/三声 \longrightarrow \overset{yì}{一} + 一声/二声/三声$$

例如：(For example：)

yī tiān ⟶ yì tiān　　yīzhí ⟶ yìzhí　　yī zhǒng ⟶ yì zhǒng
一　天　　　　　　　　一直　　　　　　一　种

2. "一"在第四声前面时，变为第二声。
   When "一" is followed by a fourth tone, it changes to the second tone.

$$\overset{yī}{一} + 四声 \longrightarrow \overset{yí}{一} + 四声$$

例如：(For example：)

yī cì ⟶ yí cì　　yī biàn ⟶ yí biàn　　yīhuìr ⟶ yíhuìr
一　次　　　　　　一　遍　　　　　　一会儿

3. "一"在两个相同的动词之间时变为轻声。
   When "一" is between two identical verbs, it changes to the neutral tone.
   例如：(For example：)

kàn yi kàn　　xiǎng yi xiǎng　　cháng yi cháng
看 一 看　　想 一 想　　尝 一 尝

● "不 bù"的变调(Tone change of "不 bù") ●

1. "不"在第四声前面时变为第二声。
When "不" is located before a fourth tone, it changes to the second tone.

bù　　　　　bú
不 + 四声 ⟶ 不 + 四声

例如：(For example：)

bù yào ⟶ bú yào　　　bù jiàn ⟶ bú jiàn　　　bù shì ⟶ bú shì
不 要　　　 不 要　　　 不 见　　　 不 见　　　 不 是　　　 不 是

2. "不"在两个相同的动词或形容词中间时变为轻声。
When "不" is located between two identical verbs or adjectives, it changes to the neutral tone.

例如：(For example：)

shì bu shì　　hǎo bu hǎo　　qù bu qù
是 不 是　　好 不 好　　去 不 去

3. "不"在动词和补语中间,变为轻声。
When "不" is located between a verb and a complement, it changes to the neutral tone.

例如：(For example：)

tīng bu jiàn　　mǎi bu dào　　chī bu xià
听 不 见　　买 不 到　　吃 不 下

说明：本书"一"和"不"的声调按变调规则标写。
In this book the tones of "一" and "不" are marked in accordance with the rules of tone changes.

韵母 er(Final "er")

韵母 er 不跟声母相拼,总是单独成音节。
The final "er" alone forms a syllable and never follows an initial.

例如：(For example：)

értóng　　dì-èr　　ěrduo
儿童　　第二　　耳朵

儿化韵(Retroflex finals)

韵母 er 有时跟其他韵母结合成儿化韵母。儿化韵母在拼写时要在原韵母的后面加"r"。
The final "er" sometimes can be attached to another final to form a retroflex final. In spelling, an "r" is added to the end of the original final.

zhèr　　huār　　xiǎoháir
这儿　　花儿　　小孩儿

汉语音节表（Syllabary of Chinese）

声母＼韵母	a	o	e	-i	er	ai	ei	ao	ou	an	en	ang	eng	ong	i	ia	iao	ie	iou(-iu)	ian	in	iang	ing	iong	u	ua	uo	uai	uei(-ui)	uan	uen(-un)	uang	ueng	ü	üe	üan	ün
b	ba	bo				bai	bei	bao		ban	ben	bang	beng		bi		biao	bie		bian	bin		bing		bu												
p	pa	po				pai	pei	pao	pou	pan	pen	pang	peng		pi		piao	pie		pian	pin		ping		pu												
m	ma	mo	me			mai	mei	mao	mou	man	men	mang	meng		mi		miao	mie	miu	mian	min		ming		mu												
f	fa	fo					fei		fou	fan	fen	fang	feng												fu												
d	da		de			dai	dei	dao	dou	dan	den	dang	deng	dong	di	dia	diao	die	diu	dian			ding		du		duo		dui	duan	dun						
t	ta		te			tai	tei	tao	tou	tan		tang	teng	tong	ti		tiao	tie		tian			ting		tu		tuo		tui	tuan	tun						
n	na		ne			nai	nei	nao	nou	nan	nen	nang	neng	nong	ni		niao	nie	niu	nian	nin	niang	ning		nu		nuo			nuan				nü	nüe		
l	la	lo	le			lai	lei	lao	lou	lan		lang	leng	long	li	lia	liao	lie	liu	lian	lin	liang	ling		lu		luo			luan	lun			lü	lüe		
g	ga		ge			gai	gei	gao	gou	gan	gen	gang	geng	gong											gu	gua	guo	guai	gui	guan	gun	guang					
k	ka		ke			kai	kei	kao	kou	kan	ken	kang	keng	kong											ku	kua	kuo	kuai	kui	kuan	kun	kuang					
h	ha		he			hai	hei	hao	hou	han	hen	hang	heng	hong											hu	hua	huo	huai	hui	huan	hun	huang					
j															ji	jia	jiao	jie	jiu	jian	jin	jiang	jing	jiong										ju	jue	juan	jun
q															qi	qia	qiao	qie	qiu	qian	qin	qiang	qing	qiong										qu	que	quan	qun
x															xi	xia	xiao	xie	xiu	xian	xin	xiang	xing	xiong										xu	xue	xuan	xun
zh	zha		zhe	zhi		zhai	zhei	zhao	zhou	zhan	zhen	zhang	zheng	zhong											zhu	zhua	zhuo	zhuai	zhui	zhuan	zhun	zhuang					
ch	cha		che	chi		chai		chao	chou	chan	chen	chang	cheng	chong											chu	chua	chuo	chuai	chui	chuan	chun	chuang					
sh	sha		she	shi		shai	shei	shao	shou	shan	shen	shang	sheng												shu	shua	shuo	shuai	shui	shuan	shun	shuang					
r			re	ri				rao	rou	ran	ren	rang	reng	rong											ru	rua	ruo		rui	ruan	run						
z	za		ze	zi		zai	zei	zao	zou	zan	zen	zang	zeng	zong											zu		zuo		zui	zuan	zun						
c	ca		ce	ci		cai		cao	cou	can	cen	cang	ceng	cong											cu		cuo		cui	cuan	cun						
s	sa		se	si		sai		sao	sou	san	sen	sang	seng	song											su		suo		sui	suan	sun						
	a	o	e		er	ai	ei	ao	ou	an	en	ang	eng		yi	ya	yao	ye	you	yan	yin	yang	ying	yong	wu	wa	wo	wai	wei	wan	wen	wang	weng	yu	yue	yuan	yun

汉语词类（Parts of Speech）

词类 Parts of speech		例词 Examples
míngcí 名词（Noun）		guójiā 国家（country）　péngyou 朋友（friend）　shū 书（book） shìqing 事情（thing）　shàngwǔ 上午（morning）　zhuōzi 桌子（table）
dài 代 cí 词（Pronoun）	rénchēngdàicí 人称代词（Personal pronoun）	wǒ 我（I）　nǐ 你（you）　tā 他（he）　tā 她（she）
	zhǐshìdàicí 指示代词（Demonstrative pronoun）	zhè 这（this）　nà 那（that）　zhèr 这儿（here）　nàr 那儿（there）
	yíwèndàicí 疑问代词（Interrogative pronoun）	shuí 谁（who）　shénme 什么（what）　nǎ 哪（which）　nǎr 哪儿（where）
dòngcí 动词（Verb）		kàn 看（look）　qù 去（go）　xǐhuan 喜欢（like） shì 是（is）　yǒu 有（have）　chī 吃（eat）
zhùdòngcí 助动词（Auxiliary verb）		néng 能（can）　huì 会（can） yīnggāi 应该（should）　yào 要（must）
xíngróngcí 形容词（Adjective）		dà 大（big）　xiǎo 小（small）　hǎo 好（good） lěng 冷（cold）　kuài 快（quick）　màn 慢（slow）
shùcí 数词（Numeral）		yī 一（1）　èr 二（2）　bǎi 百（hundred） wàn 万（ten thousand）　líng 零（0）　bàn 半（half）
liàng 量 cí 词（Measure word）	míngliàngcí 名量词（Nominal measure word）	ge 个（a most common used m.w.）　tiáo 条（m.w. for slim things）　běn 本（copy） zhāng 张（m.w. for paper, ticket, table, etc.）　yuán 元（yuan）　kè 克（gram）
	dòngliàngcí 动量词（Verbal measure word）	cì 次（time）　biàn 遍（time）　huí 回（time）

词类 Parts of speech		例词 Examples		
fùcí 副词 (Adverb)		hěn 很（very）　zhēn 真（really）　yòu 又（besides）　hái 还（still） cái 才（used to indicate something has just happened）　dàgài 大概（approximately）		
jiècí 介词 (Preposition)		cóng 从（from）　gēn 跟（used to introduce the object of comparison） duì 对（to）　guānyú 关于（about）　wèi 为（for）　bǐ 比（than）		
liáncí 连词 (Conjunction)		hé 和（and）　huòzhě 或者（or）　nàme 那么（then） ránhòu 然后（afterwards）　dànshì 但是（but）　rúguǒ 如果（if）		
zhù 助 cí 词 (Particle)	jiégòuzhùcí 结构助词 (Structural particle)	de 的	de 得	de 地
	用例 (Example of usage)	wǒ de shū 我的书 (my book)	qǐ de zǎo 起得早 (get up early)	rènzhēn de xuéxí 认真地学习 (study hard)
	dòngtàizhùcí 动态助词 (Aspectual particle)	zhe 着	le 了	guo 过
	用例 (Example of usage)	zuòzhe 坐着 (be seated)	chīle 吃了 (have eaten)	qùguo 去过 (have been to some place)
	yǔqìzhùcí 语气助词 (Modal particle)	ma 吗	ne 呢	ba 吧
	用例 (Example of usage)	Qù ma? 去吗？ (Do you go?)	Shénme ne? 什么呢？ (What?)	Qù ba! 去吧！ (Let's go together.)
tàncí 叹词 (Interjection)		wèi 喂（hello (of greeting)）　āiyā 哎呀（expressing dissatisfaction） à 啊（expressing astonishment or admiration）		
nǐshēngcí 拟声词 (Onomatopoeia)		hāhā 哈哈（used to describe laughter）　pīngpāng 乒乓（used for rattling or clattering sound） hūhū 呼呼（used for the loud sound of wind or something like it）		

词类简称表（Abbreviations of parts of speech）

名词	（名）	noun
专有名词	（专名）	proper noun
代词	（代）	pronoun
动词	（动）	verb
助动词	（助动）	auxiliary verb
形容词	（形）	adjective
数词	（数）	numeral
量词	（量）	measure word
副词	（副）	adverb
介词	（介）	preposition
连词	（连）	conjunction
助词	（助）	particle
叹词	（叹）	interjection
拟声词	（拟声）	onomatopoeia

汉语句子成分（Sentence Elements）

句 子 成 分 (Sentence elements)	例 句 (Examples)
zhǔyǔ 主语 （Subject） 主语是谓语陈述的对象。 Subject is the element which is described by the predicate.	△ Tā qù Běijīng le. 他 去 北京 了。 (He has gone to Beijing.) △ Jīntiān hěn rè. 今天 很 热。 (It is hot today.) △ Zhèli shì jiàoshì. 这里 是 教室。 (Here is a classroom.) △ Huār kāi le. 花儿 开 了。 (The flowers are in bloom.)
wèiyǔ 谓语 （Predicate） 谓语是陈述主语的。 Predicate is the element which tells something about the subject.	△ Tā lái le. 他 来 了。 (He has come yet.) △ Yéye hěn jiànkāng. 爷爷 很 健康。 (Grandfather is very healthy.) △ Wǒ shì jiàoshī. 我 是 教师。 (I am a teacher.) △ Bàba zài gōngsī. 爸爸 在 公司。 (My father is in the company.)
bīnyǔ 宾语 （Object） 宾语表示动作的对象等。 Object is the element affected by the action.	△ Wǒ měi tiān xuéxí Hànyǔ. 我 每 天 学习 汉语。 (I study Chinese every day.) △ Tā qù xuéxiào le. 他 去 学校 了。 (He has gone to the school.) △ Tā xǐhuan lǚyóu. 他 喜欢 旅游。 (He likes traveling.) △ Wǒ sòng tā yì běn cídiǎn. 我 送 他 一 本 词典。 (I gave him a dictionary.)

句 子 成 分 (Sentence elements)	例 句 (Examples)	
dìngyǔ 定语 (Attributive) 定语修饰、限制主语或宾语。 Attributive modifies or restricts the subject or the object.	△ Nǐ de shū zài zhèli. 你 的 书 在 这里。 (Your book is here.) △ Zhè běn shū shì tā de. 这 本 书 是 他 的。 (This book is his.) △ Zhè shì xīn de shū. 这 是 新 的 书。 (This is a new book.) △ Wǒ xǐhuan hóng huā. 我 喜欢 红 花。 (I like red flowers.)	
zhuàngyǔ 状语 (Adverbial) 状语修饰、限制谓语。 Adverbial modifies or restricts the predicate.	△ Wǒ měi tiān liù diǎn qǐchuáng. 我 每 天 六 点 起床。 (I get up at six every day.) △ Tā zài jiàoshì fùxí. 他 在 教室 复习。 (He is reviewing in the classroom.) △ Jīntiān tā bù lái. 今天 他 不 来。 (He would not come today.) △ Tā hěn piàoliang. 她 很 漂亮。 (She is very pretty.)	
bǔyǔ 补语 (Complement) 补语补充说明动词或形容词。 Complement gives additional explanation or description to the verb or adjective.	(Resultant complement) 结果补语	△ Wǎnfàn zuòhǎo le. 晚饭 做好 了。 (The supper is ready.) △ Zhuōzi cā gānjìng le. 桌子 擦 干净 了。 (The table has been wiped clean.) △ Yīfu fàngzài yīguì li. 衣服 放在 衣柜 里。 (The clothes are put in the wardrobe.)
	(Degree complement) 程度补语	△ Tā pǎo de tài màn. 他 跑 得 太 慢。 (He is running too slowly.) △ Yǔ xià de bú dà. 雨 下 得 不 大。 (The rain is not too heavy.) △ Tiānqì hǎojí le. 天气 好极 了。 (The weather is perfect.)

句　子　成　分 (Sentence elements)		例　句 (Examples)
bǔyǔ 补语　(Complement)	可 能 补 语 (Potential complement)	△ Tā de huà wǒ tīng de dǒng. 　他 的 话 我 听 得 <u>懂</u>。 (I understood what he said.) △ Zhè kuài shǒubiǎo xiū de hǎo. 　这 块 手表 修 得 <u>好</u>。 (This watch can be repaired.) △ Shízài chī bu xià le. 　实在 吃 不 <u>下</u> 了。 (I really can't eat any more.)
	数 量 补 语 (Quantitative complement)	△ Wǒ qùle liǎng cì Hángzhōu. 　我 去了 <u>两 次</u> 杭州。 (I have been to Hangzhou twice.) △ Tā bǐ wǒ gāo sān límǐ. 　他 比 我 高 <u>三 厘米</u>。 (He is three centimeters taller than I.) △ Wǒ xuéle sān nián Hànyǔ. 　我 学了 <u>三 年</u> 汉语。 (I've learned Chinese for three years.)
	趋 向 补 语 (Directional complement)	△ Tā mǎilaile yí shù xiānhuā. 　他 <u>买来</u>了 一 束 鲜花。 (He bought a bunch of flowers.) △ Tā ná huilai yì běn zázhì. 　她 拿 <u>回来</u> 一 本 杂志。 (She brought a magazine back.) △ Gàoshi yǐjīng tiē chuqu le. 　告示 已经 贴 <u>出去</u> 了。 (The notice has been posted up.)

汉语语序 (Word Order)

一、在汉语里,语序是非常重要的语法手段。一般是主语在前面,谓语在后面。宾语在动词谓语的后面。

In Chinese, word order is one of the more important grammar factors. Usually the subject precedes the predicate and the object follows the verbal predicate.

主语——谓语——宾语

　　　Wǒ　shì　xuésheng.
△　我　是　学生。　　(I am a student.)

　　　Xiǎo　Lǐ　zài　jiàoshì.
△　小　李　在　教室。　　(Xiao Li is in the classroom.)

　　　Tā　yǒu　gēge.
△　他　有　哥哥。　(He has an elder brother.)

　　　Wǒ　xuéxí　Rìyǔ.
△　我　学习　日语。　(I am learning Japanese.)

　　　Tā　lái　Shànghǎi　le.
△　他　来　上海　了。　　(He has come to Shanghai.)

二、定语一定在主语或宾语的前面。

The attributive always precedes the subject or object.

(定语)——主语——谓语——宾语

　　　　Wǒ　tàitai　shì　jiàoshī.
△　(我)　太太　是　教师。　　(My wife is a teacher.)

　　　Bàba　de　bàngōngshì　zài　nàli.
△　(爸爸)　的　办公室　在　那里。　(My father's office is there.)

　　　Báisè　de　huār　kāi　le.
△　(白色)　的　花儿　开　了。　(The white flowers are in bloom.)

　　　Xīn　de　zázhì　zài　shūjià　shang.
△　(新)　的　杂志　在　书架　上。　(The new magazine is on the bookshelf.)

　　　Nà　běn　shū　diū　le.
△　(那本)　书　丢　了。　(That book was lost.)

主语——谓语——(定语)——宾语

　　　Wǒ　yǒu　Hànyǔ　shū.
△　我　有　(汉语)　书。　　(I have a Chinese book.)

　　　Wǒ　xǐhuan　báisè　de　huār.
△　我　喜欢　(白色)　的　花儿。　(I like white flowers.)

　　　Wǒ　rènshi　nàge　rén.
△　我　认识　(那个)　人。　(I know that person.)

　　　Tā　mǎile　xiǎo　huāpíng.
△　他　买了　(小)　花瓶。　(He bought a small vase.)

　　　Wǒ　kànle　yǒuqù　de　xiǎoshuō.
△　我　看了　(有趣)　的　小说。　(I have read an interesting book.)

三、状语一定在动词谓语或形容词谓语的前面。

The adverbial always precedes the verbal predicate or adjective predicate.

主语——[状语]——谓语——宾语

△ 　Tā　zuótiān　qùle　Nánjīng.
　　他　[昨天]　去了　南京。　　(He went to Nanjing yesterday.)

△ 　Wǒ　hěn　xǐhuan　méihuā.
　　我　[很]　喜欢　梅花。　　(I like plum blossoms very much.)

△ 　Tā　zài　jiàoshì　zuò　zuòyè.
　　他　[在　教室]　做　作业。　　(He is doing the exercises in the classroom.)

△ 　Wǒmen　kuài　zǒu　ba.
　　我们　[快]　走　吧。　　(Let's hurry up.)

△ 　Tā　fēicháng　piàoliang.
　　她　[非常]　漂亮。　　(She is very pretty.)

△ 　Zhèli　zhēn　rènao.
　　这里　[真]　热闹。　　(It is really bustling here.)

△ 　Zhège　bù　hǎochī.
　　这个　[不]　好吃。　　(This one is not tasty.)

四、补语一定在动词谓语或形容词谓语的后面。

The complement always comes after the verbal predicate or adjective predicate.

主语——谓语——〈补语〉——宾语

△ 　Zhuōzi　cā　gānjìng　le.
　　桌子　擦　〈干净〉　了。　　(The desk has been wiped clean.)

△ 　Shū　fàngzài　shūjià　shang.
　　书　放〈在　书架　上〉。　　(The book was put on the bookshelf.)

△ 　Tā　chàng　de　hǎo.
　　他　唱　得　〈好〉。　　(He sang very well.)

△ 　Wǒ　dúle　sì　biàn　kèwén.
　　我　读了　〈四　遍〉　课文。　　(I have read the text four times.)

△ 　Tā　nálaile　bàozhǐ.
　　他　拿〈来〉了　报纸。　　(He brought back the newspaper.)

△ 　Wǒ　lèi　de　yàomìng.
　　我　累　得　〈要命〉。　　(I am dead tired.)

△ 　Wǒ　mángjí　le.
　　我　忙〈极〉　了。　　(I am terribly busy.)

△ 　Tā　piàoliang　jí　le.
　　她　漂亮　〈极〉　了。　　(She is extraordinarily beautiful.)

汉语句子类型(Types of Sentences)

一、按谓语的性质分类,汉语中主语和谓语都有的句子可分为四种:

Sentences with subjects and predicates can be divided into four types according to their predicates:

1. 名词谓语句　　　　　由名词、名词词组或数量词组作谓语的句子叫名词谓语句。

   Sentence with noun predicate　The predicate of this type of sentences is formed using a noun, a noun phrase or a numeral-measure word phrase.

   Jīntiān xīngqīsān.
   △ 今天　星期三。　(Today is Wednesday.)

   Tā Zhōngguórén.
   △ 他　中国人。　(He is Chinese.)

   Míngtiān qíngtiān.
   △ 明天　晴天。　(It will be fine tomorrow.)

   Xiànzài shí diǎn.
   △ 现在　十　点。　(It is ten o'clock now.)

2. 动词谓语句　　　　　由动词作谓语的句子叫动词谓语句。

   Sentence with verbal predicate　The predicate of this type of sentences is formed using a verb.

   Tā bā diǎn chūfā.
   △ 他 八　点　出发。　(He will start off at eight o'clock.)

   Wǒ mǎile shuǐguǒ.
   △ 我　买了　水果。　(I have bought some fruits.)

   Wǒ yǐjīng fùxí le.
   △ 我　已经　复习　了。　(I have reviewed.)

   Tā míngnián bìyè.
   △ 她　明年　毕业。　(She will graduate next year.)

3. 形容词谓语句　　　　由形容词作谓语的句子叫形容词谓语句。

   Sentence with adjective predicate　The predicate of this type of sentences is formed using an adjective.

   Zhège jiàoshì hěn dà.
   △ 这个　教室　很　大。　(This classroom is very big.)

   Zhè xīguā fēicháng tián.
   △ 这　西瓜　非常　甜。　(This watermelon is very sweet.)

   Zhèli hěn gānjìng.
   △ 这里　很　干净。　(It is very clean here.)

   Zhège cài bù hǎochī.
   △ 这个　菜不　好吃。　(This dish is not tasty.)

17

4. 主谓谓语句　　　　　　　由主谓词组作谓语的句子叫主谓谓语句。

Sentence with a sub-　　The predicate of this type of sentences is formed using a subject

ject-predicate phrase　　– predicate phrase.

as predicate

Wǒ tóu téng.
△ 我 头 疼。　（I have a headache.）

Jīntiān tiānqì qínglǎng.
△ 今天 天气 晴朗。　（It is fine today.）

Tā xīnqíng bù hǎo.
△ 他 心情 不 好。　（He is in a bad mood.）

Huáng Shān fēngjǐng yōuměi.
△ 黄 山 风景 优美。　（The scenery of Huangshan Mountain is beautiful.）

二、按语气分类,汉语句子可分为四种:

Sentences can be divided into four types according to their functions:

1. 陈述句　　　　　　　叙述事情或说明看法的句子叫陈述句。句末用句号(。)。

Declarative sentence　A declarative sentence is used to state a thing or a view. A full

stop should be put at the end of the sentence.

Tā shì xuésheng.
△ 他 是 学生。　（He is a student.）

Tā zài jiàoshì xuéxí.
△ 他 在 教室 学习。　（He is studying in the classroom.）

Wǒ bú huì Yīngyǔ.
△ 我 不 会 英语。　（I can't speak English.）

Tā shì ge hǎorén.
△ 他 是 个 好人。　（He is a good man.）

2. 疑问句　　　　　　　提出问题的句子叫疑问句。句末用问号(?)。

Interrogative sentence　An interrogative sentence is used to ask a question. A question

mark should be put at the end of the sentence.

Zhè shì shénme?
△ 这 是 什么?　（What is this?）

Nǐ shì xuésheng ma?
△ 你 是 学生 吗?　（Are you a student?）

Nǐ qù bu qù?
△ 你 去 不 去?　（Will you go or not?）

Nǐ wèi shénme chídào?
△ 你 为 什么 迟到?　（Why are you late?）

3. 祈使句　　　　　　　　　提出要求的句子叫祈使句。句末用句号(。)或感叹号(!)。

   Imperative sentence　　An imperative sentence is used to make a demand or request. A full stop or an exclamation mark should be put at the end of the sentence.

   　　　Qǐng　zuò!
   △　请　　坐!　(Sit down, please.)

   　　　Kuài zǒu!
   △　快　　走!　(Hurry up!)

   　　　Wǒmen　yìqǐ　zǒu ba!
   △　我们　　一起　走　吧!　(Let's go together.)

   　　　Bié　wàngjì　zuò zuòyè.
   △　别　忘记　做　作业。　(Don't forget your exercises.)

4. 感叹句　　　　　　　　　抒发感情的句子叫感叹句。句末用感叹号(!)。

   Exclamatory sentence　Exclamatory sentence is used to express feelings. An exclamation mark should be put at the end of the sentence.

   　　　Zhèli　fēngjǐng　tài měi le!
   △　这里　风景　太　美　了!　(What beautiful scenery here!)

   　　　Jīntiān　zhēn　rè a!
   △　今天　　真　热　啊!　(What a hot day today!)

   　　　Wǒ　lèijí　le!
   △　我　累极　了!　(I am dead tired!)

   　　　Tā　duōme　piàoliang　a!
   △　她　多么　　漂亮　　啊!　(How beautiful she is!)

汉字基本笔画(Basic Strokes of Chinese Characters)

笔画名称 (Stroke name)	笔画及运笔方向 (Stroke and direction)	例 字 (Examples)
点 diǎn	╲	六 主 江 我 兴
横 héng	一 →	二 十 不 木 上
竖 shù	∣ ↓	中 米 忙 下 外
撇 piě	丿 ↙	人 火 丈 个 欠
捺 nà	╲ ↘	八 大 介 及 又
提 tí	╱ ↗	河 打 习 录 次
钩 gōu	⌐ ⌐ ╲ ∪ ∟ → ↓ ↘ ∪ ↳	买 小 找 心 儿
折 zhé	⌐ ∟ ╱ → ∟ ↙	口 日 山 母 么

汉字笔顺规则（ Rules of Stroke-order of Chinese Characters ）

笔顺规则 (Stroke-order rule)	例 字 (Examples)	笔画顺序 (Stroke order)
先横后竖 (横 precedes 竖)	十	一　十
先撇后捺 (撇 precedes 捺)	人	丿　人
从上到下 (From top to bottom)	立	丶　二　亠　立　立
从左到右 (From left to right)	川	丿　川　川
先外后内 (Outside precedes inside)	同	丨　冂　冂　冋　同　同
先外后内再封口 (Outside precedes inside, the sealing stroke is last)	田	丨　冂　日　囲　田
先中间后两边 (Middle precedes the two sides)	小	亅　小　小

说明:汉字的运笔方向一般来说总是从左边、上边开始,到右边、下边结束。但是也有例外的,例如"边、进、延"这类字是从右边开始书写的。又如"戈、我、求"这类字的点(丶)虽然在上面,却是最后才写的。所以除了掌握一般规则以外,还要了解每个字的书写习惯。

Notes：The stroke direction of Chinese characters usually starts from left or top and ends at right or bottom. But there are some exceptions. For words like "边", "进" and "延", the stroke order starts from the right. And for words like "戈", "我" and "求", although "点" (丶) in these characters is found at top, it is the last to be written. Therefore we should know the stroke-order for each character besides the rules of the stroke-order.

Chinese for Foreigners

外国人学汉语

Daily Conversations
日 常 会 话

1 打 招 呼
Dǎ Zhāohu

GREETINGS

Nǐ zǎo!
1. A：你 早！ — Good morning.

Zǎoshang hǎo!
B：早上   好！ — Good morning.

Wǎnshang hǎo!
2. A：晚上   好！ — Good evening.

Nǐ hǎo!
B：你 好注1！ — Good evening.

Wǎn'ān!
3. A：晚安！ — Good night.

(Qǐng) zǎo diǎnr xiūxi.
B：（请） 早 点儿 休息。 — Good night.

Huānyíng!
4. A：欢迎！ — Welcome.

Xièxie.
B：谢谢。 — Thank you.

5. A：您_{注2} 身体 好 吗？
Nín shēntǐ hǎo ma?
How are you?

B：我 很 好，你 呢？
Wǒ hěn hǎo, nǐ ne?
I am fine. How about you?

A：我 也 很 好，谢谢。
Wǒ yě hěn hǎo, xièxie.
I am fine too. Thanks.

B：你 先生 身体 好 吗？
Nǐ xiānsheng shēntǐ hǎo ma?
How is your husband?

A：他 还 可以。谢谢。
Tā hái kěyǐ. Xièxie.
He is OK. Thank you.

B：最近 忙 吗？
Zuìjìn máng ma?
Are you busy these days?

A：很 忙。你 呢？
Hěn máng. Nǐ ne?
Yes, very busy. How about you?

B：（我）不 太 忙。
Wǒ bú tài máng.
Not too busy.

6. A：好久 没 见面 了。
Hǎojiǔ méi jiànmiàn le.
Long time no see.

B：是 的，好久 不 见 了。
Shì de, hǎojiǔ bú jiàn le.
Yes, we haven't seen each other for a long time.

A：最近 去 哪里 了？
Zuìjìn qù nǎli le?
Where have you been recently?

B：去 北京 出差 了。
Qù Běijīng chūchāi le.
I've been to Beijing on business.

A：向 你 太太 问 好。
Xiàng nǐ tàitai wèn hǎo.
Please give my regards to your wife.

B：我 也 向 你 先生 问 好。
Wǒ yě xiàng nǐ xiānsheng wèn hǎo.
Give mine to your husband too.

A：再见。
Zàijiàn.
Good-bye.

B：再会。
Zàihuì.
Good-bye.

7. A：明天 见。
Míngtiān jiàn.
See you tomorrow.

B：Bāi bai.
Bye.

8. A:
Nàme, huí(tóu) jiàn.
那么，回（头）见。　　　　　Then, see you later.

B:
Yíhuìr jiàn.
一会儿 见。　　　　　　　See you later.

☆ 注 释（Notes） ☆

1. "你好"是常用的问候语，什么时候都可以用。回答时也说"你好"。
   "你好" is a common greeting and can be used anytime when people meet each other. The answer for "你好" is also "你好".

2. "您"是"你"的敬语。
   "您" is an honorific of "你".

☆ 句型提示（Sentence pattern references） ☆

1. 您身体好吗？　　　　　　　请参看 293 页句型 1。
2. 我很好，你呢？　　　　　　请参看 315 页句型 48。
3. 最近去哪里了？　　　　　　请参看 296 页句型 8。
4. 去北京出差了。　　　　　　请参看 312 页句型 41。
5. 向你太太问好。　　　　　　请参看 361 页句型 151。

☆ 词语用法举例（Examples for usage of the words） ☆

1. 好久没见面了
   Wǒ hǎojiǔ méi qù Nánjīng Lù le.
   (1) 我 好久 没 去 南京 路 了。

   Wǒ hǎojiǔ méi chī Zhōngguócài le.
   (2) 我 好久 没 吃 中国菜 了。 （中国菜：Chinese food）

   Bǐ'ěr lái Shànghǎi hǎojiǔ le.
   (3) 比尔 来 上海 好久 了。

   Tā chūqu hǎojiǔ le.
   (4) 他 出去 好久 了。 （出去：go out）

2. 向你太太问好
   Tā xiàng wàiguó péngyou jièshào xuéxiào de qíngkuàng.
   (1) 他 向 外国 朋友 介绍 学校 的 情况。 （介绍：introduce）

   Tā xiàng lǎoshī shuōmíng chídào de yuányīn.
   (2) 他 向 老师 说明 迟到 的 原因。 （迟到：be late）

   Wǒ xiàng tā shuōle duìbuqǐ.
   (3) 我 向 他 说了 对不起。 （对不起：sorry）

   Wǒ xiàng Xiǎo Wáng dàoqiàn le.
   (4) 我 向 小 王 道歉 了。 （道歉：apologize）

27

3．一会儿见

          Yíhuìr wǒ zài lái.
（1）一会儿　我　再　来。（再：again）

          Yíhuìr wǒ gàosu nǐ.
（2）一会儿　我　告诉　你。（告诉：tell）

          Yíhuìr wǒ chūqu.
（3）一会儿　我　出去。

          Yíhuìr wǒ gěi nǐ.
（4）一会儿　我　给　你。（给：give）

☆　词　语（Word list）　☆

1.	wǒ 我	（代）	I,me	2.	nǐ 你	（代）	you
3.	nín 您	（代）	you（respectful form of 你)	4.	tā 他	（代）	he,him
5.	tā 她	（代）	she,her	6.	zǎo 早	（形）	early
7.	diǎnr 点儿	（量）	a little,a bit	8.	xiūxi 休息	（动）	rest
9.	hěn 很	（副）	very	10.	máng 忙	（形）	busy
11.	jiànmiàn 见面	（动）	meet each other	12.	zhèli /zhèr 这里/这儿	（代）	here
13.	nàli /nàr 那里/那儿	（代）	there	14.	nǎli /nǎr 哪里/哪儿	（代）	where
15.	chūchāi 出差	（动）	be on a business trip	16.	qù 去	（动）	go

☆　练　习（Exercises）　☆

一、完成对话（Complete the conversations）

1．A：你父母（fùmǔ/parents）身体好吗？

    B：＿＿＿＿＿＿＿＿＿＿＿＿。

2．A：好久没见面了，你去哪里了？

    B：＿＿＿＿＿＿＿＿＿＿＿＿。

3．A：你最近忙吗？

    B：＿＿＿＿＿＿＿＿＿＿＿＿。

4．A：＿＿＿＿＿＿＿＿＿＿＿＿？

    B：他出差了。

二、把下列句子改成疑问句（Change the following sentences into questions）

1．他工作很忙。

2．她先生出差了。

3．他身体很好。

4．贝克(Bèikè)先生回(huí/return)英国(Yīngguó)了。

三、替换练习（Substitution exercises）

1．他去北京出差了。 　　　西安(Xī'ān) 　　　旅游(lǚyóu/tour)

　　　　　　　　　　　　广州(Guǎngzhōu) 　工作(gōngzuò/work)

　　　　　　　　　　　　北京大学(dàxué) 　学习(xuéxí/study)

　　　　　　　　　　　　英国(Yīngguó) 　　留学(liúxué/study abroad)

2．向你太太问好 　　　你先生

　　　　　　　　　你父母

　　　　　　　　　周(Zhōu)先生

四、会话（Conversation）

大卫·布朗：小刘(Xiǎo Liú)，你好！

刘　明　村：早！布朗(Bùlǎng)先生。你好久没来这里了，出差了吗？

大卫·布朗：不，去桂林(Guìlín)旅游了。你呢？

刘　明　村：我很忙，没去旅游。你太太也去桂林了吗？

大卫·布朗：是的。

刘　明　村：你太太好吗？

大卫·布朗：她很好。你父母身体好吗？

刘　明　村：很好，谢谢。请向你太太问好。

大卫·布朗：谢谢。

刘　明　村：再见。

大卫·布朗：再见。

☆　　**练习答案**(Key to the exercises)　　☆

一、1．很好，谢谢

　　2．我去北京出差了

　　3．很忙

　　4．你先生去哪里了

二、1．他工作忙吗？

　　2．她先生出差了吗？

　　3．他身体好吗？

　　4．贝克先生回英国了吗？

2　Xìngmíng
姓名 注1

NAME

1. A: Nín guì xìng?
   您 贵 姓？　　　May I know your surname?

   B: Miǎn guì, xìng Zhāng.
   免 贵， 姓 张。　　My surname is Zhang.

2. A: Nǐ xìng shénme?
   你 姓 什么？　　　What is your surname?

   B: Wǒ xìng Wáng.
   我 姓 王。　　　　My surname is Wang.

3. A: Nǐ jiào shénme míngzi?
   你 叫 什么 名字？　What is your name?

   B: Wǒ jiào Zhāng Xiǎoyīng.
   我 叫 张 晓英。　　My name is Zhang Xiaoying.

4. A: Nǐ de péngyou jiào shénme
   你 的 朋友 叫 什么　What is your friend's name?

   míngzi?
   名字？

   B: Tā jiào Chén Jiànguó.
   他 叫 陈 建国。　　His name is Chen Jianguo.

5. A: Nà wèi xiānsheng shì shuí?
　　那[注2]位 先生 是 谁? —— Who is that gentleman?

　 B: Tā shì Xīnghuá Gōngsī de Zhōu
　　他是 兴华 公司 的 周 —— He is Mr. Zhou Sirong of Xinghua Company.

　　Sīróng xiānsheng.
　　思荣 先生。

6. A: Nǎ wèi shì Lǐ Míng lǎoshī?
　　哪 位 是 李 明 老师? —— Who is Teacher Li Ming?

　 B: Zuòzhe nà wèi jiù shì.
　　坐着 那 位 就 是[注3]。 —— That gentleman sitting there.

7. A: Nín shì Wáng tàitai ma?
　　您 是 王 太太 吗? —— Are you Mrs. Wang?

　 B: Bù, wǒ xiānsheng xìng Huáng.
　　不，我 先生 姓 黄。 —— No, my husband's surname is Huang.

　 A: Duìbuqǐ.
　　对不起。 —— I am sorry.

　 B: Méi guānxi.
　　没 关系。 —— No problem.

8. A: Nǐ rènshi Bèikè tàitai ma?
　　你 认识 贝克 太太 吗? —— Do you know Mrs. Baker?

　 B: Rènshi, tā shì wǒ de línjū.
　　认识，她 是 我 的 邻居。 —— Yes. She is my neighbor.

　 A: Nǐ rènshi Kē'ēn xiānsheng ma?
　　你 认识 科恩 先生 吗? —— Do you know Mr. Cohen?

　 B: Zǎo jiù rènshi le. Tā shì wǒ
　　早 就 认识 了。他 是 我 —— Yes, I have known him for a long time. He is

　　de hǎo péngyou.
　　的 好 朋友。 —— my good friend.

　 A: Nǐ rènshi zhège xuéxiào de
　　你 认识 这个 学校 的 —— Do you know the principal of this school?

　　xiàozhǎng ma?
　　校长 吗?

　 B: Bú rènshi. Méi jiànguo miàn.
　　不 认识。没 见过 面。 —— No, I've never met him.

☆ 注 释(Notes) ☆

1. 中国人的姓在前，名在后。单姓多，复姓少。单名、双名都有。

   In Chinese the surname comes first and the given name follows the surname. Most surnames have only one Chinese character; a few of surnames have two characters. Given

names may consist of one or two characters.

2．"这、那、哪"有两种读音：zhè/zhèi、nà/nèi、nǎ/něi。口语常读 zhèi、nèi、něi。

"这"，"那" and "哪" have two pronunciations：zhè/zhèi, nà/nèi and nǎ/něi. In spoken language they are usually pronounced as zhèi, nèi and něi respectively.

3．"就"在这里加强肯定语气。"就是"的后面省略了"李明老师"。

"就" is used here to emphasize an affirmative tone. "李明老师" is omitted after "就是".

☆　句型提示（Sentence pattern references）　☆

1．他是兴华公司的周思荣先生。　　　请参看 304 页句型 21、22。
2．坐着那位就是。　　　　　　　　　请参看 308 页句型 34。
3．早就认识了。　　　　　　　　　　请参看 379 页句型 193。
4．没见过面。　　　　　　　　　　　请参看 310 页句型 37。

☆　词语用法举例（Examples for usage of the words）　☆

1．没关系

（1）A：麻烦你了。（Máfan nǐ le.）（Sorry for giving you trouble.）

　　B：没关系。（Méi guānxi.）

（2）A：打扰您了。（Dǎrǎo nín le.）（Sorry for disturbing you.）

　　B：没关系。（Méi guānxi.）

（3）A：下雨了。（Xià yǔ le.）（下：fall）

　　B：没关系，我有伞。（Méi guānxi, wǒ yǒu sǎn.）（伞：umbrella）

（4）A：你感冒了，能去吗？（Nǐ gǎnmào le, néng qù ma?）（感冒：catch cold　能：can）

　　B：没关系，能去。（Méi guānxi, néng qù.）

2．你认识贝克太太吗

（1）你认识坐着的那个人吗？（Nǐ rènshi zuòzhe de nàge rén ma?）

（2）我认识你的邻居。（Wǒ rènshi nǐ de línjū.）

（3）我不认识去豫园的路。（Wǒ bú rènshi qù Yùyuán de lù.）（路：way）

（4）我不认识这个汉字。（Wǒ bú rènshi zhège Hànzì.）（汉字：Chinese character）

☆　词　语（Word list）　☆

1. 先生 xiānsheng （名）mister（Mr.）; gentleman; husband
2. 同志 tóngzhì （名）comrade
3. 师傅 shīfu （名）master, skilled worker
4. 夫人 fūren （名）wife, Mrs.
5. 太太 tàitai （名）wife, Mrs.
6. 女士 nǚshì （名）lady, Ms.
7. 小姐 xiǎojie （名）Miss
8. 医生 yīshēng （名）doctor
9. 司机 sījī （名）driver
10. 学生 xuésheng （名）student
11. 同学 tóngxué （名）schoolmate
12. 同事 tóngshì （名）colleague
13. 这位 zhè wèi （代）this（person）
14. 这个 zhège （代）this
15. 那位 nà wèi （代）that（person）
16. 那个 nàge （代）that
17. 哪位 nǎ wèi （代）who, which one
18. 哪个 nǎge （代）which, who
19. 谁 shuí/shéi （代）who, whom
20. 男人 nánrén （名）man
21. 女人 nǚrén （名）woman
22. 老人 lǎorén （名）old man/woman, the aged
23. 年轻人 niánqīngrén （名）young people
24. 孩子 háizi （名）child
25. 男孩 nánhái （名）boy
26. 女孩 nǚhái （名）girl

☆　练　习（Exercises）　☆

一、替换练习（Substitution exercises）

1. 这是我的<u>邻居</u> <u>布朗太太</u>。

女朋友　　李丽平(Lǐ Lìpíng)
太太　　　良子(Liángzǐ)
同事　　　中村(Zhōngcūn)
老师　　　马天齐(Mǎ Tiānqí)

2. 你认识<u>布朗太太</u>吗?

王东(Wáng Dōng)
坐着的那个人
她的先生
你的邻居

3. <u>坐着那位</u>就是李明老师。

站(zhàn/stand)着那位
拿(ná/carry)着包(bāo/bag)那位
带(dài/accompany)着孩子那位

看（kàn/read）着书（shū/book）那位

二、对下列画线部分提问（Form questions for the following underlined part）

1. 我姓李，叫丽平。

2. 那个人是马天齐的同学。

3. 那位是司机。

4. 我们公司的司机姓高（Gāo）。

三、回答问题（Answer the following questions）

1. 你叫什么名字？

2. 你的汉语老师是谁？

3. 你的邻居姓什么？

4. 你认识你先生的同事吗？

四、会话（Conversation）

玛　丽：你好。我是玛丽·布朗（Mǎlì·Bùlǎng），美国（Měiguó）人。

于雪来：你好，布朗太太。我叫于雪来（Yú Xuělái）。这是我的儿子（érzi/son）。

玛　丽：你好。你叫什么名字？

明　明：我叫郭明明（Guō Míngming）。

玛　丽：妈妈姓于，儿子姓郭？

于雪来：我的先生姓郭。中国女人结婚（jiéhūn/marry）后（hòu/after）不改（gǎi/change）姓。

☆　**练习答案**（Key to the exercises）　☆

二、1. 你姓什么？叫什么名字？

2. 那个人是谁？

3. 哪位是司机？

4. 你们公司的司机姓什么？

3 Jièshào
介绍

INTRODUCTION

1. A: Wǒ gěi nǐmen jièshào yíxià.
我 给 你们 介绍 一下 注1。   Let me introduce to you.

Zhè wèi shì Gélín xiānsheng.
这 位 是 格林 先生。   This is Mr. Green.

Zhè wèi shì Lǐ Yīng xiǎojie.
这 位 是 李 英 小姐。   This is Miss Li Ying.

B: Zhè shì wǒ de míngpiàn.
这 是 我 的 名片。   This is my business card.

C: Rènshi nǐ, hěn gāoxìng.
认识 你, 很 高兴。   Glad to meet you.

B: Wǒ yě hěn gāoxìng.
我 也 很 高兴。   Glad to meet you too.

C: Qǐng duō bāngzhù.
请 多 帮助。   Hope to have your help.

B: Yě qǐng nín duō guānzhào.
也 请 您 多 关照。   Me too.

A: Gélín xiānsheng shì Měiguó
格林 先生 是 美国   Mr. Green is the Sales Manager of Baker

Bèikè Gōngsī de xiāoshòubù
贝克 公司 的 销售部   Co., USA.

zhǔrèn.
主任。

Lǐ Yīng xiǎojie shì Shànghǎi
李 英 小姐 是 上海　　　Miss Li Ying is the Public Relations Manager

Dàhuá Gōngsī de gōngguānbù
大华 公司 的 公关部　　　of Dahua Company.

zhǔrèn.
主任。

2. A: Wǒ lái jièshào yíxià.
我 来 注2 介绍 一下。　　Let me introduce.

Zhè wèi shì Zhāng tàitai. Tā
这 位 是 张 太太。她　This is Mrs. Zhang. Her husband is a doctor

de xiānsheng zài Huàshān Yīyuàn
的 先生 在 华山 医院　working at Huashan Hospital.

gōngzuò, shì yīshēng.
工作， 是 医生。

Zhè wèi shì Dài'ěr tàitai. Tā
这 位 是 戴尔 太太。她　This is Mrs. Dale. Her husband is working in

de xiānsheng zài Luódé Gōngsī
的 先生 在 罗德 公司　Rohde Company. He is the Sales Manager

gōngzuò, shì xiāoshòu kēzhǎng.
工作， 是 销售 科长。　there.

B: Jiàndào nǐ hěn gāoxìng.
见到 你 很 高兴。　　Nice to meet you.

C: Wǒ gāng dào Shànghǎi, qǐng
我 刚 到 上海， 请　I came to Shanghai just now. I may need your

duō guānzhào.
多 关照。　　　　　　help.

B: Yǒu shénme yào bāngmáng de,
有 什么 要 帮忙 的，　Please feel free to let me know if you need

qǐng shuō yì shēng, bié
请 说 一 声， 别　help.

kèqi.
客气。

3. A: Gébì de Shǐmìsī xiānsheng
隔壁 的 史密斯 先生　What is the nationality of Mr. Smith, the man

shì nǎ guó rén?
是 哪 国 人?　　　　next to us?

B: Shì Yīngguórén.
是 英国人。　　　　　He is British.

Tā cóng nǎli lái?
A：他 从 哪里 来？　　　　　Where did he come from?

Tā cóng Lúndūn lái.
B：他 从 伦敦 来。　　　　　He came from London.

Tā de tàitai yě shì
A：他 的 太太 也 是　　　　　Is his wife also British?

Yīngguórén ma?
英国人 吗？

Bù, tā shì Měiguórén.
B：不，她 是 美国人。　　　　No, she is American.

☆ 注 释（Notes） ☆

1. 这里的"一下"在动词后面表示动作短促。如：看一下、听一下、考虑一下。

   "一下" after a verb indicates that the action is short. For example "看一下"（take a look），"听一下"（listen for a short while），"考虑一下"（think for a moment）.

2. "来"在动词前面表示要做某件事。"我来介绍一下"和"我介绍一下"意思一样。

   "来" before a verb is to express "going to do something". "我来介绍一下" and "我介绍一下" have the same meaning.

☆ 句型提示（Sentence pattern references） ☆

1. 我给你们介绍一下。　　　　　请参看 321 页句型 60。
2. 我给你们介绍一下。　　　　　请参看 314 页句型 45。
3. 请多帮助。　　　　　　　　　请参看 391 页句型 216。
4. 她的先生在华山医院工作。　　请参看 305 页句型 25。
5. 他从伦敦来。　　　　　　　　请参看 356 页句型 139。

☆ 词语用法举例（Examples for usage of the words） ☆

1. 我也很高兴

   Tā tàitai yě shì jiàoshī.
   （1）他 太太 也 是 教师。　　（教师：teacher）

   Xiǎo Lǐ yě shì Běijīngrén.
   （2）小 李 也 是 北京人。

   Wǒ yě hěn máng.
   （3）我 也 很 忙。

   Xīméng yě qù Guǎngzhōu.
   （4）西蒙 也 去 广州。

2. 我刚到上海。

Tā gāng qù Hángzhōu.
(1) 他　刚　去　杭州。

Xiǎo Chén gāng jiéhūn.
(2) 小　陈　刚　结婚。

Tāmen gāng rènshi.
(3) 他们　刚　认识。

Huìyì gāng kāishǐ.
(4) 会议　刚　开始。（会议:meeting　开始:start）

3. 有什么要帮忙的

Yǒu shénme hǎochī de?
(1) 有　什么　好吃　的?　（好吃:delicious）

Yǒu shénme hǎowán de?
(2) 有　什么　好玩　的?　（好玩:amusing, interesting）

Yǒu shénme wèntí?
(3) 有　什么　问题?　（问题:question）

Jīntiān yǒu shénme kèren lái?
(4) 今天　有　什么　客人　来?

☆　词　语（Word list）　☆

1.	zìwǒ jièshào 自我 介绍		introduce oneself	2.	hùxiāng jièshào 互相 介绍	introduce each other
3.	fùzérén 负责人	（名）	person in charge	4.	jīnglǐ 经理 （名）	manager
5.	zhíyuán 职员	（名）	office staff	6.	fānyì 翻译 （名/动）	interpreter; interpret
7.	yuànzhǎng 院长	（名）	president	8.	xiàozhǎng 校长 （名）	president, principal
9.	jiàodǎo zhǔrèn 教导 主任	（名）	dean of studies	10.	xuéyuàn 学院 （名）	college
11.	dàxué 大学	（名）	university	12.	zhōngxué 中学 （名）	middle school, secondary school
13.	xiǎoxué 小学	（名）	primary school	14.	gōngsī 公司 （名）	company
15.	gōngchǎng 工厂	（名）	factory	16.	bànshìchù 办事处 （名）	office
17.	bàngōngshì 办公室	（名）	office	18.	Jiānádà 加拿大 （专名）	Canada
19.	Fǎguó 法国	（专名）	France	20.	Déguó 德国 （专名）	Germany
21.	Xībānyá 西班牙	（专名）	Spain	22.	Yìdàlì 意大利 （专名）	Italy
23.	Hélán 荷兰	（专名）	Netherlands	24.	Hánguó 韩国 （专名）	South Korea, Republic of Korea
25.	Cháoxiǎn 朝鲜	（专名）	Korea; Democratic People's Republic of Korea	26.	Tàiguó 泰国 （专名）	Thailand

27. 新加坡 （专名） Singapore   *Xīnjiāpō*

28. 俄罗斯 （专名） Russia   *Éluósī*

29. 澳大利亚 （专名） Australia   *Àodàlìyà*

30. 日本 （专名） Japan   *Rìběn*

☆ 练 习(Exercises) ☆

一、替换练习(Substitution exercises)

他是贝克公司的销售部主任。

李先生	翻译
李舒(Lǐ Shū)先生	公司的经理
这个美国人	我先生的同事
我妹妹	大华公司的职员
她	我家的保姆(bǎomǔ/house-keeper)

二、完成对话(Complete the conversations)

1. A：＿＿＿＿＿＿＿＿＿＿＿＿＿，这位是刘一生(Liú Yīshēng)，他是＿＿＿＿＿＿＿＿＿＿＿＿＿。

    B：＿＿＿＿＿＿＿＿＿＿＿＿＿，这是我的名片。

2. A：你好，我找这里的经理。

    B：＿＿＿＿＿＿＿＿＿＿＿＿＿。

3. A：你在哪里工作？

    B：＿＿＿＿＿＿＿＿＿＿＿＿＿。

4. A：＿＿＿＿＿＿＿＿＿＿＿＿＿？

    B：我是加拿大人。

三、会话(Conversations)

大　卫：玛丽！

玛　丽：什么事？

大　卫：这位是我们的司机小林(Xiǎo Lín)。这是我的太太玛丽。

林立强：布朗太太，您好。

玛　丽：你好，小林师傅。

大　卫：小林是上海人。

玛　丽：我刚来上海，请你多帮助。

林立强：好的。有什么要帮忙的，请告诉我，别客气。

玛　丽：谢谢。

玛　丽：我来介绍，这位是小于，于……

于雪来：于雪来。我是你们的邻居。

大　卫：你好。

玛　　丽：这是我先生,他叫大卫(Dàwèi)。

于雪来：布朗先生,你好。

玛　　丽：她的先生姓郭。他们有一个儿子。

大　　卫：郭先生在哪里工作?

于雪来：他是律师(lǜshī/lawyer),在律师事务所(shìwùsuǒ/office)工作。

大　　卫：我太太刚来上海,请你多多帮助她。谢谢。

于雪来：别客气。

☆　**练习答案**(Key to the exercises)　☆

二、1. A：我来介绍一下　北方(Běifāng)中学的老师

　　　　B：你好

　　2. B：我就是

　　3. B：我在华山医院工作

　　4. A：你是哪国人

4 时间 Shíjiān　　　　TIME

1. A：Xiànzài jǐ diǎn?
现在 几 点?　　　　What is the time?

B：Jiǔ diǎn.
· 九 点。　　　　Nine o'clock.

Jiǔ diǎn guò wǔ fēn.
· 九 点 过 五 分。　　　　Five past nine.

Chà shí fēn liù diǎn.
· 差 十 分 六 点。　　　　Ten to six.

Qī diǎn yí kè.
· 七 点 一 刻。　　　　A quarter past seven.

Wǔ diǎn sān kè.
· 五 点 三 刻。　　　　A quarter to six.

Liǎng diǎn bàn.
· 两 点 半。　　　　Half past two.

2. A：Xiànzài jǐ diǎn le?
现在 几 点 了?　　　　What time is it now?

B：Xiànzài shíyī diǎn le.
现在 十一 点 了。　　　　It's eleven o'clock already.

3. A：
Xuéxiào shàngwǔ jǐ diǎn shàngkè?
学校 上午 几 点 上课？
What time do the classes begin in the morning?

B：
Bā diǎn.
八 点。
Eight o'clock.

A：
Xuéxiào xiàwǔ jǐ diǎn fàngxué?
学校 下午 几 点 放学？
What time does the school close in the afternoon?

B：
Sì diǎn bàn.
四 点 半。
Half past four.

4. A：
Huìyì jǐ diǎn kāishǐ?
会议 几 点 开始？
What time will the meeting start?

B：
Shàngwǔ jiǔ diǎn bàn (kāishǐ).
上午 九 点 半 （开始）。
(It will start at) Half past nine in the morning.

A：
Zhège huì(yì) yào kāi duō jiǔ?
这个 会（议） 要 开 多 久？
How long would the meeting last?

B：
(Yào kāi) liǎng ge xiǎoshí.
（要 开） 两 注1 个 小时。
(It will last) Two hours.

5. A：
Cóng zhèli dào chēzhàn yào zǒu duō cháng shíjiān?
从 这里 到 车站 要 走 多 长 时间？
How long would it take to the bus stop on foot?

B：
(Yào) èrshí fēnzhōng zuǒyòu.
（要） 二十 分钟 左右。
(It takes) About 20 minutes.

6. A：
Nǐ xiānsheng chūchāi yào qù jǐ tiān?
你 先生 出差 要 去 几天？
How many days will your husband be away on business?

B：
Qù sì-wǔ tiān ba.
去 四五 天 吧。
Maybe four or five days.

7. A：
Nǐ lái Shànghǎi duō jiǔ le?
你 来 上海 多 久 了？
How long have you been in Shanghai?

B：
Láile yì nián líng sān ge yuè le.
来了 一 年 零 三 个 月 了。
(I've been here for) One year and three months already.

8. A：
Nǐ dǎsuan zài Xiānggǎng dāi jǐ ge xīngqī?
你 打算 在 香港 待 注2 几 个 星期？
How many weeks will you stay in Hong Kong?

B：
(Wǒ dǎsuan dāi) sān ge xīngqī.
（我 打算 待） 三 个 星期。
(I am going to stay for) Three weeks.

☆ 注 释(Notes) ☆

1. "两"和"二"都表示数词"2",但用法有些不同。
   (1) 量词前一般用"两",不用"二"。例如"两个小时"、"两个人"不说"二个小时"、"二个人"。
   (2) 序数用"二",不用"两"。"第二"不说"第两"。
   (3) 个位数和十位数用"二",不用"两"。例如"十二"、"二十"。
   (4) "百"前一般用"二",也可用"两";"千、万"前多用"两"。
   "两" and "二" both indicate numeral "2". But they have different usage.
   (1) We usually use "两", not "二", before a measure word. For example, we should say "两个小时" and "两个人", not "二个小时" and "二个人".
   (2) Use "二", not "两", for ordinal number. For example, we should say "第二", not "第两".
   (3) For one-digit number and two-digit number, use "二", not "两". For example, "十二" and "二十".
   (4) Before "百", we usually use "二" and sometimes use "两". Before "千" and "万", "两" is always used.

2. "待"是口语,书面语是"逗留"。
   "待" is used in spoken Chinese and "逗留" shall be used in written Chinese.

☆ 句型提示(Sentence pattern references) ☆

1. 现在几点? 请参见 297 页句型 10。
2. 现在几点了? 请参看 380 页句型 195。
3. 从这里到车站要走多长时间? 请参看 356 页句型 141。
4. 你先生出差要去几天?
   你打算在香港待几个星期? 请参看 298 页句型 11。
5. 来了一年零三个月了。 请参看 350 页句型 128。
6. 来了一年零三个月了。 请参看 309 页句型 36。

☆ 词语用法举例(Examples for usage of the words) ☆

1. 这个会(议)要开多久
   Qù gōngsī yào zǒu èrshí fēnzhōng.
   (1) 去 公司 要 走 二十 分钟。
   Qù Hángzhōu yào liǎng ge xiǎoshí.
   (2) 去 杭州 要 两 个 小时。
   Jìdào Rìběn de xìn yào qī tiān.
   (3) 寄到 日本 的 信 要 七 天。 (寄到日本的信:a letter to Japan)

Diànfèi yào liǎngbǎi kuài.
(4) 电费 要 两百 块。 (电费:charge for electricity)

2. 去四五天吧

Tā chūchāi yǐjīng qī-bā tiān le.
(1) 他 出差 已经 七八 天 了。 (已经:already)

Xiǎo Zhōu chūqu liǎng-sān ge xiǎoshí le.
(2) 小 周 出去 两三 个 小时 了。

Tā zài Měiguó zhùle sān-sì nián.
(3) 他 在 美国 住了 三四 年。 (住:live)

Wǔ-liù ge yuè qián tā qù Rìběn le.
(4) 五六 个 月 前 他 去 日本 了。

3. 你打算在香港待几个星期

Wǒ dǎsuan míngnián qù Měiguó.
(1) 我 打算 明年 去 美国。

Lǐ Guófēng dǎsuan zhège yuè mǎi fángzi.
(2) 李 国峰 打算 这个 月 买 房子。 (买:buy 房子:house)

Zhāng Qīng dǎsuan xià ge yuè jiéhūn.
(3) 张 清 打算 下 个 月 结婚。 (下个月:next month)

Tā dǎsuan qù Fǎguó liúxué.
(4) 他 打算 去 法国 留学。

☆ 词 语 (Word list) ☆

1. 一(1) (数) one
2. 二(2) (数) two
3. 三(3) (数) three
4. 四(4) (数) four
5. 五(5) (数) five
6. 六(6) (数) six
7. 七(7) (数) seven
8. 八(8) (数) eight
9. 九(9) (数) nine
10. 十(10) (数) ten
11. 零(0) (数) zero
12. 百 (数) hundred
13. 千 (数) thousand
14. 万 (数) ten thousand
15. 亿 (数) one hundred million
16. 三 分 之 一 one third
17. 百 分 之 二十 twenty percent
18. 一半 (数) half
19. 秒 (量) second
20. 倍 (量) time
21. 钟 (名) clock
22. 手表 (名) watch

44

☆ 练 习(Exercises) ☆

一、用汉语说出下列时间(Say the following time in Chinese)
7:13am　　10:50am　　11:15am　　3:30pm　　9:28pm

二、用汉语说出下列数字(Say the following numbers in Chinese)
123　　53786　　2222　　5001　　3～4 个　　11～19　　400～499

三、回答问题(Answer the following questions)
1. 美国的中学早上几点钟开始上课?
2. 你要在中国待多久?
3. 从纽约坐飞机(zuò fēijī/take a flight)到上海要多长时间?
4. 你学了多长时间汉语(Hànyǔ)?

四、会话(Conversation)
于雪来：你早上几点起床(qǐchuáng/get up)?
玛　丽：六点半。
于雪来：你先生早上几点出门(chūmén/leave home)?
玛　丽：八点。
于雪来：从你家到公司要多长时间?
玛　丽：要一个小时。
于雪来：你先生每天(měi tiān/ every day)几点回家(huí jiā/go home)?
玛　丽：七点半左右。
于雪来：晚上你们几点睡觉(shuìjiào/go to bed)?
玛　丽：十一点左右。
于雪来：你的朋友在上海待了几天?
玛　丽：待了三天。

☆ 练习答案(Key to the exercises) ☆

一、早上七点十三分；　　　　　　　　上午十点五十分/差十分十一点；
　　上午十一点十五分/十一点一刻；　　下午三点半；
　　晚上九点二十八分
二、一百二十三；　　　　　　　　　　五万三千七百八十六；
　　两千二百二十二；　　　　　　　　五千零一；
　　三四个；　　　　　　　　　　　　十几；
　　四百多

5 日期

Rìqī

DATE

1. A：今天 是注1几 号注2？
   Jīntiān shì jǐ hào?

   What is the date today?

   B：十 月 四 号。
   Shí yuè sì hào.

   October the fourth.

   A：昨天 几 号？
   Zuótiān jǐ hào?

   What was the date yesterday?

   B：三 号。
   Sān hào.

   The third.

   A：明天 星期 几？
   Míngtiān xīngqī jǐ?

   What day will it be tomorrow?

   B：星期四。
   Xīngqīsì.

   Thursday.

   A：几 月 几 号 是 国庆 节？
   Jǐ yuè jǐ hào shì Guóqìng Jié?

   What date is National Day?

   B：十 月 一 号。
   Shí yuè yī hào.

   October the first.

2. A：你 儿子 是 哪 年 生 的？
   Nǐ érzi shì nǎ nián shēng de?

   When was your son born?

B：Shì yījiǔbālíng nián shēng de.
是 一九八〇 年 生 的。　He was born in 1980.

A：Nǐ nǚ'ér de shēngrì shì jǐ
你 女儿 的 生日 是 几　When is your daughter's birthday?

yuè jǐ hào?
月 几 号？

B：Sān yuè shí'èr hào.
三 月 十二 号。　March 12th.

3. A：Nǐ shì shénme shíhou lái
你 是 什么 时候 来　When did you come to Shanghai?

Shànghǎi de?
上海 的？

B：Wǒ shì shàng ge yuè lái
我 是 上 个 月 来　I came to Shanghai last month.

Shànghǎi de.
上海 的。

A：Nǐ zhǔnbèi shénme shíhou huí
你 准备 什么 时候 回　When are you going to return to England?

Yīngguó?
英国？

B：Zhège yuèdǐ huòzhě xià ge
这个 月底 或者 下 个　The end of this month or the beginning of

yuèchū.
月初。　next month.

A：Kèlākè xiānsheng dǎsuan
克拉克 先生 打算　When does Mr. Clark plan to leave

shénme shíhou líkāi Shànghǎi?
什么 时候 离开 上海？　Shanghai?

B：Xià ge xīngqī.
下 个 星期。　Next week.

4. A：Zhè jiàn shì shénme shíhou néng
这 件 事 什么 时候 能　When can this job be completed?

zuòhǎo?
做好？

B：Hái yào wǔ tiān.
还 要 五 天。　In five days.

5. A：Zài guò yí ge yuè jiù shì
再 过 一 个 月 就 是　The New Year is one month away. Are you

xīnnián le. Nǐ huí Měiguó ma?
新年 了。你 回 美国 吗？　going to return to America?

Yào　huí　de.
B：要　回　的。　　　　　　　　　　Yes，we will.

Shénme　shíhou　yào　fù　fángzū?
6. A：什么　时候　要　付　房租?　　When should I pay the rent?

Zhège　yuè　wǔ　hào　yǐqián（yào
B：这个　月　五　号　以前（要　　（You shall pay the rent）Before the fifth of

fù　fángzū）.
付　房租）。　　　　　　　　this month.

Wǒ　shénme　shíhou　néng　dédào
7. A：我　什么　时候　能　得到　　When will I have your reply?

dáfù?
答复?

Guò　jǐ　tiān　gěi　nǐ　dáfù.
B：过　几　天　给　你　答复。　　I will give you my reply in several days.

☆　注　释（Notes）　☆

1. 这里的"是"可以省略。
　"是" here can be omitted.

2. 表示某一天，口语用"号"，书面语用"日"。
　"号" is used to indicate the date in spoken Chinese and "日" in written Chinese.

☆　句型提示（Sentence pattern references）　☆

1. 你准备什么时候回英国?
　克拉克先生打算什么时候离开上海?　请参看 333～334 页句型 87、88。
2. 这件事什么时候能做好?　　　　　请参看 336 页句型 94。
3. 这件事什么时候能做好?　　　　　请参看 346 页句型 118。
4. 还要五天。　　　　　　　　　　　请参看 375 页句型 183。
5. 这个月五号以前要付房租。　　　　请参看 332 页句型 85。

☆　词语用法举例（Examples for usage of the words）　☆

1. 你准备什么时候回英国

Tā　zhǔnbèi　hòutiān　huí　guó.
（1）他　准备　后天　回　国。　（回国：return to one's own country）

Tā　zhǔnbèi　xià　xīngqī　qù　Nánjīng.
（2）他　准备　下　星期　去　南京。

Wáng Jiànhuá zhǔnbèi shí'èr hào líkāi Sūzhōu.
(3) 王 建华 准备 十二 号 离开 苏州。

Zhèng Yùwén zhǔnbèi qù Àomén kàn péngyou.
(4) 郑 玉文 准备 去 澳门 看 朋友。

2. 这个月底或者下个月初

Wǒ shí hào huòzhě shíyī hào chūfā.
(1) 我 十 号 或者 十一 号 出发。   (出发：set out)

Wǒ xiǎng mǎi diǎnr píngguǒ huòzhě lí.
(2) 我 想 买 点儿 苹果 或者 梨。   (苹果：apple 梨：pear)

Tā dǎsuan qù Měiguó huòzhě Yīngguó liúxué.
(3) 他 打算 去 美国 或者 英国 留学。

Hóngsè de huòzhě lánsè de dōu xíng.
(4) 红色 的 或者 蓝色 的 都 行。   (红色：red 蓝色：blue)

3. 这件事什么时候能做好

Fàn shénme shíhou néng zuòhǎo?
(1) 饭 什么 时候 能 做好?

Zuòyè shénme shíhou néng zuòhǎo?
(2) 作业 什么 时候 能 做好?   (作业：exercise)

Yīfu shénme shíhou néng xǐhǎo?
(3) 衣服 什么 时候 能 洗好?

Fángjiān shénme shíhou néng dǎsǎo hǎo?
(4) 房间 什么 时候 能 打扫 好?   (房间：room 打扫：clean)

4. 再过一个月就是新年了

Zài guò wǔ tiān jiù shì wǒ de shēngrì.
(1) 再 过 五 天 就 是 我 的 生日。

Zài guò shí tiān jiù kāixué le.
(2) 再 过 十 天 就 开学 了。 (开学：school term begins)

Zài guò shí fēnzhōng jiù dào Guìlín le.
(3) 再 过 十 分钟 就 到 桂林 了。

Zài guò yíhuìr jiù xiàbān.
(4) 再 过 一会儿 就 下班。 (下班：get off work)

5. 这个月五号以前要付房租

Zhège xīngqītiān wǒ yào qù gōngsī.
(1) 这个 星期天 我 要 去 公司。

Xià ge xīngqī wǒ yào chūchāi.
(2) 下 个 星期 我 要 出差。

Tā yào dòng shǒushù.
(3) 他 要 动 手术。   (动手术：undergo operation)

Sān diǎn yǐqián yào dào jīchǎng.
(4) 三 点 以前 要 到 机场。   (机场：airport)

☆　词　语（Word list）　☆

1.	早上 zǎoshang	（名）	morning	2.	上午 shàngwǔ	（名）	morning

1. 早上 zǎoshang （名） morning
2. 上午 shàngwǔ （名） morning
3. 中午 zhōngwǔ （名） noon
4. 下午 xiàwǔ （名） afternoon
5. 白天 báitiān （名） day time
6. 傍晚 bàngwǎn （名） evening, nightfall, dusk
7. 晚上 wǎnshang （名） evening, night
8. 半夜 bànyè （名） midnight
9. 前天 qiántiān （名） the day before yesterday
10. 后天 hòutiān （名） the day after tomorrow
11. 星期一 xīngqīyī （名） Monday
12. 星期二 xīngqī'èr （名） Tuesday
13. 星期三 xīngqīsān （名） Wednesday
14. 星期四 xīngqīsì （名） Thursday
15. 星期五 xīngqīwǔ （名） Friday
16. 星期六 xīngqīliù （名） Saturday
17. 星期天／日 xīngqītiān/rì （名） Sunday
18. 上　个　星期 shàng ge xīngqī last week
19. 这个　星期 zhège xīngqī this week
20. 下　个　星期 xià ge xīngqī next week
21. 上　个　月 shàng ge yuè last month
22. 这个　月 zhège yuè this month
23. 下　个　月 xià ge yuè next month
24. 月初 yuèchū （名） the beginning of the month
25. 月中 yuèzhōng （名） the middle of the month
26. 月底 yuèdǐ （名） the end of the month
27. 去年 qùnián （名） last year
28. 今年 jīnnián （名） this year
29. 明年 míngnián （名） next year
30. 年初 niánchū （名） the beginning of the year
31. 年底 niándǐ （名） the end of the year
32. 节日 jiérì （名） holiday, festival
33. 以后 yǐhòu （名） after, later
34. 纪念日 jìniànrì （名） commemoration day

☆　练　习（Exercises）　☆

一、替换练习（Substitution exercises）

1. 我<u>这个月五号以前</u>要<u>付房租</u>。

十一点以前	回家
国庆节以后	去美国出差
年底	给他答复
新年以前	离开中国

2. 再过<u>一个月</u>就是<u>新年</u>了。

两天	我的生日

十天 　　　　　　　　我们的结婚纪念日

三个星期 　　　　　　中秋节（Zhōngqiū Jié）

四分钟 　　　　　　　八点

二、对下列画线部分提问（Form questions for the following underlined part）

1．李平打算<u>下星期三</u>回国。

2．他是<u>一九七九年</u>生的。

3．王老师的儿子是<u>今年五月</u>来上海的。

4．史密斯（Shǐmìsī）先生<u>二十号</u>出发。

三、选择正确的词语（Select the correct words）

1．36 小时是_____。

　　A. 一天半　　　　　B. 一半天　　　　　C. 一个半天

2．14 天是_____。

　　A. 二个星期　　　　B. 两个星期　　　　C. 二星期

3．100 天是_____。

　　A. 三多月　　　　　B. 三月多　　　　　C. 三个多月

4．400 天是_____。

　　A. 一年多　　　　　B. 一多年　　　　　C. 一个多年

四、会话（Conversation）

于雪来：你们是什么时候来上海的？

玛　丽：我先生来中国已经三年了。我是上个月来上海的。

于雪来：你的汉语很好啊。你学了多久？

玛　丽：在美国学了一年多。

于雪来：下星期我们打算去西安（Xī'ān）旅游。

玛　丽：去多久？

于雪来：去四五天。你准备什么时候回美国？

玛　丽：准备下个月底回去。

于雪来：明天是星期天，我们带孩子去公园（gōngyuán/park）好吗？

玛　丽：好的。几点出门？

于雪来：早上九点在公寓（gōngyù/apartment house）门口（ménkǒu/gate）等（děng/wait）。

☆．练习答案（Key to the exercises）　☆

二、1．李平打算什么时候回国？

　　2．他是哪年生的？

　　3．王老师的儿子是几月来上海的？

　　4．史密斯先生几号出发？

三、1．A　　2．B　　3．C　　4．A

6 　Zài　Shípǐndiàn
在 食品店　　IN A FOOD STORE

1. A： Nín yào mǎi shénme?
您 要 买 什么？　　May I help you?

   B： Zhè zhǒng nǎitáng duōshao qián yì jīn?注1
这 种 奶糖 多少 钱 一 斤注1？　　How much is this toffee per *jin* ?

   A： Èrshíwǔ kuài (yì jīn).
二十五 块 （一 斤）。　　25 *yuan* (per *jin*).

   B： Zhè zhǒng ne?
这 种 呢？　　How about this?

   A： Èrshíbā kuài (yì jīn).
二十八 块 （一 斤）。　　28 *yuan* (per *jin*)

   B： Gè yào yì jīn.
各 要 一 斤。　　I'll take one *jin* of each.

   A： Yígòng wǔshísān kuài. (Nín de qián) zhèng hǎo.
一共 五十三 块。（您 的 钱） 正 好。　　All together 53 *yuan* . (Your money is) Just right.

2. A： Yì píng kělè duōshao qián?
一 瓶 可乐 多少 钱？　　How much is a bottle of Cola?

Liù kuài qián (yì píng).
B：六 块 钱（一 瓶）。　　　　　　Six *yuan* (a bottle).

Yào liǎng píng.
A：要 两 瓶。　　　　　　　　　I'll take two bottles.

(Qǐng fù) shí'èr kuài. Shōu nín
B：（请 付）十二 块。收 您　　12 *yuan* please. You gave me 15 *yuan* and

shíwǔ kuài, zhǎo nín sān kuài.
十五 块，找 您 三 块。　　here is three *yuan* change for you.

Zhè shì shénme?
3. A：这 是 什么？　　　　　　　What is this?

Wǔxiāngdòu, shì Shànghǎi tèchǎn.
B：五香豆， 是 上海 特产。　Wuxiangdou (spiced bean), a special product

with Shanghai flavor.

Duōshao qián yì bāo?
A：多少 钱 一 包？　　　　　How much for a packet?

Shí kuài (yì bāo).
B：十 块（一 包）。　　　　Ten *yuan* (per packet).

Yào wǔ bāo.
A：要 五 包。　　　　　　　Five packets please.

(Shōu nín) yìbǎi kuài. Zhè
B：（收 您）一百 块。这　100 from you. Here is your change. Please

shì zhǎotou, qǐng diǎn yíxià.
是 找头， 请 点 一下。　check it.

Hái yào bié de ma?
还 要 别 的 吗？　　　　Anything else?

Gòu le, jiù mǎi zhèxiē.
A：够 了，就注2 买 这些。　No, that's all.

☆　注　释(Notes)　☆

1. 口语中"500 克(kè)"说"一斤"。"斤、块、瓶、包"是量词。
   In spoken Chinese "一斤" means 500 gram. "斤"，"块"，"瓶" and "包" are all measure words.

2. "就"在这里表示限定范围。
   "就" here is used to define the scope.

☆　句型提示(Sentence pattern references)　☆

1. 您要买什么？　　　　　　　　　请参看 331 页句型 83。
2. 这种呢？　　　　　　　　　　　请参看 302 页句型 19。

3. 一瓶可乐多少钱?   请参看 298 页句型 12。

4. 够了,就买这些。   请参看 374 页句型 181。

☆ 词语用法举例 (Examples for usage of the words) ☆

1. 您要买什么

(1) Nǐ yào chī Zhōngguócài ma?
你 要 吃 中国菜 吗? (吃:eat)

(2) Nǐ yào kàn diànshì ma?
你 要 看 电视 吗? (电视:TV)

(3) Wǒ yào qù Xī'ān wán.
我 要 去 西安 玩。 (玩:have fun)

(4) Mèimei yào dào wàimian qù wán.
妹妹 要 到 外面 去 玩。 (外面:outside)

(5) Wǒ yào mǎi zhège.
我 要 买 这个。

2. 各要一斤

(1) Qiānbǐ hé máobǐ gè yào liǎng zhī.
铅笔 和 毛笔 各 要 两 支。 (铅笔:pencil 毛笔:writing brush)

(2) Píjiǔ hé pútaojiǔ gè mǎile sì píng.
啤酒 和 葡萄酒 各 买了 四 瓶。 (啤酒:beer)

(3) Měi rén gè yào yì wǎn fàn.
每 人 各 要 一 碗 饭。

(4) Měi yàng gè ná liǎng tào.
每 样 各 拿 两 套。 (套:量词)

3. 请点一下

(1) Qǐng diǎn yíxià chūxí de rénshù.
请 点 一下 出席 的 人数。

(2) Qǐng diǎn yíxià xíngli.
请 点 一下 行李。 (行李:luggage)

(3) Wǒ diǎnguo le, xíngli dōu qí le.
我 点过 了,行李 都 齐 了。 (齐:all ready)

(4) Zhè shì yìqiān kuài, wǒ diǎnguo le.
这 是 一千 块, 我 点过 了。

4. 就买这些

(1) Xíngli jiù fàngzài zhèli ba.
行李 就 放在 这里 吧。 (放:put)

(2) Jiù zài zhèli tíngchē ba.
就 在 这里 停车 吧。 (停车:park the car)

Nǐ jiù zài jiā wán ba.
（3）你 就 在 家 玩 吧。

Wǒ jiù zài ménkǒu děng nǐ.
（4）我 就 在 门口 等 你。

☆ 词 语（Word list）☆

mǎi dōngxi
1. 买 东西　　　shopping

kāishuǐ
3. 开水　（名）boiling water

kuàngquánshuǐ
5. 矿泉水　（名）mineral water

lǜchá
7. 绿茶　（名）green tea

lóngjǐngchá
9. 龙井茶　（名）Longjing tea

kāfēi
11. 咖啡　（名）coffee

suānniúnǎi
13. 酸牛奶　（名）yogurt

miànbāo
15. 面包　（名）bread

diǎnxin
17. 点心　（名）refreshments, snack

shuǐguǒtáng
19. 水果糖　（名）fruit drops

mìjiàn
21. 蜜饯　（名）candied fruit, preserved fruit

huángyóu
23. 黄油　（名）butter

guàntou
25. 罐头　（名）can, tin

yǐnliào
2. 饮料　（名）drink

lěngkāishuǐ
4. 冷开水　（名）cool boiled water

hóngchá
6. 红茶　（名）black tea

mòlìhuāchá
8. 茉莉花茶　（名）jasmine tea

wūlóngchá
10. 乌龙茶　（名）Wulong tea

niúnǎi
12. 牛奶　（名）milk

chéngzhī
14. 橙汁　（名）orange juice

dàngāo
16. 蛋糕　（名）cake

huāshēngtáng
18. 花生糖　（名）peanut brittle

qiǎokèlì
20. 巧克力　（名）chocolate

fēngmì
22. 蜂蜜　（名）honey

guǒjiàng
24. 果酱　（名）jam

kè
26. 克　（量）gram

☆ 练 习（Exercises）☆

一、完成对话（Complete the conversations）
1. A：_____？
　 B：我要牛奶、橙汁和可乐。
　 A：您要买多少？
　 B：_____买两瓶。
2. A：这种蛋糕_____？
　 B：三块两毛。
　 A：我要四块。
　 B：好的，_____十二块八。还要别的吗？
　 A：_____。给你二十块。

55

B：＿＿＿＿＿＿＿＿＿＿＿七块两毛。

二、替换练习（Substitution exercises）

1. 这种<u>奶糖</u>多少钱一<u>斤</u>？

面包	个（量词）	
矿泉水	瓶	
罐头	罐（量词）	
点心	盒（hé，量词）	
饮料	杯（bēi，量词）	

2. <u>奶糖</u>和<u>水果糖</u>各要<u>一斤</u>。

牛奶	酸奶	两瓶
咖啡	红茶	一杯
龙井茶	乌龙茶	一包
杯子（cup）	碗（wǎn/bowl）	五个

三、请用汉语说（Say the numbers in Chinese）

　　2.40 元　　344.55 元　　7.50 元　　12 003 元

四、会话（Conversation）

于雪来：玛丽,你去哪儿？

玛　丽：我去买牛奶。

于雪来：我也要买,我们一起（yìqǐ/together）去吧。

玛　丽：好啊。昨天在你家吃的蛋糕很好吃。是在哪里买的？

于雪来：在前面那家面包店买的。你看,那个就是。

（到了面包店）

售货员：你要买什么？

玛　丽：要一个这种蛋糕。多少钱？

售货员：八块五。这种小饼干（bǐnggān/biscuit）很好吃。您要吗？

玛　丽：好吧。多少钱一袋（dài，量词）？

售货员：九块两毛。

玛　丽：小于,你不买吗？

于雪来：我家里有（yǒu/have）面包了。今天不买。

玛　丽：就买这些,一共十七块七毛,给你。

售货员：正好。谢谢。

☆　　**练习答案（Key to the exercises）**　　☆

一、1. A：您要买什么　B：各

　　2. A：多少钱一块　B：一共　A：不要了　B：找您

三、两元四角/两块四毛；　　　　三百四十四元五角五分/三百四十四块五毛五；

　　七元五角/七块五；　　　　　一万两千零三元/一万两千零三块。

7   Zài   Shuǐguǒdiàn 在 水果店   IN A FRUIT SHOP

Zhè lí kàn shangqu búcuò, tián
A：这 梨 看 上去 不错，甜   These pears look good. Are they sweet?

bu tián?
不 甜?

Zhè shì zhèngzōng Tiānjīn yālí,
B：这 是 正宗 天津 鸭梨，   They are genuine Tianjin Yali, quite fragrant

yòu tián yòu xiāng.
又 甜 又 香。   and sweet.

Duōshao qián yì jīn?
A：多少 钱 一 斤?   How much are they per *jin* ?

Shí kuài (qián) sān jīn.
B：十 块 (钱) 三 斤。   Ten *yuan* for three *jin* .

Kěyǐ tiāo ma?
A：可以 挑 吗?   Can I take my pick?

Qǐng suíbiàn tiāo ba.
B：请 随便 挑 吧。   Please pick whichever you like.

Jiù yào zhèxiē.
A：就 要 这些。   I'll take these.

B：
Sì jīn liù liǎng, zài jiā yí
四 斤 六 两[注1]，再 加 一
ge, mǎi wǔ jīn, hǎo ma?
个，买 五 斤，好 吗？

They weigh four *jin* and six *liang*. Add one more for five *jin*, OK?

A：
Hǎo ba.
好 吧。

OK.

B：
Zhènghǎo wǔ jīn. Hái yào bié
正好 五 斤。还 要 别
de ma? Zhè shì Huángyán mìjú,
的 吗？这 是 黄岩 蜜橘，
hěn xīnxiān.
很 新鲜。

Exactly five *jin*. Anything else? These are Huangyan oranges, very fresh.

A：
Suān ma?
酸 吗？

They aren't sour, are they?

B：
Bù suān. Nín xiān chángchang.
不 酸。您 先 尝尝。

Not at all. You can try it first.

A：
Bù zěnme suān, hǎochī. Yě yào
不 怎么 酸，好吃。也 要
wǔ jīn.
五 斤。

It tastes good, not really sour. I want five *jin* too.

B：
Wǔ jīn bàn, kěyǐ ma?
五 斤 半，可以 吗？

They weigh five *jin* and a half. Is it ok?

A：
Tài duō le, wǔ jīn gòu le.
太 多 了，五 斤 够 了。

It's too much. Five *jin* is enough.

B：
Hǎo de. Zhènghǎo wǔ jīn. Wǔ kuài
好 的。正好 五 斤。五 块
sān jīn, wǔ jīn shì bā kuài sān,
三 斤，五 斤 是 八 块 三，
yígòng èrshísì kuài jiǔ máo.
一共 二十四 块 九 毛[注2]。

OK. Exactly five *jin*. Five *yuan* for three *jin*, then five *jin* costs eight *yuan* and three *jiao*.

Totally 24 *yuan* and nine *jiao*.

☆ 注 释 (Notes) ☆

1. 口语 50 克说 1 两。
   In spoken Chinese "一两"(one *liang*) means 50 gram.
2. 人民币的计算单位是"元"、"角"、"分"。口语中常用"块"、"毛"、"分"。"毛"或"分"在最后常常省略。
   The Chinese monetary units are the "元"，"角"and "分". In spoken Chinese people usually use their equivalents "块"，"毛"and "分". "毛" and "分" are often omitted when they are at the end.

☆ **句型提示**(Sentence pattern references) ☆

1. 这梨看上去不错,甜不甜?   请参看 341 页句型 106。
2. 这梨看上去不错,甜不甜?   请参看 301 页句型 16。
3. 又甜又香。   请参看 383 页句型 201。
4. 可以挑吗?   请参看 294 页句型 3。
5. 请随便挑吧。   请参看 392 页句型 218。
6. 太多了,五斤够了。   请参看 365 页句型 160。

☆ **词语用法举例**(Examples for usage of the words) ☆

1. 这梨看上去不错

  (1) 这个 菜 的 味道 不错。 (菜:dish)
      Zhège cài de wèidao búcuò.

  (2) 这 本 小说 很 不错。
      Zhè běn xiǎoshuō hěn búcuò.

  (3) 你 的 照相机 很 不错。 (照相机:camera)
      Nǐ de zhàoxiàngjī hěn búcuò.

  (4) 他 的 学习 成绩 不错。
      Tā de xuéxí chéngjì búcuò.

2. 请随便挑吧

  (1) 请 随便 坐 吧。
      Qǐng suíbiàn zuò ba.

  (2) 我 这些 书, 你 可以 随便 拿去 看。
      Wǒ zhèxiē shū, nǐ kěyǐ suíbiàn náqu kàn.

  (3) A: 你 要 喝 点儿 什么? (喝:drink)   B: 随便 吧。
      Nǐ yào hē diǎnr shénme?   Suíbiàn ba.

3. 不怎么酸

  (1) 今天 不 怎么 热。 (热:hot)
      Jīntiān bù zěnme rè.

  (2) 质量 不 怎么 好。 (质量:quality)
      Zhìliàng bù zěnme hǎo.

  (3) 这个 菜 不 怎么 好吃。
      Zhège cài bù zěnme hǎochī.

  (4) 这儿 的 交通 不 怎么 方便。 (方便:convenient)
      Zhèr de jiāotōng bù zěnme fāngbiàn.

4. 五斤够了

  (1) 我 吃 一 碗 就 够 了。
      Wǒ chī yì wǎn jiù gòu le.

（2）A：<ruby>再<rt>Zài</rt></ruby> <ruby>喝<rt>hē</rt></ruby> <ruby>一<rt>yì</rt></ruby> <ruby>杯<rt>bēi</rt></ruby> <ruby>吧<rt>ba</rt></ruby>!　　B：<ruby>够<rt>Gòu</rt></ruby> <ruby>了<rt>le</rt></ruby>，<ruby>谢谢<rt>xièxie.</rt></ruby>。

（3）A：<ruby>买<rt>Mǎi</rt></ruby> <ruby>钢琴<rt>gāngqín,</rt></ruby>，<ruby>一万<rt>yíwàn</rt></ruby> <ruby>块<rt>kuài</rt></ruby> <ruby>钱<rt>qián</rt></ruby> <ruby>够<rt>gòu</rt></ruby> <ruby>吗<rt>ma?</rt></ruby>?　（钢琴：piano）

　　　B：<ruby>够<rt>Gòu</rt></ruby> <ruby>了<rt>le.</rt></ruby>。

☆　词　语（Word list）　☆

1.	苹果 píngguǒ	（名）	apple	2.	梨 lí	（名）	pear
3.	香蕉 xiāngjiāo	（名）	banana	4.	桃子 táozi	（名）	peach
5.	橘子 júzi	（名）	tangerine	6.	菠萝 bōluó	（名）	pineapple
7.	西瓜 xīguā	（名）	watermelon	8.	葡萄 pútáo	（名）	grape
9.	柿子 shìzi	（名）	persimmon	10.	柠檬 níngméng	（名）	lemon
11.	樱桃 yīngtáo	（名）	cherry	12.	草莓 cǎoméi	（名）	strawberry
13.	栗子 lìzi	（名）	chestnut	14.	哈密瓜 hāmìguā	（名）	Hami melon
15.	香瓜 xiāngguā	（名）	muskmelon	16.	猕猴桃 míhóutáo	（名）	kiwi fruit
17.	芒果 mángguǒ	（名）	mango	18.	椰子 yēzi	（名）	coconut
19.	荔枝 lìzhī	（名）	litchi	20.	桂圆 guìyuán	（名）	longan
21.	橄榄 gǎnlǎn	（名）	olive	22.	杏子 xìngzi	（名）	apricot
23.	杨梅 yángméi	（名）	red bayberry	24.	橙子 chéngzi	（名）	orange

☆　练　习（Exercises）　☆

一、对画线部分提问（Form questions for the following underlined part）

1. 这哈密瓜<u>很甜</u>。

2. 香蕉<u>不怎么新鲜</u>。

3. 两斤<u>够了</u>。

二、用括号中的词语完成句子（Complete sentences with the words in brackets）

1. 栗子很好吃，＿＿＿＿＿＿＿＿＿＿吧。（随便）

2. 这是别人（biéren/other person）的东西，不能＿＿＿＿＿＿＿＿＿＿。（随便）

3. 你买的荔枝＿＿＿＿＿＿＿＿＿＿。（看上去）

4. A：这些苹果有几斤？　　B：＿＿＿＿＿＿＿＿＿＿。（正好）

5. 我买了桃子,你_____。(尝尝)

三、会话(Conversation)

小　贩:新鲜的荔枝,刚从广东(Guǎngdōng)来的。

玛　丽:这荔枝多少钱一斤?

小　贩:这些大(dà/big)的十七块,小(xiǎo/small)的十二块。

玛　丽:大的看上去好一点儿。我尝尝可以吗?

小　贩:尝吧。

玛　丽:不错,很甜。要一斤吧。

小　贩:这是一斤二两,可以吗?

玛　丽:太多了,一斤够了。

小　贩:好吧。收您二十块,找您三块。

☆　**练习答案**(Key to the exercises)　☆

一、1. 这哈密瓜甜不甜?

　　2. 香蕉新鲜不新鲜?

　　3. 两斤够不够? /两斤够吗?

二、1. 请随便吃

　　2. 随便拿回去

　　3. 看上去不错

　　4. 正好五斤

　　5. 尝尝吧

8

Zài　Càichǎng
在　　菜场

IN A FOOD MARKET

1. A：
Zhè huángguā tǐng xīnxiān, mǎi
这　黄瓜　挺　新鲜，买
diǎnr　ba.
点儿　吧。

These cucumbers are very fresh. Would you like some?

B：
Yào sān jīn.
要　三　斤。

I want three *jin*.

A：
Duōle yìdiǎnr, kěyǐ ma?
多了　一点儿，可以　吗?

A little bit more, OK?

B：
Duōshao?
多少?

How much?

A：
Sān jīn bàn.
三　斤　半。

Three *jin* and a half.

B：
Kěyǐ.
可以。

All right.

A：
Zhènghǎo qī kuài qián. Hái
正好　七　块　钱。还注1
yào bié de ma?
要　别　的　吗?

It's seven *yuan* exactly. Do you need anything else?

B：
Zài yào liǎng ge yángcōng.
再注2 要　两　个　洋葱。

Two onions also.

Zhège shì huài de, gěi wǒ
这个 是 坏 的，给 我
huàn yí ge.
换 一 个。

This one is bad. Please change it for me.

Yǒu qīngjiāo ma?
有 青椒 吗？

Do you have green peppers?

A: Duìbuqǐ, qīngjiāo màiguāng le.
对不起，青椒 卖光 了。

Sorry, green peppers are all sold out.

2. A: Zhè shì shénme yú? Shì héyú
这 是 什么 鱼？是 河鱼
háishi hǎiyú?
还是 海鱼？

What fish is this? Is it freshwater fish or sea fish?

B: Zhè jiào lúyú, shì héyú.
这 叫 鲈鱼，是 河鱼。

This is perch. It's freshwater fish.

A: Yào yì tiáo dà de.
要 一 条 大 的。

Give me a big one.

3. A: Wǔshí kuài yì jīn, yòu dà
五十 块 一 斤，又 大
yòu xīnxiān de xiā!
又 新鲜 的 虾！

Big and fresh shrimps! 50 yuan for one jin!

B: Tài guì le, piányi diǎnr,
太 贵 了，便宜 点儿，
sìshíwǔ kuài ba.
四十五 块 吧。

It's too expensive. Can you make it a little cheaper? Say 45 yuan?

A: Bú guì de. Hǎo ba, sìshíbā
不 贵 的。好 吧，四十八
kuài, zěnmeyàng?
块，怎么样？

I don't think it is expensive. But, all right, how about 48 yuan?

B: Wǒ qiántiān mǎi yě shì
我 前天 买 也 是
sìshíwǔ kuài.
四十五 块。

I bought it for 45 yuan the day before yesterday.

A: Hǎo ba, piányi diǎnr màigěi
好 吧，便宜 点儿 卖给
nǐ. Yào duōshao?
你。要 多少？

All right. Just give it to you cheaply. How many do you want?

B: Yào yì jīn.
要 一 斤。

I want one jin.

☆　注　释(Notes)　☆

1. "还"在这里表示范围的扩大。

　"还" indicates an enlargement of the scope.

2. "再"在这里表示完成一个动作以后,将重复这个动作。例如:"再去一次"、"再吃一碗"、"再看一遍"。

　"再" here means to repeat the action after its completion. For example "再去一次(go once more)","再吃一碗(eat one bowl more)" and "再看一遍(read one more time)"。

☆　句型提示(Sentence pattern references)　☆

1. 这黄瓜挺新鲜。　　　　　　　　请参看 366 页句型 163。
2. 再要两个洋葱。　　　　　　　　请参看 368 页句型 168。
3. 青椒卖光了。　　　　　　　　　请参看 347 页句型 120。

☆　词语用法举例(Examples for usage of the words)　☆

1. 正好七块钱

　(1) Tǐzhòng zhènghǎo yìbǎi jīn.
　　　体重　　正好　一百　斤。

　(2) Tā lái de shíhou zhènghǎo qī diǎn.
　　　他来的时候　正好　七点。

　(3) Wǒ de gōngzī zhènghǎo liǎngqiān kuài.
　　　我的工资　正好　两千　块。　(工资：salary)

　(4) Yǒu sān zhāng piào, zhènghǎo měi rén yì zhāng.
　　　有三张票,　正好　每人一张。　(张：量词　票：ticket)

2. 还要别的吗

　(1) Wǒ hái yào yì jīn qíncài.
　　　我还要一斤芹菜。

　(2) Tā hái dǎsuan qù Àodàlìyà.
　　　他还打算去澳大利亚。

　(3) Wǒ hái yào zài kàn yí cì.
　　　我还要再看一次。

　(4) Lǐ Yǒng hái huì Fǎyǔ.
　　　李勇还会法语。　(法语：French)

3. 再要两个洋葱

　(1) Gēn wǒ zài dú yí cì.
　　　跟我再读一次。　(跟：follow　读：read aloud)

64

Zài gěi wǒ yì bēi.
(2) 再 给 我 一 杯。

Jīnnián wǒ dǎsuan zài qù yí cì Huáng Shān.
(3) 今年 我 打算 再 去 一 次 黄 山。

Mèimei zhǔnbèi zài mǎi yí jiàn dàyī.
(4) 妹妹 准备 再 买 一 件 大衣。 （大衣：coat）

4. 要一条大的

Wǒ yào hóng de.
(1) 我 要 红 的。

Tā xǐhuan xián de.
(2) 他 喜欢 咸 的。 （咸：salty）

Cháng de guì, duǎn de piányi.
(3) 长 的 贵, 短 的 便宜。 （长：long 短：short）

Dà de hǎokàn, xiǎo de bù hǎokàn.
(4) 大 的 好看, 小 的 不 好看。 （好看：good looking）

☆ 词 语（Word list） ☆

fānqié/xīhóngshì
1. 番茄/西红柿（名）　tomato

qīngcài
2. 青菜　（名）　green vegetables

luóbo
3. 萝卜　（名）　radish

húluóbo
4. 胡萝卜　（名）　carrot

bōcài
5. 菠菜　（名）　spinach

yángbáicài/juǎnxīncài
6. 洋白菜/卷心菜（名）　cabbage

tǔdòu
7. 土豆　（名）　potato

huángguā
8. 黄瓜　（名）　cucumber

dōngguā
9. 冬瓜　（名）　wax gourd

yángcōng
10. 洋葱　（名）　onion

sǔn
11. 笋　（名）　bamboo shoot

qīngjiāo
12. 青椒　（名）　green pepper

làjiāo
13. 辣椒　（名）　hot pepper, chili

huācài
14. 花菜　（名）　cauliflower

mógu
15. 蘑菇　（名）　mushroom

xiānggū
16. 香菇　（名）　Xianggu mushroom

qíncài
17. 芹菜　（名）　celery

jiǔcài
18. 韭菜　（名）　leek

qiézi
19. 茄子　（名）　egg plant

máodòu
20. 毛豆　（名）　green soy bean

biǎndòu
21. 扁豆　（名）　hyacinth bean, haricot bean

dāodòu
22. 刀豆　（名）　sword bean

dòuyá
23. 豆芽　（名）　bean sprouts

jiāngdòu
24. 豇豆　（名）　cowpea

lián'ǒu
25. 莲藕　（名）　lotus root

yùtou
26. 芋头　（名）　taro

dòufu
27. 豆腐　（名）　bean curd

dòufugān
28. 豆腐干　（名）　dried bean curd

29. 葱　　（名）　scallion （cōng）

30. 姜　　（名）　ginger （jiāng）

31. 大蒜　（名）　garlic （dàsuàn）

32. 鱼　　（名）　fish （yú）

33. 虾　　（名）　shrimp （xiā）

34. 螃蟹　（名）　crab （pángxiè）

☆　**练　习**(Exercises)　☆

一、替换练习(Substitution exercises)

1. 这<u>番茄</u>多少钱一<u>斤</u>?

花菜	斤
青菜	把(bǎ, 量词)
豆腐	盒(hé, 量词)
豆腐干	块(kuài, 量词)

2. 再要<u>两个</u> <u>洋葱</u>。

三只(zhī, 量词)	螃蟹
一块	姜
一把	葱
三个	胡萝卜
一条(tiáo, 量词)	鱼
半个	冬瓜

二、用括号中的词语完成句子(Complete sentences with the words in brackets)

1. A：有蘑菇吗?　　　B：对不起，_____。（动词＋光）

2. A：香蕉呢?　　　　B：昨天_____。（动词＋光）

3. 这个土豆太小，_____。（换）

4. 这个番茄不红，_____。（换）

三、对画线部分提问(Form questions for the following underlined part)

1. 这是<u>鲈鱼</u>。

2. 这是<u>韭菜</u>。

3. 虾<u>十八块钱</u>一斤。

4. 这菠菜<u>很新鲜</u>。

四、会话(Conversation)

玛　丽：大闸蟹(dàzháxiè/Dazha crab)多少钱一斤?

小　贩：六十块。你要多少?

玛　丽：六十块，太贵了。上星期买是五十二块。

小　贩：货色(huòsè/quality)不一样，这些好。你看这只，又大又肥(féi/fat)。

玛　丽：五十二块吧。

小　贩：你多买就便宜一点儿。要多少?

玛　丽：两斤。

小　贩：五十五块吧,怎么样?

玛　丽：好吧,可以挑吗?

小　贩：随便挑。都是好的。

玛　丽：这些够了。

小　贩：这些不到两斤,再加一只吧。

玛　丽：好吧。那只太小,换一只吧。

小　贩：好的。

☆　练习答案(Key to the exercises)　☆

二、1. 蘑菇卖光了

　　2. 吃光了

　　3. 给我换个大的

　　4. 给我换个红的

三、1. 这是什么鱼?

　　2. 这是什么菜?

　　3. 虾多少钱一斤?

　　4. 这波菜新鲜吗?

9 Zài Chāoshì 在 超市　IN A SUPERMARKET

Huānyíng guānglín.
A：欢迎 光临注。

Welcome!

Nǎli yǒu lánzi?
B：哪里 有 篮子?

Where are the baskets?

Nàli yǒu lánzi hé shǒutuīchē.
A：那里 有 篮子 和 手推车。

There are baskets and pushcarts there.

Zhèli de shāngpǐn néng bu néng
B：这里 的 商品 能 不 能

dǎ zhékòu?
打 折扣?

Can you offer a discount on the goods sold here?

Zhèli de shāngpǐn bù néng jiǎnjià.
A：这里 的 商品 不 能 减价。

There is no discount for the goods sold here.

Xiàwǔ liù diǎn yǐhòu miànbāo dǎ
下午 六 点 以后 面包 打

bā zhé.
八 折。

But there is 20% off on bread after 6 pm.

Qǐngwèn, xiāmi fàngzài nǎr?
B：请问, 虾米 放在 哪儿?

Excuse me, where are the dried shrimps located?

(Zài) qiánmian.
A：（在） 前面。

Right ahead.

68

Cháyè zài nǎr?
B：茶叶 在 哪儿？
Where is the tea?

Zài yòumian de jiàzi shang.
A：在 右面 的 架子 上。
On the shelf in your right side.

Zài nǎr fù qián?
B：在 哪儿 付 钱？
Where is the cashier?

Qǐng dào nàbian shōukuǎnchù fù
A：请 到 那边 收款处 付
Make your payment at the cash desk over

qiǎn.
钱。
there, please.

Yígòng yìbǎi wǔshísān kuài.
C：一共 一百 五十三 块。
All together 153 *yuan*.

Shōu nín liǎngbǎi kuài. Yǒu sān
收 您 两百 块。 有 三
I take 200 *yuan* from you. Do you have three

kuài qián ma?
块 钱 吗？
yuan ?

Yǒu de.
B：有 的。
Yes, I do.

Zhèyàng, wǒ zhǎo nín wǔshí kuài.
C：这样， 我 找 您 五十 块。
Then, I give you 50 *yuan* change.

Zhèli de dōngxi bǐjiào piányi.
B：这里 的 东西 比较 便宜。
The goods here are cheap.

Huānyíng zài lái.
C：欢迎 再 来。
Welcome to come again.

☆ 注 释 (Note) ☆

"光临"是"来"的敬语。

"光临" has the same meaning as "来", but shows respect and politeness.

☆ 句型提示 (Sentence pattern references) ☆

1. 虾米放在哪儿？ 请参看 349 页句型 124。
2. 茶叶在哪儿？ 请参看 304 页句型 23、24。

☆ 词语用法举例 (Examples for usage of the words) ☆

1. 下午六点以后面包打八折

Kěyǐ dǎ diǎnr zhékòu ma?
（1）可以 打 点儿 折扣 吗？

Bā zhé màigěi nǐ ba.
（2）八 折 卖给 你 吧。

（3）换季　减价，全部　打　六　折。　（换季：season change）
Huànjì jiǎnjià, quánbù dǎ liù zhé.

（4）拆迁　减价，全部　五　折。
Chāiqiān jiǎnjià, quánbù wǔ zhé.

（拆迁：have old buildings pulled down and arrange their occupants to move elsewhere）

2. 这里的东西比较便宜

（1）这儿　比较　安静。　（安静：quiet）
Zhèr bǐjiào ānjìng.

（2）浦东　的　发展　比较　快。
Pǔdōng de fāzhǎn bǐjiào kuài.

（3）乘　地铁　比较　快。
Chéng dìtiě bǐjiào kuài.

（4）李　志刚　的　日语　比较　流利。　（流利：fluent）
Lǐ Zhìgāng de Rìyǔ bǐjiào liúlì.

☆　词　语（Word list）　☆

1.	酒 jiǔ	（名）	alcoholic drink	2.	盐 yán	（名）	salt
3.	油 yóu	（名）	oil	4.	酱油 jiàngyóu	（名）	soy bean sauce
5.	辣酱油 làjiàngyóu	（名）	pungent sauce	6.	辣酱 làjiàng	（名）	thick chili sauce
7.	醋 cù	（名）	vinegar	8.	糖 táng	（名）	sugar
9.	胡椒 húrjiāo	（名）	pepper	10.	芥末 jièmo	（名）	mustard
11.	麻油 máyóu	（名）	sesame oil	12.	咖喱 gālí	（名）	curry
13.	味精 wèijīng	（名）	gourmet powder, monosodium glutamate	14.	生粉 shēngfěn	（名）	starch
15.	鸡蛋 jīdàn	（名）	egg	16.	鸡 jī	（名）	chicken
17.	鸭 yā	（名）	duck	18.	猪肉 zhūròu	（名）	pork
19.	牛肉 niúròu	（名）	beef	20.	火腿 huǒtuǐ	（名）	ham
21.	香肠 xiāngcháng	（名）	sausage	22.	榨菜 zhàcài	（名）	tsatsai, hot pickled mustard tuber
23.	紫菜 zǐcài	（名）	laver	24.	花生 huāshēng	（名）	peanut
25.	红枣 hóngzǎo	（名）	red date, dried Chinese date, jujube	26.	莲子 liánzǐ	（名）	lotus seed
27.	黄豆 huángdòu	（名）	soybean	28.	核桃 hétao	（名）	walnut

☆ 练 习（Exercises） ☆

一、对画线部分提问（Form questions for the following underlined part）

1. 这里的东西<u>不能减价</u>。

2. 在这里买面包可以<u>打八五折</u>。

3. 奶粉（nǎifěn/milk powder）放在<u>左边的架子上</u>。

4. 这里有<u>龙井、乌龙茶和茉莉花茶</u>。

二、替换练习（Substitution exercises）

1. 在<u>收款处</u>付钱。　　超市　　　　买东西
　　　　　　　　　　　　办公室　　　　工作
　　　　　　　　　　　　咖啡馆　　　　跟朋友见面
　　　　　　　　　　　　家里　　　　　学习汉语

2. <u>虾米</u>放在<u>架子上</u>。　鸡蛋　　　　冰箱（bīngxiāng/refrigerator）里
　　　　　　　　　　　　青菜　　　　篮子里
　　　　　　　　　　　　苹果　　　　桌子（zhuōzi/table）上
　　　　　　　　　　　　酱油　　　　厨房（chúfáng/kitchen）里

三、会话（Conversation）

于雪来：玛丽，这里有篮子。

玛　丽：我要买的东西比较多，有手推车吗？

于雪来：那里有。在大超市里东西的品种（pǐnzhǒng/assortment, category）比较多。

玛　丽：在超市买东西不用（búyòng/not need）说话（shuōhuà/talk），只（zhǐ/only）用（yòng/use）手（shǒu/hand）拿就可以了。

于雪来：哈哈（hāhā）。

玛　丽：请问，调料（tiáoliào/seasoning）在哪儿？

服务员：在那边第三（dì-sān/third）个架子上。

于雪来：玛丽，刚才（gāngcái/just now）你说（shuō/speak）了汉语！

玛　丽：真的（zhēn de/really）！还是（háishi/still）要说汉语啊。

☆ 练习答案（Key to the exercises） ☆

一、1. 这里的东西能不能减价？

　　2. 在这里买面包能打折吗？/在这里买面包能打几折？

　　3. 奶粉放在哪里？/奶粉放在什么地方？

　　4. 这里有什么茶叶？

10 Chéng Chūzū Qìchē
乘 出租 汽车　TAKING A TAXI

1. A： Nín (yào) qù nǎr?
   您 （要） 去 哪儿? — Where to?

   B： (Wǒ yào dào) Wàitān.
   （我 要 到） 外滩。 — (I am going to) The Bund.

   A： (Shì) Nánjīng Lù Wàitān ma?
   （是） 南京 路 外滩 吗? — Is the Bund at Nanjing Rd. ?

   B： Shì de.
   是 的。 — Yes.

   (Qǐng) xiàng zuǒ zhuǎn.
   （请） 向 左 转。 — Turn left, please.

   Jiù zài zhèli tíngchē ba.
   就 在 这里 停车 吧。 — Here we are.

2. A： Wǒ yào qù Huáihǎi Xīlù,
   我 要 去 淮海 西路, — I am going to Huaihai Xilu (West Huaihai

   Xīnhuá Lù fùjìn.
   新华 路 附近。 — Rd.), close to Xinhua Rd.

   B： Hǎo de, qǐng jìhǎo ānquándài.
   好 的, 请 系好 安全带。 — All right. Please fasten your seat belt.

   A： (Qǐng) xiàng yòu guǎi, ránhòu
   （请） 向 右 拐, 然后 — Please turn right, then go straight ahead.

   yìzhí xiàng qián kāi.
   一直 向 前 开。

Guòle qiánmian de shízì lùkǒu
过了 前面 的 十字 路口　　Stop just after the next intersection.

tíngchē ba.
停车 吧。

B: Nín yòng xiànjīn (fù) háishi
您 用 现金（付）还是　　Will that be cash or card?

yòng kǎ?
用 卡?

A: (Wǒ yòng) xiànjīn (fù).
（我 用）现金（付）。　　Cash.

3. A: Xiān qù Gǔběi Xīnqū, wǒ jiē
先 去 古北 新区，我 接　　Go to Gubei Xinqu（New Gubei District）first

ge péngyou zài qù Shànghǎi
个 朋友，再 去 上海　　to pick up a friend of mine. Then go to the

Zhíwùyuán.
植物园。　　Shanghai Botanical Garden.

B: Hǎo de, zhīdao le.
好 的，知道 了。　　Yes, I know.

A: Zài nà zuò dàlóu qiánmian
在 那 座 大楼 前面　　Stop in front of that building.

tíngchē.
停车。

(Qǐng) zài zhèli děng yíxià.
（请）在 这里 等 一下。　　Wait a moment here, please.

4. A: Wǒ yǒu jíshì, (qǐng) kāi
我 有 急事，（请）开　　I am in a hurry. Please drive fast.

(de) kuài diǎnr.
（得）快 点儿。

B: (Wǒ) jǐnliàng gǎn ba.
（我）尽量注 赶 吧。　　Well, I'll try my best.

5. A: Wǒ yǐjīng wǎn le, kěyǐ kāi
我 已经 晚 了，可以 开　　Can you drive a little faster? I am already late.

de kuài diǎnr ma?
得 快 点儿 吗?

B: Nín chéng jǐ diǎn de fēijī?
您 乘 几 点 的 飞机?　　What's the departure time of your flight?

A: Jiǔ diǎn yí kè. Láibují
九 点 一 刻。来不及　　A quarter past nine. We can't make it, can

le ba?
了 吧?　　we?

B：Fàngxīn ba, láidejí.
放心 吧，来得及。 　　Don't worry. We can make it.

A：(Qǐng) zhùyì ānquán.
（请） 注意 安全。 　　Be careful, please.

B：Jīchǎng dào le. (Chēfèi shì)
机场 到 了。（车费 是） 　　Here we are at the airport. That'll be 52

Wǔshí'èr kuài. Zhè shì fāpiào.
五十二 块。这 是 发票。 　　*yuan* . This is your receipt.

Bié wàngle nín de dōngxi.
别 忘了 您 的 东西。 　　Don't forget your belongings.

☆ 注　释(Note) ☆

"尽量"表示在一定的范围内尽力达到最大的限度。

"尽量"means to do something to the best of one's ability or to try one's best.

Wǒ jǐnliàng zǎo diǎnr qù.
（1）我 尽量 早 点儿 去。 I'll go as early as possible.

Qǐng nǐ jǐnliàng cānjiā.
（2）请 你 尽量 参加。 Please try your best to participate.

☆ 句型提示(Sentence pattern references) ☆

1. 请向左转。 　　　　　　　　　　请参看 360 页句型 150。
2. 先去古北新区,我接个朋友,再去上海 　请参看 384 页句型 203。
　植物园。
3. 请开得快点儿。 　　　　　　　　请参看 343 页句型 112。

☆ 词语用法举例(Examples for usage of the words) ☆

1. 我要去淮海西路,新华路附近

Shípǐndiàn zài Liánhuá Chāoshì fùjìn.
（1）食品店 在 联华 超市 附近。

Wǒ jiā zhùzài Guótài Diànyǐngyuàn fùjìn.
（2）我 家 住在 国泰 电影院 附近。 （电影院：cinema）

Chāoshì fùjìn yǒu yínháng.
（3）超市 附近 有 银行。

Zhèr fùjìn yǒu yīyuàn ma?
（4）这儿 附近 有 医院 吗? （医院：hospital）

2. 我尽量赶吧

Jǐnliàng zǎo diǎnr chūfā ba.
（1）尽量 早 点儿 出发 吧。

(2) Jǐnliàng kuài diǎnr kāishǐ gōngzuò ba.
尽量 快 点儿 开始 工作 吧。

(3) Jīntiān jǐnliàng duō zuò diǎnr ba.
今天 尽量 多 做 点儿 吧。

(4) Nǐ zhīdao de jǐnliàng gàosu wǒ.
你 知道 的 尽量 告诉 我。

3. 我尽量赶吧

(1) Wǒ jiǔ diǎn qián gǎndào gōngsī le.
我 九 点 前 赶到 公司 了。

(2) Tā zài fēijī qǐfēi qián gǎndào jīchǎng le.　(起飞:take off)
他 在 飞机 起飞 前 赶到 机场 了。

(3) Tā cóng Běijīng gǎnlai cānjiā huìyì.
他 从 北京 赶来 参加 会议。

(4) Wǒ yào gǎn qī diǎnzhōng de huǒchē, bù chī zǎofàn le.　(火车:train)
我 要 赶 七 点钟 的 火车, 不 吃 早饭 了。

4. 来不及了吧

(1) Kuài zǒu ba, láibují le.
快 走 吧, 来不及 了。

(2) Xiànzài qù yǐjīng láibují le.
现在 去 已经 来不及 了。

(3) Zhǐ yǒu èrshí fēnzhōng, láibují chī zǎofàn le.
只 有 二十 分钟, 来不及 吃 早饭 了。

(4) Zǒulù qù láibují le.
走路 去 来不及 了。

5. 放心吧,来得及

(1) Màn diǎnr zǒu, láidejí.　(慢:slowly)
慢 点儿 走, 来得及。

(2) Xiànzài chūfā láidejí.
现在 出发 来得及。

(3) Hái yǒu yí ge xiǎoshí, láidejí.
还 有 一 个 小时, 来得及。

(4) Chéng chē qù dehuà láidejí.
乘 车 去 的话 来得及。

6. 请注意安全

(1) Qǐng zhùyì xiūxi, bié tài lèi le.　(累:tired)
请 注意 休息, 别 太 累 了。

(2) Yào zhùyì yíngyǎng.　(营养:nutrition)
要 注意 营养。

(3) Lǎorén yào zhùyì tiānqì biànhuà, jiājiǎn yīfu.
老人 要 注意 天气 变化, 加减 衣服。

(4) Xià yǔ lù huá, qǐng zhùyì!
下 雨 路 滑, 请 注意!

☆ 词 语 (Word list) ☆

1. hónglǜdēng 红绿灯 （名） traffic light
2. hóngdēng 红灯 （名） red light
3. lǜdēng 绿灯 （名） green light
4. mǎlù 马路 （名） street, road
5. gōnglù 公路 （名） highway
6. gāosù gōnglù 高速 公路（名） express way
7. jiē 街 （名） street
8. rénxíng héngdào 人行 横道（名） zebra crossing, crosswalk
9. gāojiàlù 高架路 （名） viaduct
10. tiānqiáo 天桥 （名） overhead walk
11. tíngchēchǎng 停车场 （名） parking lot
12. jiāotōng jǐngchá 交通 警察（名） traffic police
13. xúnjǐng 巡警 （名） patrolman
14. jiāotōng dǔsè 交通 堵塞 traffic jam
15. guò mǎlù 过 马路 cross a street
16. jiào chē 叫 车 get a taxi
17. qǐbùfèi 起步费 （名） minimum fare
18. diàotóu 掉头 （动） turn around
19. dàochē 倒车 （动） back the car
20. qìyóu 汽油 （名） gasoline
21. jiāyóu 加油 （动） fuel
22. chāochē 超车 （动） overtake other vehicles on the road

☆ 练 习 (Exercises) ☆

一、替换练习(Substitution exercises)

1. 请<u>开</u>得<u>快</u>点儿。

走	慢
说	清楚(qīngchu/clear)
唱(chàng/sing)	大声(dàshēng/ loud)
洗(xǐ/wash)	干净(gānjìng/clean)

2. <u>乘</u> <u>几点</u>的<u>飞机</u>?

坐	早上十点半	火车
看	晚上八点一刻	电影
听(tīng/listen)	七点半	新闻(xīnwén/news)
乘	四点半	飞机

3. 向<u>左</u> <u>拐</u>。

右	转
前	走
东(dōng/east)	开
上	看

二、用括号中的词语完成句子(Complete sentences with the words in brackets)

1. 师傅,我要迟到(chídào/late)了,请_____。(尽量)

2. A:现在去火车站吗？　　B:不,_____。(先……再……)

3. A:要转弯(zhuǎnwān/turn)吗？　　B:不,_____。(一直)

4. 八点钟上班,现在已经七点三刻了,_____。(来不及)

三、回答问题(Answer the following questions)

1. 美国的高速公路怎么样？

2. 在中国你自己开车吗？

3. 你出去常坐出租车吗？

四、会话(Conversation)

于雪来:师傅,到延安(Yán'ān)路,江苏(Jiāngsū)路附近。

司　机:好,请系好安全带。

于雪来:师傅,能开得快点儿吗？我们有急事。

玛　丽:六点钟能到吗？

司　机:六点钟来得及。过了这个路口(lùkǒu/intersection),我们就上高架。上了高架就快了。

玛　丽:上海交通堵塞厉害(lìhai/terrible)吗？

于雪来:上下班时间比较堵。

于雪来:向左拐。在这里停车吧。

司　机:好,车费是十四块。

于雪来:师傅,给你。

司　机:谢谢,别忘了你们的东西。

玛　丽:再见。

☆　　**练习答案**(Key to the exercises)　　☆

二、1. 尽量开(得)快点儿

　　2. 先去超市买些东西再去火车站

　　3. 一直向前走

　　4. 来不及了

11 乘 公共 汽车 TAKING A BUS
Chéng Gōnggòng Qìchē

1. A：请问， 到 南浦 大桥
Qǐngwèn, dào Nánpǔ Dàqiáo

坐 几 路注1 车？
zuò jǐ lù chē?

Excuse me, which bus goes to Nanpu Bridge?

B：（乘） 四十三 路， 到
(Chéng) sìshísān lù, dào

终点 就 行 了。
zhōngdiǎn jiù xíng le.

Take Bus No. 43 to its terminus.

A：还 要 换 车 吗？
Hái yào huàn chē ma?

Do I need to change buses on my way there?

B：不用 了。
Búyòng le.

No, you don't need to.

A：四十三 路 车站 在 哪里？
Sìshísān lù chēzhàn zài nǎli?

Where is the No. 43 bus stop?

B：过了 这 条 马路， 向
Guòle zhè tiáo mǎlù, xiàng

左 一 拐 就 是。
zuǒ yì guǎi jiù shì.

Cross this road and turn left. The bus stop will be there.

2. A: Qù Yángpǔ Dàqiáo chéng zhè lù chē duì ma?
去 杨浦 大桥 乘 这 路 车 对 吗?

Is this the right bus for Yangpu Bridge?

B: Duì, shàng chē ba.
对, 上 车 吧。

Yes, please get in.

A: Chēpiào duōshao qián?
车票 多少 钱?

What is the fare?

B: Liǎng kuài.
两 块。

Two *yuan*.

Yángpǔ Dàqiáo dào le, qǐng xià chē.
杨浦 大桥 到 了, 请 下 车。

It's the terminal, Yangpu Bridge. Everyone off, please.

3. A: Qù Huádōng Shīfàn Dàxué chéng shénme chē hǎo?
去 华东 师范 大学 乘 什么 车 好?

Which bus goes to East China Normal University?

B: Xiān chéng jiǔshísān lù, dào Tiánlín Lù, zài huàn èr'èrsì lù ba.
先 乘 九十三 路, 到 田林 路, 再 换 二二四 路 吧。

Take Bus No. 93 to Tianlin Rd. , then change to Bus No. 224 there.

4. A: Dào Jiāotōng Dàxué hái yǒu jǐ zhàn?
到 交通 大学 还 有 几 站?

How many more stops until Jiaotong University?

B: Hái yǒu sān zhàn.
还 有 三 站。

There are three stops to go.

A: (Rúguǒ) dào le, (jiù) qǐng gàosu wǒ yì shēng.
(如果) 到 了, (就) 请 告诉 我 一 声注2。

Please tell me when we get there.

B: Xià yí zhàn shì Jiāotōng Dàxué, xià chē de chéngkè qǐng zhǔnbèi.
下 一 站 是 交通 大学, 下 车 的 乘客 请 准备。

Next stop is Jiaotong University. Please prepare to get off.

Duìbuqǐ,　qǐng　ràng　yi　ràng.
A：对不起， 请 让 一 让。　　Excuse me, please let me get off.

Xiàyízhàn　shì　Jìng'ān　Sì　ma?
5. A：下一站 是 静安 寺 吗?　　Is Jing'ansi temple the next stop ?

Jìng'ān　Sì　hái　méi　dào.
B：静安 寺 还 没 到。　　Not yet.

Wǒmen　zuò　gōnggòng　qìchē
6. A：我们 坐 公共 汽车　　Let's take a bus there.

qù　ba.
去 吧。

Dào　nàr　hěn　jìn, zuò
B：到 那儿 很 近, 坐　　It's a very short distance. Walking is prefera-

gōnggòng　qìchē　bùrú　zǒulù.
公共 汽车 不如 走路。　　ble to taking a bus.

☆ 注 释 (Notes) ☆

1. "路"指公共汽车的行车路线。
   "路" means the bus' route.

2. "声"是量词,表示声音发出的次数。
   "声" is a measure word to indicate the times of sound emitted.

☆ 句型提示 (Sentence pattern references) ☆

1. 不用了。　　　　　　　　请参看 333 页句型 86。
2. 向左一拐就是。　　　　　请参看 386 页句型 206。
3. (如果)到了,(就)请告诉我一声。　请参看 388 页句型 210。
4. 坐公共汽车不如走路。　　请参看 326 页句型 73。

☆ 词语用法举例 (Examples for usage of the words) ☆

1. 到终点就行了

Dào　nàr　hěn　jìn, zǒulù　qù　jiù　xíng　le.
(1) 到 那儿 很 近, 走路 去 就 行 了。

Qiánmian　yǒu　dìtiězhàn,　chéng　dìtiě　qù　jiù　xíng　le.
(2) 前面 有 地铁站, 乘 地铁 去 就 行 了。 (地铁:subway)

Bàozhǐ　fàngzài　zhèr　jiù　xíng　le.
(3) 报纸 放在 这儿 就 行 了。 (报纸:newspaper)

Zhè jiàn shì, wǒ yí ge rén zuò jiù xíng le.
(4) 这 件 事, 我 一 个 人 做 就 行 了。

2. 还要换车吗

Chéng chē dào zhōngdiǎnzhàn, hái yào zǒu shí fēnzhōng.
(1) 乘 车 到 终点站, 还 要 走 十 分钟。

Xiàle bān hái yào kāihuì.
(2) 下了 班 还 要 开会。

Zuòle fàn hái yào xǐ yīfu.
(3) 做了 饭 还 要 洗 衣服。

Qùle yínháng hái yào qù càichǎng.
(4) 去了 银行 还 要 去 菜场。

3. 去杨浦大桥乘这路车对吗

Nǐ shì Měiguórén, duì ma?   Duì.
(1) A: 你 是 美国人, 对 吗?   B: 对。

Zhège zì zhèyàng xiě, duì bu duì?   Bú duì.
(2) A: 这个 字 这样 写, 对 不 对?   B: 不 对。

4. 上车吧

Dàjiā dōu shàng chē le.
(1) 大家 都 上 车 了。

Lǐ Mín shàng fēijī le.
(2) 李 民 上 飞机 了。

Tā shàngle chuán jiù shuìjiào.
(3) 他 上了 船 就 睡觉。

Huǒchē yào kāi le, wǒmen shàng chē ba.
(4) 火车 要 开 了, 我们 上 车 吧。

5. (如果)到了,(就)请告诉我一声

Yǒu shénme yào bāngmáng de, qǐng shuō yì shēng.
(1) 有 什么 要 帮忙 的, 请 说 一 声。

Nǐ zǒu de shíhou, qǐng gàosu wǒ yì shēng.
(2) 你 走 的 时候, 请 告诉 我 一 声。

Nǐ míngtiān qǐchuáng de shíhou, jiào wǒ yì shēng.
(3) 你 明天 起床 的 时候, 叫 我 一 声。 (叫:call)

Nǐ hǎn yì shēng, wǒ jiù huì lái de.
(4) 你 喊 一 声, 我 就 会 来 的。 (喊:call)

☆ 词 语(Word list) ☆

1. 无人 售票车(名) bus without a conductor
   (wúrén shòupiàochē)

2. 起点站 (名) starting station
   (qǐdiǎnzhàn)

3. 终点站 (名) terminal
   (zhōngdiǎnzhàn)

4. 头班车 (名) first bus
   (tóubānchē)

5. 末班车 (名) last bus
   (mòbānchē)

6. 上下 车门(名) passenger door
   (shàngxià chēmén)

7. 车内 广播 (名) intercom on bus
   (chēnèi guǎngbō)

8. 司机 (名) driver
   (sījī)

9. 售票员 (名) conductor
   (shòupiàoyuán)

10. 急刹车 (动) brake sharp
    (jíshāchē)

11. 高峰 时间 (名) rush time
    (gāofēng shíjiān)

12. 自行车 (名) bicycle
    (zìxíngchē)

13. 摩托车 (名) motorcycle
    (mótuōchē)

14. 小客车 (名) minibus
    (xiǎokèchē)

15. 卡车 (名) truck
    (kǎchē)

16. 车祸 (名) car accident, traffic accident
    (chēhuò)

17. 交通 事故(名) traffic accident
    (jiāotōng shìgù)

18. (拥)挤 (形) crowded, packed
    ((yōng)jǐ)

19. 坐 过 站 go past the stop
    (zuò guò zhàn)

20. 挤 (动) crowd, pack, push
    (jǐ)

☆ 练 习(Exercises) ☆

一、对画线部分提问(Form questions for the following underlined part)

1. 去鲁迅(Lǔ Xùn)公园坐十八路车。

2. 二十路车的终点站在中山(Zhōngshān)公园。

3. 到交通大学的乘客请在徐家汇(Xújiāhuì)站下车。

4. 还有一站就到体育馆(tǐyùguǎn)了。

5. 二二四路不到火车站。

6. 末班车是晚上十点半。

二、回答问题(Answer the following questions)

1. 你在中国坐过公共汽车吗?

2. 美国人上班坐公共汽车吗?

3. 美国的公共汽车拥挤吗?

4. 纽约(Niǔyuē)的地铁怎么样?

三、会话(Conversation)

玛 丽:小于,我们坐出租车吧。

于雪来:不用。公共汽车很方便,不用换车。

玛 丽:人多吗?

82

于雪来：现在是中午,车上不会挤。

玛　丽：车站远吗?

于雪来：就在前面。

玛　丽：车来了。

于雪来：这是无人售票车,从前门上。

玛　丽：这儿有座位(zuòwèi/seat)。我们坐几站?

于雪来：四站。在美国,你常(cháng/often)坐公共汽车吗?

玛　丽：不常坐。我常常坐地铁、出租车。

于雪来：下一站就到了。

玛　丽：对不起,请让一下。

☆　练习答案(Key to the exercises)　☆

一、1. 去鲁迅公园坐几路车?

　　2. 二十路车的终点站在什么地方?

　　3. 到交通大学在哪个站下车?

　　4. 到体育馆还有几站?

　　5. 二二四路车到不到火车站? / 二二四路车到火车站吗?

　　6. 末班车是几点钟?

12 问 路 ASKING FOR DIRECTIONS
Wèn Lù

1. A：请问， 到 友谊 商店 怎么 走？
Qǐngwèn, dào Yǒuyì Shāngdiàn zěnme zǒu?

Excuse me, can you tell me how to get to the Friendship Store?

B：一直 往 前 走。
Yìzhí wǎng qián zǒu.

Go straight ahead, please.

2. A：请问， 第一 百货 商店 在 哪儿？
Qǐngwèn, Dì-yī Bǎihuò Shāngdiàn zài nǎr?

Excuse me, where is the First Department Store?

B：就 在 前面， 过了 十字 路口 就 是。
Jiù zài qiánmian, guòle shízì lùkǒu jiù shì.

Just go ahead. It is after the intersection.

3. A：去 上海 商城 是 往 右 拐 吗？
Qù Shànghǎi Shāngchéng shì wǎng yòu guǎi ma?

Shall I turn right to get to Shanghai Centre?

Xià ge guǎijiǎo wǎng yòu
B：下 个 拐角 往 右
Yes, turn right at the next corner.

jiù shì.
就 是。

4. A：
Xīnhuá Shūdiàn zài nàbian ma?
新华 书店 在 那边 吗？
Is Xinhua Bookstore over there?

B：
Shì, wǎng qián zǒu yìdiǎnr,
是， 往 前 走 一点儿，
Yes. Go ahead a little. There is a post office

yǒu ge yóujú, yóujú de
有 个 邮局， 邮局 的
there. It is next to the post office.

pángbiān jiù shì.
旁边 就 是。

5. A：
Qǐngwèn, qù Shànghǎi Túshūguǎn,
请问， 去 上海 图书馆，
Excuse me, is this the way to the Shanghai

zǒu zhè tiáo lù duì ma?
走 这 条 路 对 吗？
Library?

B：
Duì, dào hónglǜdēng nàr zài
对， 到 红绿灯 那儿 再
Yes. Go to the traffic light, and then turn left

xiàng zuǒ guǎi.
向 左 拐。
there.

A：
Lí zhèr yuǎn ma?
离 这儿 远 吗？
Is it far from here?

B：
Bú tài yuǎn, zǒu shí fēnzhōng
不 太 远， 走 十 分钟
Not very far. Just about ten minutes' walk.

zuǒyòu jiù dào le.
左右 就 到 了。

6. A：
Pǔdōng lí zhèr yuǎn ma?
浦东 离 这儿 远 吗？
Is Pudong far from here?

B：
Yuǎnzhe ne.
远着 呢。
It is quite a long way from here.

7. A：
Duìbuqǐ, qù Jìng'ān Sì gāi注
对不起， 去 静安 寺 该注
Excuse me, how to get to Jing'ansi?

zěnme zǒu?
怎么 走？

B：
Qǐng kàn zhè zhāng dìtú.
请 看 这 张 地图。
Please look at this map.

A：
Qǐng nǐ gěi wǒ huà yì zhāng
请 你 给 我 画 一 张
Please draw a sketch-map for me.

jiǎndān de lùxiàntú.
简单 的 路线图。

B：Hǎo ba. Dì-èr ge shízì lùkǒu
好 吧。第二 个 十字 路口
All right. Turn left at the second intersection.

wǎng zuǒ guǎi.
往 左 拐。

8. A：Duìbuqǐ, wǒ mílù le. Zhè
对不起，我 迷路 了。这
Excuse me, I lost my way. Where are we now?

shì shénme dìfang?
是 什么 地方？

B：Zhè shì Yán'ān Dōnglù, nǐ
这 是 延安 东路，你
This is Yan'an Donglu (East Yan'an Rd.).

yào qù nǎr?
要 去 哪儿？
Where are you going?

A：Wǒ xiǎng qù Rénmín Guǎngchǎng.
我 想 去 人民 广场。
I am going to People's Square.

B：Wǒ yě qù Rénmín Guǎngchǎng,
我 也 去 人民 广场，
I am going to People's Square too. Let's go together.

yìqǐ zǒu ba.
一起 走 吧。

9. A：Dìtiězhàn shì zài qiánmian ma?
地铁站 是 在 前面 吗？
Excuse me, is the subway station just ahead?

B：Duìbuqǐ, wǒ yě bù zhīdao,
对不起，我 也 不 知道，
Sorry, I don't know either. Please ask some-one else.

nǐ wènwen biéren ba.
你 问问 别人 吧。

☆ 注 释 (Note) ☆

"该"表示按照情理或习惯必须怎么做。

"该" indicates how or what one must or should do according to obligation or custom.

(1) Yǐjīng jiǔ diǎn le, wǒ gāi qù gōngsī le.
已经 九 点 了，我 该 去 公司 了。
It is nine o'clock already. I should go to my company.

(2) Yǐjīng shí'èr diǎn le, nǐ gāi shuìjiào le.
已经 十二 点 了，你 该 睡觉 了。
It is 12 o'clock now. It's time for you to go to bed.

☆ 句型提示 (Sentence pattern references) ☆

1. 到友谊商店怎么走？　　　　　　　　请参看 300 页句型 14。
2. 浦东离这儿远吗？　　　　　　　　　请参看 357 页句型 142。

3. 请你给我画一张简单的路线图。　　　　请参看 320 页句型 59。

☆　**词语用法举例**（Examples for usage of the words）　☆

1. 到友谊商店怎么走

(1) Zhège yīn zěnme fā?
这个 音 怎么 发?

(2) Zhège zì zěnme xiě?
这个 字 怎么 写?

(3) Zhège cài zěnme zuò?
这个 菜 怎么 做?

(4) Qiánbāo diū le, zěnme bàn?
钱包 丢 了, 怎么 办?　　（钱包:wallet　丢了:lost　办:do）

2. 过了十字路口就是

(1) Guò mǎlù shí yào zǒu héngdàoxiàn.
过 马路 时 要 走 横道线。

(2) Guòle Nánpǔ Dàqiáo jiù dào le.
过了 南浦 大桥 就 到 了。

(3) Guò liǎng-sān tiān nín zài lái kànkan ba.
过 两三 天 您 再 来 看看 吧。

(4) Guò jǐ tiān zài shuō ba.
过 几 天 再 说 吧。

3. 到红绿灯那儿再向左拐

(1) Wǒ zài shízì lùkǒu nàr děng nǐ.
我 在 十字 路口 那儿 等 你。

(2) Wǒ gāng cóng Wáng lǎoshī nàr lái.
我 刚 从 王 老师 那儿 来。

(3) Xiǎo Lǐ nàr yǒu Shànghǎi dìtú.
小 李 那儿 有 上海 地图。

(4) Tā nàr yǒu hǎochī de.
他 那儿 有 好吃 的。

4. 离这儿远吗

(1) Zhèr lí jīchǎng hěn jìn.
这儿 离 机场 很 近。

(2) Pǔdōng lí zhèr hěn yuǎn.
浦东 离 这儿 很 远。

(3) Wǒ jiā lí gōngsī hěn jìn.
我 家 离 公司 很 近。

(4) Xuéxiào lí wǒ jiā bù yuǎn.
学校 离 我 家 不 远。

5. 走十分钟左右就到了

(1) 　Wǒ zài Rìběn zhùle sān nián zuǒyòu.
　　我 在 日本 住了 三 年 左右。

(2) 　Měi ge yuè de shuǐfèi yào yìbǎi kuài zuǒyòu.
　　每 个 月 的 水费 要 一百 块 左右。　（水费：charge for water）

(3) 　Tā dàgài wǔshí suì zuǒyòu.
　　他 大概 五十 岁 左右。　（岁：year (of age)）

(4) 　Zhè suǒ xuéxiào yǒu liǎngbǎi rén zuǒyòu.
　　这 所 学校 有 两百 人 左右。

☆ 词 语（Word list） ☆

1.	qián 前	（名）	ahead, front	2.	hòu 后	（名）	behind, back
3.	zuǒ 左	（名）	left	4.	yòu 右	（名）	right
5.	dōng 东	（名）	east	6.	nán 南	（名）	south
7.	xī 西	（名）	west	8.	běi 北	（名）	north
9.	wàimian 外面	（名）	outside	10.	lǐmian 里面	（名）	inside
11.	duìmiàn 对面	（名）	opposite	12.	pángbiān 旁边	（名）	beside, next
13.	lùkǒu 路口	（名）	crossing, intersection	14.	rénxíngdào 人行道	（名）	sidewalk
15.	dānxíngdào 单行道	（名）	one-way	16.	jìnzhǐ tōngxíng 禁止 通行		closed to traffic
17.	qiáo 桥	（名）	bridge	18.	shízì lùkǒu 十字 路口	（名）	intersection, cross-roads
19.	dīngzì lùkǒu 丁字 路口	（名）	T-shaped intersection	20.	guòjiāng suìdào 过江 隧道		cross-river tunnel

☆ 练 习（Exercises） ☆

一、替换练习（Substitution exercises）

1. <u>邮局的旁边</u>就是<u>车站</u>。　　　超级市场的左边　　　　银行
　　　　　　　　　　　　　　　　　　过了十字路口　　　　　邮局
　　　　　　　　　　　　　　　　　　前面第一条马路　　　　淮海路
　　　　　　　　　　　　　　　　　　前面那座大楼　　　　　图书馆

2. <u>走十分钟</u>就<u>到邮局</u>了。　　　　乘地铁半个小时　　　　到公司
　　　　　　　　　　　　　　　　　　跑（pǎo/run）几分钟　　　累

88

学一会儿	会 (master, be good at)
坐飞机两个小时	到日本
3. <u>邮局</u>离这儿<u>很远</u>。 体育馆	非常远
地铁站	不太远
车站	很近

二、用括号中的词语完成句子(Complete sentences with the words in brackets)

1. A：去体育馆怎么走？　　B：_____。（一直）
2. A：哪儿有超市？　　B：_____。（往）
3. A：菜场远吗？　　B：_____。（离）
4. 你去哪儿？我们_____。（一起）
5. 晚上十点了,孩子_____。（该）

三、会话(Converstions)

玛　丽：请问,2 号楼在哪儿？
路人一：对不起,我也不知道,你问问别人吧。
玛　丽：去 2 号楼怎么走？
路人二：你到第一个路口向左转。
玛　丽：谢谢。

玛　丽：这是 2 号楼吗？
路人三：不是。你走错(cuò/wrong)了。2 号楼在那边。
玛　丽：离这儿远吗？
路人三：不远了。
玛　丽：啊,这个路口有指路牌(zhǐlùpái/signpost)。

☆　　**练习答案**(Key to the exercises)　　☆

二、1. 一直向前走　　2. 往东走,前面就是　　3. 菜场离这儿不太远
　　4. 一起走吧　　5. 该睡觉了

13　打　电话₁　MAKING A TELEPHONE CALL₁

Dǎ　Diànhuà

1. A：喂_{注1}，你好。　　　　Hello.
   Wèi,　　nǐ　hǎo.

   B：你好，布朗太太在　　Hello. Is Mrs. Brown in?
   Nǐ　hǎo, Bùlǎng tàitai zài
   家吗？
   jiā　ma?

   A：不在，她出去了。　　Sorry. She is out.
   Bú zài, tā chūqu le.

   B：她什么时候回来？　　When will she come back?
   Tā shénme shíhou huílai?

   A：我不知道，您有什么　I don't know. Anything I can help with?
   Wǒ bù zhīdao, nín yǒu shénme
   事？
   shì?

   B：我是露西，请让她　This is Lucy speaking. Please ask her to call
   Wǒ shì Lùxī, qǐng ràng tā
   给我回个_{注2}电话。　me back.
   gěi wǒ huí ge diànhuà.

   A：好的，请告诉我您　Sure. Would you please tell me your phone
   Hǎo de, qǐng gàosu wǒ nín

de diànhuà hàomǎ.
的 电话 号码。 number?

Liùsìsānwǔbālíng'èr, xièxie, zàijiàn.
B：6 4 3 5 8 0 2，谢谢，再见。 6435802. Thanks. Bye – bye.

Wèi, Chén lǎoshī zài ma?
2. A：喂，陈 老师 在 吗? Hello. Is Teacher Chen in?

Wǒ jiù shì. Nín shì nǎ wèi?
B：我 就 是。您 是 哪 位? Yes, speaking. Who is calling?

Wèi, Dīng yīshēng zài ma?
3. A：喂，丁 医生 在 吗? Hello. Is Dr. Ding in?

Zài, qǐng děng yíxià.
B：在，请 等 一下。 Yes, a moment please.

Wèi, Zhāng xiānsheng zài ma?
4. A：喂，张 先生 在 吗? Hello. Is Mr. Zhang in?

Tā bú zài, guò yíhuìr zài
B：他 不 在，过 一会儿 再 Sorry. He is not in this moment. Please call

dǎlai ba.
打来 吧。 him later.

Wèi, wǒ zhǎo Lǐ xiānsheng.
5. A：喂，我 找 李 先生。 Hello. May I speak to Mr. Li?

Qǐng nǐ děng yíxià, bié
B：请 你 等 一下，别 Hold on, please.

guàduàn diànhuà.
挂断 电话。

Tā zǒukāi le, tā huílai
他 走开 了，他 回来 Sorry, he is out. He will call you back when

mǎshàng gěi nín diànhuà.
马上 给 您 电话。 he returns.

Wèi, nǐ shì Dàzhòng Gōngsī
6. A：喂，你注3是 大众 公司 Hello. Is this Dazhong Company?

ma?
吗?

Bú shì, nǐ dǎcuò le.
B：不 是，你 打错 了。 No, you dialed the wrong number.

Wú xiānsheng, nín de diànhuà.
7. A：吴 先生，您 的 电话。 Mr. Wu, you are wanted on the phone.

Xièxie.
B：谢谢。 Thank you.

Yǒu shénme shì qǐng dǎ
8. A：有 什么 事 请 打 If there is anything, please call me.

diànhuà gěi wǒ.
电话　给　我。

　　Hǎo de.
B：好　的。　　　　　　　　All right.

Guò jǐ tiān wǒ dǎ diànhuà
9. A：过　几　天　我　打　电话　　I will phone you in several days to give you

dáfù nǐ.
答复　你。　　　　　　　　my reply.

　　Hǎo, wǒ děng nín diànhuà.
B：好，我　等　您　电话。　　Well, I will be waiting.

Zhè shì Huáyuán Dàshà, tīngdào
10. 这　是　华园　大厦，听到　This is Huayuan Mansions. Please dial the

líng xiǎng yǐhòu, qǐng bō
铃　响　（以）后，请　拨　extension number after you hear the tone. If

fēnjī hàomǎ. Cháhào qǐng bō
分机　号码。查号　请　拨　you don't know the extension number, please

líng.
零。　　　　　　　　　　dial zero.

Nín hǎo, zhèli shì
11. 您　好，这里　是　　　Hello. This is 6473158. Please leave your

liùsìqīsānyāowǔbā, tīngdào "dī"
6 4 7 3 1 5 8，听到 "嘀"　message after you hear the beep.

de yì shēng yǐhòu, qǐng liúyán.
的一　声　以后，请　留言。

Duìbuqǐ, nín bō de hàomǎ
12. 对不起，您　拨　的　号码　Sorry. The number you dialed does not exist.

shì kōnghào, qǐng cháxún.
是　空号，请　查询。　　Please check it.

Duìbuqǐ, nín bō de yònghù
13. 对不起，您　拨　的　用户　Sorry. The number you dialed is switched off.

yǐ guānjī, qǐng shāohòu zài bō.
已　关机，请　稍后　再　拨。Please dial later.

Duìbuqǐ, nín bō de yònghù
14. 对不起，您　拨　的　用户　Sorry. The number you dialed has no answer.

méiyǒu yìngdá.
没有　应答。

☆　**注　释**(Notes)　☆

1. 在打电话的时候，"喂"一般读成"wéi"。

In phone conversation, "喂" is pronounced as "wéi".

2. "回个电话"是"回一个电话"的意思,动词和宾语之间的数词"一"可以省略。

"回个电话" has the same meaning as "回一个电话". The numeral "一" between a verb and an object can be omitted.

Wǒ qù mǎi běn shū.
(1) 我 去 买 本 书。 I am going to buy a book.

Xiàwǔ wǒ kànle chǎng diànyǐng.
(2) 下午 我 看了 场 电影。 I saw a movie this afternoon.

3. 打电话的时候,无论询问的是人还是单位,都用"你"来称呼对方。"你"和"是"常常省略。

In telephone talk we usually use "你" to address the other side no matter it is a person or an organization. "你" and "是" are often omitted.

Wèi, nǐ shì Dàzhòng Gōngsī ma?
(1) 喂, 你 是 大众 公司 吗? Hello. Is this Dazhong Company?

Wèi, Dàzhòng Gōngsī ma?
(2) 喂, 大众 公司 吗? Hello. Is this Dazhong Company?

☆ 句型提示(Sentence pattern references) ☆

1. 布朗太太在家吗?　　　　　　请参看 304 页句型 23、24。
2. 别挂断电话。　　　　　　　　请参看 393 页句型 221。

☆ 词语用法举例(Examples for usage of the words) ☆

1. 请告诉我您的电话号码

Qǐng gàosu Lǐ Míng xiàwǔ liǎng diǎn kāihuì.
(1) 请 告诉 李 明 下午 两 点 开会。

Zhè jiàn shì shì tā gàosu wǒ de.
(2) 这 件 事 是 他 告诉 我 的。

Zhè jiàn shì wǒ méi gàosu tā.
(3) 这 件 事 我 没 告诉 他。

Chēhuò de shì bié gàosu tā.
(4) 车祸 的 事 别 告诉 她。

2. 过一会儿再打来吧

Nǐ zhème máng, wǒ guò yíhuìr zài lái ba.
(1) 你 这么 忙, 我 过 一会儿 再 来 吧。

Nǐ xiān zǒu ba, wǒ guò yíhuìr jiù lái.
(2) 你 先 走 吧, 我 过 一会儿 就 来。

Zhè zhāng bàozhǐ, wǒ hái méi kànwán, guò yíhuìr gěi nǐ.
(3) 这 张 报纸, 我 还 没 看完, 过 一会儿 给 你。

Gāngcái tíngdiàn le, guòle yíhuìr yòu yǒu diàn le.
(4) 刚才 停电 了，过了 一会儿 又 有 电 了。

3. 别挂断电话

Yǔ zhème dà, bié chūqu le.
(1) 雨 这么 大，别 出去 了。

Zhèxiē píngguǒ huài le, bié chī le.
(2) 这些 苹果 坏 了，别 吃 了。

Tài guì le, bié mǎi le.
(3) 太 贵 了，别 买 了。

Zài gōnggòng chǎngsuǒ bié chōuyān.
(4) 在 公共 场所 别 抽烟。 （抽烟：smoke）

4. 你打错了

Wǒ xiěcuò le, zěnme bàn?
(1) 我 写错 了，怎么 办？

Wǒ kàncuò le rìqī.
(2) 我 看错 了日期。

Yíngyèyuán suàncuò le, duō shōule wǒ shí kuài qián.
(3) 营业员 算错 了，多 收了 我 十 块 钱。

Nǐ tīngcuò le, shì "yī", bú shì "qī".
(4) 你 听错 了，是 "一"，不 是 "七"。

5. 听到铃响(以)后

Shōudào māma de xìn hòu, tā mǎshàng huí jiā le.
(1) 收到 妈妈 的 信 后，他 马上 回 家 了。 （收到：receive）

Jiēdào diànhuà hòu, tā mǎshàng qù yīyuàn le.
(2) 接到 电话 后，他 马上 去 医院 了。

Kànle guǎnggào yǐhòu, tā jiù qù mǎi le.
(3) 看了 广告 以后，他 就 去 买 了。 （广告：advertisement）

Fàngxué yǐhòu wǒ qù mǎi dōngxi le.
(4) 放学 以后 我 去 买 东西 了。

☆ 词 语 (Word list) ☆

diànhuàbù
1. 电话簿 （名）telephone directory

zǒngjī
2. 总机 （名）switchboard

fēnjī
3. 分机 （名）extension

gōngyòng diànhuà
4. 公用 电话 （名）public telephone

tóubì diànhuà
5. 投币 电话 （名）pay phone

cíkǎ diànhuà
6. 磁卡 电话 （名）card phone

shǒujī
7. 手机 （名）mobile phone

chuánzhēnjī
8. 传真机 （名）fax machine

mángyīn
9. 忙音 （名）a tone which means the number is engaged

zhànxiàn
10. 占线 （动）the line is busy, the number is engaged

11. jiē diànhuà
接　电话　　answer the phone call

12. diànhuà huài le　the phone is out of
电话　坏　了　order

13. guónèi chángtú diànhuà　domestic long - dis-
国内　长途　电话(名)tance call

14. guójì chángtú diànhuà　International long -
国际　长途　电话(名)distance call

☆　练　习(Exercises)　☆

一、替换练习(Substitution exercises)

1. 请她给我回个电话。

打	个	电话
写	封(fēng,量词)	信(xìn/letter)
泡(pào)	杯	茶(泡茶:make tea)
买	盒	饭

2. 过一会儿再打来吧。

过两天	去你家玩
过半个小时	休息
明天	去公园
下个星期	开会

二、用括号中的词语完成句子(Complete sentences with the words in brackets)

1. 这是大华公司。请＿＿＿＿＿＿＿＿＿＿。（拨）

2. 他不在,请＿＿＿＿＿＿＿＿＿＿。（再）

3. 他马上就来,请＿＿＿＿＿＿＿＿＿＿。（别）

4. 电话铃响了,谁＿＿＿＿＿＿＿＿＿＿?（接）

三、完成对话(Complete the conversations)

1. A：喂,＿＿＿＿＿＿＿＿＿＿＿＿＿＿＿?

　B：他不在,出差了。

　A：＿＿＿＿＿＿＿＿＿＿＿＿＿＿?

　B：下星期一回来。请问您是哪位?

　A：我是＿＿＿＿＿＿＿＿＿＿＿＿。

　B：好的,等他回来＿＿＿＿＿＿＿＿＿＿。

2. A：(这里是)大华公司。＿＿＿＿＿＿＿＿＿＿＿?

　B：我找顾宁。

　A：他走开了。＿＿＿＿＿＿＿＿＿＿＿。

　B：请他给我回个电话。我叫李丽平。

　A：他知道＿＿＿＿＿＿＿＿＿＿吗?

　B：他有我的电话号码。

3. A：你好,我是李丽平,顾宁回来了吗?

　B：他回来了,＿＿＿＿＿＿＿＿＿。顾宁,来接电话。

四、会话（Conversations）

郭明明：喂？谁啊？

玛　丽：是明明吗？我是玛丽。你妈妈在吗？

郭明明：妈妈不在。您有什么事吗？

玛　丽：我过一会儿再打来吧。

郭明明：好的。啊！等一等,妈妈回来了。妈妈,快点儿,电话！

于雪来：谁来的电话？

郭明明：是玛丽阿姨（āyí/aunt）

于雪来：玛丽,你好。什么事啊？

玛　丽：是这样。你知道音乐厅（yīnyuètīng/concert hall）的电话号码吗？

于雪来：我也不知道。你可以打114问。

玛　丽：114是什么？

于雪来：114是电话查号台（cháhàotái/directory inquiries）。

玛　丽：明白了。谢谢。

服务员：您好,这里是114查号台,请讲。

玛　丽：我想问上海音乐厅的电话号码。

服务员：请稍等。请记录（jìlù/record, write down）:53866666。

☆　**练习答案**（Key to the exercises）　☆

二、1. 拨分机号码　　　　2. 过一会儿再打来

　　3. 别挂断电话　　　　4. 去接电话

三、1. A：李明在吗　他什么时候回来　王小良

　　　B：叫他打电话给你

　　2. A：你找谁　请过一会儿再打来吧　你的电话号码

　　3. B：请你等一下

14 Dǎ Diànhuà
打 电话₂ MAKING A TELEPHONE CALL₂

1. A： Wèi, shì Gōngyù Guǎnlǐchù
喂， 是 公寓 管理处
ma?
吗？

Hello. Is this the Management Office of the Apartment Building?

B： Shì de, yǒu shénme shì ma?
是 的， 有 什么注 事 吗？

Yes, may I help you?

A： Wǒ shì yāosìlíng'èr shì, kōngtiáo
我 是 1 4 0 2 室， 空调
huài le, qǐng lái xiūlǐ.
坏 了， 请 来 修理。

This is Apt. 1402. The air conditioning is out of order. Please come to fix it.

B： Nǐmen shénme shíhou zài jiā?
你们 什么 时候 在 家？

All right. When will you be home?

A： Xiàwǔ sān diǎn yǐhòu.
下午 三 点 以后。

After 3 pm.

B： Hǎo de, wǒmen xiàwǔ sān
好 的， 我们 下午 三
diǎn qù.
点 去。

OK. We will be there at 3 pm.

2. A：Wèi, zhèli shì Bìchún Gōngsī.
喂，这里 是 碧纯 公司。
Hello. This is Bichun Company.

B：Nǐ hǎo, qǐng sòng sì tǒng shuǐ lai.
你 好，请 送 四 桶 水 来。
Please send four large bottles of（pure）water here.

A：Nín shì nǎli?
您 是 哪里?
Where are you?

B：Xiāngshān Gōngyù sānlíngsì, wǒ xìng Lǐ.
香山 公寓 304，我 姓 李。
Apt. 304 of Xiangshan Building. My surname is Li.

A：Míngtiān shàngwǔ shí diǎn sòng- qu kěyǐ ma?
明天 上午 十 点 送 去 可以 吗?
Can I deliver the water at 10 am tomorrow morning?

B：Míngtiān shàngwǔ wǒ bú zài jiā, xiàwǔ liǎng diǎn sònglai hǎo ma?
明天 上午 我 不 在 家，下午 两 点 送来 好 吗?
Sorry. I will not be home then. Is 2 pm OK for you?

A：Hǎo de.
好 的。
Sure.

3. B：Wèi, Bìchún Gōngsī ma?
喂，碧纯 公司 吗?
Hello. Is that Bichun Company?

Wǒ yùdìng de shuǐ wèi shénme hái méi sònglai?
我 预订 的 水 为 什么 还 没 送来?
The water I ordered hasn't come yet. Why?

A：Sòng shuǐ de chē yǐjīng chūfā le, kěnéng lù shang dǔchē, mǎshàng huì dào de.
送 水 的 车 已经 出发 了，可能 路 上 堵车，马上 会 到 的。
The delivery van is on way there. Maybe there is traffic jam. It will be there soon.

4. A：Wèi, (zhèli shì) Shūcài Gōngsī, qǐng jiǎng.
喂，（这里 是）蔬菜 公司，请 讲。
Hello. This is Vegetable Company. May I help you?

Wǒ yào yì qiānkè fānqié、
B: 我 要 一 千克 番茄、

liǎng qiānkè tǔdòu, liǎng ge
两 千克 土豆, 两 个

juǎnxīncài, qǐng sònglai. Wǒ
卷心菜, 请 送来。我

shì Guānghuá Gōngyù liùlíngqī,
是 光华 公寓 607,

wǒ shì Nánxī·Bèikè.
我 是 南希·贝克。

Zhīdao le, jīntiān xiàwǔ sì
A: 知道 了, 今天 下午 四

diǎn sòngqu.
点 送去。

I need one kilogram of tomatoes, two kilograms of potatoes and two cabbages. Please deliver them to me. My address is Apt. 607, Guanghua Building. My name is Nancy Baker.

I see. We will deliver these items to you at four o'clock this afternoon.

☆ 注 释(Note) ☆

这里的"什么"指不肯定的事物。"什么"可以省略,句子的意思不变。
"什么" here indicates something undefined. "什么" can be omitted, and the meaning of the sentence would not change.

☆ 句型提示(Sentence pattern references) ☆

1. 我预订的水为什么还没送来? 请参看 299 页句型 13。
2. 可能路上堵车。 请参看 339 页句型 101。
3. 马上会到的。 请参看 335 页句型 91。

☆ 词语用法举例(Examples for usage of the words) ☆

1. 空调坏了

Xǐyījī huài le, jīntiān bù xǐ yīfu le.
(1) 洗衣机 坏 了, 今天 不 洗 衣服 了。

Wǒ jiā de rèshuǐqì huài le.
(2) 我 家 的 热水器 坏 了。

Zhèxiē xiāngjiāo huài le, bié chī le.
(3) 这些 香蕉 坏 了,别 吃 了。

Nàge xiǎoháir gēn huàirén xué huài le.
(4) 那个 小孩儿 跟 坏人 学 坏 了。 (坏人:bad person
学:learn)

2. 我预订的水为什么还没送来

(1) Shí'èr diǎn le, tā hái méi shuìjiào.
十二 点 了，他 还 没 睡觉。

(2) Dōu jiǔ diǎn le, tā hái méi qǐchuáng.
都 九 点 了，他 还 没 起床。

(3) Wǒ hái méi chīguo Rìběncài.
我 还 没 吃过 日本菜。

(4) Tā dàxué hái méi bìyè.
他 大学 还 没 毕业。 （毕业：graduate）

3. 可能路上堵车

(1) Míngtiān kěnéng xià yǔ.
明天 可能 下 雨。

(2) Qiánmian kěnéng chū jiāotōng shìgù le.
前面 可能 出 交通 事故 了。

(3) Méi jiàndào tā, kěnéng bìng le.
没 见到 他，可能 病 了。

(4) Zhème rè, kěnéng shì kōngtiáo huài le.
这么 热，可能 是 空调 坏 了。

4. 马上会到的

(1) Míngtiān huì xià yǔ de.
明天 会 下 雨 的。

(2) Xiàbān shíjiān gōnggòng qìchē huì hěn jǐ de.
下班 时间 公共 汽车 会 很 挤 的。

(3) Tā dāying le, huì lái de.
他 答应 了，会 来 的。 （答应：promise）

(4) Jiàndào nǐ, māma huì hěn gāoxìng de.
见到 你，妈妈 会 很 高兴 的。

☆ 词 语（Word list） ☆

1.	diàndēng 电灯	（名）	electric light	2.	kāiguān 开关	（名） switch
3.	rèshuǐqì 热水器	（名）	water heater	4.	méiqìlú 煤气炉	（名） gas cooker
5.	xǐyījī 洗衣机	（名）	washing machine	6.	diànfànguō 电饭锅	（名） electric rice cooker
7.	wēibōlú 微波炉	（名）	microwave oven	8.	diànshìjī 电视机	（名） television set
9.	lùxiàngjī 录像机	（名）	video, video recorder	10.	yīnxiǎng 音响	（名） Hi-fi
11.	diànshàn 电扇	（名）	fan, electric fan	12.	diànbīngxiāng 电冰箱	（名） refrigerator

13.	xīchéngqì 吸尘器	（名）	vacuum cleaner	14.	zìláishuǐ 自来水	（名）	running water, tap – water
15.	shuǐguǎn 水管	（名）	water pipe	16.	shuǐlóngtóu 水龙头	（名）	tap, faucet
17.	zuòcè 坐厕	（名）	lavatory, water closet	18.	lòushuǐ 漏水		water leakage
19.	tíngshuǐ 停水		cut off the water	20.	tíngdiàn 停电		blackout, power failure
21.	diànhuà yùdìng 电话　预订		make reservation by phone				

☆ 练 习（Exercises） ☆

一、完成对话（Complete the conversations）

1. A：这里是大众（Dàzhòng）出租汽车公司。

   B：我要＿＿＿＿＿＿＿＿＿＿＿。今天下午三点。

   A：您在哪里上车?

   B：＿＿＿＿＿＿＿＿＿＿＿。

   A：您要到哪里?

   B：＿＿＿＿＿＿＿＿＿＿＿。

2. A：喂,是管理处吗?

   B：是,＿＿＿＿＿＿＿＿＿＿＿?

   A：＿＿＿＿＿＿＿＿＿＿＿。

   B：好的,您什么时候在家?

   A：＿＿＿＿＿＿＿＿＿＿＿。

3. A：是大华公司吗?

   B：不是,＿＿＿＿＿＿＿＿＿＿＿。

   A：对不起。

二、用括号中的词语完成句子（Complete sentences with the words in brackets）

1. A：他会来吗?　　　　　B：雨下得很大,＿＿＿＿＿＿＿＿＿。（不会）

2. A：他在哪儿?　　　　　B：＿＿＿＿＿＿＿＿＿。（可能）

3. A：你去过西安吗?　　　B：＿＿＿＿＿＿＿＿＿。（没）

4. A：你爸爸呢? 回家了吗?　B：＿＿＿＿＿＿＿＿＿。（还没）

三、替换练习（Substitution exercises）

1. <u>送</u>两桶水<u>来</u>。　　　　送　　　　一张电影票

　　　　　　　　　　　　买　　　　一斤水果

　　　　　　　　　　　　拿　　　　啤酒

2. <u>送</u>两桶水<u>去</u>。　　　　送　　　　电风扇

寄	一封信
拿	几个肉包子（ròubāozi/steamed bun with meat stuffing）

四、会话（Conversation）

玛　丽：是管理处吗？

管理处：是的。您有什么事？

玛　丽：我家的水管漏了。麻烦你们来修一修。

管理处：您是……

玛　丽：啊，我是4号楼302室的。

管理处：哪个地方的水管？

玛　丽：厨房里的。

管理处：您今天下午在家吗？

玛　丽：在的。

管理处：那么，我们两点钟去，行吗？

玛　丽：好的。麻烦你们。还有，我的电话也不好。

管理处：修电话要找电信公司，您拨112吧。

玛　丽：谢谢。

☆　　练习答案（Key to the exercises）　　☆

一、1. B：一辆车　大华公寓二号楼门口　浦东

　　2. B：您有什么事　A：我家门铃坏了，请来修理　下午一点以后

　　3. B：你打错了

二、1. 他不会来了

　　2. 可能在办公室

　　3. 没去过

　　4. 还没回来

15
Zài   Xǐyīdiàn
在 洗衣店   IN A LAUNDRY

A：Shīfu,   yǒu jǐ jiàn yīfu yào xǐ.
师傅，有 几 件 衣服 要 洗。   Hello, sir. I'd like to have these clothes washed.

B：Hǎo de,   shénme yīfu?
好 的， 什么 衣服？   Yes. What clothes?

A：Sān jiàn chènyī, liǎng tiáo kùzi.
三 件 衬衣， 两 条 裤子。   Three shirts and two pairs of pants.

Zhè yóuzì néng bu néng qùdiào?
这 油渍 能 不 能 去掉？   Can you get rid of this oily dirt?

B：Néng qùdiào.
能 去掉。   Yes, we can.

A：Zhè jiàn   nídàyī yào gānxǐ.
这 件 呢大衣 要 干洗。   And I want to have this woolen coat dry

Zhè jiàn shàngyī qǐng yùn yíxià.
这 件 上衣 请 熨 一下。   cleaned. Please have this jacket ironed. When

Shénme shíhou kěyǐ qǔ?
什么 时候 可以 取？   can I pick them up?

B：Sān tiān yǐhòu lái ba.
三 天 以后 来 吧。   In three days.

A：
Wǒ yào chūchāi, kuài diǎnr
我 要 出差, 快 点儿
xíng ma?
行 吗?

Is it possible to speed it up? I am going on a business trip.

B：
Nàme, hòutiān lái ba.
那么注1, 后天 来 吧。

If so, you can pick them up the day after tomorrow.

A：
Néng bu néng zài kuài diǎnr?
能 不 能 再注2 快 点儿?
Wǒ děngzhe chuān ne.
我 等着 穿 呢。

May I get them even earlier? I need to wear them.

B：
Zuì kuài yě yào hòutiān shàngwǔ.
最 快 也 要 后天 上午。

The morning of the day after tomorrow is the earliest time.

A：
Xiànzài fù qián ma?
现在 付 钱 吗?

Should I pay now?

B：
Qǐng xiànzài fù.
请 现在 付。

Yes, please.

Zhè shì fāpiào, qǐng shōuhǎo.
这 是 发票, 请 收好。
Qǔ yīfu de shíhou qǐng bié
取 衣服 的 时候 请 别
wàngle dài fāpiào lai.
忘了 带 发票 来。

This is the receipt. Please keep it. Don't forget to bring the receipt with you when you pick your clothes up.

☆　注　释(Notes)　☆

1. "那么"在这里是连词,承接上文的语意,引出表示结果的下文。口语中常说"那"。
   "那么"is a conjunction here. It continues the meaning from the proceeding paragraph and draws a conclusion in the following paragraph. In spoken language, we often use "那".
2. "再"是副词,在这里表示程度增加。
   "再"is an adverb. It indicates an increase in degree.

☆　句型提示(Sentence pattern references)　☆

1. 什么衣服?　　　　　　请参看 295 页句型 6。
2. 这油渍能不能去掉?　请参看 301 页句型 16。
3. 能去掉。　　　　　　请参看 335 页句型 92。
4. 什么时候可以取?　　请参看 336 页句型 94。

☆ 词语用法举例(Examples for usage of the words) ☆

1. 什么时候可以取

(1) Zhè běn shū shénme shíhou kěyǐ chūbǎn?
    这 本 书 什么 时候 可以 出版?

(2) Shénme dìfang kěyǐ mǎidào nǎilào?
    什么 地方 可以 买到 奶酪? (奶酪: fromage)

(3) Shíwǔ hào de jīpiào xiànzài kěyǐ yùdìng le.
    十五 号 的 机票 现在 可以 预订 了。 (机票: air ticket)

(4) Wǒmen kěyǐ sònghuò shàngmén.
    我们 可以 送货 上门。 (送货上门:deliver goods to customers)

2. 快点儿行吗

(1) Bāng ge máng, xíng ma?
    帮 个 忙, 行 吗?

(2) Péi wǒ shàng yīyuàn, xíng ma?
    陪 我 上 医院, 行 吗? (陪:accompany)

(3) Bāng wǒ jiào liàng chē, xíng ma?
    帮 我 叫 辆 车, 行 吗?

(4) Yòng yíxià nǐ de diànhuà, xíng ma?
    用 一下 你 的 电话, 行 吗?

3. 我等着穿呢

(1) Qǐng kuài diǎnr sòng shuǐ lai, wǒ děngzhe shāofàn ne.
    请 快 点儿 送 水 来, 我 等着 烧饭 呢。 (烧饭:prepare a meal)

(2) Qǐng yòng kuàijiàn jìlai, wǒ děngzhe yòng.
    请 用 快件 寄来, 我 等着 用。 (快件:express mail)

(3) Kuài qù mǎi cháyè, wǒ děngzhe pàochá ne.
    快 去 买 茶叶, 我 等着 泡茶 呢。

(4) Zhè kuài shǒubiǎo néng kuài diǎnr xiūhǎo ma? Wǒ děngzhe yòng.
    这 块 手表 能 快 点儿 修好 吗? 我 等着 用。

4. 最快也要后天上午

(1) Zuì zǎo yě děi shí'èr tiān.
    最 早 也 得 十二 天。

(2) Zuì chí èrshí hào dáfù nǐ.
    最 迟 二十 号 答复 你。 (迟: late)

(3) Zuì shǎo yě yào yìqiān kuài.
    最 少 也 要 一千 块。

(4) Zuì duō gěi nǐ yìbǎi kuài.
    最 多 给 你 一百 块。

5. 请别忘了带发票来

(1) Xiàwǔ yào xià yǔ, bié wàngle dài yǔsǎn.
    下午 要 下 雨, 别 忘了 带 雨伞。

Xià chē shí bié wàngle ná bāo.
（2）下 车 时 别 忘了 拿 包。

Chūmén shí bié wàngle guāndēng.
（3）出门 时 别 忘了 关灯。　（关灯：turn off the light）

Chīwán fàn bié wàngle chī yào.
（4）吃完 饭 别 忘了 吃 药。　（吃药：take medicine）

☆　词　语（Word list）　☆

1. 熨斗 yùndǒu	（名）	iron, flatiron	
3. 肥皂 féizào	（名）	soap	
5. 毛衣 máoyī	（名）	woolen sweater	
7. 连衣裙 liányīqún	（名）	one piece dress, frock	
9. 睡衣 shuìyī	（名）	pajamas	
11. T恤 T xù	（名）	T-shirt	
13. 夹克 jiákè	（名）	jacket	
15. 滑雪衫 huáxuěshān	（名）	skiing jacket	
17. 雨衣 yǔyī	（名）	raincoat	
19. 内裤 nèikù	（名）	underpants, briefs	
21. 连裤袜 liánkùwà	（名）	panty-hose	
23. 围巾 wéijīn	（名）	scarf	
25. 旗袍 qípáo	（名）	*chi-pao*, mandarin gown	
27. 拉链 lāliàn	（名）	zipper	
29. 晾 衣服 liàng yīfu		dry clothes in the air	
31. 折 衣服 zhé yīfu		fold clothes	

2. 洗衣粉 xǐyīfěn （名） washing powder
4. 西服 xīfú （名） western style clothes, suit
6. 裙子 qúnzi （名） skirt
8. 背心 bèixīn （名） vest, waistcoat
10. 运动服 yùndòngfú （名） sportswear
12. 风衣 fēngyī （名） windcheater, windbreaker
14. 牛仔裤 niúzǎikù （名） jeans
16. 游泳衣 yóuyǒngyī （名） swimming suit
18. 内衣 nèiyī （名） underwear, underclothes
20. 袜子 wàzi （名） socks, stockings
22. 手帕 shǒupà （名） handkerchief
24. 丝巾 sījīn （名） silk scarf
26. 围裙 wéiqún （名） apron
28. 衣架 yījià （名） clothes hanger
30. 晒（衣服）shài(yīfu) （动） dry clothes in the sun

☆　练　习（Exercises）　☆

一、替换练习（Substitution exercises）

1. 什么<u>衣服</u>?　　　　　　电影

水果(shuǐguǒ)

公司

报纸

2. 三天以后来取。　　　一年　　　　　　　回国

三点钟　　　　　　在家等你

来中国　　　　　　看了很多中国电影

学习汉语　　　　　认识了很多中国朋友

二、用括号中的词语完成句子(Complete sentences with the words in brackets)

1. A：你的衣服是什么时候送来的?　　B：＿＿＿＿＿＿＿＿＿＿。（以前）

2. A：您要洗多少衣服?　　　　　　B：大衣和衬衣＿＿＿＿＿＿。（各）

3. 你买酱油回来了吗? 我＿＿＿＿＿＿＿＿。（等着）

三、完成对话(Complete the conversations)

1. A：这个地方脏(zāng/dirty)了,能洗掉吗?

B：＿＿＿＿＿＿＿＿＿＿＿＿＿。

A：＿＿＿＿＿＿＿＿＿＿＿＿＿?

B：五天以后。

2. A：什么时候可以取?

B：＿＿＿＿＿＿＿＿＿＿＿＿＿。

A：＿＿＿＿＿＿＿＿＿＿＿＿＿?

B：对不起,不能更快了。

四、会话(Conversation)

服务员：布朗太太,要洗衣服吗?

玛　丽：是的。这红酒(red wine)渍能洗掉吗?

服务员：红酒渍是洗不掉的。

玛　丽：那怎么办?

服务员：我们试试看(shìshi kàn/try)吧。

玛　丽：好吧。这里洗毛衣多少钱一件?

服务员：十五块钱。请您拿好发票,三天以后来取。

玛　丽：好的。

☆　**练习答案**(Key to the exercises)　☆

二、1. 是三天以前送来的　　2. 各两件　　3. 等着用

三、1. B：能洗掉　　A：什么时候可以取

2. B：两天以后　　A：能不能快点儿

16 Zài Lǐfàdiàn 在 理发店 AT THE BARBER'S

1. A: Qǐng jìn, qǐng zhèbian zuò,
请 进，请 这边 坐，

qǐng shāo děng yíhuìr.
请 稍 等 一会儿。

Come in please. Please sit here and wait a moment.

   B: Yào děng duō jiǔ?
要 等 多 久？

How long will it be?

   A: Dàyuē yí kè zhōng. Xíng
大约 一 刻 钟。行

ma?
吗？

About 15 minutes. Is that OK?

   B: Xíng, wǒ děngzhe.
行，我 等着。

OK, I will wait.

2. A: Lúndào nín le, qǐng dào
轮到 您 了，请 到

zhèbian lai.
这边 来。

It is your turn. Please come over here.

   B: Wǒ yào xǐtóu、 chuīfēng.
我 要 洗头、 吹风。

I want a shampoo and blow-dry.

3. A：Xǐguo tóu le ma?
洗过 头 了 吗？ — Did you have a shampoo?

B：Wǒ xǐguo tóu le, dān chuīfēng.
我 洗过 头 了, 单 吹风。 — Yes, I had a shampoo. Blow-dry only, please.

4. A：Chuīfēng ma?
吹风 吗？ — A blow-dry?

B：Dān xǐtóu jiù kěyǐ le注, búyòng chuīfēng.
单 洗头 就 可以 了注, 不用 吹风。 — A shampoo only. No blow-dry.

A：Qǐng bǎ yǎnjìng zhāi xialai.
请 把 眼镜 摘 下来。 — Please take off your glasses.

5. A：(Nín yào) jiǎn shénme yàngzi?
(您 要) 剪 什么 样子？ — How do you want your haircut?

B：Hé xiànzài yíyàng.
和 现在 一样。 — The same as it is.

(Qǐng) jiǎn de duǎn yìdiǎnr.
(请) 剪 得 短 一点儿。 — Cut it short, please.

A：Yào xiāobáo yìxiē ma?
要 削薄 一些 吗？ — Do you want it thinner?

B：Nǐ kànzhe bàn ba.
你 看着 办 吧。 — Do as you think fit.

6. A：Jīntiān shì jiǎn tóufa háishi tàng tóufa?
今天 是 剪 头发 还是 烫 头发？ — A haircut or permanent for you today?

B：Yào jiǎn tóufa.
要 剪 头发。 — A haircut.

(Qǐng) bié jiǎn de tài duǎn.
(请) 别 剪 得 太 短。 — Don't make it too short, please. Just a trim.

Shāowēi xiū yíxià jiù kěyǐ le.
稍微 修 一下 就 可以 了。

7. A：Wǒ yào tàng tóufa.
我 要 烫 头发。 — I want a perm.

B：Nín yào tàng shénme fàxíng?
您 要 烫 什么 发型？ — Which hairstyle do you want for the perm?

Nǐ gěi wǒ shèjì ba.
A：你 给 我 设计 吧。　　　Please design a style for me.

Wǒ xiǎng rǎn tóufa.
8. A：我 想 染 头发。　　　I'd like to have my hair dyed.

Rǎn shénme yánsè?
B：染 什么 颜色?　　　Which color would you prefer?

Rǎn hēisè.
A：染 黑色。　　　Black, please.

Zhèyàng, nín mǎnyì ma?
B：这样， 您 满意 吗?　　　Here you are. How do you like it?

Hěn hǎo.
A：很 好。　　　It's very good.

☆　注 释(Note)　☆

"就可以了"或者"就行了"表示达到这种程度就够了。

"就可以了"or "就行了"means that it is enough to reach this degree or this level.

Dài wǔbǎi kuài qù jiù xíng le.
(1) 带 五百 块 去 就 行 了。

It is sufficient to take 500 *yuan* with you.

Zhè jiàn shì wǒmen liǎng ge rén zuò jiù xíng le.
(2) 这 件 事 我们 两 个 人 做 就 行 了。

Just two of us are enough for handling this work.

☆　句型提示(Sentence pattern references)　☆

1. 我洗过头了。　　　请参看 309 页句型 36。
2. 请把眼镜摘下来。　　　请参看 326 页句型 74。
3. 请把眼镜摘下来。　　　请参看 353 页句型 134。
4. 和现在一样　　　请参看 365 页句型 159。
5. 请剪得短一点儿。　　　请参看 343 页句型 112。

☆　词语用法举例(Examples for usage of the words)　☆

1. 请把眼镜摘下来

Qǐng bǎ chuāng dǎkāi.
(1) 请 把 窗 打开。　（窗：window）

Qǐng bǎ tóufa jiǎnduǎn.
(2) 请 把 头发 剪短。

Tā bǎ tóufa tàng le.
(3) 她 把 头发 烫 了。

Dìdi bǎ bēizi dǎsuì le.
(4) 弟弟 把 杯子 打碎 了。（打碎：break）

Mèimei bǎ qiǎokèlì chīguāng le.
(5) 妹妹 把 巧克力 吃光 了。

Nǐ bǎ zhè bēi jiǔ hēle ba.
(6) 你 把 这 杯 酒 喝了 吧。

2. 你看着办吧

Jīnwǎn yǒu sì ge péngyou lái, yào mǎi duōshao cài, nǐ kànzhe bàn ba.
(1) 今晚 有 四 个 朋友 来，要 买 多少 菜，你 看着 办 吧。

Mǎi shénme huā hǎo, nǐ kànzhe bàn ba.
(2) 买 什么 花 好，你 看着 办 吧。

Xiǎoháir de dōngxi, nǐ kànzhe mǎi ba.
(3) 小孩儿 的 东西，你 看着 买 吧。

Zhǐ yǒu zhème yìdiǎnr qián, nǐ kànzhe yòng ba.
(4) 只 有 这么 一点儿 钱，你 看着 用 吧。

3. 别剪得太短

Yán bié fàng de tài duō.
(1) 盐 别 放 得 太 多。

Jiǔ bié hē de tài duō.
(2) 酒 别 喝 得 太 多。

Ròu bié shāo tài jiǔ.
(3) 肉 别 烧 太 久。（烧：cook）

Chá bié pào tài nóng.
(4) 茶 别 泡 太 浓。（浓：thick）

☆ 词 语（Word list）☆

lǐfàdiàn
1. 理发店 （名） barber shop, beauty salon

měiróngyuàn
2. 美容院 （名） beauty salon

lǐfàshī
3. 理发师 （名） barber, hairdresser

jiǎn tóufa
4. 剪 头发 cut hair

zuò tóufa
5. 做 头发 set hair

jiǎfà
6. 假发 （名） wig

jiǎndāo
7. 剪刀 （名） scissors

shūzi
8. 梳子 （名） comb

shūtóu
9. 梳头 （动） comb one's hair

zhào jìngzi
10. 照 镜子 look at oneself in the mirror

xǐfàshuǐ
11. 洗发水 （名） shampoo

xiāngbō
12. 香波 （名） shampoo

xiāngzào
13. 香皂 （名） perfumed soap, toilet soap

yānzhi
14. 胭脂 （名） rouge

	chúngāo				kǒuhóng		
15.	唇膏	（名）	lipstick	16.	口红	（名）	lipstick

	xiāngshuǐ				dìngxíngshuǐ		
17.	香水	（名）	perfume	18.	定型水	（名）	hair spray

	hùfūshuāng				hùfàsù		
19.	护肤霜	（名）	face cream	20.	护发素	（名）	hair conditioner

	zā biànzi			liú liúhǎir	
21.	扎 辫子	plait/braid one's hair	22.	留 刘海儿	have a fringe/bang

☆　练　习 (Exercises)　☆

一、替换练习 (Substitution exercises)

1. 轮到你 洗头 了。　　　　　　他　　　　　　　　讲故事 (gùshi/story)
　　　　　　　　　　　　　　　李丽平　　　　　　　请客 (qǐngkè/give dinner)
　　　　　　　　　　　　　　　日本队 (duì/team)　　发球 (fāqiú/serve a ball)
　　　　　　　　　　　　　　　你　　　　　　　　　读

2. 剪得短一点儿。　　　　　　　削　　　　　　　　薄
　　　　　　　　　　　　　　　染　　　　　　　　黄
　　　　　　　　　　　　　　　烫　　　　　　　　卷 (juǎn/curl)

二、用括号中的词语完成句子 (Complete sentences with the words in brackets)

1. 我不要套餐 (tàocān/set meal) , ＿＿＿＿＿＿＿＿＿＿＿＿。（单）

2. 买这样的衣服不用一百块, ＿＿＿＿＿＿＿＿＿＿＿＿。（就可以了）

3. 这是我的电话号码, 有什么事＿＿＿＿＿＿＿＿＿＿＿＿。（就行了）

4. A：面条里要不要放辣椒？　　　B：＿＿＿＿＿＿＿＿＿＿＿＿。（稍微）

5. 不要剪得太短, ＿＿＿＿＿＿＿＿＿＿＿＿。（稍微）

三、把下列句子变成疑问句 (Change the following sentences into interrogative sentences)

1. 我要烫头发。

2. 我要剪到耳朵 (ěrduo/ear)。

3. 我不要削薄。

4. 这个发型很好看。

四、会话 (Conversations)

洗头小姐：您好。洗头吗？

玛　　丽：是的。还要剪一下。

洗头小姐：好。您用哪种洗发水？

玛　　丽：我习惯 (xíguàn/be accustomed to) 用欧莱雅 (Ōuláiyǎ) 的。

洗头小姐：去冲洗 (chōngxǐ/rinse) , 请到这边来。

玛　　丽：好的。

洗头小姐：我给您按摩（ànmó/massage）一下吧。

玛　　丽：谢谢。

发 型 师：您要剪什么样子？

玛　　丽：我喜欢（xǐhuan/like）现在的发型，剪短一点儿就可以了。

发 型 师：不想换一个样子？

玛　　丽：不换。现在这个发型很好。

发 型 师：好了，您看看行吗？

玛　　丽：很好。

☆　练习答案（Key to the exercises）　☆

二、1. 单要一个汉堡包（hànbǎobāo/hamburger）

　　2. 七十多块就可以了

　　3. 打个电话就行了

　　4. 稍微放一点儿吧

　　5. 稍微剪一点儿吧

三、1. 您要烫发吗？

　　2. 您要剪多短？

　　3. 您要削薄头发吗？

　　4. 这个发型好看吗？/这个发型好看不好看？

17 Qù Fàndiàn 去 饭店 GOING TO A RESTAURANT

Wǒ yǒu diǎnr è le.
A：我 有 点儿 饿 了。　　　　I am a bit hungry.

Shí'èr diǎn guò le, wǒmen qù
B：十二 点 过 了，我们 去　　It is after 12 o'clock. Let's go for lunch.

chī fàn ba.
吃 饭 吧。

Fùjìn nǎ jiā fàndiàn hǎo?
A：附近 哪 家 饭店 好?　　　Which restaurant is good around here?

Nǐ xiǎng chī Zhōngguócài háishi
B：你 想 吃 中国菜 还是　　Do you want Chinese food or western food?

xīcān?
西餐?

Wǒ xiǎng chī Zhōngguócài.
A：我 想 吃 中国菜。　　　　I'd like Chinese food.

Nàme, qù Xīnyǎ Yuècàiguǎn ba,
B：那么，去 新雅 粤菜馆 吧，　So, let's go to Xinya Cantonese Restaurant.

nàr de Guǎngdōngcài hěn yǒumíng.
那儿 的 广东菜 很 有名。　　Its Cantonese food is very famous.

A：Guǎngdōngcài hé Shànghǎicài bù
广东菜　　和　上海菜　不
yíyàng ma?
一样　吗？

Are Cantonese cuisine and Shanghainese cuisine not the same?

B：Yǒu yìdiǎnr bùtóng.
有　一点儿　不同。

There are a few differences.

A：Shànghǎicài, nǎ jiā fàndiàn hǎo?
上海菜，　哪　家　饭店　好？

Which restaurant is good for Shanghainese cuisine?

B：Shànghǎicài yào shǔ Yùyuán de
上海菜　　要　数注1　豫园　的
Lǎofàndiàn zuì yǒumíng.
老饭店　最　有名。

Talking about Shanghainese cuisine, the Laofandian Restaurant (Old Restaurant) in Yu Garden is the most famous.

A：Jīntiān xiān chángchang Guǎngdōng-
今天　先　尝尝注2　广东
cài ba, gǎitiān zài qù chī
菜 吧，改天　再　去　吃
Shànghǎicài.
上海菜。

Let's try the Cantonese food today and taste the Shanghainese food some other day.

B：Xīnyǎ Yuècàiguǎn hěn jìn, wǒmen
新雅　粤菜馆　很　近，我们
zǒuzhe qù ba.
走着　去　吧。

The Xinya Cantonese Restaurant is nearby. Let's walk there.

A：Shànghǎi hái yǒu nǎxiē yǒumíng
上海　还　有　哪些　有名
de fàndiàn?
的　饭店？

Are there other well-known restaurants in Shanghai?

B：Yǒumíng de fàndiàn kě duō le.
有名　的　饭店　可　多　了。

There are quite a lot.

A：Tīngshuō Shànghǎi de xiǎochī
听说　上海　的　小吃
hěn yǒumíng, shì ma?
很　有名，　是　吗？

I've heard that the Shanghainese snacks are very good. Is it true?

B：Shì de, Yùyuán li yǒu gè zhǒng
是　的，豫园　里　有　各　种
gè yàng de xiǎochī.
各　样　的　小吃。

Yes. There are various snacks in Yu Garden.

A：Zuì yǒumíng de shì shénme?
最　有名　的　是　什么？

What kind of snack is the most famous?

Yào shǔ xiǎolóngbāozi le.
B：要　数　小笼包子　了。

It should be the Xiaolongbaozi (stuffed bun in small steamer).

☆　注　释 (Notes)　☆

1. "要数"表示谁或者什么在一定的范围中是最突出的。

"要数" indicates the superlative one within the scope.

Qìhòu zuì hǎo de chéngshì yào shǔ Kūnmíng le.
（1）气候　最　好　的　城市　要　数　昆明　了。／气候要数昆明最好。

It is Kunming the city that has the best weather.

Zhège bān chéngjì zuì hǎo de xuésheng yào shǔ tā le.
（2）这个　班　成绩　最　好　的　学生　要　数　他　了。／这个班成绩要数他最好。

It is him who is the best student in this class.

2. "尝尝"表示吃一点儿辨别滋味的意思。

"尝尝" means to taste, to try the flavor of food.

Wǒ xiǎng chángchang Rìběncài.
（1）我　想　尝尝　日本菜。　I'd like to try Japanese cuisine.

Nǐ lái chángchang xiándàn.
（2）你　来　尝尝　咸淡。　Please taste it to see if it's salty enough.

☆　句型提示 (Sentence pattern references)　☆

1. 我有点儿饿了。　　　　　　　请参看 341 页句型 107。
2. 我们去吃饭吧。　　　　　　　请参看 311 页句型 39。
3. 你想吃中国菜还是西餐?　　　请参看 301 页句型 17。
4. 我想吃中国菜。　　　　　　　请参看 331 页句型 82。
5. 我们走着去吧。　　　　　　　请参看 311 页句型 40。
6. 听说上海的小吃很有名,是吗?　请参看 317 页句型 52。

☆　词语用法举例 (Examples for usage of the words)　☆

1. 广东菜和上海菜不一样吗

Shànghǎihuà hé pǔtōnghuà bù yíyàng.
（1）上海话　和　普通话　不　一样。

Rìběnrén de shēnghuó xíguàn hé Zhōngguórén bù yíyàng.
（2）日本人　的　生活　习惯　和　中国人　不　一样。

Jiějie de xìnggé hé mèimei bù yíyàng.
（3）姐姐　的　性格　和　妹妹　不　一样。

Zhège diàn de jiàqian hé nàge diàn bù yíyàng.
（4）这个　店　的　价钱　和　那个　店　不　一样。（价钱:price）

2. 上海菜要数豫园的老饭店最有名

Wǒmen zhè jǐ ge rén li tā zuì gāo.
(1) 我们 这 几 个 人 里 他 最 高。

Zhège diàn de dōngxi zuì guì.
(2) 这个 店 的 东西 最 贵。

Wǒ zuì xǐhuan chī xiā.
(3) 我 最 喜欢 吃 虾。

Tā zuì xiǎng qù guówài lǚxíng.
(4) 他 最 想 去 国外 旅行。

3. 改天再去吃上海菜

Wǒ jīntiān hěn máng, gǎitiān zài hé nǐ liáotiān.
(1) 我 今天 很 忙， 改天 再 和 你 聊天。 （聊天：chat）

Wǒ míngtiān yào kǎoshì, gǎitiān zài gěi nǐ dǎ diànhuà.
(2) 我 明天 要 考试， 改天 再 给 你 打 电话。 （考试：take an examination）

Jīntiān bùxíng, gǎitiān ba.
(3) 今天 不行， 改天 吧。

Zhè cì wǒ lái fù qián, gǎitiān nǐ zài qǐngkè ba.
(4) 这 次 我 来 付 钱， 改天 你 再 请客 吧。

4. 我们走着去吧

Lǎoshī zhànzhe jiǎngkè.
(1) 老师 站着 讲课。 （讲课：give lessons）

Xuésheng kànzhe shū huídá wèntí.
(2) 学生 看着 书 回答 问题。

Tā xiàozhe dāying le.
(3) 他 笑着 答应 了。 （笑：smile, laugh）

Bié tǎngzhe kàn shū.
(4) 别 躺着 看 书。 （躺：lie）

☆ 词 语（Word list） ☆

dāozi				chāzi			
1. 刀子	（名）	knife		2. 叉子	（名）	fork	
kuàizi				sháozi			
3. 筷子	（名）	chopsticks		4. 勺子	（名）	spoon	
bēizi				pánzi			
5. 杯子	（名）	cup		6. 盘子	（名）	plate, dish, tray	
wǎn				cānjīn			
7. 碗	（名）	bowl		8. 餐巾	（名）	napkin	
yáqiān				kāipíngqì			
9. 牙签	（名）	toothpick		10. 开瓶器	（名）	bottle opener	
wèidao				xián			
11. 味道	（名）	taste		12. 咸	（形）	salty	

dàn				tián			
13. 淡	（形）	light, tasteless, weak, without enough salt		14. 甜	（形）	sweet	
suān				kǔ			
15. 酸	（形）	sour, tart		16. 苦	（形）	bitter	
xiāng				chòu			
17. 香	（形）	scented, appetizing (smell)		18. 臭	（形）	stinking, foul	
là				xīnxiān			
19. 辣	（形）	spicy, hot		20. 新鲜	（形）	fresh	
xiān				nóng			
21. 鲜	（形）	fresh, delicious, tasty		22. 浓	（形）	thick, dense	
chóu				xī			
23. 稠	（形）	thick, dense		24. 稀	（形）	thin, watery	
yìng				ruǎn			
25. 硬	（形）	hard, tough		26. 软	（形）	soft	
lǎo				nèn			
27. 老	（形）	overcooked, overdone		28. 嫩	（形）	tender, (of food) under done	
shú				shēng			
29. 熟	（形）	ripe, cooked, done		30. 生	（形）	unripe, raw, un-cooked	
tàng				rè			
31. 烫	（形）	very hot, scalding		32. 热	（形）	hot	
liáng				wēn			
33. 凉	（形）	cool, cold		34. 温	（形）	warm	
huǒguō				zhèngzōng			
35. 火锅	（名）	chafing-dish		36. 正宗	（形）	genuine, real	
kuàicāntīng				zìzhùcān			
37. 快餐厅	（名）	fast food restaurant		38. 自助餐	（名）	buffet	
lěngcānhuì				tàocān			
39. 冷餐会	（名）	buffet dinner, buffet reception		40. 套餐	（名）	set meal	
héfàn				mántou			
41. 盒饭	（名）	box lunch		42. 馒头	（名）	steamed bread	

☆ 练 习（Exercises） ☆

一、替换练习（Substitution exercises）

1. 你想吃 中国菜还是西餐？　　喝　　　　　咖啡　　茶
　　　　　　　　　　　　　　喜欢吃　　　甜的　　咸的
　　　　　　　　　　　　　　想　　　　　去饭店吃　在家里吃
　　　　　　　　　　　　　　想　　　　　在这儿坐　要包房(bāofáng/booth)

2. 有名的饭店可多了。　　　四川菜　　　辣
　　　　　　　　　　　　　广东菜　　　好吃
　　　　　　　　　　　　　小于做的菜味道　好
　　　　　　　　　　　　　意大利的咖啡　香

二、用括号中的词语完成对话（Complete the following conversations with the words in bracket）

1. A：去酒吧（jiǔbā/bar）喝一杯吧。

B：今天我有点儿累，＿＿＿＿＿＿＿＿＿＿＿＿。（改天）

2. A：现在有时间吗？

　 B：对不起，我现在要出去，＿＿＿＿＿＿＿＿＿＿＿。（改天）

3. A：美国最有名的山是哪一座？

　 B：＿＿＿＿＿＿＿＿＿＿＿＿。（要数）

4. A：你们公司谁的英语最好？

　 B：＿＿＿＿＿＿＿＿＿＿＿＿。（要数）

5. A：听说美国的奶酪(nǎilào)有很多种，是吗？

　 B：是啊，＿＿＿＿＿＿＿＿＿＿＿＿＿＿。（各种各样）

6. A：这里有西餐馆吗？

　 B：＿＿＿＿＿＿＿＿＿＿＿＿。（附近）

三、回答问题(Answer the following questions)

1. 你喜欢吃猪肉还是牛肉？

2. 你喜欢吃什么鱼？

3. 你喜欢喝什么茶？

4. 你喜欢吃中国菜吗？

四、会话(Conversation)

于雪来：走了这么多路，我有点儿累了。

玛　丽：我也是。我们找个地方坐坐吧。

于雪来：我知道附近有个快餐厅，去那里坐坐？

玛　丽：好吧。我不喜欢吃快餐，不过，喝杯茶休息休息也好。

于雪来：我要一杯红茶，你呢？

玛　丽：我要一杯橙汁。

于雪来：你来中国以后，吃过中国菜吗？

玛　丽：吃过很多次。在美国的时候也常吃。

于雪来：在美国吃的中国菜和在上海吃的一样吗？

玛　丽：有点儿不一样。不太正宗。要吃正宗的中国菜还是要来中国呀。

☆　**练习答案**(Key to the exercises)　☆

二、1. 改天再去吧

　 2. 改天谈(tán/talk)吧

　 3. 美国最有名的山要数落基山(Luòjī Shān/Rocky Mountains)了

　 4. 英语最好的要数老李了

　 5. 美国有各种各样的奶酪

　 6. 附近没有(西餐馆)

18 在 饭店 IN A RESTAURANT

Zài Fàndiàn

1. A: 请问 几 位注1？

Qǐngwèn jǐ wèi?

How many in your party?

B: 六 个 人。

Liù ge rén.

Six.

A: 请 这边 坐。

Qǐng zhèbian zuò.

Please sit here.

这 是 菜单。几 位 喝 什么 茶？

Zhè shì càidān. Jǐ wèi hē shénme chá?

This is the menu. What tea do you like?

B: （要） 龙井（茶）。

（Yào） lóngjǐng（chá）.

Longjing Tea, please.

A: 请 点 菜 吧。

Qǐng diǎn cài ba.

May I take your order?

B: 你们 这里 有 哪些 特色 菜?

Nǐmen zhèli yǒu nǎxiē tèsè cài?

What are your specialties?

A：Yǒu guǎngshì kǎoyā、 kǎorǔzhū.
有　广式　烤鸭、烤乳猪。　　We have Cantonese roast duck and roast piglet.

B：Nà jiù yào zhè liǎng ge cài ba.
那就要　这　两　个　菜　吧。　　OK. We'll take these two dishes.

Hái yào yí ge qīngchǎo xiārén、
还　要　一　个　清炒　虾仁、　　And the stir-fried shrimp dish and a stir-fried

yí ge qīngcài chǎo mógu.
一　个　青菜　炒　蘑菇。　　vegetables with mushrooms as well.

A：Yào lěngcài ma?
要　冷菜　吗?　　Any cold dishes?

B：Lěngcài, yào liángbàn qíncài
冷菜,　要　凉拌　芹菜　　Tossed celery and jellyfish with sauce for cold

hé liángbàn hǎizhésī.
和　凉拌　海蜇丝。　　dishes.

A：Yào shénme tāng?
要　什么　汤?　　What soup would you like?

B：Yào jīróng yùmǐtāng ba.
要　鸡茸　玉米汤　吧。　　Corn soup with minced chicken.

A：Hē shénme jiǔ?
喝　什么　酒?　　What wine would you like to drink?

B：Lái sān píng píjiǔ.
来注2 三　瓶　啤酒。　　Give us three bottles of beer.

A：Yǐnliào yào shénme?
饮料　要　什么?　　What kind of soft drink would you like?

B：Liǎng guàn chéngzhī.
两　罐　橙汁。　　Two cans of orange juice.

C：Cài yào qīngdàn diǎnr, bié
菜　要　清淡　点儿,　别　　Cook the dishes blandly, not too oily.

tài yóunì.
太　油腻。

B：Wǒmen yǒu diǎnr shì, qǐng
我们　有　点儿　事,　请　　We have something to do later. Please hurry.

kuài diǎnr shàngcài.
快　点儿　上菜。

2. C：Wèidao zhēn búcuò.
味道　真　不错。　　It's delicious.

B：Chǎofàn qǐng gěi (wǒmen) fēn
炒饭.　请　给　(我们)　分　　Please serve the fried rice for us.

yíxià.
一下。

Zhège chèdiào ba.
C：这个 撤掉 吧。　　　　　Remove this dish please.

Qǐng jiézhàng.
B：请 结账。　　　　　　　Can I have my bill, please?

Wǒ qǐngkè, ràng wǒ lái fù
C：我 请客，让 我 来注3 付　　Be my guest please.
qián.
钱。

☆　**注 释**(Notes)　☆

1. "位"是量词,用于人,含有敬意。一般用"个"。
   "位"is a measure word to be used for counting human beings with respect. "个" is used under common occasions.
2. 这里的"来"是代替某个有具体意义的动词。常用于口语。
   "来"here replaces another verb which indicates a real action. It is usually used in spoken language.
3. "来＋动词"表示要做某件事。"来"省略后意思不变。
   "来＋verb"indicates going to do something. The meaning keeps the same when "来" is omitted.

☆　**句型提示**(Sentence pattern references)　☆

1. 我们有点儿事。　　　　　　请参看 343 页句型 110。
2. 请快点儿上菜。　　　　　　请参看 342 页句型 109。
3. 让我来付钱。　　　　　　　请参看 330 页句型 81。

☆　**词语用法举例**(Examples for usage of the words)　☆

1. 请点菜吧

   Diǎn nǐ xǐhuan chī de ba.
   (1) 点 你 喜欢 吃 的 吧。

   Bié diǎn tài là de cài.
   (2) 别 点 太 辣 的 菜。

   Kēzhǎng diǎn míng jiào Xiǎo Lǐ qù.
   (3) 科长 点 名 叫 小 李 去。　(点名:to mention somebody by name)

   Wǒ dǎ diànhuà dào guǎngbō diàntái diǎnle yì shǒu gē.
   (4) 我 打 电 话 到 广 播 电 台 点了 一 首 歌。
   (广播电台:radio station　点歌:request a song)

2. 来三瓶啤酒

　　Lái yì pán Yángzhōu chǎofàn.
（1）来 一 盘 扬州 炒饭。

　　Lái liǎng guàn píngguǒzhī.
（2）来 两 罐 苹果汁。

　　Lái bēi kāfēi, zěnmeyàng?
（3）来 杯 咖啡，怎么样?

　　Wǒ kě le, lái bēi shuǐ ba.
（4）我 渴 了，来 杯 水 吧。

3. 让我来付钱

　　Ràng wǒ bāng nǐ ba.
（1）让 我 帮 你 吧。

　　Ràng wǒ kànkan.
（2）让 我 看看。

　　Ràng wǒ yě shìshi.
（3）让 我 也 试试。

　　Zuòyè zuòhǎo le, ràng wǒ chūqu wán ba.
（4）作业 做好 了，让 我 出去 玩 吧。

4. 让我来付钱

　　Wǒ lái qǐngkè.
（1）我 来 请客。

　　Nǐ yě lái chángchang.
（2）你 也 来 尝尝。

　　Ràng tā yě lái kànkan.
（3）让 他 也 来 看看。

　　Wǒmen lái kāi ge xīnnián wǎnhuì ba.
（4）我们 来 开 个 新年 晚会 吧。 （晚会:party）

☆ 词 语 (Word list) ☆

1. 做 饭 (zuò fàn)		to do cooking, to prepare a meal, to cook rice	2. 做 菜 (zuò cài)		to prepare dishes
3. 烹调 (pēngtiáo)	（动）	cook	4. 炸 (zhá)	（动）	deep-fry
5. 蒸 (zhēng)	（动）	steam	6. 烤 (kǎo)	（动）	roast
7. 煎 (jiān)	（动）	fry in shallow oil	8. 炒 (chǎo)	（动）	stir-fry
9. 煮 (zhǔ)	（动）	boil	10. 红烧 (hóngshāo)	（动）	braise in soy sauce
11. 大 火 (dà huǒ)	（名）	cooking with roaring fire	12. 小 火 (xiǎo huǒ)	（名）	cooking with weak fire

13.	guō 锅	（名）	pot, pan, wok	14.	càidāo 菜刀	（名）	kitchen knife
15.	zhēnbǎn 砧板	（名）	chopping block, chopping board	16.	qiē 切	（动）	cut
17.	duò 剁	（动）	chop, cut	18.	chéng 盛	（动）	fill, ladle
19.	bàn 拌	（动）	mix thoroughly	20.	kuài 块	（名）	piece, lump, chunk
21.	tiáo 条	（名）	long narrow piece	22.	sī 丝	（名）	shred
23.	piàn 片	（名）	slice	24.	dīng 丁	（名）	cube, dice
25.	mò 末	（名）	ground, minced	26.	mòyú 墨鱼	（名）	cuttlefish
27.	xuěyú 鳕鱼	（名）	cod	28.	lúyú 鲈鱼	（名）	perch
29.	yóuyú 鱿鱼	（名）	squid	30.	dàiyú 带鱼	（名）	hairtail
31.	mányú 鳗鱼	（名）	conger eel, river eel	32.	huángyú 黄鱼	（名）	yellow croaker
33.	qīngyú 青鱼	（名）	black carp	34.	liányú 鲢鱼	（名）	silver carp
35.	sānwényú 三文鱼	（名）	salmon	36.	máidān 埋单	（动）	bring the bill, pay the bill

☆　练　习（Exercises）　☆

一、替换练习（Substitution exercises）

1. 让我 来付吧。　　　　她们　　　　　看看
　　　　　　　　　　　　孩子　　　　　自己（zìjǐ/oneself）洗衣服
　　　　　　　　　　　　爸爸　　　　　先吃
　　　　　　　　　　　　他　　　　　　点菜

2. 来一个 炒虾仁。　　　两个　　　　　冷菜
　　　　　　　　　　　　五罐　　　　　可乐
　　　　　　　　　　　　一壶（hú, 量词）绿茶
　　　　　　　　　　　　一个　　　　　热汤

二、回答问题（Answer the following questions）

1. 你喜欢喝什么酒？

2. 你喜欢吃冷菜还是热菜？

3. 你能看懂中国的菜单吗？

4. 你会用汉语点菜了吗？

5. 你喜欢吃咸的还是甜的？

三、完成对话(Complete the conversations)

1. A：请问几位？

   B：_____。

2. A：_____？

   B：我们这里的特色菜是炒鸡。

3. A：要什么饮料？

   B：_____。

四、会话(Conversation)

服务员：欢迎光临，请问有几位？

玛　丽：两个人。

服务员：请这边坐。要喝什么茶？

玛　丽：茉莉花茶。

服务员：现在点菜吗？

玛　丽：你们这儿有什么特色菜？

服务员：辣子鸡(làzijī/chilly chicken)和松鼠黄鱼(sōngshǔ huángyú/sweet and sour yellow croak-er)。

玛　丽：琳达，你能吃辣的吗？

琳　达：很辣吗？

服务员：不是很辣。

琳　达：那好吧，尝一尝。要一个辣子鸡。

服务员：我们这儿的鲈鱼很新鲜，要不要来一条？

玛　丽：不用了。再来一个炒双菇(shuānggū/fresh and dry xianggu mushrooms)、一个三鲜(sānxiān/three delicacies)豆腐。

琳　达：三鲜是什么意思(yìsi/meaning)？

服务员：三鲜就是火腿、鲜肉、海产(hǎichǎn/sea food)。你们喝什么饮料？

琳　达：我就喝茶。

玛　丽：我也是。还要两碗米饭。

服务员：好的，请稍等。

☆　　**练习答案(Key to the exercises)**　　☆

三、1. 五个人

　　2. 你们有什么特色菜

　　3. 要三瓶可乐

19 Yùdìng Jiǔxí 预订 酒席 MAKING A RESERVATION FOR TABLE

Wǒ xiǎng yùdìng jiǔxí.
1. A：我　想　预订 酒席。 I'd like to make a reservation.

Shénme shíhou?
B：什么　时候? When do you need it?

Hòutiān wǎnshang qī diǎn.
A：后天　晚上　七　点。 At seven o'clock in the evening the day after

tomorrow.

Nín yào yùdìng duōshao qián
B：您　要　预订　多少　钱 How much do you wish to spend per table?

yì zhuō de?
一　桌　的?

Yìqiān kuài zuǒyòu de dìng
A：一千　块　左右　的　订 About 1,000 yuan for each table. Totally

sān zhuō.
三　桌。 three tables.

B: Yào Shànghǎicài háishi Sìchuāncài?
要 上海菜 还是 四川菜? Do you want Shanghai or Sichuan cuisine?

A: Yào Sìchuāncài ba.
要 四川菜 吧。 I'd like Sichuan cuisine.

B: Yào zhǔnbèi shénme jiǔ hé
要 准备 什么 酒 和 What kind of wine and soft drinks should we

yǐnliào?
饮料? prepare?

A: Pútaojiǔ hé wēishìjì, gè 注
葡萄酒 和 威士忌, 各 Please prepare several bottles of grape wine

zhǔnbèi jǐ píng ba.
准备 几 瓶 吧。 and whiskey for each table.

Kělè hé kuàngquánshuǐ, měi
可乐 和 矿泉水, 每 And give each table two bottles of cola and

zhuō gè yào liǎng píng.
桌 各 要 两 瓶。 mineral water.

Yìqiān kuài bāokuò jiǔ hé
一千 块 包括 酒 和 Does 1,000 yuan cover the wine and soft

yǐnliào ma?
饮料 吗? drinks?

B: Bù, jiǔ hé yǐnliào zhào yǐnyòng
不, 酒 和 饮料 照 饮用 No. The wine and soft drinks will be charged

de shùliàng lìngwài suàn.
的 数量 另外 算。 separately.

A: Dìngjīn shì duōshao?
订金 是 多少? How much is the deposit?

B: Qǐng yùfù liùbǎi kuài.
请 预付 六百 块。 Please deposit 600 yuan.

Qǐng liúxia nín de xìngmíng
请 留下 您 的 姓名 Please leave us your name and telephone

hé diànhuà hàomǎ.
和 电话 号码。 number.

2. A: Wǒ qiántiān yùdìngle jiǔxí,
我 前天 预订了 酒席, I made a reservation the day before yesterday

xiànzài xiǎng qǔxiāo.
现在 想 取消。 and now I want to cancel it.

B: Hǎo de, dìngjīn tuìhuán gěi nín.
好 的, 订金 退还 给 您。 Well. Here is the refund of your deposit.

3. A: Wǒ xiǎng yùdìng xīngqīwǔ xiàwǔ
我 想 预订 星期五 下午 I'd like to book a table for eight at 6 pm on

　　　　liù diǎn bā ge rén de zuòwèi,
　　六 点 八 个 人 的 座位，　　Friday. Is that OK?

　　　　yǒu ma?
　　有 吗?

　　　　Duìbuqǐ, yǐjīng yùdìng mǎn le.
B：**对不起，已经 预订 满 了。**　　Sorry, all the tables are booked.

☆　注　释(Note)　☆

"各"在这里作副词用，表示分别做或分别具有的意思。
"各"is an adverb here. It means to do something respectively or to have something respectively.

☆　句型提示(Sentence pattern references)　☆

1. 葡萄酒和威士忌,各准备几瓶吧。　　请参看 363 页句型 157。
2. 酒和饮料照饮用的数量另外算。　　请参看 359 页句型 146。
3. 请留下您的姓名和电话号码。　　请参看 352 页句型 131。

☆　词语用法举例(Examples for usage of the words)　☆

1. 要准备什么酒和饮料
　　　　Wǒ zhèngzài zhǔnbèi kǎoshì.
　(1) 我 正在 准备 考试。

　　　　Māma zài zhǔnbèi wǎnfàn.
　(2) 妈妈 在 准备 晚饭。

　　　　Míngtiān de bǐsài, nǐmen zhǔnbèi hǎole ma?
　(3) 明天 的 比赛，你们 准备 好了 吗? （比赛:competition, match）

　　　　Lǚxíng de dōngxi, yǐjīng zhǔnbèi hǎo le.
　(4) 旅行 的 东西，已经 准备 好 了。

2. 一千块包括酒和饮料吗
　　　　Zhè suǒ xuéxiào yǒu wǔbǎi rén zuǒyòu, bāokuò jiàoshī hé xuésheng.
　(1) 这 所 学校 有 五百 人 左右，包括 教师 和 学生。

　　　　Měi rén yìqiān kuài, bāokuò zhùsùfèi hé huǒshífèi.
　(2) 每 人 一千 块，包括 住宿费 和 伙食费。

　　　（住宿费:accommodation expenses　伙食费:food expenses）

　　　　Bāokuò shǒutíbāo, yígòng shí jiàn xíngli.
　(3) 包括 手提包，一共 十 件 行李。

　　　　Bāokuò jiàoshī, yígòng èrshí ge rén.
　(4) 包括 教师，一共 二十 个 人。

3. 酒和饮料照饮用的数量另外算

(1) Wǒ gěi shēngbìng de nǎinai lìngwài zuò cài.
我 给 生病 的 奶奶 另外 做 菜。

(2) Tā dǎsuan lìngwài mǎi fángzi jiéhūn.
他 打算 另外 买 房子 结婚。

(3) Bù máfan nǐ le, wǒ lìngwài xiǎng bànfǎ.
不 麻烦 你 了, 我 另外 想 办法。

(4) Zhè zhāng huàr gěi tā ba, wǒ lìngwài huà yì zhāng gěi nǐ.
这 张 画儿 给 他 吧, 我 另外 画 一 张 给 你。

(画儿:painting, picture 画:paint, draw)

4. 请留下您的姓名和电话号码

(1) Qǐng liúxia nǐ de fángjiān hàomǎ.
请 留下 你 的 房间 号码。

(2) Qǐng liúxia nǐ zài Měiguó de diànhuà hàomǎ.
请 留下 你 在 美国 的 电话 号码。

(3) Tā liúxia yì zhāng tiáozi jiù zǒu le.
他 留下 一 张 条子 就 走 了。 (条子:brief information notes, message)

(4) Tā chūguó le, liúxia yì běn shū gěi nǐ.
他 出国 了, 留下 一 本 书 给 你。

☆ 词 语 (Word list) ☆

1. báizhǎnjī 白斩鸡 (名) soft-boiled chicken
2. cuìpíjī 脆皮鸡 (名) crisp-skin chicken
3. chǐzhī jīkuài 豉汁 鸡块 (名) steamed chicken with fermented soy bean sauce
4. gālíjī 咖喱鸡 (名) chicken curry
5. zhájītuǐ 炸鸡腿 (名) deep-fried chicken legs
6. jiàngbào jīdīng 酱爆 鸡丁 (名) quick-fried chicken dice with thick soy bean sauce
7. yāoguǒ jīdīng 腰果 鸡丁 (名) diced chicken with cashew nut
8. hóngshāo hǎishēn 红烧 海参 (名) braised sea cucumber in brown sauce
9. fúróng xiārén 芙蓉 虾仁 (名) stir-fried shrimp meat with egg white
10. tángcùyú 糖醋鱼 (名) sweet and sour fish
11. gǔlǎoròu 古老肉 (名) Gulao pork (sweet and sour pork)
12. yúxiāng ròusī 鱼香 肉丝 (名) Yuxiang (fragrant as fish) shredded pork
13. hóngshāo shīzitóu 红烧 狮子头 (名) braised pork balls
14. qīngjiāo niúròu 青椒 牛肉 (名) beef with green peppers
15. fānqié niúròu 番茄 牛肉 (名) beef with tomatoes
16. dāodòu ròupiàn 刀豆 肉片 (名) sliced pork with sword bean
17. hóngshāo qiézi 红烧 茄子 (名) braised eggplant
18. qíncài ròusī 芹菜 肉丝 (名) shredded pork with celery

129

19. 清蒸 鲈鱼（名）　qīngzhēng lúyú　steamed perch
20. 麻婆 豆腐（名）　mápó dòufu　stir-fried bean curd in hot sauce
21. 炒素（菜）（名）　chǎosù(cài)　stir-fried vegetables
22. 火腿 菜汤（名）　huǒtuǐ càitāng　ham and vegetable soup
23. 香菇 肉片汤（名）　xiānggū ròupiàntāng　mushroom and sliced pork soup
24. 春卷 （名）　chūnjuǎn　spring roll
25. 馄饨 （名）　húntun　wonton, dumpling soup
26. 饺子 （名）　jiǎozi　dumpling
27. 什锦 炒面（名）　shíjǐn chǎomiàn　assorted fried noodles, assorted chow mein
28. 什锦 炒饭（名）　shíjǐn chǎofàn　assorted fried rice
29. 叉烧 炒面（名）　chāshāo chǎomiàn　fried noodles with grilled pork
30. 牛肉 汤面（名）　niúròu tāngmiàn　noodles in beef soup
31. 荤菜 （名）　hūncài　food which contains meat or fish
32. 素菜 （名）　sùcài　food which contains only vegetables, vegetable dish
33. 菜 （名）　cài　dish
34. 清淡 （形）　qīngdàn　light, bland
35. 油腻 （形）　yóunì　oily
36. 加热 （动）　jiārè　heat, warm up

☆　练　习（Exercises）　☆

一、替换练习（Substitution exercises）

1. 留下电话号码。
　　　　　　　一封信
　　　　　　　几句话
　　　　　　　您的地址

2. 照饮用的数量 另外算钱。
　　妈妈的话　　　　　　做
　　这个样子　　　　　　做一件衬衣
　　老师说的　　　　　　做
　　中国人的习惯　　　　做菜

二、用括号中的词语完成对话（Complete the following conversations with the words in brackets）

1. A：去西安的飞机票买了吗？
　 B：_____。（预订）

2. A：你认识路吗？
　 B：不认识，不过我有地图。_____。（照）

3. A：请五个客人，要多少个菜？
　 B：_____。（准备）

三、会话(Conversations)

于雪来：今年元旦(Yuándàn/New Year's Day)，我们到饭店吃一顿(dùn, 量词)吧。

郭　放：好啊。请弟弟一家一起去吧。

于雪来：去哪个饭店好？

郭　放：杏花楼(Xìnghuālóu)吧。那儿的菜有特色。

于雪来：那好，我下午就去预订。

于雪来：你好。我想预订一月一号的酒席。

服务员：一月一号，中午还是晚上？

于雪来：中午。

服务员：订几桌？

于雪来：一桌，七个人。

服务员：我们有八百八十元一桌的，也有九百八十元一桌的，您要哪一种？

于雪来：我能先看看菜单吗？

服务员：当然可以。都是八菜一汤，六荤二素。

于雪来：包括酒和饮料吗？

服务员：送两瓶啤酒和一瓶可乐，别的酒和饮料要另外算钱。

于雪来：嗯，要八百八十元一桌的吧。有包房吗？

服务员：有的。

于雪来：那要包房吧。订金多少？

服务员：一百元。请您留下电话号码。

☆　**练习答案**(Key to the exercises)　☆

二、1. B：已经预订了

　　2. B：照地图走就可以了

　　3. B：准备六个菜吧

20　Zài　Yóuzhèngjú　在　邮政局　IN A POST OFFICE

1. A: Qǐngwèn,　jìdào　Běijīng　de
请问，　寄到　北京　的

xìn,　tiē　yí　kuài　èr
信，　贴　一　块　二

yóupiào,　duì　ma?
邮票，　对　吗?

Excuse me, is this 1.2 *yuan* stamp the correct postage for this letter to Beijing?

B: Duì,　jìdào　wàidì　dōu　shì
对，寄到　外地　都　是

yí　kuài　èr.
一　块　二。

Yes. One *yuan* and two *jiao* for a letter to any place outside this city.

A: Běnshì　ne?
本市　呢?

How much inside this city?

B: Běnshì　bā　máo.
本市　八　毛。

Eight *jiao* inside the city.

2. A: Jìdào　Yīngguó　de　xìn,　yào
寄到　英国　的　信，要

duōshao　qián?
多少　钱?

How much is a letter to England?

B: Hángkōng　xìn　yào　liù　kuài.
航空　信　要　六　块。

Six *yuan* by airmail.

Qǐng bǎ xìn gěi wǒ chēng
请 把 信 给 我 称

yíxià.
一下。

Please let me weigh your letter.

(Zhè fēng xìn) chāozhòng le,
(这 封 信) 超重 了,

yào liù kuài wǔ.
要 六 块 五。

It is over weight. It needs six *yuan* and five *jiao*.

3. A: Nǐ yào jì píngxìn háishi
你 要 寄 平信 还是

guàhàoxìn?
挂号信?

Are you going to mail a regular letter or a registered one?

B: (Wǒ yào jì) guàhàoxìn.
(我 要 寄) 挂号信。

Registered.

4. A: Zhèr yǒu míngxìnpiàn mài ma?
这儿 有 明信片 卖 吗?

Do you have postcards?

B: Yǒu, yào jǐ zhāng?
有, 要 几 张?

Yes. How many do you want?

A: Yào wǔ zhāng.
要 五 张。

I want five.

(Qǐng) gěi wǒ wǔ ge xìnfēng
(请) 给 我 五 个 信封

hé yì dāo xìnzhǐ.
和 一 刀 信纸。

Please give me five envelopes and 100 sheets of letter paper.

5. A: Wǒ yào jì bāoguǒ.
我 要 寄 包裹。

I'd like to send this package.

B: Lǐmian zhuāng de shì shénme?
里面 装 的注 是 什么?

Qǐng dǎkāi ràng wǒ kànkan.
请 打开 让 我 看看。

What's in it? Please open it and let me have a look.

A: (Lǐmian) shì yīfu hé yàopǐn.
(里面) 是 衣服 和 药品。

Clothes and medicine.

B: Méiyǒu jiā xìn ba? Bāoguǒ li
没有 夹 信 吧? 包裹 里

bù zhǔn fàngjìn xìnjiàn.
不 准 放进 信件。

Is there a letter inside? Letters are not allowed in packages.

A: Zhǐ shì yīfu hé yàopǐn.
只 是 衣服 和 药品。

No, clothes and medicine only.

B: Kěyǐ le, qǐng bāohǎo zài
可以 了, 请 包好 再

nálai.
拿来。

OK. Please wrap it up, and then bring it to me.

Zhèyàng xíng le ma?
A：这样　行　了　吗？　　　Is this OK?

Qǐng zā de jiēshi diǎnr.
B：请　扎　得　结实　点儿。　　Please tie it fast.

☆　注　释(Note)　☆

"动词＋的"相当于一个名词,可以看作"的"后面省略了一个名词。"装的"就是"装的东西"。

"Verb＋的"is regarded as a noun. The noun after "的" is omitted. "装的" means "装的东西".

Tā ná de shì shénme?
(1) 他 拿 的 是 什么？　What does he hold?

Qiáng shang guà de shì shénme?
(2) 墙　上　挂　的　是　什么？　What is hung on the wall?

☆　句型提示(Sentence pattern references)　☆

1. 寄到北京的信　　　　　　　请参看 349 页句型 125。
2. 请打开让我看看。　　　　　请参看 313 页句型 43。
3. 请包好再拿来。　　　　　　请参看 384 页句型 203。

☆　词语用法举例(Examples for usage of the words)　☆

1. 寄到北京的信

Wǒ bǎ shūcài nádào chúfáng qu le.
(1) 我 把 蔬菜 拿到 厨房 去 了。

Nǐ bǎ ròu fàngdào bīngxiāng li ba.
(2) 你 把 肉 放到 冰箱 里 吧。

Nǐ bǎ jīntiān de bàozhǐ fàngdào shénme dìfang le?
(3) 你 把 今天 的 报纸 放到 什么 地方 了?

Cóng zhèr zǒudào chēzhàn yào bàn ge xiǎoshí.
(4) 从 这儿 走到 车站 要 半 个 小时。

2. 寄到外地都是一块二

Tāmen dōu shì wàiguórén.
(1) 他们 都 是 外国人。

Zhèxiē shū dōu shì lǎoshī de.
(2) 这些 书 都 是 老师 的。

Shǔjià wǒmen dōu qù lǚxíng.
(3) 暑假 我们 都 去 旅行。　（暑假:summer holiday)

Dàjiā dōu shuō tā shì hǎo xuésheng.
(4) 大家 都 说 他 是 好 学生。 （大家：all, everybody）

3. 这儿有明信片卖吗

Nǎr yǒu mài Zhōngguó zìhuà de?
(1) 哪儿 有 卖 中国 字画 的？ （字画：calligraphy and painting）

Chāoshì li yǒu túshū mài.
(2) 超市 里 有 图书 卖。 （图书：books）

Nǎr yǒu mài hèniánkǎ de?
(3) 哪儿 有 卖 贺年卡 的？

Zhèr yǒu nǎilào mài ma?
(4) 这儿 有 奶酪 卖 吗？

4. 里面装的是什么

Nǐ kǒudài li zhuāng de shì shénme?
(1) 你 口袋 里 装 的 是 什么？ （口袋：pocket）

Lǎoshī shǒu li ná de shì shénme?
(2) 老师 手 里 拿 的 是 什么？

Qiáng shang tiē de shì wǒ érzi huà de huàr.
(3) 墙 上 贴 的 是 我 儿子 画 的 画儿。 （墙：wall）

Zhèr guà de quán shì tàitai de yīfu.
(4) 这儿 挂 的 全 是 太太 的 衣服。 （挂：hang）

5. 包裹里不准放进信件

Jiàoshì li bù zhǔn chōuyān.
(1) 教室 里 不 准 抽烟。

Xiǎoháir bù zhǔn hē jiǔ.
(2) 小孩儿 不 准 喝 酒。

Bù zhǔn luàn rēng lājī.
(3) 不 准 乱 扔 垃圾。 （乱扔：throw about 垃圾：garbage, litter）

Bù zhǔn wúzhèng jiàshǐ.
(4) 不 准 无证 驾驶。 （驾驶：drive）

6. 请包好再拿来

Yào xǐle shǒu zài chī fàn.
(1) 要 洗了 手 再 吃 饭。

Yīnggāi shuāle yá zài shuìjiào.
(2) 应该 刷了 牙 再 睡觉。 （刷牙：brush teeth）

Tīng yíhuìr yīnyuè zài shuìjiào.
(3) 听 一会儿 音乐 再 睡觉。

Tài lèi le, xiūxi yíhuìr zài zuò fàn ba.
(4) 太 累 了，休息 一会儿 再 做 饭 吧。

☆　词　语（Word list）　☆

1. 信纸　　　（名）letter paper
   <small>xìnzhǐ</small>
2. 信封　　　（名）envelope
   <small>xìnfēng</small>
3. 信箱　　　（名）mail box
   <small>xìnxiāng</small>
4. 电子 邮件（名）e-mail
   <small>diànzǐ yóujiàn</small>
5. 传真　　　（名）fax
   <small>chuánzhēn</small>
6. 汇款　（动/名）remit money, remittance
   <small>huìkuǎn</small>
7. 特快 专递（名）express delivery
   <small>tèkuài zhuāndì</small>
8. 印刷品　　（名）printed matter
   <small>yìnshuāpǐn</small>
9. 贺年卡　　（名）New Year card, season's greeting card
   <small>hèniánkǎ</small>
10. 糨糊　　　（名）paste
    <small>jiànghu</small>
11. 胶水　　　（名）glue
    <small>jiāoshuǐ</small>
12. 邮政 编码（名）postcode
    <small>yóuzhèng biānmǎ</small>
13. 订 报纸　　subscribe a newspaper
    <small>dìng bàozhǐ</small>
14. 柜台　　　（名）counter
    <small>guìtái</small>
15. 秤　　　　（名）balance, scale, steelyard
    <small>chèng</small>
16. 集邮　　　（动）philately, stamp collecting
    <small>jíyóu</small>

☆　练　习（Exercises）　☆

一、回答问题（Answer the following questions）

1. 从中国寄到美国的信要贴多少钱邮票？

2. 从纽约寄到旧金山的信要贴多少钱邮票？

3. 你旅行的时候，有没有买风景明信片的习惯？

4. 你常常给朋友写信吗？

二、按照中国方式写一个信封（Write an envelope in Chinese way）

样板（Sample）：

```
200001

              上海市　福州路 390 号
              海文音像出版社
              薛××小姐收


                          北京大华公司于寄
                              100025
```

三、用"把"改写下列句子（Use "把" to rewrite the following sentences）

1. 给我那张报纸。

2. 小王吃完了昨天买的面包。

3. 屋子里有点儿热,请打开空调。

4. 请你叫小林到办公室来。

四、模仿造句(Make sentences following the patterns)

1. 动词1 + 好 + 再 + 动词2

请包好再拿来。 做好作业再休息。

_____

2. 处所 + 动词 + 的 + 是 + 名词

里面装的是食品。 手上拿的是他的照片。

_____

3. 处所 + 不准 + 动词

包裹里不准放信件。 房间里不准抽烟。

_____

五、填量词(Fill in the brackets with measure words)

一( )信封 一( )信纸 一( )邮票
一( )信 一( )包裹 一( )明信片

六、会话(Conversation)

玛丽:这封信寄挂号要多少钱?

职员:请把信放在秤上称一下。请付三块三毛。

玛丽:多久能寄到广州?

职员:四五天吧。

玛丽:太慢了。

职员:那么您寄特快专递吧。两天就能收到。

玛丽:好吧。多少钱?

职员:十五块。请填一下这张表。

玛丽:填好了。

职员:请拿好收据。

☆ **练习答案**(Key to the exercises) ☆

三、1. 把那张报纸给我。

2. 小王把昨天买的面包吃完了。

3. 屋子里有点儿热,请把空调打开。

4. 请你把小林叫到办公室来。

五、一(个)信封 一(张)信纸 一(张)邮票 一(封)信 一(个)包裹
一(张)明信片

137

21　在 银行₁　IN A BANK₁
Zài Yínháng

1. A：**在 哪里 兑换 外币?**
   Zài nǎli duìhuàn wàibì?
   Where is for foreign money exchange?

   B：**请 到 2 号 窗口。**
   Qǐng dào èr hào chuāngkǒu.
   Go to the window No.2, please.

2. A：**我 要注 把 美元 换成 人民币。**
   Wǒ yào bǎ měiyuán huànchéng rénmínbì.
   I want to change my US dollars into Renminbi.

   B：**请 填 这 张 兑换单。**
   Qǐng tián zhè zhāng duìhuàndān.
   Please fill in this exchange form.

   A：**今天 美元 对 人民币 的 兑换率 是 多少?**
   Jīntiān měiyuán duì rénmínbì de duìhuànlǜ shì duōshao?
   What is the exchange rate today between American dollar and Renminbi?

   B：**(是) 一 比 七 点 八。**
   (Shì) yī bǐ qī diǎn bā.
   One dollar for seven point eight RMB.

   您 换 多少?
   Nín huàn duōshao?
   How much do you want to change?

A：Yìqiān měiyuán.
一千　美元。
1,000 dollars.

B：Yígòng qīqiān bābǎi kuài, qǐng diǎn yíxià.
一共　七千　八百　块，请　点　一下。
It's 7,800 *yuan* in all. Please check it.

A：Wǒ xiǎng yào diǎnr língqián.
我　想注　要　点儿　零钱。
I want to have some small bills.

3. A：Wǒ xiǎng bǎ zhè zhāng zhīpiào huànchéng xiànjīn.
我　想　把　这　张　支票　换成　现金。
I'd like to cash this check.

B：Qǐng zài zhèr qiānmíng.
请　在　这儿　签名。
Please sign your name here.

4. A：Yínháng shàngwǔ jǐ diǎn kāimén?
银行　上午　几　点　开门？
What time does the bank open in the morning?

B：Bā diǎn bàn.
八　点　半。
Eight thirty.

A：Xiàwǔ jǐ diǎn guānmén?
下午　几　点　关门？
What time does the bank close in the afternoon?

B：Wǔ diǎn.
五　点。
Five o'clock.

A：Xiànzài qù láibují le ba?
现在　去　来不及　了　吧？
It is too late to get there, isn't it?

B：Láidejí, kuài zǒu ba.
来得及，快　走　吧。
You can make it. Hurry up!

5. A：Yínháng xīngqītiān xiūxi ma?
银行　星期天　休息　吗？
Does the bank close on Sundays?

B：Bù xiūxi.
不　休息。
No.

☆　注　释(Note)　☆

"要＋动词"有很多意思，在这里是表示意愿。和"想＋动词"意思差不多。否定的时候，一般不用"不要"而用"不想"。

"要＋verb" has many meanings. Here it expresses a wish or desire. This meaning is close to the meaning of "想＋verb". For its negative form, we usually use "不想" instead of "不要".

(1) Nǐ yào/xiǎng chī shénme?
你　要／想　吃　什么？　What do you want to eat?

(2) Wǒ shénme yě bù xiǎng chī.
我　什么　也　不　想　吃。　I don't want to eat anything.

139

☆　句型提示 (Sentence pattern references)　☆

1. 我要把美元换成人民币。　　　　请参看 327 页句型 75。
2. 现在去来不及了吧?　　　　　　请参看 340 页句型 103。

☆　词语用法举例 (Examples for usage of the words)　☆

1. 我想要点儿零钱

　　　　　Wǒ　xiǎng　qù　Xīnjiāpō　lǚxíng.
　(1) 我　　想　　去　新加坡　旅行。

　　　　　Dìdi　xiǎng　kǎo　dàxué.
　(2) 弟弟　　想　　考　大学。　　(考:take the entrance examination)

　　　　　Mèimei　xiǎng　xué　tán　gāngqín.
　(3) 妹妹　　想　　学　弹　钢琴。　　(弹:play)

　　　　　Māma　xiǎng　mǎi　yí　jiàn　dàyī.
　(4) 妈妈　　想　买　一　件　大衣。

2. 银行上午几点开门

　　　　　Chāoshì　jǐ　diǎn　kāimén?
　(1) A: 超市　　几　点　开门?

　　　　　Zǎoshang　qī　diǎn.
　　　 B: 早上　　七　点。

　　　　　Bǎihuò　shāngdiàn　shí　diǎn　kāimén.
　(2) 百货　商店　十　点　开门。

　　　　　Túshūguǎn　yì　kāimén,　wǒ　jiù　jìnqu.
　(3) 图书馆　一　开门,　我　就　进去。　　(进去:go into, enter)

3. 下午几点关门

　　　　　Kèren　zǒu　le,　guānmén　ba.
　(1) 客人　走　了,　关门　吧。

　　　　　Chāoshì　guānmén　le.
　(2) 超市　关门　了。

　　　　　Shí'èr　diǎn　le,　shāngdiàn　dōu　guānmén　le.
　(3) 十二　点　了,　商店　都　关门　了。

　　　　　Luósēndiàn　èrshísì　xiǎoshí　bù　guānmén.
　(4) 罗森店　二十四　小时　不　关门。

4. 快走吧

　　　　　Kuài　qǐchuáng!　Yào　chídào　le.
　(1) 快　起床!　要　迟到　了。

　　　　　Kuài　bāng　wǒ　yíxià.
　(2) 快　帮　我　一下。

Kuài ná zhǐxiěyào lai.
(3) 快 拿 止血药 来。 (止血药:haemostatic, styptic)

Chē mǎshàng yào kāi le, kuài shàng chē ba.
(4) 车 马上 要 开 了, 快 上 车 吧。

5. 银行星期天休息吗

Wǒmen gōngsī jīntiān xiūxi, qǐng míngtiān lái ba.
(1) 我们 公司 今天 休息, 请 明天 来 吧。

Jīntiān wǒ xiūxi, búyòng qù gōngsī.
(2) 今天 我 休息, 不用 去 公司。

Nǐ gǎnmào bù qīng, hǎohāor xiūxi ba.
(3) 你 感冒 不 轻, 好好儿 休息 吧。 (轻:slight)

Wǎnshang zǎodiǎnr xiūxi, bié tài lèi le.
(4) 晚上 早点儿 休息, 别 太 累 了。

Zǒule yí ge xiǎoshí le, xiūxi yíxià zài zǒu ba.
(5) 走了 一 个 小时 了, 休息 一下 再 走 吧。

☆ 词 语 (Word list) ☆

1. 中国 银行 (名) Bank of China
2. 建设 银行 (名) Construction Bank
3. 交通 银行 (名) Bank of Communications
4. 工商 银行 (名) Industrial and Commercial Bank
5. 外汇 牌价 (名) foreign exchange quotation
6. 美元 (名) American dollar
7. 英镑 (名) pound sterling
8. 欧元 (名) Euro
9. 日元 (名) Japanese yen
10. 卢布 (名) ruble
11. 港币 (名) Hong Kong dollar
12. 硬币 (名) coin
13. 钞票 (名) bill, notes
14. 元／块 (量) yuan
15. 角／毛 (量) jiao
16. 分 (量) fen

☆ 练 习 (Exercises) ☆

一、替换练习 (Substitution exercises)
1. 把美元 换成 人民币。

旅行支票	换	现金
单人房	换	双人房
这个句子	翻译	英语
头发	染	褐色 (hèsè/brown)

2. 把<u>十块钱</u>错<u>看</u>成<u>一百块</u>。

这个故事	写	一本书
小李	认	小王
"体"字	写	"休"字
一	听	七

二、用括号中的词语完成句子(Complete the following sentences with the words in brackets)

1. 这是找给你的钱,＿＿＿＿＿＿＿＿＿＿。（点）
2. 取包裹的时候要＿＿＿＿＿＿＿＿＿＿。（签名）
3. 人民币快用完了,我要去＿＿＿＿＿＿＿＿＿＿。（兑换）
4. 你有没有零钱? ＿＿＿＿＿＿＿＿＿＿。（换）

三、完成对话(Complete the conversations)

1. A:＿＿＿＿＿＿＿＿＿? 　B:换钱请到三号窗口。
2. A:＿＿＿＿＿＿＿＿＿? 　B:一美元换七元八毛人民币。
3. A:＿＿＿＿＿＿＿＿＿? 　B:银行早上九点钟开门。

四、会话(Conversations)

玛　丽:小姐,这张支票请换成现金。
职　员:请在这儿签名。
玛　丽:这样写可以吗?
职　员:可以。这是您换的钱,一共是八百七十二块三毛一分。请点一下。
玛　丽:好的,没错。

妮　娜:小姐,我要把这两百美元换成人民币。今天的兑换率是多少?
职　员:一美元换七元九角七分人民币。请您填这张表。
妮　娜:用英文填可以吗?
职　员:用中文、英文都可以。
妮　娜:填好了,你看这样对吗?
职　员:对。这是一千五百九十四块。请点一下。
妮　娜:没错。

☆　**练习答案**(Key to the exercises)　☆

二、1. 请点一下　2. 在包裹单上签名　3. 银行兑换　4. 我想把十块钱换成零钱
三、1. A:在哪里兑换外币　2. A:美元对人民币的兑换率是多少
　　3. A:银行早上几点开门

22 Zài Yínháng
在 银行₂   IN A BANK₂

1. A： Wǒ yào kāi ge cúnkuǎn hùtóu.
我 要 开 个 存款 户头。
I'd like to open an account.

B： Nín cún huóqī háishi dìngqī?
您 存 活期 还是 定期?
Do you want a current account or fixed deposit account?

A： Dìngqī de lìxī shì duōshao?
定期 的 利息 是 多少?
What is the interest rate for fixed deposit?

B： Cún yì nián shì bǎi fēn zhī
存 一 年 是 百 分 之
3.78% for a one-year term.

sān diǎn qī bā.
三 点 七 八。

A： Huóqī ne?
活期 呢?
What about a current account?

B： Bǎi fēn zhī yī diǎn sì sì.
百 分 之 一 点 四 四。
1.44%.

A： Wǒ xiǎng cún dìngqī.
我 想 存 定期。
I want a fixed-term deposit account.

B：Qǐng tián cúnkuǎndān.
请　填　存款单。
Please fill in the deposit form.

Yào liú mìmǎ ma?
要　留　密码　吗?
Do you need a password?

A：Yào de. Jǐ wèi shù?
要　的。几　位　数?
Yes. How many digits?

B：Liù wèi shù.
六　位　数。
Six digits.

2. A：Wǒ xiǎng qǔ diǎnr qián.
我　想　取　点儿　钱。
I want to withdraw some money from my account.

B：Qǐng xiān qǔ ge xùhào.
请　先　取　个　序号.
Please take a sequential number.

A：Xùhào wǒ náhǎo le.
序号　我　拿好注　了。
Well, I've got it.

B：Qǐng bǎ zhège hé cúnzhé
请　把　这个　和　存折
Please take it and your deposit book to the

yìqǐ jiāogěi yíngyèyuán.
一起　交给　营业员。
clerk.

3. A：Wǒ yào qǔ qián.
我　要　取　钱。
I'd like to take some money out of my account.

B：Nín qǔ duōshao qián?
您　取　多少　钱?
How much do you want?

A：Liǎngqiān kuài.
两千　块。
2000 *yuan* .

B：Zhè shì liǎngqiān kuài, qǐng nín
这　是　两千　块，请　您
Here is 2000 *yuan* . Please check it.

diǎn yíxià.
点　一下。

4. A：Zhè dìngqī cúnkuǎn méi dàoqī,
这　定期　存款　没　到期，
This fixed deposit is not yet due. Can I take

kěyǐ qǔ chulai ma?
可以　取　出来　吗?
the money out?

B：Dìngqī cúnkuǎn méi dàoqī, yào
定期　存款　没　到期，要
Yes, but we will need your ID.

yǒu shēnfènzhèng cái néng qǔ
有　身份证　才　能　取

(qián).
(钱)。

☆　注　释(Note)　☆

"好"放在动词后面,表示动作圆满完成的意思。否定时用"没+动词+好"。

When "好" is after a verb it indicates the action has been perfectly completed. For its negative form, we use the pattern "没+verb+好".

　　　Jìhuà　dìnghǎo　le.
(1) 计划　订好　了。　The plan has been worked out.

　　　Jīntiān　de　zuòyè　zuòhǎo　le.
(2) 今天　的　作业　做好　了。　Today's exercises have been finished.

　　　Fángjiān　méi　shōushi　hǎo.
(3) 房间　没　收拾　好。　The room has not been tidied up yet.

☆　句型提示(Sentence pattern references)　☆

1. 这定期存款没到期。　　　　　请参看 309 页句型 36。
2. 要有身份证才能取钱。　　　　请参看 371 页句型 175。

☆　词语用法举例(Examples for usage of the words)　☆

1. 你存活期还是定期

　　　　Nǐ　shì　Zhōngguórén　háishi　Rìběnrén?
(1) 你　是　中国人　还是　日本人?

　　　　Nǐ　xǐhuan　tián　de　háishi　xián　de?
(2) 你　喜欢　甜　的　还是　咸　的?

　　　　Jīntiān　shì　xīngqīsān　háishi　xīngqīsì?
(3) 今天　是　星期三　还是　星期四?

　　　　Xú　Fāng　míngtiān　chūfā　háishi　hòutiān?
(4) 徐　芳　明天　出发　还是　后天?

2. 序号我拿好了

　　　Wǒ　shāohǎo　fàn　le.
(1) 我　烧好　饭　了。

　　　Wǒ　xǐhǎo　yīfu　le.
(2) 我　洗好　衣服　了。

　　　Tā　xiěhǎo　lùnwén　le.
(3) 他　写好　论文　了。　(论文:paper, thesis)

　　　Nǐ　bànhǎo　shǒuxù　le　ma?
(4) 你　办好　手续　了　吗?　(办手续:go through formalities)

　　　Qù　Xī'ān　de　piào　wǒ　mǎihǎo　le.
(5) 去　西安　的　票　我　买好　了。

3. 请把这个和存折一起交给营业员

Qǐng bǎ zhè fēng xìn jiāogěi xiàozhǎng.
(1) 请 把 这 封 信 交给 校长。

Wénjiàn wǒ jiāogěi kēzhǎng le.
(2) 文件 我 交给 科长 了。（文件：documents）

Bàn qiānzhèng yào jiāo sìbǎi kuài.
(3) 办 签证 要 交 四百 块。（签证：visa）

Měi ge rén yīnggāi yīfǎ jiāo shuì.
(4) 每 个 人 应该 依法 交 税。（依法：according to law　税：tax）

4. 要有身份证才能取钱

Yào zuòwán zuòyè cái néng kàn diànshì.
(1) 要 做完 作业 才 能 看 电视。

Yào dǎsǎo wán bàngōngshì cái néng huí jiā.
(2) 要 打扫 完 办公室 才 能 回 家。

Yào bànwán shì cái néng xiūxi.
(3) 要 办完 事 才 能 休息。

Xué wàiyǔ yào duō shuō cái néng xuéhuì.
(4) 学 外语 要 多 说 才 能 学会。

☆　词　语（Word list）　☆

1. 储蓄 chǔxù	（名/动）	save	2. 存钱 cúnqián	（动） deposit money
3. 取钱 qǔqián	（动）	withdraw money	4. 信用卡 xìnyòngkǎ	（名） credit card
5. 自动 取款机 zìdòng qǔkuǎnjī	（名）	cash dispenser	6. 账号 zhànghào	（名） account number
7. 到期 dàoqī	（动）	become due	8. 本金 běnjīn	（名） principal, capital
9. 电汇 diànhuì	（动）	remittance by telegram	10. 利率 lìlǜ	（名） interest rate
11. 利息 lìxī	（名）	interest	12. 贷款 dàikuǎn	（名/动） loan
13. 挂失 guàshī	（动）	report a loss	14. 划拨 huàbō	（动） transfer (money)

☆　练　习（Exercises）　☆

一、用"要……才能……"回答问题（Use "要……才能……" to answer the following questions）

1. 爸爸什么时候才能回家？

2. 这本书什么时候才能出版？

3. 这个工程（gōngchéng/project）要多长时间才能完成？

4. 买这样的房子要多少钱？

二、用汉语说出下面的数字（Say the numbers in Chinese）

35412.11 元　　5398.50 元　　　880054 元　　98.6%　　8.25%

三、完成对话（Complete the conversations）

1. A：您要取多少钱？　　　B：＿＿＿＿＿＿＿＿＿＿＿＿。

2. A：您要存定期还是活期？　　　B：＿＿＿＿＿＿＿＿＿＿＿。

3. A：＿＿＿＿＿＿＿＿＿＿＿？　　　B：三年定期的利率是百分之三点零五。

四、会话（Conversation）

于雪来：小姐,这张定期存单到期了。我要取出来。

职　员：本金五千元,利息八百三十六元,一共五千八百三十六元,请点一下。

于雪来：我想办一张信用卡。

职　员：那边有开户申请书（shēnqǐngshū/application form）,先填好再来。

于雪来：填好了,给你。

职　员：要有一百元本金,才能开户。

于雪来：就把这五千块钱存进去吧。

职　员：您的身份证？

于雪来：给你。

职　员：请在这里签字。请留密码。

于雪来：几位数？

职　员：六位。按（àn/key in, input）完密码请按确认（quèrèn/confirm）键（jiàn/key）。

于雪来：好了。

职　员：请再按一遍（biàn,量词）。好了。请拿好您的卡。

☆　练习答案（Key to the exercises）　☆

一、1. 爸爸要下了班才能回家。

　　2. 要过两三个月才能出版。

　　3. 要两年才能完成。

　　4. 要八十万才能买到（这样的房子）。

二、三万五千四百十二元一角一分;　　　五千三百九十八元五角;

　　八十八万零五十四元;　　　　　　　百分之九十八点六;

　　百分之八点二五

三、1. B：一万块

　　2. B：我要存活期

　　3. A：三年定期的利息是多少

23 住址 ADDRESS

Zhùzhǐ

1. A: 你 家 住在 哪里?
   Nǐ jiā zhùzài nǎli?
   Where do you live?

   B: 我 住在 徐汇 区 漕宝 路。
   Wǒ zhùzài Xúhuì Qū Cáobǎo Lù.
   I live on Caobao Rd. , Xuhui District.

   A: 靠近 哪里?
   Kàojìn nǎli?
   Near what place?

   B: 在 华厦 宾馆 附近。
   Zài Huáxià Bīnguǎn fùjìn.
   Near Huaxia Hotel.

   A: 你 一直 住在 那里 吗?
   Nǐ yìzhí zhùzài nàli ma?
   Have you lived there for a long time?

   B: 不, 我 原来注 住在 普陀区。
   Bù, wǒ yuánlái zhùzài Pǔtuó Qū.
   No, I lived in Putuo District before.

   A: 什么 时候 搬家 的?
   Shénme shíhòu bānjiā de?
   When did you move?

   B: 是 三 年 前 搬 的。
   Shì sān nián qián bān de.
   Three years ago.

2. A: 你家的 门牌 是 多少 号?
   Nǐ jiā de ménpái shì duōshao hào?
   What's your building number?

B：二十 号。
Èrshí hào.

20.

A：你 住 几 楼？几 号 房间？
Nǐ zhù jǐ lóu? Jǐ hào fángjiān?

Which floor do you live on? And what's the apartment number?

B：（我 住）六 楼 603 室。
(Wǒ zhù) liù lóu liùlíngsān shì.

I live in Apt. 603 on the sixth floor.

A：你 家 的 电话 号码 是 多少？
Nǐ jiā de diànhuà hàomǎ shì duōshao?

May I know your home phone number?

B：6 7 8 4 5 1 3。
Liùqībāsìwǔyāosān.

6784513.

3. A：你 做 什么 工作？
Nǐ zuò shénme gōngzuò?

What do you do for work?

B：我 是 公司 职员。
Wǒ shì gōngsī zhíyuán.

I am an office worker in a company.

A：你 的 工作 单位 在 哪里？
Nǐ de gōngzuò dānwèi zài nǎli?

Where is your company?

B：在 西藏 中路。
Zài Xīzàng Zhōnglù.

On Xizang Zhonglu (Middle Xizang Rd.).

A：（公司）离 家 远 吗？
(Gōngsī) lí jiā yuǎn ma?

Is your company far from your home?

B：很 远。每 天 乘 地铁 上班。
Hěn yuǎn. Měi tiān chéng dìtiě shàngbān.

Yes, very far. I take the subway to work every day.

A：你 儿子 的 学校 离 家 近 吗？
Nǐ érzi de xuéxiào lí jiā jìn ma?

Is your son's school close to your home?

B：不 太 近。他 每 天 骑 自行车 去 学校。
Bú tài jìn. Tā měi tiān qí zìxíngchē qù xuéxiào.

Not really close. He goes to school by bicycle every day.

☆　注　释（Note）　☆

"原来"在这里表示以前某一时期,有现在已经不是这样的意思。

"原来"here indicates that something existed or happened in the past but no longer exists or happens now.

（1）Zhèli　yuánlái　shì　sēnlín.
这里　原来　是　森林。　Here once was a forest.

（2）Tā　yuánlái　shì　jiàoshī.
他　原来　是　教师。　He was a teacher.

☆　句型提示（Sentence pattern references）　☆

1. 是三年前搬的。	请参看 381 页句型 197。
2. 每天乘地铁上班。	请参看 306 页句型 30。
3. 不太近。	请参看 366 页句型 161。

☆　词语用法举例（Examples for usage of the words）　☆

1. 靠近哪里

（1）Hāmì　Lù　kàojìn　dòngwùyuán.
哈密　路　靠近　动物园。

（2）Měiguó　lǐngshìguǎn　kàojìn　nǎli?
美国　领事馆　靠近　哪里?

（3）Bàozhǐ　fàngzài　kàojìn　shāfā　de　zhuōzi　shang.
报纸　放在　靠近　沙发　的　桌子　上。　（沙发：sofa）

（4）Wǒ　de　zuòwèi　kàojìn　chuāngkǒu.
我　的　座位　靠近　窗口。

2. 你一直住在那里吗

（1）Tā　yìzhí　dāng　yīshēng.
他　一直　当　医生。　（当医生：be a doctor）

（2）Lín　Zhìqiáng　duì　gōngzuò　yìzhí　hěn　rènzhēn.
林　志强　对　工作　一直　很　认真。　（认真：conscientious）

（3）Tā　de　háizi　yìzhí　shēngbìng.
他　的　孩子　一直　生病。　（生病：be sick）

（4）Tā　yìzhí　děngzhe.
他　一直　等着。

3. 你的工作单位在哪里

（1）Wǒ　bā　diǎn　yào　qù　dānwèi.
我　八　点　要　去　单位。

Bàba hé māma zài tóng yí ge dānwèi gōngzuò.
(2) 爸爸 和 妈妈 在 同 一 个 单位 工作。

Tā zuówǎn zài dānwèi jiābān.
(3) 他 昨晚 在 单位 加班。 (加班:work overtime)

Tā xiǎng zhǎo ge hǎo de gōngzuò dānwèi.
(4) 她 想 找 个 好 的 工作 单位。

4. 每天乘地铁上班

Wǒ měi tiān chéng gōnggòng qìchē dào gōngsī.
(1) 我 每 天 乘 公共 汽车 到 公司。

Kēzhǎng chéng fēijī qù Xiānggǎng le.
(2) 科长 乘 飞机 去 香港 了。

Xiǎo Chén shì chéng huǒchē qù Guìlín de.
(3) 小 陈 是 乘 火车 去 桂林 的。

Wǒ xiǎng chéng chuán huí Rìběn.
(4) 我 想 乘 船 回 日本。

5. 他每天骑自行车去学校

Tā huì qí mǎ.
(1) 他 会 骑 马。 (马:horse)

Gēge qízài mǎ shang pāizhào.
(2) 哥哥 骑在 马 上 拍照。 (拍照:take photo)

Wǒ bú huì qí zìxíngchē.
(3) 我 不 会 骑 自行车。

Shūshu qí mótuōchē qù huǒchēzhàn le.
(4) 叔叔 骑 摩托车 去 火车站 了。

☆ 词 语 (Word list) ☆

tōngxùn dìzhǐ
1. 通讯 地址 (名) address

jiātíng zhùzhǐ
2. 家庭 住址 (名) home address

dānwèi dìzhǐ
3. 单位 地址 (名) office address

shěng
4. 省 (名) province

shì
5. 市 (名) city

qū
6. 区 (名) district

shìqū
7. 市区 (名) urban district

jiāoqū
8. 郊区 (名) suburbs

xiàn
9. 县 (名) county

zhōuwéi
10. 周围 (名) around, surrounding

gōngyuán
11. 公园 (名) park

túshūguǎn
12. 图书馆 (名) library

diànyǐngyuàn
13. 电影院 (名) cinema

jùchǎng
14. 剧场 (名) theater

guǎngchǎng
15. 广场 (名) square

fángzi
16. 房子 (名) house

17. 房屋　　（名）　house
_{fángwū}

18. 房租　　（名）　rent
_{fángzū}

☆　练　习(Exercises)　☆

一、用括号中的词语改写句子(Rewrite the following sentences with the words in brackets)

1. 这本书是他的,现在他送给了我。（原来）

2. 一年前我在复旦大学学习,现在在上海师范大学学习。（原来）

3. 我住在这里三年了,没有搬过家。（一直）

4. 大学毕业以后,他在这个公司工作,没有换过单位。（一直）

5. 他的家在静安寺附近。（靠近）

二、用括号中的词语完成句子(Complete sentences with the words in brackets)

1. 现在住的房子太小了,孩子出生以后,我们要＿＿＿＿＿＿＿＿＿＿＿＿。（搬）

2. A：附近有邮局吗? B：没有。＿＿＿＿＿＿＿＿＿＿＿＿。（离）

3. A：你骑自行车上班吗? B：不,＿＿＿＿＿＿＿＿＿＿＿＿。（乘）

4. A：你住在哪儿? B：＿＿＿＿＿＿＿＿＿＿＿＿。（地址）

三、回答问题(Answer the following questions)

1. 你家住哪儿?

2. 你住在市区还是郊区?

3. 你家的门牌号码是多少?

4. 你一直住在那里吗?

5. 附近有银行和超市吗?

6. 你住的大楼有几层(céng/storey)? 你住在第几层?

7. 你现在的房子一个月房租是多少?

四、会话(Conversation)

刘达生：雪来、小郭,我搬家了,明天请你们来我的新家坐坐。

于雪来：是吗? 你原来住在华山路上,很不错的地方啊。为什么要搬?

刘达生：住在市区是很方便,可房子太小。

郭　放：新房子在哪儿?

刘达生：在莘庄。

于雪来：那恭喜(gōngxǐ/congratulate)你了。

刘达生：谢谢。你们明天一定来啊。这是地址。

郭　放：梅园小区33号503室。好,我们一定去。

刘达生：是一栋(dòng,量词)绿色(lǜsè/green)的大楼。很好找的。

于雪来：坐什么车去?

刘达生：坐地铁。我家离地铁站只有十分钟路。

郭　放：挺方便的嘛。

☆　**练习答案**(Key to the exercises)　☆

一、1. 这本书原来是他的,现在他送给了我。

　　2. 我原来在复旦大学学习,现在在上海师范大学学习。

　　3. 我一直住在这里,没有搬过家。

　　4. 大学毕业以后他一直在这个公司工作,没换过单位。

　　5. 他的家靠近静安寺。

二、1. 搬家

　　2. 邮局离这儿很远

　　3. 我乘公共汽车上班

　　4. 我的地址是……

24 约会
Yuēhuì

MAKING AN APPOINTMENT

1. A：你　星期六　晚上　有
　　Nǐ　xīngqīliù　wǎnshang　yǒu
　　空　吗？
　　kòng　ma?

Are you free this Saturday evening?

B：有　空。有　什么　事　吗？
　　Yǒu kòng. Yǒu shénme shì ma?

Yes. What's happening?

A：我　想　去　你　家　坐坐注1。
　　Wǒ xiǎng qù nǐ jiā zuòzuo.

I'd like to go to see you.

B：欢迎。　你　几　点　来？
　　Huānyíng. Nǐ jǐ diǎn lái?

Good! When will you come?

A：晚上　　八　点　　左右
　　Wǎnshang bā diǎn zuǒyòu
　　方便　　吗？
　　fāngbiàn ma?

About eight p.m. Is that convenient for you?

B：晚上　　我　一般　都　在
　　Wǎnshang wǒ yìbān dōu zài
　　家。你　什么　时候　来
　　jiā. Nǐ shénme shíhou lái
　　都　行。我　等　你。
　　dōu xíng. Wǒ děng nǐ.

I'm usually at home in the evening. You may come any time. I will be waiting for you.

2. A: Míngtiān xiàwǔ nǐ yǒu shíjiān ma?
明天 下午 你 有 时间 吗?　　Are you available tomorrow afternoon?

B: Duìbuqǐ wǒ yǒu diǎnr shì,
对不起, 我 有 点儿 事,　　Sorry, I am busy.

méi kòng.
没 空。

3. A: Jīnwǎn yìqǐ chī wǎnfàn ba.
今晚 一起 吃 晚饭 吧。　　How about having dinner together this evening?

B: Duìbuqǐ, wǒ yǒu bié de
对不起, 我 有 别 的　　Sorry, I have an appointment already.

yuēhuì.
约会。

A: Nàme, wǒ gǎitiān zài yuē nǐ
那么, 我 改天 再 约 你　　Then let's make an arrangement for another

ba.
吧。　　day.

B: Guò liǎng tiān wǒ dǎ diànhuà
过 两注2 天 我 打 电话　　I'll call you soon.

gěi nǐ.
给 你。

4. A: Xīngqītiān yìqǐ qù Pǔdōng wán,
星期天 一起 去 浦东 玩,　　Let's go to Pudong for fun this Sunday. Is it

hǎo ma?
好 吗?　　all right?

B: Nà tài hǎo le! Wǒ dài
那 太 好 了! 我 带　　That's fine! May I bring a friend with me?

péngyou yìqǐ qù, kěyǐ ma?
朋友 一起 去, 可以 吗?

A: Hǎo de. (Qǐng nǐ de péngyou)
好 的。(请 你 的 朋友)　　Sure. Please invite your friend to go with

gēn wǒmen yìqǐ qù ba.
跟 我们 一起 去 吧。　　us.

B: Nàme, bā diǎn bàn zài sìshí'èr
那么, 八 点 半 在 四十二　　So, let's meet at the terminal of Bus No. 42 at

lù zhōngdiǎnzhàn jiànmiàn ba.
路 终点站 见面 吧。　　eight thirty.

A: Hǎo de, bújiàn-búsàn.
好 的, 不见不散。　　OK. See you there.

5. A：<ruby>明天<rt>Míngtiān</rt></ruby> <ruby>的<rt>de</rt></ruby> <ruby>会议<rt>huìyì</rt></ruby> <ruby>改在<rt>gǎizài</rt></ruby> <ruby>后天<rt>hòutiān</rt></ruby> <ruby>下午<rt>xiàwǔ</rt></ruby>。<ruby>请<rt>Qǐng</rt></ruby> <ruby>您<rt>nín</rt></ruby> <ruby>出席<rt>chūxí</rt></ruby>。
   Tomorrow's meeting is changed to the afternoon of the day after tomorrow. Please be there.

   B：<ruby>对不起<rt>Duìbuqǐ</rt></ruby>，<ruby>我<rt>wǒ</rt></ruby> <ruby>很<rt>hěn</rt></ruby> <ruby>忙<rt>máng</rt></ruby>，<ruby>不<rt>bù</rt></ruby> <ruby>能<rt>néng</rt></ruby> <ruby>出席<rt>chūxí</rt></ruby>。
   Sorry, I can't attend it since I am very busy.

6. A：<ruby>后天<rt>Hòutiān</rt></ruby> <ruby>出发<rt>chūfā</rt></ruby> <ruby>吗<rt>ma</rt></ruby>?
   Are we leaving the day after tomorrow?

   B：<ruby>能<rt>Néng</rt></ruby> <ruby>不<rt>bu</rt></ruby> <ruby>能<rt>néng</rt></ruby> <ruby>出发<rt>chūfā</rt></ruby>，<ruby>要<rt>yào</rt></ruby> <ruby>看<rt>kàn</rt></ruby> <ruby>天气<rt>tiānqì</rt></ruby> <ruby>好<rt>hǎo</rt></ruby> <ruby>不<rt>bu</rt></ruby> <ruby>好<rt>hǎo</rt></ruby>。
   It depends on the weather.

☆ 注 释 (Notes) ☆

1. 动词重叠表示动作的时间短,或表示轻松的意思。
   The repeat of a verb expresses that the action lasts for a short time or the action will be carried out with ease.

   (1) <ruby>寒假<rt>Hánjià</rt></ruby> <ruby>我<rt>wǒ</rt></ruby> <ruby>想<rt>xiǎng</rt></ruby> <ruby>去<rt>qù</rt></ruby> <ruby>西安<rt>Xī'ān</rt></ruby> <ruby>玩玩<rt>wánwan</rt></ruby>。
   I want to take a tour to Xi'an in the winter vacation.

   (2) <ruby>让<rt>Ràng</rt></ruby> <ruby>我<rt>wǒ</rt></ruby> <ruby>看看<rt>kànkan</rt></ruby>。
   Let me have a look.

2. "两"在这儿表示概数。
   "两" here is just an approximate number.

   (1) <ruby>多<rt>Duō</rt></ruby> <ruby>读<rt>dú</rt></ruby> <ruby>两<rt>liǎng</rt></ruby> <ruby>遍<rt>biàn</rt></ruby> <ruby>就<rt>jiù</rt></ruby> <ruby>能<rt>néng</rt></ruby> <ruby>记住<rt>jìzhù</rt></ruby>。
   Read it several more times then you can memorize it.

   (2) <ruby>我<rt>Wǒ</rt></ruby> <ruby>再<rt>zài</rt></ruby> <ruby>看<rt>kàn</rt></ruby> <ruby>两<rt>liǎng</rt></ruby> <ruby>页<rt>yè</rt></ruby> <ruby>就<rt>jiù</rt></ruby> <ruby>睡觉<rt>shuìjiào</rt></ruby>。
   I'll go to bed after reading some more pages.

☆ 句型提示 (Sentence pattern references) ☆

1. 我带朋友一起去,可以吗?　　　　　请参看 294 页句型 3。
2. 请你的朋友跟我们一起去吧。　　　　请参看 363 页句型 157。

☆ 词语用法举例(Examples for usage of the words) ☆

1. 你星期六晚上有空吗

(1) Yǒu kòng qǐng dào wǒ jiā lái wán.
有 空 请 到 我 家 来 玩。

(2) Míngtiān yǒu kòng dehuà, wǒ xiǎng kàn chǎng diànyǐng.
明天 有 空 的话，我 想 看 场 电影。

(3) Gōngzuò hěn duō, zhěngtiān dōu méi kòng.
工作 很 多， 整天 都 没 空。 (整天：the whole day)

(4) Zuìjìn hěn máng, yìzhí méi kòng.
最近 很 忙， 一直 没 空。

2. 我想去你家坐坐

(1) Wǒ qùqu jiù lái.
我 去去 就 来。

(2) Nǐ de qiānbǐ jiègěi wǒ yòngyong, kěyǐ ma?
你 的 铅笔 借给 我 用用， 可以 吗?

(3) Wǒ xiǎng chángchang Shànghǎi de xiǎochī.
我 想 尝尝 上海 的 小吃。

(4) Kànkan diànshì, tīngting yīnyuè, zhēn shūfu.
看看 电视， 听听 音乐， 真 舒服。 (舒服：comfortable)

3. 晚上八点左右方便吗

(1) Nǐ fāngbiàn dehuà, wǒ xiànzài qù nǐ nàr.
你 方便 的话，我 现在 去 你 那儿。

(2) Rúguǒ fāngbiàn, jiègěi wǒ yìdiǎnr qián.
如果 方便， 借给 我 一点儿 钱。 (借给：lend)

(3) Rúguǒ bù fāngbiàn, jiù suàn le.
如果 不 方便， 就 算 了。 (算了：forget it)

(4) Bù fāngbiàn dehuà, nǐ búyòng lái.
不 方便 的话， 你 不用 来。

4. 晚上我一般都在家

(1) Wǎnshang yìbān dōu yào jiābān.
晚上 一般 都 要 加班。

(2) Wǒ yìbān shíyī diǎn shuìjiào.
我 一般 十一 点 睡觉。

(3) Tā chūchāi yìbān dōu chéng fēijī.
他 出差 一般 都 乘 飞机。

(4) Wǒ yìbān yì nián huí yí cì lǎojiā.
我 一般 一 年 回 一 次 老家。

5. 你什么时候来都行

(1) Shuí zuò dōu xíng.
谁 做 都 行。

(2) Chī shénme dōu xíng.
吃 什么 都 行。

　　　　Shénme　yánsè　dōu　xíng.
（3）什么　颜色　都　行。

　　　　Fàngzài　nǎli　dōu　xíng.
（4）放在　哪里　都　行。

6. 星期天一起去浦东玩,好吗

　　　　Chéng　chūzūchē　qù,　hǎo　ma?
（1）乘　出租车　去,　好　吗?

　　　　Shǔjià　qù　Dōngběi　wán,　hǎo　ma?
（2）暑假　去　东北　玩,　好　吗?

　　　　Jīntiān　chī　Guǎngdōngcài,　hǎo　ma?
（3）今天　吃　广东菜,　好　吗?

　　　　Yìqǐ　qù　kàn　jīngjù,　hǎo　ma?
（4）一起　去　看　京剧,　好　吗?　　（京剧:Beijing Opera）

7. 我带朋友一起去,可以吗

　　　　Xià　yǔ　le,　xìnghǎo　wǒ　dàile　yǔsǎn.
（1）下　雨　了,　幸好　我　带了　雨伞。　（幸好:fortunately）

　　　　Zāogāo!　Wàngjì　dài　qiánbāo　le.
（2）糟糕!　忘记　带　钱包　了。　（糟糕:What bad luck!）

　　　　Míngtiān　dài　háizi　qù　dòngwùyuán.
（3）明天　带　孩子　去　动物园。

　　　　Nǐ　bú　rènshi　lù,　wǒ　dài　nǐ　qù　ba.
（4）你　不　认识　路,　我　带　你　去　吧。

8. 我带朋友一起去,可以吗

　　　　Wǒ　yòng　yíxià　zhège　diànhuà,　kěyǐ　ma?
（1）我　用　一下　这个　电话,　可以　吗?

　　　　Wǒ　kàn　yíxià　nǐ　de　yǐngjí,　kěyǐ　ma?
（2）我　看　一下　你　的　影集,　可以　吗?　（影集:photo album）

　　　　Zài　zhèr　zuò　yíxià,　kěyǐ　ma?
（3）在　这儿　坐　一下,　可以　吗?

　　　　Wǒ　xiǎng　chōu　zhī　yān,　kěyǐ　ma?
（4）我　想　抽　支　烟,　可以　吗?

☆　词　语（Word list）　☆

1.	bàifǎng 拜访	（动） pay a visit	2.	fǎngwèn 访问	（动） visit, call on
3.	kànwàng 看望	（动） visit, see, call on	4.	chuànmén 串门	（动） drop in, informal visit
5.	yuē 约	（动） make an appointment, invite or ask in advance	6.	děnghòu 等候	（动） wait
7.	fāngbiàn 方便	（形） convenient	8.	bù fāngbiàn 不 方便	inconvenient
9.	gǎiqī 改期	（动） change the date	10.	yíhàn 遗憾	（名/形） sorry, regret, pity

11.	wùbì 务必	（副）	must, be sure to	12.	dì-èr tiān 第二 天	the next day
13.	zhè cì 这 次		this time	14.	shàng cì 上 次	last time
15.	xià cì 下 次		next time	16.	dāying 答应	（动） promise, agree
17.	jùjué 拒绝	（动）	reject, refuse	18.	shīyuē 失约	（动） fail to keep an appointment
19.	tíqián 提前	（动）	do something in advance	20.	tuīchí 推迟	（动） postpone

☆ 练 习（Exercises） ☆

一、替换练习（Substitution exercises）

1. <u>明天的会议</u>改在<u>后天下午</u>。　　一点钟的约会　　两点半
　　　　　　　　　　　　　　　　　他乘的飞机　　　半小时以后起飞
　　　　　　　　　　　　　　　　　明天的课　　　　后天
　　　　　　　　　　　　　　　　　上午的会　　　　下午

2. <u>你什么时候来都行</u>。　　　　　去什么地方旅行　　可以
　　　　　　　　　　　　　　　　　用什么笔写　　　　没问题
　　　　　　　　　　　　　　　　　点什么菜　　　　　行
　　　　　　　　　　　　　　　　　用什么洗衣粉　　　洗不掉

3. 我带<u>朋友</u> <u>去</u>。　　　　　　儿子　　　　　　去动物园
　　　　　　　　　　　　　　　　　太太　　　　　　出席公司的新年晚会
　　　　　　　　　　　　　　　　　孩子　　　　　　看病
　　　　　　　　　　　　　　　　　秘书　　　　　　参加会议

二、用括号中的词语改写句子（Rewrite the following sentences with the words in brackets）

1. 我现在到你家可以吗？（方便）

2. 她只喝果汁,不喝酒。（什么都）

3. 北京人大多喝花茶,上海人大多喝绿茶。（一般）

4. 这几天我没空,过几天再去逛街吧。（改天）（逛街:stroll around streets）

5. 我不是一个人来的,小王也来了。（一起）

6. 广州的会议十二号举行,我们十号出发。（提前）

7. 原来一点二十分的飞机改在两点二十分起飞。（推迟）

三、完成对话（Complete the conversations）

1. A：＿＿＿＿＿＿＿＿＿＿＿＿？

　　B：今天晚上我有事。

　　A：那么,＿＿＿＿＿＿＿＿＿＿＿。

2. A：你这个星期天有空吗？

　　B：有空。＿＿＿＿＿＿＿＿＿＿＿？

A：我想带孩子去动物园。_____?

B：好啊。我们一起去吧。

3．A：明天的会议你参加不参加?

　　B：对不起,_____。

4．A：明天的茶话会(cháhuàhuì/tea party)你带孩子去吗?

　　B：不,_____。

四、会话(Conversations)

玛　丽：老师,对不起,明天有朋友来,不上课行吗?

老　师：那么什么时候上课?

玛　丽：改在后天吧。

老　师：还是上午十点到十二点吗?

玛　丽：是的。方便吗?

老　师：早一点儿行吗? 因为我跟朋友约好十二点钟一起吃饭。

玛　丽：那么就九点半到十一点吧,早一点儿结束。

老　师：好的。没问题。

李丽平：小于,我又到上海了,我们见一面吧。

于雪来：好啊。什么时候?

李丽平：今天晚上,方便吗?

于雪来：今晚不行,我没空,儿子的学校要开家长(jiāzhǎng/parent)会。明天吧。

李丽平：好,你来花园饭店(Huāyuán Fàndiàn/Garden Hotel)行吗?

于雪来：行,在哪里都行。

李丽平：那么我在一楼咖啡厅(kāfēitīng/coffee house)等你。不见不散。

于雪来：好,不见不散。

☆　练习答案(Key to the exercises)　☆

二、1. 我现在到你家方便吗?

　　2. 她只喝果汁,什么酒都不喝。

　　3. 北京人一般喝花茶,上海人一般喝绿茶。

　　4. 这几天我没空,改天再去逛街吧。

　　5. 我是和小王一起来的。

　　6. 广州的会议十二号举行,我们提前两天出发。

　　7. 原来一点二十分的飞机推迟一个小时起飞。

三、1. A：今晚有空吗　　我改天再约你吧

　　2. B：有什么事吗　　A：你也一起去,好吗

　　3. B：我没空,不能参加

　　4. B：不带孩子去

25 家庭 *Jiā tíng*

FAMILY

1. A: Nǐ jiā yǒu jǐ kǒu rén?
你 家 有 几 口 人?

How many members are there in your family?

B: (Yǒu) sān kǒu rén. Wǒ
(有) 三 口 人。我

xiānsheng、 nǚ'ér hé wǒ.
先生、 女儿 和 我。

There are three members: my husband, my

daughter and me.

A: Nǐ xiānsheng zài nǎli gōngzuò?
你 先生 在 哪里 工作?

What does your husband do?

B: Tā zài yínháng gōngzuò.
他 在 银行 工作。

He works in a bank.

A: Nǐ nǚ'ér ne?
你 女儿 呢?

And your daughter?

B: Nǚ'ér (zhèng)zài dàxué dú
女儿 (正)在 大学 读

fǎlǜ, sān niánjí le.
法律, 三 年级 了。

She is a junior university student in law

school.

2. A: Nǐ fùmǔ zhùzài nǎli?
你 父母 住在 哪里?

Where do your parents live?

B: (Tāmen) zhùzài Méihuāyuàn,
(他们) 住在 梅花苑,

They live in Meihuayuan near my home.

lí　wǒ　jiā　hěn　jìn.
离 我 家 很 近。

A：Nǐ　fùmǔ　hái　gōngzuò　ma?
你 父母 还注 工作 吗？　　　Are your parents still working?

B：Fùqīn　hái　zài　gōngzuò,　mǔqīn
父亲 还 在 工作, 母亲　　My father is still working but my mother has

yǐjīng　tuìxiū　le.
已经 退休 了。　　　　　　retired.

A：Nǐ　fùmǔqīn　duō　dà　niánjì　le?
你 父母亲 多 大 年纪 了？　How old are your parents?

B：Fùqīn　jīnnián　wǔshíbā　suì,
父亲 今年 五十八 岁,　　My father is 58 years old this year and my

mǔqīn　wǔshíliù　suì.
母亲 五十六 岁。　　　　mother is 56.

3. A：Nǐ　yǒu　xiōngdì　jiěmèi　ma?
你 有 兄弟 姐妹 吗？　　　Do you have any brothers or sisters?

B：Wǒ　yǒu　yí　ge　gēge.
我 有 一 个 哥哥。　　　　I have an elder brother.

A：Nǐ　gēge　duō　dà?
你 哥哥 多 大？　　　　　How old is your brother?

B：Gēge　bǐ　wǒ　dà　sì　suì,
哥哥 比 我 大 四 岁,　　My elder brother is four years older than me,

sānshí'èr　suì　le.
三十二 岁 了。　　　　　and he is now 32 years old.

A：Nǐ　gēge　jiéhūnle　ma?
你 哥哥 结婚了 吗？　　　Is your elder brother married?

B：Tā　jiéhūn　wǔ　nián　le,　sǎozi
他 结婚 五 年 了, 嫂子　Yes, he has been married for five years. His

shì　gēge　de　tóngxué.
是 哥哥 的 同学。　　　　wife was his classmate.

A：Zhège　xiǎo　gūniang　shì　shuí?
这个 小 姑娘 是 谁？　　Who is that little girl?

B：Tā　shì　wǒ　gēge　de　nǚ'ér.
她 是 我 哥哥 的 女儿。　She is my brother's daughter.

A：Nǐ　gēge　de　nǚ'ér　hěn
你 哥哥 的 女儿 很　　　Your brother's daughter is very beautiful.

piàoliang.
漂亮。

B：(Tā)　bùjǐn　piàoliang,　érqiě
(她) 不仅 漂亮, 而且　　She is not only beautiful, but also smart.

　　　　hěn　cōngming.
　　　很　　聪明。

4. A：你　的　朋友　杰克　有
　　　Nǐ　de　péngyou　Jiékè　yǒu
　　　几　个　孩子?
　　　jǐ　ge　háizi?

How many children does your friend Jack have?

　　B：他　有　两　个　孩子，一
　　　Tā　yǒu　liǎng　ge　háizi，yí
　　　个　儿子、一　个　女儿。
　　　ge　érzi、yí　ge　nǚ'ér.

He has two children, a son and a daughter.

　　A：他们　几　岁　了?
　　　Tāmen　jǐ　suì　le?

How old are they?

　　B：大　的　十二　岁，小　的
　　　Dà　de　shí'èr　suì，xiǎo　de
　　　八　岁。
　　　bā　suì.

The elder is twelve years old and the younger is eight.

☆　注　释(Note)　☆

"还"在这里表示动作或状态没有变化。

"还" here indicates that the action is going on or the situation remains unchanged.

　　　　Tā　hái　zhùzài　Běijīng.
(1) 他　还　住在　北京。　He still lives in Beijing.
　　　　Tā　hái　méi　bìyè.
(2) 她　还　没　毕业。　She hasn't graduated yet.

☆　句型提示(Sentence pattern references)　☆

1. 你家有几口人?　　　　　　　请参看 305 页句型 26。
2. 女儿(正)在大学读法律。　　请参看 308 页句型 33。
3. 你父母亲多大年纪了?　　　请参看 303 页句型 20。
4. 哥哥比我大四岁。　　　　　请参看 322 页句型 64。
5. 她不仅漂亮,而且很聪明。　请参看 384 页句型 202。

☆　词语用法举例(Examples for usage of the words)　☆

1. 你父母住在哪里
　　　　Lín　Méiyīng　zhùzài　xuéxiào.
　(1) 林　梅英　住在　学校。

(2)
Wǒ zhùzài shí'èr lóu.
我　住在　十二　楼。

(3)
Tā zhùzài Huátíng Bīnguǎn.
他　住在　华亭　宾馆。　　（宾馆：hotel）

(4)
Lǐ Zhìhǎi zài Měiguó zhùle sān nián.
李　志海　在　美国　住了　三　年。

2. 你父母还工作吗

(1)
Wǒ hái zhùzài Hóngqiáo Lù, méi bānjiā.
我　还　住在　虹桥　路，没　搬家。

(2)
Jǐ nián méi jiànmiàn, nǐ hái shì lǎoyàngzi.
几　年　没　见面，你　还　是　老样子。　　（老样子：look the same）

(3)
Jiǔ diǎn le, tā hái méi huí jiā.
九　点　了，他　还　没　回　家。

(4)
Tā hái méi tuìxiū.
他　还　没　退休。

3. 母亲已经退休了

(1)
Yǐjīng bā diǎn le, kuài qǐchuáng!
已经　八　点　了，快　起床！

(2)
Tā yǐjīng qīshí suì le, shēntǐ hái hěn jiēshi.
他　已经　七十　岁　了，身体　还　很　结实。　　（结实：strong）

(3)
Tā qù Běijīng yǐjīng yí ge xīngqī le, hái méi lái diànhuà.
他　去　北京　已经　一　个　星期　了，还　没　来　电话。

(4)
Wǒ lái Shànghǎi yǐjīng bàn nián le.
我　来　上海　已经　半　年　了。

☆ 词　语（Word list） ☆

1.	bàba 爸爸	（名）	father, papa	2.	māma 妈妈　（名）mother, mom
3.	yéye 爷爷	（名）	grandfather(paternal)	4.	nǎinai 奶奶　（名）grandmother (paternal)
5.	wàigōng 外公	（名）	grandfather(maternal)	6.	wàipó 外婆　（名）grandmother (maternal)
7.	zhàngfu 丈夫	（名）	husband	8.	qīzi 妻子　（名）wife
9.	gēge 哥哥	（名）	elder brother	10.	jiějie 姐姐　（名）elder sister
11.	dìdi 弟弟	（名）	younger brother	12.	mèimei 妹妹　（名）younger sister
13.	bóbo 伯伯	（名）	uncle (father's elder brother)	14.	bómǔ 伯母　（名）aunt (wife of father's elder brother)
15.	shūshu 叔叔	（名）	uncle(father's younger brother)	16.	shěnshen 婶婶　（名）aunt (wife of father's younger brother)
17.	gūgu 姑姑	（名）	aunt(father's sister)	18.	gūfù 姑父　（名）uncle (husband of father's sister)

19. jiùjiu 舅舅 （名） uncle (mother's brother)	20. jiùmā 舅妈 （名） aunt (wife of mother's brother)
21. yímā 姨妈 （名） aunt (mother's elder sister)	22. āyí 阿姨 （名） aunt (mother's younger sister)
23. yífù 姨父 （名） uncle (husband of mother's sister)	24. jiārén 家人 （名） family member
25. qīnqi 亲戚 （名） relatives	26. nánpéngyou 男朋友 （名） boyfriend
27. nǔpéngyou 女朋友 （名） girlfriend	28. hǎopéngyou 好朋友 （名） good friend
29. lǎopéngyou 老朋友 （名） old friend	30. xiàoyǒu 校友 （名） school mate, alumnus, alumna
31. zhǎngbèi 长辈 （名） persons in senior generation, senior family members	32. xiǎobèi 小辈 （名） persons in junior generation, junior family members
33. xīnláng 新郎 （名） bridegroom	34. xīnniáng(zi) 新娘(子)（名） bride
35. xìngfú 幸福 （形） happy	36. àiqíng 爱情 （名） love
37. líhūn 离婚 （动） divorce	38. dānshēn 单身 （名） unmarried, single

☆ 练 习(Exercises) ☆

一、替换练习(Substitution exercises)

1. 这个小姑娘是谁?　　　　　这个男孩子
　　　　　　　　　　　　　　那个女人
　　　　　　　　　　　　　　前面那个男人
　　　　　　　　　　　　　　坐着那位老人

2. 嫂子是哥哥的同学。　　李明　　姐姐　　男朋友
　　　　　　　　　　　　王勇　　校长　　儿子
　　　　　　　　　　　　他　　　妈妈　　同事
　　　　　　　　　　　　她　　　经理　　太太

3. 哥哥比我大三岁。　　丈夫　　妻子　　大一岁
　　　　　　　　　　　妹妹　　我　　　小两岁
　　　　　　　　　　　他　　　我　　　小一点儿
　　　　　　　　　　　科长　　你　　　大很多

二、回答问题(Answer the following questions)

1. 你有兄弟姐妹吗?

2. 你有几个孩子? 他们几岁了?

3. 你孩子在哪里学习?

4. 在你们国家,年轻人多大结婚?

三、会话（Conversations）

玛　丽：小于，请进！

于雪来：孩子还没回来吗？

玛　丽：还没呢。

于雪来：星期六你有空吗？

玛　丽：有空，什么事？

于雪来：你想知道中国人结婚的风俗（fēngsú/custom），是不是？

玛　丽：是啊（a）。

于雪来：我弟弟星期六结婚，你跟我一起去参加婚礼（hūnlǐ/wedding）吧。

玛　丽：太好了。你弟弟多大？

于雪来：二十八了。新娘子二十四岁。

于雪来：这是我爸爸、妈妈，这位是玛丽。

玛　丽：你们好，恭喜恭喜。

于　父：欢迎欢迎。请随便坐。听雪来说你是从美国来的。

玛　丽：是的。我是小于的邻居。新郎呢？

于　父：去接（jiē/meet）新娘子了。

玛　丽：我可以看看新房（xīnfáng/bridal chamber）吗？

于雪来：当然可以。来，这边来。

玛　丽：新房真（zhēn/really）漂亮。

26 看 朋友 VISITING FRIENDS

Kàn péngyou

1. A: Tīngshuō nǐ bānjiā le, shì ma?
听说 你 搬家 了，是 吗？
I heard that you had moved. Is that true?

B: Shì de. Yǒu kòng qǐng dào wǒ jiā wán.
是 的。有 空 请 到 我 家 玩。
Yes. Please drop in when you are free.

A: Hǎo de, zhège xīngqītiān fāngbiàn ma?
好 的，这个 星期天 方便 吗？
Well. Is it convenient for you this coming Sunday?

B: Zhège xīngqītiān zhěngtiān zài jiā, wǒ děng nǐ.
这个 星期天 整天 在 家，我 等 你。
I'll be home all day this Sunday. I'll wait for you.

2. (A àn ménlíng)
(A 按 门铃)
(Ring the bell)

A: Wǒ shì Wáng Wěi.
我 是 王 伟。
It's Wang Wei.

Qǐng jìn! Qǐng zuò!
B：请 进！请 坐！ Come in. Sit down please.

Xiǎng hē diǎnr shénme? Kāfēi
想 喝 点儿 什么？ 咖啡 What do you want to drink? Coffee or tea?

háishi chá? Yě yǒu kělè.
还是 茶？也 有 可乐。 Cola?

Nàme, wǒ hē chá ba.
A：那么， 我 喝 茶 吧。 Well, I prefer tea.

Qǐng hē chá! Chī diǎnr
B：请 喝 茶！吃 点儿 Here is your tea. And have some refresh-

diǎnxin ba!
点心 吧！ ments please.

Xièxie. Bié zhāngluo le.
A：谢谢。 别 张罗注1 了。 Thank you. Please don't bother.

Qǐng suíbiàn xiē, bié kèqi.
B：请 随便 些， 别 客气注2。 Please make yourself at home.

Chōuyān ma?
抽烟 吗？ Do you smoke?

Bù, bù chōu.
A：不， 不 抽。 No.

Nǐ zuìjìn zěnmeyàng?
B：你 最近 怎么样？ How are things going?

Wǒ zuìjìn máng de hěn.
A：我 最近 忙 得 很。 I have been very busy recently.

Nǐ bàba māma bú zài jiā ma?
你 爸爸 妈妈 不 在 家 吗？ Aren't your parents at home?

Tāmen shàngbān qù le.
B：他们 上班 去 了。 No, they have gone to work.

Kètīng zhēn dà. Yǒu jǐ ge
A：客厅 真 大。有 几 个 The living room is quite big. How many rooms

fángjiān?
房间？ are there?

Yǒu sān ge fángjiān, hái yǒu
B：有 三 个 房间， 还 有 Three rooms plus a kitchen and a washroom.

chúfáng hé wèishēngjiān.
厨房 和 卫生间。

Nǐ de diànnǎo fàngzài nǎli?
A：你 的 电脑 放在 哪里？ Where do you put your computer?

Diànnǎo fàngzài shūfáng li.
B：电脑 放在 书房 里。 The computer is in the study.

A：书橱 里 放着 什么？
Shūchú li fàngzhe shénme?
What are there inside the bookcase?

B：书橱 里 放着 书、杂志、
Shūchú li fàngzhe shū、 zázhì、
There are books, magazines, newspapers and

报纸 等等。
bàozhǐ děngděng.
so on inside the bookcase.

A：这个 花瓶 很 漂亮。
Zhège huāpíng hěn piàoliang.
This vase is very nice.

B：这 是 妈妈 给 我 的。
Zhè shì māma gěi wǒ de.
It's a gift from my mother.

A：这 是 谁 的 房间？
Zhè shì shuí de fángjiān?
Whose room is this?

B：这 是 我 儿子 的 房间。
Zhè shì wǒ érzi de fángjiān.
This is my son's room.

A：这 是 你 儿子 的 照片儿 吗？
Zhè shì nǐ érzi de zhàopiānr ma?
Is this a picture of your son?

B：是 他 小 时候 的 照片儿。
Shì tā xiǎo shíhou de zhàopiānr.
Yes, it's a picture taken in his childhood.

A：这里 交通 方便 吗？
Zhèli jiāotōng fāngbiàn ma?
Are the transportation facilities around this area good?

B：还 算 方便。
Hái suàn fāngbiàn.
Not bad.

A：我 想 用 一 用 洗手间。
Wǒ xiǎng yòng yi yòng xǐshǒujiān.
May I use your washroom?

B：洗手间 在 那边。 请 吧。
Xǐshǒujiān zài nàbian. Qǐng ba.
Of course, the washroom is over there.

☆　注　释 (Notes)　☆

1. "张罗"在这里指对客人的招待,如倒茶、拿点心等等。"别张罗"有时也说"别客气"。
   "张罗" here means to greet and look after the guests such as serving tea or refreshments. Sometimes "别客气" has the same meaning as "别张罗".

   A：请 喝 咖啡。 Have some coffee, please.
   Qǐng hē kāfēi.

   B：谢谢, 别 张罗/别 客气。 Thank you. Don't bother, please.
   Xièxie, bié zhāngluo/bié kèqi.

2. "别客气"在这里表示请对方不要拘束的意思。
   "别客气" here is used to ask the guests not to restrain themselves and make themselves at home.

☆　句型提示（Sentence pattern references）　☆

1. 书橱里放着书、杂志、报纸等等。　　　请参看 309 页句型 35。
2. 这是妈妈给我的。　　　　　　　　　　请参看 320 页句型 58。
3. 还算方便。　　　　　　　　　　　　　请参看 324 页句型 69。
4. 我想用一用洗手间。　　　　　　　　　请参看 313 页句型 44。

☆　词语用法举例（Examples for usage of the words）　☆

1. 请随便些，别客气

    （1）A：<ruby>请<rt>Qǐng</rt></ruby> <ruby>吃<rt>chī</rt></ruby> <ruby>点儿<rt>diǎnr</rt></ruby> <ruby>水果<rt>shuǐguǒ</rt></ruby>。<ruby>别<rt>Bié</rt></ruby> <ruby>客气<rt>kèqi</rt></ruby>。

        B：<ruby>我们<rt>Wǒmen</rt></ruby> <ruby>是<rt>shì</rt></ruby> <ruby>老朋友<rt>lǎopéngyou</rt></ruby>，<ruby>你<rt>nǐ</rt></ruby> <ruby>别<rt>bié</rt></ruby> <ruby>张罗<rt>zhāngluo</rt></ruby> <ruby>了<rt>le</rt></ruby>。

    （2）A：<ruby>你<rt>Nǐ</rt></ruby> <ruby>别<rt>bié</rt></ruby> <ruby>客气<rt>kèqi</rt></ruby>，<ruby>多<rt>duō</rt></ruby> <ruby>吃<rt>chī</rt></ruby> <ruby>点儿<rt>diǎnr</rt></ruby>。

        B：<ruby>我<rt>Wǒ</rt></ruby> <ruby>已经<rt>yǐjīng</rt></ruby> <ruby>饱<rt>bǎo</rt></ruby> <ruby>了<rt>le</rt></ruby>。

2. 我最近忙得很

    （1）<ruby>那个<rt>Nàge</rt></ruby> <ruby>店<rt>diàn</rt></ruby> <ruby>的<rt>de</rt></ruby> <ruby>东西<rt>dōngxi</rt></ruby> <ruby>贵<rt>guì</rt></ruby> <ruby>得<rt>de</rt></ruby> <ruby>很<rt>hěn</rt></ruby>。

    （2）<ruby>弟弟<rt>Dìdi</rt></ruby> <ruby>从来<rt>cónglái</rt></ruby> <ruby>不<rt>bú</rt></ruby> <ruby>复习<rt>fùxí</rt></ruby>，<ruby>懒<rt>lǎn</rt></ruby> <ruby>得<rt>de</rt></ruby> <ruby>很<rt>hěn</rt></ruby>。　（懒：lazy）

    （3）<ruby>走了<rt>Zǒule</rt></ruby> <ruby>几<rt>jǐ</rt></ruby> <ruby>个<rt>ge</rt></ruby> <ruby>小时<rt>xiǎoshí</rt></ruby> <ruby>的<rt>de</rt></ruby> <ruby>路<rt>lù</rt></ruby>，<ruby>累<rt>lèi</rt></ruby> <ruby>得<rt>de</rt></ruby> <ruby>很<rt>hěn</rt></ruby>。

    （4）<ruby>没<rt>Méi</rt></ruby> <ruby>吃<rt>chī</rt></ruby> <ruby>早饭<rt>zǎofàn</rt></ruby>，<ruby>现在<rt>xiànzài</rt></ruby> <ruby>饿<rt>è</rt></ruby> <ruby>得<rt>de</rt></ruby> <ruby>很<rt>hěn</rt></ruby>。

3. 他们上班去了（来……了）

    （1）<ruby>孩子们<rt>Háizimen</rt></ruby> <ruby>上学<rt>shàngxué</rt></ruby> <ruby>去<rt>qù</rt></ruby> <ruby>了<rt>le</rt></ruby>。

    （2）<ruby>太太<rt>Tàitai</rt></ruby> <ruby>买<rt>mǎi</rt></ruby> <ruby>东西<rt>dōngxi</rt></ruby> <ruby>去<rt>qù</rt></ruby> <ruby>了<rt>le</rt></ruby>。

    （3）<ruby>昨天<rt>Zuótiān</rt></ruby> <ruby>儿子<rt>érzi</rt></ruby> <ruby>一家<rt>yìjiā</rt></ruby> <ruby>看<rt>kàn</rt></ruby> <ruby>我<rt>wǒ</rt></ruby> <ruby>来<rt>lái</rt></ruby> <ruby>了<rt>le</rt></ruby>。

    （4）<ruby>美国<rt>Měiguó</rt></ruby> <ruby>总统<rt>zǒngtǒng</rt></ruby> <ruby>到<rt>dào</rt></ruby> <ruby>上海<rt>Shànghǎi</rt></ruby> <ruby>访问<rt>fǎngwèn</rt></ruby> <ruby>来<rt>lái</rt></ruby> <ruby>了<rt>le</rt></ruby>。

☆　词　语（Word list）　☆

1. <ruby>门<rt>mén</rt></ruby>　　（名）　door　　　　　2. <ruby>窗<rt>chuāng</rt></ruby>　　（名）　window

	chuānglián			

3. 窗帘　（名）　curtain

4. 地毯　（名）　carpet (dìtǎn)

5. 桌子　（名）　table, desk (zhuōzi)

6. 椅子　（名）　chair (yǐzi)

7. 凳子　（名）　stool, bench (dèngzi)

8. 沙发　（名）　sofa, settee (shāfā)

9. 茶几　（名）　tea table, side table (chájī)

10. 柜子　（名）　cabinet, cupboard (guìzi)

11. 衣柜　（名）　wardrobe (yīguì)

12. 碗柜　（名）　kitchen cupboard (wǎnguì)

13. 花瓶　（名）　vase (huāpíng)

14. 床　（名）　bed (chuáng)

15. 床头柜　（名）　bedside cupboard (chuángtóuguì)

16. 台灯　（名）　desk lamp, reading lamp (táidēng)

17. 枕头　（名）　pillow (zhěntou)

18. 枕套　（名）　pillow-case, pillowslip (zhěntào)

19. 被子　（名）　quilt (bèizi)

20. 床单　（名）　sheet (chuángdān)

21. 毛巾　（名）　towel (máojīn)

22. 浴巾　（名）　bath towel (yùjīn)

23. 淋浴　（动）　shower (línyù)

24. 浴缸　（名）　bathtub (yùgāng)

25. 脸盆　（名）　washbowl, washbasin (liǎnpén)

26. 手纸　（名）　toilet paper (shǒuzhǐ)

27. 烟灰缸　（名）　ashtray (yānhuīgāng)

28. 垃圾桶　（名）　garbage can (lājītǒng)

29. 走廊　（名）　corridor, passage (zǒuláng)

30. 阳台　（名）　balcony (yángtái)

☆ 练　习（Exercises）☆

一、替换练习（Substitution exercises）

1. 书桌 放在 书房里。

花瓶	放在	茶几上
电话	放在	台灯的旁边
大衣	挂在	衣柜里
汽车	停在	门口

2. 客厅里 放着 一个柜子。

茶几上	放着	两个杯子
他的手里	拿着	一束(shù,量词)花
墙上	挂着	一幅(fú,量词)画儿
前面	停着	一辆(liàng,量词)车

二、完成对话（Complete the conversations）

1. A：有空请到我家玩。

B：＿＿＿＿＿＿＿＿＿＿＿＿＿＿＿＿＿＿＿。

2．A：我可以进来吗？

B：＿＿＿＿＿＿＿＿＿＿＿＿＿＿＿＿＿＿＿＿！

3．A：你想喝点儿什么？

B：＿＿＿＿＿＿＿＿＿＿＿＿＿＿＿＿＿＿＿＿。

4．A：你最近工作忙吗？

B：＿＿＿＿＿＿＿＿＿＿＿＿＿＿＿＿＿＿＿＿。

5．A：你是什么时候搬家的？

B：＿＿＿＿＿＿＿＿＿＿＿＿＿＿＿＿＿＿＿＿。

三、回答问题(Answer the following questions)

1．你家有几个房间？

2．你家的客厅大吗？

3．你家有书房吗？

4．今天的报纸放在哪里？

5．你的书桌(shūzhuō/desk)上放着什么？

6．你家的墙上挂着什么？

四、会话(Conversation)

于雪来：我是雪来。请开门(kāi mén/open the door)。

刘志红：请进！

于雪来：你的新家真大！有几个房间？

刘志红：三室一厅。来，我带你看看。这是卧室(wòshì/bedroom)。

于雪来：这里朝南(cháo nán/face south)吗？

刘志红：对，朝南。两个房间朝南，一个朝北。这是儿子的房间。

于雪来：儿子出去了吗？

刘志红：今天他加班。

于雪来：他在哪儿工作？

刘志红：他在百货商店工作。

于雪来：你还有一个女儿，是吗？

刘志红：是的，她在北京读大学。

☆　**练习答案**(Key to the exercises)　☆

二、1．好啊，有空我一定(yídìng/certainly)去　　2．请进

3．我想喝咖啡　　4．最近我忙得很　　5．是今年三月搬的

27 做客 Zuòkè BEING A GUEST

1. A: Zhège xīngqīliù wǎnshang dào
这个 星期六 晚上 到
wǒ jiā chī dùn biànfàn, hǎo ma?
我 家 吃 顿 便饭，好 吗？

Would you please come to my home and have dinner with us in Saturday evening?

B: Hǎo de, xièxie. Wǒ tài
好 的，谢谢。我 太
gāoxìng le!
高兴 了!

Fine, thanks. I am very glad (to be invited).

2. A: Huānyíng, kuài qǐng jìn.
欢迎， 快 请 进。

Welcome! Please come in.

B: Zhè shì gěi nǐ de lǐwù. Bú shì
这 是 给 你 的 礼物。不 是
shénme hǎo dōngxi, qǐng shōuxia.
什么 好 东西，请 收下。

This is a gift to you. It's not expensive.

Please accept it.

A: Nǐ tài kèqi le, zhēn bù
你 太 客气 了注1， 真 不
hǎoyìsi.
好意思。

It's very kind of you.

B：只是 一点儿 心意。
Zhǐshì yìdiǎnr xīnyì.
It's just a token of my friendship.

A：谢谢。 请 随便 坐， 不
Xièxie. Qǐng suíbiàn zuò, bú
要 拘束。
yào jūshù.
Thanks. Sit down please and make yourself at home.

B：你 家 很 宽敞、 很
Nǐ jiā hěn kuānchang、 hěn
干净 啊。
gānjìng a.
Your house is roomy and clean.

A：哪里，哪里注2。
Nǎli, nǎli.
You are flattering me.

3. C：菜 做好 了，请 吧。
Cài zuòhǎo le, qǐng ba.
The dinner is ready. Let's eat.

B：我 就 不 客气 了。
Wǒ jiù bú kèqi le.
Well, I'll help myself.

A：这 是 我 太太 的 拿手
Zhè shì wǒ tàitai de náshǒu
菜， 尝尝 吧。
cài, chángchang ba.
This is my wife's best dish. Please try it.

B：真 好吃!
Zhēn hǎochī!
It's delicious.

A：那么， 多 吃 点儿 吧。
Nàme, duō chī diǎnr ba.
别 客气。
Bié kèqi.
Then, don't hesitate to have some more please.

C：这个 菜 有 点儿 辣，
Zhège cài yǒu diǎnr là,
没 关系 吧?
méi guānxi ba?
This dish is a little bit hot. It doesn't matter, does it?

B：我 不 太 喜欢 辣 的
Wǒ bú tài xǐhuan là de
东西。
dōngxi.
I don't really like the spicy food.

A：那么， 不要 勉强。
Nàme, búyào miǎnqiǎng.
If so, don't force yourself.

C：再 吃 一点儿 吧。
Zài chī yìdiǎnr ba.
Have some more please.

B：已经 吃了 很 多 了。
Yǐjīng chīle hěn duō le.
I have had enough.

Chī de hěn bǎo le.
吃 得 很 饱 了。

I am full and could not have any more.

Zài yě chī bu xià le.
再 也 吃 不 下 了。

A: Lái, zài hē yì bēi.
来，再 喝 一 杯。

Come on, drink one more cup.

B: Bù néng zài hē le. Zài hē jiù
不 能 再 喝 了。再 喝 就

I can not have any more. Otherwise I will be

yào zuì le.
要 醉 了。

drunk.

Jīntiān de cài hěn hǎochī. Xièxie.
今天 的 菜 很 好吃。谢谢。

The dishes are very tasty today. Thanks.

4. B: Jīntiān guò de hěn yúkuài.
今天 过 得 很 愉快。

I had a pleasant time today. But it's late now.

Shíjiān bù zǎo le, wǒ gāi
时间 不 早 了，我 该

I'd better be off.

zǒu le.
走 了。

A: Máng shénme, zài zuò yí-
忙 什么，再 坐 一

Don't be in a hurry. Please stay for a while.

huìr ba.
会儿 吧。

B: Jīntiān dǎrǎo nǐmen le.
今天 打扰 你们 了。

I really bothered you today.

A: Nǎr de huà, yǒu shíjiān
哪儿 的 话注2，有 时间

You shouldn't say that. Please drop in when

cháng lái wán.
常 来 玩。

you have time.

B: Nàme, wǒ zǒu le.
那么，我 走 了。

Well, I must say good bye now.

A: Màn zǒu.
慢 走。

Take care.

B: Búyòng sòng le, qǐng huí
不用 送 了，请 回

I can see myself out. Thank you.

ba.
吧。

☆ 注 释(Notes) ☆

1. 在收到礼物或者得到别人的款待时,用"你太客气了"来表示感谢。回答别人的感谢时,也可以用"你太客气了"。

"你太客气了" is used to express your thanks when you are given a gift or served or entertained by someone else. To answer the thanks from someone you may also say "你太客气了".

Zhè shì xīnnián lǐwù, qǐng shōuxia.
A：这 是 新年 礼物，请 收下。　This is a gift for the New Year. Please take it.

Xièxie, nín tài kèqi le.
B：谢谢，您 太 客气 了。　You are so kind. Thanks.

Xièxie nǐ de kuǎndài.
A：谢谢 你 的 款待。　Thank you for your hospitality.

Nǐ tài kèqi le.
B：你 太 客气 了。　Don't mention it.

2. "哪里,哪里"用来回答别人对自己的感谢或者夸奖。也可以说"哪儿的话"。

"哪里,哪里" is used to respond someone's thanks or praise. "哪儿的话" can be used too.

Xièxie nǐ de bāngzhù.
A：谢谢 你 的 帮助。　Thank you for your help.

Nǎli, nǎli. Xiǎo shìqing.
B：哪里，哪里。小 事情。　Don't mention it. It's nothing.

Nǐ érzi gāngqín tán de búcuò.
A：你 儿子 钢琴 弹 得 不错。　Your son plays piano very well.

Nǎr de huà, hái chà de yuǎn ne.
B：哪儿 的 话，还 差 得 远 呢。　Thanks. He still has a long way to go.

☆　句型提示 (Sentence pattern references)　☆

1. 我太高兴了!　　　　　　　　　　　请参看 394 页句型 223。
2. 这是我太太的拿手菜,尝尝吧。　　　请参看 315 页句型 47。
3. 这个菜有点儿辣。　　　　　　　　　请参看 341 页句型 107。
4. 吃得很饱了。　　　　　　　　　　　请参看 343 页句型 112。
5. 再也吃不下了。　　　　　　　　　　请参看 345 页句型 115。
6. 再喝就要醉了。　　　　　　　　　　请参看 385 页句型 205。

☆　词语用法举例 (Examples for usage of the words)　☆

1. 我太高兴了

Zhèli de fēngjǐng tài měi le!
(1) 这里 的 风景 太 美 了!

Zhè běn xiǎoshuō tài bàng le.
(2) 这 本 小说 太 棒 了!

Zhōngguócài tài hǎochī le!
(3) 中国菜 太 好吃 了!

Nǐ néng péi wǒ qù, tài hǎo le!
(4) 你 能 陪 我 去，太 好 了!

2. 真不好意思

(1) Wǒ chídào le, zhēn bù hǎoyìsi.
我　迟到　了，真　不　好意思。

(2) Xièxie nǐ de lǐwù, zhēn bù hǎoyìsi.
谢谢　你　的　礼物，真　不　好意思。

(3) Wǒ nácuò nǐ de bǐ le, bù hǎoyìsi.
我　拿错　你　的　笔了，不　好意思。

(4) Zhè shìr wǒ wàng le, bù hǎoyìsi.
这　事儿我　忘　了，不　好意思。

3. 只是一点儿心意

(1) Dìdi bú zuò zuòyè, zhǐshì wán.
弟弟　不　做　作业，只是　玩。

(2) Nàge xiǎoháir mílù le, zhǐshì kū, shuō bu chū huà.
那个　小孩儿　迷路　了，只是　哭，说　不　出　话。　　（哭：cry）

(3) Shān shang zhǐshì shítou, yì kē cǎo yě méiyǒu.
山　上　只是　石头，一　棵　草　也　没有。

(4) Zhuōzi shang zhǐshì shū, méiyǒu bié de dōngxi.
桌子　上　只是　书，没有　别　的　东西。

4. 这是我太太的拿手菜

(1) Tā zuò cài hěn náshǒu.
他　做　菜　很　拿手。

(2) Zuò yīfu, tā fēicháng náshǒu.
做　衣服，她　非常　拿手。

(3) Zhè shì tā de náshǒu hǎoxì.
这　是　他　的　拿手　好戏。　　（拿手好戏：specialty, forte）

(4) Tàitai de náshǒucài shì hóngshāo xiānggūjī.
太太　的　拿手菜　是　红烧　香菇鸡。

5. 这个菜有点儿辣

(1) Jīntiān yǒu diǎnr lěng.
今天　有　点儿　冷。

(2) Zhè jiàn chènyī yǒu diǎnr cháng.
这　件　衬衣　有　点儿　长。

(3) Wǒ dùzi yǒu diǎnr téng.
我　肚子　有　点儿　疼。

(4) Zhè chá yǒu diǎnr kǔ.
这　茶　有　点儿　苦。

6. 不要勉强

(1) Nǐ bù fāngbiàn dehuà, bié miǎnqiǎng.
你　不　方便　的话，别　勉强。

Tā bú huì hē jiǔ, bié miǎnqiǎng tā.
(2) 他 不 会 喝 酒, 别 勉强 他。

Tā miǎnqiǎng pǎowán bābǎi mǐ.
(3) 他 勉强 跑完 八百 米。（米：meter）

Wǒ miǎnqiǎng zǒudào shísān lóu, lèijí le.
(4) 我 勉强 走到 十三 楼, 累极 了。

7. 再吃一点儿吧

Mǎi yìdiǎnr jìniànpǐn dài huíqu ba.
(1) 买 一点儿 纪念品 带 回去 吧。

Zài Zhōngguó shēnghuó, yào xué yìdiǎnr Hànyǔ.
(2) 在 中国 生活, 要 学 一点儿 汉语。

Wàichū lǚxíng, duō dài yìdiǎnr qián hǎo.
(3) 外出 旅行, 多 带 一点儿 钱 好。

Wǒ kě le, yào hē diǎnr shuǐ.
(4) 我 渴 了, 要 喝 点儿 水。

8. 吃得很饱了

Xiǎo Liú pǎo de hěn kuài.
(1) 小 刘 跑 得 很 快。

Nàge gūniang zhǎng de hěn piàoliang.
(2) 那个 姑娘 长 得 很 漂亮。

Tā chàng de hěn hǎo.
(3) 他 唱 得 很 好。

Yīfu xǐ de hěn gānjìng.
(4) 衣服 洗 得 很 干净。

9. 再也吃不下了

Gǎnmào le, chī bu xià.
(1) 感冒 了, 吃 不 下。

Zhè zhāng zhuōzi, shí ge rén zuò bu xià.
(2) 这 张 桌子, 十 个 人 坐 不 下。

Dōngxi tài duō, zhège dàizi zhuāng bu xià.
(3) 东西 太 多, 这个 袋子 装 不 下。（袋子：bag）

Fángjiān tài xiǎo, wǔ ge rén zhù bu xià.
(4) 房间 太 小, 五 个 人 住 不 下。

10. 再喝就要醉了

Zài xià yǔ jiù yào nào shuǐzāi le.
(1) 再 下 雨 就 要 闹 水灾 了。（闹水灾：flood）

Zài bù qǐchuáng jiù yào chídào le.
(2) 再 不 起床 就 要 迟到 了。

Cài zài bù chī jiù yào liáng le.
(3) 菜 再 不 吃 就 要 凉 了。

<pre>
        Tā zài bù lái jiù bù děng tā le.
（4）他 再 不 来 就 不 等 他 了。
</pre>

☆ 词 语（Word list）☆

1. yāoqǐng
   邀请 （动） invite

2. qǐngkè
   请客 （动） play the host, stand treat

3. yìngyāo
   应邀 （动） be invited

4. zuòkè
   做客 （动） pay a visit, be a guest

5. biànfàn
   便饭 （名） simple meal

6. bǎo
   饱 （形） have eaten one's fill, be full

7. chī bu xià
   吃 不 下 can not eat any more

8. hé kǒuwèi
   合 口味 to one's taste

9. gòu
   够 （动） be enough

10. gàocí
    告辞 （动） take leave

11. lǐwù
    礼物 （名） gift

12. sònglǐ
    送礼 （动） present gifts, send gifts

☆ 练 习（Exercises）☆

一、完成对话（Complete the conversations）

1. A：星期五晚上_____。
   B：好，我一定去。

2. A：这是一点心意，请收下。
   B：_____。

3. A：你做的菜真好吃。
   B：_____。

4. A：多吃一点儿吧。
   B：_____。

二、回答问题（Answer the following questions）

1. 你常常在家里请客吗?

2. 你自己做饭吗? 你的拿手菜是什么?

3. 去朋友家做客你一般送什么礼物?

4. 朋友家的菜不合你的口味怎么办?

三、用下列词语造句（Make sentences with the following words）

1. 打扰

2. 拘束

3. 有点儿＋形容词

4. 多＋动词

四、会话(Conversation)

于雪来：布朗先生、玛丽，快进来。

玛　丽：这是一点儿心意，请收下。

于雪来：那就谢谢了。

于雪来：来，吃饭了。

玛　丽：啊，小于，你做了这么多菜！辛苦了(xīnkǔ le/have worked hard – a Chinese phrase for expressing gratitude)！

郭　放：请尝尝炖(dùn)牛肉，这是雪来的拿手菜。

大　卫：好吃，好吃。

玛　丽：真的，比饭店里的菜还好吃。

于雪来：哪里，哪里。多吃一点儿。尝尝鸡的味道，合你们的口味吗？

玛　丽：有点儿辣。

郭　放：你不吃辣的吗？

玛　丽：我只能吃一点儿。

大　卫：我觉得(juéde/feel, think)很好吃啊。

郭　放：那就再吃一点儿。

大　卫：我吃得太多了，吃不下了。

玛　丽：时间不早了，我们该回去了。

于雪来：再喝杯茶吧。

大　卫：不用了，谢谢。今天非常高兴。

郭　放：那么请改天再来玩。

☆　**练习答案(Key to the exercises)**　☆

一、1．A：到我家吃顿便饭吧　　　2．B：你太客气了，真不好意思

　　3．B：那么，多吃点儿吧　　　4．B：吃不下了

28 Xuéxí 学习 STUDY

1. A: Nǐ huì shuō Yīngyǔ ma?
   你 会 说 英语 吗？ — Can you speak English?

   B: Wǒ huì.
   我 会。 — Yes, I can.

   A: Nǐ tàitai ne?
   你 太太 呢？ — How about your wife?

   B: Tā bú huì.
   她 不 会。 — She can't.

   A: Nǐ huì Rìyǔ ma?
   你 会 日语 吗？ — Can you speak Japanese?

   B: Huì yìdiǎnr.
   会 一点儿。 — Yes, a little.

   A: Nǐ tàitai yě huì Rìyǔ ma?
   你 太太 也 会 日语 吗？ — Can your wife speak Japanese too?

   B: Tā yìdiǎnr yě bú huì.
   她 一点儿 也注1 不 会。 — No, not a single word.

2. A: Nǐ zài xué Hànyǔ ma?
   你 在 学 汉语 吗？ — Are you learning Chinese?

B：Shì de. Gāng kāishǐ xué.
是 的。 刚 开始 学。　　Yes, I've just started my study.

A：Mǎdīng xuéle duō cháng shíjiān le?
马丁 学了 多 长 时间 了?　　How long has Martin learned Chinese?

B：Tā xuéle yì nián duō le.
他 学了 一 年 多 了。　　He has been studying it for more than one year.

A：Nǐmen zài nǎli xuéxí?
你们 在 哪里 学习?　　Where do you study?

B：Tā zài Fùdàn Dàxué xuéxí.
他 在 复旦 大学 学习。　　He is studying in Fudan University.

Wǒ qǐng Hànyǔ lǎoshī dào
我 请 汉语 老师 到　　I have a teacher to teach me Chinese at

jiā li jiāo wǒ.
家 里 教 我。　　home.

A：Měi xīngqī shàng jǐ cì kè?
每 星期 上 几 次 课?　　How many classes do you have per week?

B：Shàng sì cì kè.
上 四 次 课。　　Four classes.

A：Nǐ juéde Hànyǔ nán bu nán?
你 觉得 汉语 难 不 难?　　Do you think Chinese is difficult?

B：Wǒ juéde fāyīn hěn nán.
我 觉得 发音 很 难。　　I think its pronunciation is very difficult.

A：Chúle Hànyǔ yǐwài, hái xué
除了 汉语 以外, 还 学　　Do you take any other course besides

shénme?
什么?　　Chinese Language?

B：Hái xué Zhōngguó lìshǐ hé
还 学 中国 历史 和　　We study Chinese history and geography

dìlǐ.
地理。　　also.

A：Zhōngwén bàozhǐ nǐ kàn de
中文 报纸 你 看 得　　Can you read a Chinese newspaper?

dǒng ma?
懂注2 吗?

B：Hái kàn bu dǒng.
还 看 不 懂。　　Not right now.

A：Mǎdīng (shuō) Hànyǔ shuō
马丁 (说) 汉语 说　　How is Martin's spoken Chinese?

de zěnmeyàng?
得 怎么样?

B：他 说 得 很 好。
<small>Tā shuō de hěn hǎo.</small>
He speaks Chinese very well.

A：你 也 说 得 不错 注3。
<small>Nǐ yě shuō de búcuò.</small>
Your Chinese is good too.

B：哪里，哪里。还 不行。
<small>Nǎli, nǎli. Hái bùxíng.</small>
Thanks. But I don't think so.

☆ 注 释（Notes） ☆

1. "一+量词+也"用在否定句中，加强否定的语气。
   "一+量词+也" is used in negative sentences to strengthen the negative tone. ·

2. "动词+得+动词/形容词"表示可能。否定时用"动词+不+动词/形容词"。
   "verb+得+verb/adjective" indicates possibility. "verb+不+verb/adjective" is used to deny the possibility.

   （1）这个 箱子，我 一 个 人 拿 得 动。
   <small>Zhège xiāngzi, wǒ yí ge rén ná de dòng.</small>
   I can carry this suitcase alone.

   （2）这个 箱子，我 一 个 人 拿 不 动。
   <small>Zhège xiāngzi, wǒ yí ge rén ná bu dòng.</small>
   I can't carry this suitcase alone.

   （3）这 件 事，他 讲 得 清楚。
   <small>Zhè jiàn shì, tā jiǎng de qīngchu.</small>
   He can give a clear explanation about this matter.

   （4）这 件 事，他 讲 不 清楚。
   <small>Zhè jiàn shì, tā jiǎng bu qīngchu.</small>
   He is not able to give a clear explanation about this matter.

3. "不错"和"好"意思一样。
   "不错" has the same meaning as "好".

☆ 句型提示（Sentence pattern references） ☆

1. 你会说英语吗？   请参看 334 页句型 89。
2. 她一点儿也不会。   请参看 343 页句型 111。
3. 我觉得发音很难。   请参看 321 页句型 61。
4. 除了汉语以外，还学什么？   请参看 363 页句型 156。

☆ 词语用法举例（Examples for usage of the words） ☆

1. 你会说英语吗

   （1）我 会 烧. 中国菜。
   <small>Wǒ huì shāo Zhōngguócài.</small>

   （2）小 宝宝 会 走路 了。 （小宝宝：baby）
   <small>Xiǎo bǎobao huì zǒulù le.</small>

Xiǎo bǎobao hái bú huì shuōhuà.
(3)小 宝宝 还 不 会 说话。

Tā bú huì qí zìxíngchē.
(4)她 不 会 骑 自行车。

2. 她一点儿也不会

Zhè shì wǒ yìdiǎnr yě bù zhīdao.
(1)这 事 我 一点儿 也 不 知道。

Tā yìdiǎnr jiāwù yě bú zuò.
(2)他 一点儿 家务 也 不 做。 (家务:housework)

Zhè chū xì yìdiǎnr yě bù hǎokàn.
(3)这 出 戏 一点儿 也 不 好看。 (戏:play, show, drama)

Zhège cài yìdiǎnr yě bù hǎochī.
(4)这个 菜 一点儿 也 不 好吃。

Tā yì fēn qián yě bú làngfèi.
(5)他 一 分 钱 也 不 浪费。

Nàxiē rén wǒ yí ge yě bú rènshi.
(6)那些 人 我 一 个 也 不 认识。

Tā yì nián yě bù huí yí cì lǎojiā.
(7)他 一 年 也 不 回 一 次 老家。

Tā měi tiān xuéxí Hànyǔ, yì tiān yě bú jiànduàn.
(8)他 每 天 学习 汉语， 一 天 也 不 间断。 (间断:be interrupted)

3. 你在学汉语吗

Lǎoshī zài jiǎngkè.
(1)老师 在 讲课。

Tāmen zài kāihuì.
(2)他们 在 开会。

Bàba zài xiūlǐ zìxíngchē.
(3)爸爸 在 修理 自行车。

Xiǎo bǎobao hái zài shuìjiào.
(4)小 宝宝 还 在 睡觉。

4. 他学了一年多了

Wǒ děngle yí ge xiǎoshí le.
(1)我 等了 一 个 小时 了。

Jīnglǐ qùle sān tiān le.
(2)经理 去了 三 天 了。

Tā xuéle sì ge yuè le.
(3)他 学了 四 个 月 了。

Tiánzhōng xiānsheng zài Shànghǎi zhùle yì nián le.
(4)田中 先生 在 上海 住了 一 年 了。

5. 你觉得汉语难不难

Wǒ juéde zhège yàngzi búcuò.
(1) 我 觉得 这个 样子 不错。

Zhè bù diànyǐng, nǐ juéde zěnmeyàng?
(2) 这 部 电影，你 觉得 怎么样?

Wǒ juéde yǒu diǎnr lěng, kāi kōngtiáo hǎo ma?
(3) 我 觉得 有 点儿 冷，开 空调 好 吗?

Zhège cài, wǒ juéde yǒu diǎnr xián.
(4) 这个 菜，我 觉得 有 点儿 咸。

6. 中文报纸你看得懂吗

Zhème duō dōngxi, nǐ chī de wán ma?
(1) 这么 多 东西，你 吃 得 完 吗?

Dào nàr hěn jìn, shíwǔ fēnzhōng zǒu de dào.
(2) 到 那儿 很 近，十五 分钟 走 得 到。

Shìqing bù duō, yí ge rén zuò de liǎo.
(3) 事情 不 多，一 个 人 做 得 了。 (做得了:be able to do)

Zhè kuài shǒubiǎo xiū de hǎo.
(4) 这 块 手表 修 得 好。

7. 还看不懂

Tài duō le, wǒ chī bu wán.
(1) 太 多 了，我 吃 不 完。

Hěn yuǎn, yí ge xiǎoshí zǒu bu dào.
(2) 很 远，一 个 小时 走 不 到。

Shìqing hěn duō, yí ge rén zuò bu liǎo.
(3) 事情 很 多，一 个 人 做 不 了。

Zhè kuài shǒubiǎo tài jiù, xiū bu hǎo le.
(4) 这 块 手表 太 旧，修 不 好 了。 (旧:old, worn)

☆ 词 语 (Word list) ☆

1.	tīng lùyīn 听 录音	listen to the recording	2.	xiě Hànzì 写 汉字	write Chinese characters
3.	niàn kèwén 念 课文	read aloud the text	4.	kàn shū 看 书	read the book
5.	zuò zuòyè 做 作业	do exercises	6.	yùxí 预习 （动）	prepare lessons before class
7.	fùxí 复习 （动）	review, review lessons	8.	liànxí 练习 （名/动）	exercise
9.	shēngcí 生词 （名）	new words	10.	dǎkāi shū 打开 书	open the book
11.	héshang shū 合上 书	close the book	12.	wèntí 问题 （名）	question
13.	tíwèn 提问 （动）	ask a question	14.	huídá 回答 （动）	answer

15.	jiěshì 解释	（动）	explain	16.	shuōmíng 说明	（动/名）	explain, illustrate; explanation
17.	běnzi 本子	（名）	notebook	18.	qiānbǐ 铅笔	（名）	pencil
19.	gāngbǐ 钢笔	（名）	pen, fountain pen	20.	yuánzhūbǐ 圆珠笔	（名）	ball pen
21.	máobǐ 毛笔	（名）	writing brush	22.	zhǐ 纸	（名）	paper
23.	xiàngpí 橡皮	（名）	eraser, rubber	24.	cídiǎn 词典	（名）	dictionary, lexicon
25.	zìdiǎn 字典	（名）	dictionary	26.	kèběn 课本	（名）	textbook
27.	jiàokēshū 教科书	（名）	textbook	28.	tīng 听	（动）	listen
29.	shuō 说	（动）	speak	30.	dú 读	（动）	read
31.	xiě 写	（动）	write	32.	bèi 背	（动）	recite
33.	róngyì 容易	（形）	easy	34.	yònggōng 用功	（动/形）	diligent, hardworking
35.	nǔlì 努力	（形/动）	hardworking; make great efforts	36.	jìnbù 进步	（动/形）	progress, improve; progressive
37.	jìzhù 记住		remember, bear in mind	38.	wàngjì 忘记	（动）	forget

☆　练　习（Exercises）　☆

一、替换练习（Substitution exercises）

1. 除了汉语以外，我还学中国历史。

中国人	公司里	有外国人
教师	教室里	有学生
学课文	我们	做练习
课本	我	买了汉英词典

2. 中文报纸你看得懂吗？

中文歌(gē)	听	懂
这个箱子	拿	动
这件事	办	到
生词	记	住

3. 他汉语 说得很好。

英文歌	唱	不错
练习	做	都对
汉字	写	很好
西餐	做	不好吃

二、用括号中的词语回答问题（Answer the following questions with the words in brackets）

1. 你喜欢喝酒吗？（一点儿也）

2. 你会说法语吗？（一点儿也）

3. 你先生常常出差吗?（每……次）

4. 上海的交通怎么样?（觉得）

5. 学汉语最难的是什么?（觉得）

6. 你学汉语学了多久了?（半年）

三、选择填空（Select the appropriate phase to fill in the blanks）

| 听不清楚 | 看不懂 | 看得见 | 洗得干净 | 买得到 |
| 听不见 | 记得住 | 买不到 | 洗不干净 | 搬不动 |

1. 没开灯(kāi dēng),你＿＿＿＿＿＿＿＿吗?

2. 有油渍的衣服用洗衣机＿＿＿＿＿＿＿＿。

3. 他说得太快,我＿＿＿＿＿＿＿＿。

4. 这本书太难,我＿＿＿＿＿＿＿＿。

5. 电视机太重(zhòng/heavy),一个人＿＿＿＿＿＿＿＿。

6. 现在是十二月,＿＿＿＿＿＿＿＿西瓜了。

7. 他＿＿＿＿＿＿＿＿很长的密码。

8. 在超市里＿＿＿＿＿＿＿＿新鲜鸡蛋。

9. 小孩子自己洗衣服,＿＿＿＿＿＿＿＿吗?

10. 电话坏了,我＿＿＿＿＿＿＿＿他说的话。

四、会话（Conversation）

于雪来:安妮,你汉语说得不错啊。

安　妮:哪里,我刚学,还不行。玛丽说得比我好。

玛　丽:不,我的发音不太好。

于雪来:来中国以前,你们学了多长时间?

玛　丽:我在美国的大学里学了两年。可是,只学看和写,很少说汉语。

安　妮:我原来一点儿也不会,来上海以后才开始学汉语。

于雪来:在哪个学校?

安　妮:在上海师范大学。

玛　丽:课多吗?

安　妮:不太多,每天四节(jié,量词)课。玛丽,听说你现在请了一位老师到家里上课,是吗?

玛　丽:是的。每星期上三次课。

☆　**练习答案**(Key to the exercises)　☆

二、1. 我一点儿也不喜欢。　　2. 我一点儿也不会。
　　3. 他每个月要出差一次。　4. 我觉得上海的交通很方便。
　　5. 我觉得学汉语最难的是声调。　6. 我学汉语学了半年了。

三、1. 看得见　2. 洗不干净　3. 听不清楚　4. 看不懂　5. 搬不动
　　6. 买不到　7. 记得住　8. 买得到　9. 洗得干净　10. 听不见

29 Tiānqì 天气　　WEATHER

1. A: Tiānqì zhēn hǎo!
天气　真　好!
It's a lovely day!

B: Shì de, bù lěng yě bú rè.
是 的，不 冷 也 不 热。
Yes, it's not too cold and not too hot.

A: Zuótiān tiānqì bú tài hǎo,
昨天　天气　不 太 好,
hěn rè.
很 热。
The weather was not good yesterday. It was very hot.

B: Tīngshuō zuì gāo qìwēn yǒu
听说　最　高　气温　有
sānshíliù dù.
三十六 度注。
I heard that the maximum temperature was 36 degree Celsius.

A: Míngtiān tiānqì zěnmeyàng?
明天　天气　怎么样?
What will the weather be like tomorrow?

B: (Jù) tiānqì yùbào shuō míngtiān
(据) 天气 预报 说 明天
(shì) yīntiān, xiàwǔ xià yǔ.
(是) 阴天，下午 下 雨。
It will be overcast tomorrow and would rain tomorrow afternoon according to the weather forecast.

188

2. A: Tīngshuō Hǎinán Dǎo de xiàtiān
听说 海南 岛 的 夏天　It's said that the weather on Hainan Island is

hěn rè, shì ma?
很 热，是 吗?　very hot in summer. Is that true?

B: Shì de, érqiě xiàtiān hěn cháng.
是 的，而且 夏天 很 长。　Yes. And the summer is very long.

A: Shànghǎi nǎge jìjié zuì hǎo?
上海 哪个 季节 最 好?　Which season is the best in Shanghai?

B: Nà yào shǔ qiūtiān zuì hǎo.
那 要 数 秋天 最 好。　That's autumn.

A: Nǐ xǐhuan nǎge jìjié?
你 喜欢 哪个 季节?　What season do you like?

B: Wǒ xǐhuan xiàtiān. Kěyǐ yóuyǒng.
我 喜欢 夏天。可以 游泳。　I like summer. I can go swimming.

A: Nǐ duì Shànghǎi de tiānqì
你 对 上海 的 天气　Are you accustomed to Shanghai's climate?

xíguànle ma?
习惯了 吗?

B: Xíguàn le. Shànghǎi de tiānqì
习惯 了。上海 的 天气　Yes, I am. The climate in Shanghai is similar

hé wǒ jiāxiāng (de) chàbuduō.
和 我 家乡 （的） 差不多。　to my hometown's.

3. A: Xià yǔ le, bú qù gōngyuán le.
下 雨 了，不去 公园 了。　It's raining now. We are not going to the park.

B: Yǔ tíng le! Wǒmen zǒu ba.
雨 停 了! 我们 走 吧。　The rain has stopped. Let's go.

4. A: Kuàiyào xià xuě le.
快要 下 雪 了。　It will snow soon.

B: Ňg, tiānqì yuèláiyuè lěng le.
嗯，天气 越来越 冷 了。　Mm–hmm. It's getting colder and colder.

A: Zhèli de dōngtiān chángcháng
这里 的 冬天 常常　There are many windy days here in winter.

guā fēng.
刮 风。

B: Shì a, qiūtiān yě yǒu diǎnr
是 啊，秋天 也 有 点儿　Yes. And the climate here is a bit dry in

gānzào.
干燥。　autumn.

5. A: Mēnrè de shízài shòubuliǎo.
闷热 得 实在 受不了。　It's too muggy to bear.

B: Jīntiān méi zuótiān nàme rè.
今天 没 昨天 那么 热。　It's not so hot today as it was yesterday.

189

6. A： Jīntiān hé zuótiān yíyàng lěng.
今天 和 昨天 一样 冷。　　It is as cold today as yesterday.

B： Ǹg, Shànghǎi de dōngtiān hěn
嗯，上海 的 冬天 很　　Mm－hmm, it's rare that the winter in

shǎo zhème lěng.
少 这么 冷。　　Shanghai is so cold.

☆　注　释（Note）　☆

"有＋数量词"表示达到了某一数量。

"有＋数量词"indicates that the quantity reaches a certain value.

(1) Zhège fángjiān de miànjī yǒu sìshí píngfāngmǐ.
这个 房间 的 面积 有 四十 平方米。　　This room's area is 40 square meters.

(2) Dōngfāngmíngzhūtǎ yǒu sìbǎi liùshíbā mǐ gāo.
东方明珠塔 有 四百 六十八 米 高。　　The Oriental Pearl Tower is 468 meters high.

☆　句型提示（Sentence pattern references）　☆

1. 明天天气怎么样？　　　　　　　　　　　请参看 300 页句型 15。
2. （据）天气预报说明天（是）阴天，下午下雨。　请参看 318 页句型 53。
3. 你喜欢哪个季节？　　　　　　　　　　　请参看 318 页句型 54。
4. 快要下雪了。　　　　　　　　　　　　　请参看 307 页句型 32。
5. 天气越来越冷了。　　　　　　　　　　　请参看 381 页句型 196。
6. 今天没昨天那么热。　　　　　　　　　　请参看 324 页句型 68。
7. 今天和昨天一样冷。　　　　　　　　　　请参看 365 页句型 159。

☆　词语用法举例（Examples for usage of the words）　☆

1. 不冷也不热

(1) Zhè jiàn dàyī bù cháng yě bù duǎn, zhènghǎo.
这 件 大衣 不 长 也 不 短， 正好。

(2) Nǐ zuò de cài bù xián yě bú dàn, zhènghǎo.
你 做 的 菜 不 咸 也 不 淡， 正好。

(3) Zhè yánsè zhènghǎo, bù shēn yě bù qiǎn.
这 颜色 正好， 不 深 也 不 浅。

(4) Zhè shuāng xié bú dà yě bù xiǎo.
这 双 鞋 不 大 也 不 小。

2. （据）天气预报说

(1) （据）医生 说 不 是 什么 大病。
（Jù） yīshēng shuō bú shì shénme dàbìng.

(2) （据）报纸 说 昨天 发生了 车祸。
（Jù） bàozhǐ shuō zuótiān fāshēngle chēhuò.

(3) （据）广播 说 美国 总统 选举 还 没 结果。(总统：president
（Jù） guǎngbō shuō Měiguó zǒngtǒng xuǎnjǔ hái méi jiéguǒ. 选举：election)

(4) （据）广告 说 这 种 药 对 感冒 很 有效。 (药：medicine)
（Jù） guǎnggào shuō zhè zhǒng yào duì gǎnmào hěn yǒuxiào.

3. 那要数秋天最好

(1) 治疗 癌症，要 数 肿瘤 医院 最 好。
Zhìliáo áizhèng, yào shǔ Zhǒngliú Yīyuàn zuì hǎo.

(2) 兄弟 几 个，要 数 老二 成绩 最 好。 (老二：the second youngest
Xiōngdì jǐ ge, yào shǔ lǎo'èr chéngjì zuì hǎo. child in a family)

(3) 人口 最 多 的 城市，要 数 上海 了。
Rénkǒu zuì duō de chéngshì, yào shǔ Shànghǎi le.

(4) 东京 最 热闹 的 地方，要 数 银座 和 新宿。
Dōngjīng zuì rènao de dìfang, yào shǔ Yínzuò hé Xīnsù.

4. 我喜欢夏天

(1) 我 喜欢 一 个 人 散步。
Wǒ xǐhuan yí ge rén sànbù.

(2) 李 老师 很 喜欢 喝 咖啡。
Lǐ lǎoshī hěn xǐhuan hē kāfēi.

(3) 我 不 喜欢 看 足球 比赛。 (足球：football)
Wǒ bù xǐhuan kàn zúqiú bǐsài.

(4) 我 不 喜欢 西餐。
Wǒ bù xǐhuan xīcān.

5. 不去公园了

(1) 我 有 点儿 事，不 去 听 音乐会 了。
Wǒ yǒu diǎnr shì, bú qù tīng yīnyuèhuì le.

(2) 他 要 出差，不 能 出席 会议 了。
Tā yào chūchāi, bù néng chūxí huìyì le.

(3) 老师 生病 了，不 能 来 上课 了。
Lǎoshī shēngbìng le, bù néng lái shàngkè le.

(4) 我 下 个 月 回 国，不 学 汉语 了。
Wǒ xià ge yuè huí guó, bù xué Hànyǔ le.

6. 快要下雪了

(1) Shuǐ kuàiyào kāi le.
　　 水 　快要 　开 　了。　(开：boil)

(2) Yīnghuā kuàiyào kāi le.
　　 樱花 　快要 　开 　了。(开：blossom)

(3) Chē kuàiyào kāi le.
　　 车 　快要 　开 　了。(开：start, leave)

(4) kuàiyào shàngkè le.
　　 快要 　上课 　了。

7. 天气越来越冷了

(1) Tiān yuèláiyuè àn le.
　　 天 　越来越 　暗 了。

(2) Dìdi yuèláiyuè yònggōng le.
　　 弟弟 　越来越 　用功 　了。

(3) Rénmín shēnghuó yuèláiyuè hǎo le.
　　 人民 　生活 　越来越 　好 了。

(4) Dōngxi yuèláiyuè guì le.
　　 东西 　越来越 　贵 了。

8. 闷热得实在受不了

(1) Chǎo de shízài shòubuliǎo.
　　 吵 　得 　实在 　受不了。　　(吵：noisy)

(2) Tiāntiān yào jiābān dào shí'èr diǎn, shízài shòubuliǎo.
　　 天天 　要 加班 到 十二 点， 实在 　受不了。

(3) Rén tài duō, jǐ de shízài shòubuliǎo.
　　 人 太 多，挤 得 实在 　受不了。

(4) Tā tài luōsuo, ràng rén shòubuliǎo.
　　 他 太 啰嗦，让 人 受不了。　　(啰嗦：wordy, long-winded)

9. 今天没昨天那么热

(1) Míngming méi Fāngfang cōngming.
　　 明明 　没 方方 　聪明。

(2) Yéye méi nǎinai shēntǐ hǎo.
　　 爷爷 没 奶奶 身体 好。

(3) Xiǎo Zhāng méi Xiǎo Sòng gāo.
　　 小 张 没 小 宋 高。

(4) Xiùyīng méi Méifāng piàoliang.
　　 秀英 没 梅芳 　漂亮。

10. 上海的冬天很少这么冷

(1) Wǒ píngshí hěn shǎo guàngjiē.
　　 我 平时 很 少 　逛街。

Tā hěn shǎo qù fàndiàn chīfàn.
（2）他 很 少 去 饭店 吃饭。

Wǒ hěn shǎo mǎi jìnkǒu shāngpǐn.
（3）我 很 少 买 进口 商品。　（进口：import）

Lǎo Zhōu hěn shǎo duànliàn shēntǐ.
（4）老 周 很 少 锻炼 身体。　（锻炼：do exercises）

☆ 词 语（Word list） ☆

chūntiān			
1. 春天	（名）	spring	

dōngtiān			
2. 冬天	（名）	winter	

No.	词语	词性	英文	No.	词语	词性	英文
1.	春天 chūntiān	（名）	spring	2.	冬天 dōngtiān	（名）	winter
3.	打雷 dǎléi	（动）	thunder	4.	闪电 shǎndiàn	（名）	lightning
5.	雾 wù	（名）	fog	6.	霜 shuāng	（名）	frost
7.	闷热 mēnrè	（形）	muggy, sultry	8.	凉快 liángkuai	（形）	cool
9.	暖和 nuǎnhuo	（形）	warm	10.	潮湿 cháoshī	（形）	humid, damp
11.	阵雨 zhènyǔ	（名）	shower	12.	暴雨 bàoyǔ	（名）	torrential rain, rainstorm
13.	大雨 dàyǔ	（名）	heavy rain	14.	小雨 xiǎoyǔ	（名）	light rain, drizzle
15.	雨量 yǔliàng	（名）	rainfall	16.	晴 qíng	（形）	sunny
17.	多云 duōyún	（名）	cloudy	18.	晴 转 阴 qíng zhuǎn yīn		change from fine to overcast
19.	热带 风暴 rèdài fēngbào	（名）	tropical storm	20.	台风 táifēng	（名）	typhoon
21.	摄氏 shèshì	（名）	Celsius	22.	零 下 líng xià		below zero

☆ 练 习（Exercises） ☆

一、替换练习（Substitution exercises）

1. 上海的天气和我家乡的差不多。

今年的成绩	去年的
她做的菜	我妈妈做的
这家店里的衣服	那家店里的
她说的	中国人

2. 今天没昨天那么热。

昨天	今天	这么	冷
我的家	老王的家	那么	大

二、用括号中的词语改写句子（Rewrite the following sentences with the words in brackets）

1. 这家店里的东西太贵了。（实在）

2. 我真的不喜欢去热闹的地方。（实在）

3. 上海比北京潮湿。（……没有……＋形容词）

4. 寄挂号信比寄平信安全。（……没有……＋形容词）

5. 我不常坐公共汽车上班。（很少）

三、用"有＋数量词"回答问题（Answer the following questions with "有＋数量词"）

1. 你父亲多大年纪了？

2. 你住的大楼有几层？

3. 今天的最高气温是几度？

4. 你儿子的身高是多少？

四、会话（Conversation）

玛　丽：雨已经下了三天了，实在受不了。

于雪来：上海黄梅（huángméi）天常常下雨，你会习惯的。

玛　丽：上海冬天下雪吗？

于雪来：以前常下雪。我就是下雪的时候出生的，所以叫雪来。最近几年很少下雪了。

玛　丽：在我的家乡，最美要数下雪的时候了。

于雪来：听说黑龙江省（Hēilóngjiāng Shěng）有零下三十度呢。那儿的冰雪一定也很美。

玛　丽：真的吗？那我要去看看。你去过黑龙江吗？

于雪来：去过。我是秋天去的。冬天那么冷，我受不了，我怕冷（pà lěng/be afraid of the coldness, cannot stand the coldness）。

☆　练习答案（Key to the exercises）　☆

二、1. 这家店里的东西实在太贵了。

　　2. 我实在不喜欢去热闹的地方。

　　3. 北京没有上海潮湿。

　　4. 寄平信没有寄挂号信安全。

　　5. 我很少坐公共汽车上班。

30 生病 Shēngbìng FALLING SICK

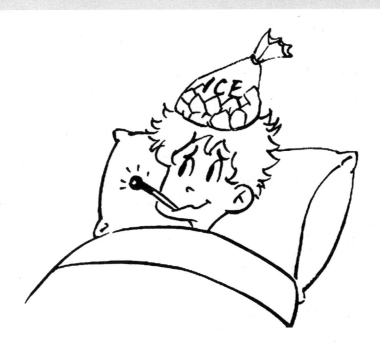

1. A：你 怎么 啦? 脸色 很 难看。
Nǐ zěnme la? Liǎnsè hěn nánkàn.
What's wrong with you? You look awful.

B：我 （身体） 很 不 舒服。
Wǒ (shēntǐ) hěn bù shūfu.
I feel unwell.

A：发烧 吗?
Fāshāo ma?
Do you have a fever?

B：好像 有 一点儿。
Hǎoxiàng yǒu yìdiǎnr.
It seems a bit.

A：是 感冒 吧?
Shì gǎnmào ba?
Maybe you've caught a cold.

B：大概 是 吧。 头疼、 鼻塞、
Dàgài shì ba. Tóuténg、 bísè、
Possibly. I have a headache, stuffy nose and

咳嗽。
késou.
cough.

A：中午 吃 饭 了 吗?
Zhōngwǔ chī fàn le ma?
Have you had lunch?

B：没有，一点儿 也 不 想 吃。
Méiyǒu, yìdiǎnr yě bù xiǎng chī.
No. I have no appetite at all.

Yào qù kàn yīshēng ma?
A：要 去 看 医生 吗？　　　　Are you going to see a doctor?

Búyòng le, wǒ zìjǐ chī diǎnr
B：不用 了，我 自己 吃 点儿　　Not necessary. I'll take some medicine

yào jiù xíng le.
药 就 行 了。　　　　　　myself. It will be all right.

Nǐ bù shūfu ma?
2. A：你 不 舒服 吗？　　　　　You don't feel very well, do you?

Wǒ hěn nánshòu.
B：我 很 难受。　　　　　　I feel sick.

Nǎli bù shūfu?
A：哪里 不 舒服？　　　　　What's wrong?

Fālěng、 ǒutù、 dùzi téng.
B：发冷、呕吐、肚子 疼。　　Chills, vomiting and pain in stomach.

Téng de lìhai ma?
A：疼 得 厉害 吗？　　　　　How is the pain?

Téng de yàomìng.
B：疼 得 要命。　　　　　　It's terrible.

Zhèyàng ba, wǒ péi nǐ qù
A：这样 吧注1，我 陪 你 去　　Then let me take you to the hospital.

yīyuàn ba.
医院 吧。

Xièxie, máfan nǐ jiào liàng
B：谢谢，麻烦 你注2 叫 辆　　Thank you. Would you please get a taxi for

chē lái.
车 来。　　　　　　　　me?

Wǒ zhè jiù qù, nǐ děng yíxià.
A：我 这 就 去，你 等 一下。　Yes. Please wait a moment. I'll go to get it.

☆ **注 释**(Notes) ☆

1. "这样吧"放在句首，表示考虑以后作出建议、选择或决定。
   When "这样吧" is put at the beginning of a sentence, it indicates a suggestion, choice or decision after consideration.

2. "麻烦你"是在请别人帮忙或向别人请教时常说的话。
   "麻烦你" is a phrase commonly used when you ask for someone's help or advice.

☆　**句型提示**（Sentence pattern references）　☆

1. 好像有一点儿。　　　　　　　　请参看 340 页句型 104。
2. 是感冒吧？大概是吧。　　　　　请参看 340 页句型 103。
3. 我陪你去医院吧。　　　　　　　请参看 393 页句型 220。

☆　**词语用法举例**（Examples for usage of the words）　☆

1. 脸色很难看

　　　　Tā de tóufa rǎnchéng hóngsè, hěn nánkàn.
（1）她 的 头发 染成 红色， 很 难看。

　　　　Zhè zhī gǒu hěn nánkàn.
（2）这 只 狗 很 难看。 （狗:dog）

　　　　Tā chàng zǒudiào le, tài nántīng le.
（3）他 唱 走调 了， 太 难听 了。 （走调:out of tune；难听:unpleasant to hear）

　　　　Shénme wèir? Zhème nánwén.
（4）什么 味儿? 这么 难闻。 （难闻:smell bad）

2. 我身体很不舒服

　　　　Wǒ dùzi yǒu diǎnr bù shūfu.
（1）我 肚子 有 点儿 不 舒服。

　　　　Zhè chènyī tài xiǎo, chuānzhe bù shūfu.
（2）这 衬衣 太 小， 穿着 不 舒服。

　　　　Zuòwèi tài xiǎo, zuò de bù shūfu.
（3）座位 太 小， 坐 得 不 舒服。

　　　　Zhěntou tài gāo, shuì de bù shūfu.
（4）枕头 太 高， 睡 得 不 舒服。

3. 好像有一点儿

　　　　Hǎoxiàng yào xià xuě.
（1）好像 要 下 雪。

　　　　Wǒ hǎoxiàng zài nǎr jiànguo tā.
（2）我 好像 在 哪儿 见过 他。

　　　　Tā hǎoxiàng shì Měiguórén.
（3）她 好像 是 美国人。

　　　　Dīng Lìlì hǎoxiàng qù Rìběn le.
（4）丁 丽莉 好像 去 日本 了。

4. 大概是吧

　　　　Nà wèi dàgài shì xiàozhǎng ba.
（1）那 位 大概 是 校长 吧。

Tā dàgài yǒu wǔshí suì le ba.
(2) 她 大概 有 五十 岁 了 吧。

Tā yǐjīng sānshí suì le, dàgài jiéhūnle ba.
(3) 她 已经 三十 岁 了, 大概 结婚了 吧。

Tā liǎnsè hěn nánkàn, dàgài shì shēngbìngle ba.
(4) 他 脸色 很 难看, 大概 是 生病了 吧。

5. 我很难受

Wǒ chī de tài bǎo, wèi hěn nánshòu.
(1) 我 吃 得 太 饱, 胃 很 难受。

Wǒ bízi bù tōngqì, hěn nánshòu.
(2) 我 鼻子 不 通气 很 难受。

Wǒ yào hé fùmǔ fēnbié, xīnli hěn nánshòu.
(3) 我 要 和 父母 分别, 心里 很 难受。　（分别：part）

Wǒ méi kǎoshang dàxué, xīnli hěn nánshòu.
(4) 我 没 考上 大学, 心里 很 难受。

6. 疼得厉害吗

Tā ké de hěn lìhai.
(1) 他 咳 得 很 厉害。

Dōngběi de dōngtiān lěng de lìhai.
(2) 东北 的 冬天 冷 得 厉害。

Bú yàojǐn, téng de bú tài lìhai.
(3) 不 要紧, 疼 得 不 太 厉害。

Zhège shāngdiàn de dōngxi guì de lìhai.
(4) 这个 商店 的 东西 贵 得 厉害。

7. 我陪你去医院吧

Wǒ bú rènde lù, nǐ péi wǒ qù, hǎo ma?
(1) 我 不 认得 路, 你 陪 我 去, 好 吗?

Tā jīntiān péi wàibīn cānguān gōngchǎng.
(2) 他 今天 陪 外宾 参观 工厂。

（外宾：foreign guests　参观：visit　工厂：factory）

Wǒ jīntiān yào péi tàitai mǎi dōngxi.
(3) 我 今天 要 陪 太太 买 东西。

Nǐ yí ge rén zài jiā, wǒ lái péi nǐ shuōshuo huà ba.
(4) 你 一 个 人 在 家, 我 来 陪 你 说说 话 吧。

8. 麻烦你叫辆车来

Wǒ bú huì shuō Hànyǔ, máfan nǐ bāng wǒ dǎ ge diànhuà.
(1) 我 不 会 说 汉语, 麻烦 你 帮 我 打 个 电话。

Máfan nǐ tì wǒ xiàng jīnglǐ qǐngjià.
(2) 麻烦 你 替 我 向 经理 请假。　（替：for, on behalf of）

Zuótiān de shì, tài máfan nǐ le.
(3) 昨天 的 事, 太 麻烦 你 了。

Máfan nín le, xièxie.
(4) 麻烦 您 了, 谢谢。

9. 麻烦你叫辆车来

Nǐ zǒu ·de shíhou jiào wǒ yì shēng.
(1) 你 走 的 时候 叫 我 一 声。

Jiào Xiǎo Hé lái jiē diànhuà.
(2) 叫 小 何 来 接 电话。

Jiào Míngming lái jiànjian kèren.
(3) 叫 明明 来 见见 客人。

Míngtiān zǎoshang wǔ diǎn jiàoxǐng wǒ, xíng ma?
(4) 明天 早上 五 点 叫醒 我, 行 吗?

☆ 词 语 (Word list) ☆

shēntǐ			
1. 身体	(名)	body	
yǎnjing			
3. 眼睛	(名)	eye	
bízi			
5. 鼻子	(名)	nose	
kǒu			
7. 口	(名)	mouth	
yáchǐ			
9. 牙齿	(名)	tooth	
bózi			
11. 脖子	(名)	neck	
ěrduo			
13. 耳朵	(名)	ear	
shǒuzhǐ			
15. 手指	(名)	finger	
jiānbǎng			
17. 肩膀	(名)	shoulder	
xiōng			
19. 胸	(名)	chest	
gān			
21. 肝	(名)	liver	
xīnzàng			
23. 心脏	(名)	heart	
jiǎo			
25. 脚	(名)	foot	
pífū			
27. 皮肤	(名)	skin	
guānjié			
29. 关节	(名)	joint	

liǎn
2. 脸 (名) face

méimao
4. 眉毛 (名) eyebrow

zuǐba
6. 嘴巴 (名) mouth

zuǐchún
8. 嘴唇 (名) lip

shétou
10. 舌头 (名) tongue

hóulong
12. 喉咙 (名) throat

shǒu
14. 手 (名) hand

shǒubì
16. 手臂 (名) arm

yāo
18. 腰 (名) waist

fèi
20. 肺 (名) lung

shèn
22. 肾 (名) kidney

tuǐ
24. 腿 (名) leg

nǎo
26. 脑 (名) brain

biǎntáoxiàn
28. 扁桃腺 (名) tonsil

xīgài
30. 膝盖 (名) knee

☆ 练 习（Exercises） ☆

一、读词组（Read the following word groups aloud）

1. 发烧　　　　发高烧　　　　发低(dī)烧(slight fever)　　　退(tuì)烧(bring down a fever, the fever is gone)

2. 头疼　　　　肚子疼　　　　牙疼　　　　　　脚疼

3. 疼得厉害　　冷得厉害　　　热得厉害　　　贵得厉害

二、用"一……也"改写句子（Rewrite the following sentences with"一……也"）

1. 房间里没有人。

2. 这个包里没有钱。

3. 这个电影没有意思。

4. 来中国以后，我没吃过北京烤鸭。（kǎoyā/roast Beijing duck）

5. 我喉咙疼，吃不下饭。

三、用括号中的词语完成对话（Complete the following conversations with the words in brackets）

1. A：下午会下雨吗？
   B：外面天很暗，＿＿＿＿＿＿＿＿＿＿＿。（大概）

2. A：老王是不是在大华公司？
   B：＿＿＿＿＿＿＿＿＿＿＿。（大概）

3. A：你看那个人是不是小林？
   B：＿＿＿＿＿＿＿＿＿＿＿。（好像）

4. A：他的脸色很黄，＿＿＿＿＿＿＿＿＿＿＿。（好像）
   B：大概是吧。

5. A：他的病怎么样？
   B：＿＿＿＿＿＿＿＿＿＿＿。（厉害）

6. A：这两天地铁挤不挤？
   B：当然，＿＿＿＿＿＿＿＿＿＿＿。（要命）

7. A：你一个人去医院吗？
   B：不，＿＿＿＿＿＿＿＿＿＿＿。（陪）

8. A：我们一起去买东西好不好？
   B：不行啊，我有工作，＿＿＿＿＿＿＿＿＿＿＿。（陪）

四、会话（Conversation）

于雪来：郭放，吃饭了。

郭　放：你们吃吧。我一点儿也不想吃。

于雪来：你怎么了？

郭　放：没什么，只是有点儿不舒服。

于雪来：哪里不舒服？

郭　放：肚子疼。

于雪来：疼得很厉害吗？

郭　放：不太厉害。大概是中午吃的东西不干净。

于雪来：要不要去医院看看？

郭　放：不用了。自己先吃药看看，如果不行再去医院吧。

郭明明：还是去医院看看吧，你的脸色很难看。

于雪来：对，我陪你去。明明，你去把爸爸的大衣拿来。

郭　放：没关系，不是很厉害。雪来，你先吃饭。吃完饭再去。

☆　**练习答案**(Key to the exercises)　☆

二、1. 房间里一个人也没有。

　　2. 这个包里一分钱也没有。

　　3. 这个电影一点儿意思也没有。

　　4. 来中国以后，我一次北京烤鸭也没吃过。

　　5. 我喉咙疼，一点儿饭也吃不下。

三、1. B：大概会下雨吧

　　2. B：大概是(在大华公司)吧

　　3. B：(那个人)好像是小林

　　4. A：好像生病了

　　5. B：病得很厉害

　　6. B：挤得要命

　　7. B：我先生陪我去

　　8. B：不能陪你去(买东西)

31　在 医院₁　Zài Yīyuàn

IN A HOSPITAL ₁

1. A：请问，在哪里挂号？
   Qǐngwèn, zài nǎli guàhào?
   Excuse me, where can I register?

   B：那边　挂号处。
   Nàbian guàhàochù.
   At the registration office over there.

2. A：我要挂号。
   Wǒ yào guàhào.
   I'd like to register.

   B：您要挂哪一科？
   Nín yào guà nǎ yì kē?
   What department do you want to register for?

   A：（我要挂）内科。
   (Wǒ yào guà) nèikē.
   The department of Internal Medicine.

   B：是初诊吗？
   Shì chūzhěn ma?
   Is this your first visit?

   A：是的，我第一次来。
   Shì de, wǒ dì-yī cì lái.
   Yes. This is the first time I've come here.

   B：请填病历卡这几栏。
   Qǐng tián bìnglìkǎ zhè jǐ lán.
   Please fill in these columns of the medical record.

   请付二十块钱诊疗费。
   Qǐng fù èrshí kuài qián zhěnliáofèi.
   Please pay 20 yuan for the diagnosis fee.

Wǒ gāi dào nǎge zhěnshì kànbìng?
A: 我 该 到 哪个 诊室 看病?　　Which consulting room shall I go to?

(Qǐng dào) dì-sān zhěnshì.
B: (请 到) 第三 诊室。　　Please go to the third consulting room.

Yīshēng, wǒ hěn nánshòu.
3. A: 医生, 我 很 难受。　　Doctor, I feel terrible.

Nǐ nǎr bù shūfu?
B: 你 哪儿 不 舒服?　　What are the symptoms?

(Wǒ) dùzi hěn téng, shàngwǔ
A: (我) 肚子 很 疼, 上午　　Severe stomachache. And I vomited three

tùle sān cì.
吐了 三 次。　　times this morning.

Shénme shíhou kāishǐ de?
B: 什么 时候 开始 的?　　When did it start?

Liǎng-sān tiān yǐqián (kāishǐ de).
A: 两三 天 以前 (开始 的)。　　About two or three days ago.

Xiān liáng yíxià tǐwēn ba.
B: 先 量 一下 体温 吧。　　Let me take your temperature first.

Sānshíbā dù bā, nǐ fāshāo le.
三十八 度 八, 你 发烧 了。　　Thirty-eight point eight degree Celsius. You

have a fever.

Guàibude yǒu diǎnr fālěng.
A: 怪不得注 有 点儿 发冷。　　So that's why I feel a bit chilly.

(Bǎ) shétou shēn chulai, gěi
B: (把) 舌头 伸 出来, 给　　Please stick out your tongue and let me have

wǒ kànkan.
我 看看。　　a look.

Jiěkāi shàngyī, ràng wǒ tīngting.
解开 上衣, 让 我 听听。　　Please unbutton your coat and let me listen.

Dào nàr tǎngxia.
到 那儿 躺下。　　Please lie down there.

Zhèr téng ma?
这儿 疼 吗?　　Is there pain here?

Bù téng.
A: 不 疼。　　No.

Zhèr ne?
B: 这儿 呢?　　What about here?

Jiù nàr téng.
A: 就 那儿 疼。　　That's it.

203

☆ 注 释(Note) ☆

"怪不得"在这里表示突然明白了某事发生的原因。

"怪不得"here expresses the sudden understanding of the reason why something happened.

Kōngtiáo méi kāi, guàibude zhème rè.
(1) 空调　没 开，怪不得 这么 热。

So that's why I feel so hot. The air conditioning is not on.

Guàibude tā Hànyǔ shuō de nàme hǎo ne, yuánlái tā shì Zhōngguórén a.
(2) 怪不得 他 汉语 说 得 那么 好 呢，原来 他 是　中国人　啊。

No wonder he speaks Chinese so well. He is Chinese!

☆ 句型提示(Sentence pattern references) ☆

1. 上午吐了三次。　　　　　　请参看 350 页句型 128。
2. 先量一下体温吧。　　　　　请参看 368 页句型 167。
3. 让我听听。　　　　　　　　请参看 330 页句型 81。
4. 到那儿躺下。　　　　　　　请参看 352 页句型 131。

☆ 词语用法举例(Examples for usage of the words) ☆

1. 我该到哪个诊室看病

Qù zhíwùyuán gāi zǒu nǎ tiáo lù?
(1) 去 植物园 该 走 哪 条 路?

Bàn zhè jiàn shì, gāi zhǎo shuí?
(2) 办 这 件 事，该 找 谁?

Gāi dào nǎli fù shuǐdiànfèi?
(3) 该 到 哪里 付 水电费?

Zhège yīn gāi zěnme fā?
(4) 这个 音 该 怎么 发?

2. 先量一下体温吧

Wǒmen xiān fùxí yíxià ba.
(1) 我们　先 复习 一下 吧。

Wǒ xiān zìwǒ jièshào yíxià.
(2) 我 先 自我 介绍 一下。

Duìbuqǐ, wǒ xiān zǒu le.
(3) 对不起，我 先 走 了。

Nǐ bù shūfu, xiān huí jiā ba.
(4) 你 不 舒服，先 回 家 吧。

3. 怪不得有点儿发冷

(1) A: Chén Míng shēngbìng le.
　　　 陈　 明　 生病　 了。

　　 B: Guàibude tā de liǎnsè zhème nánkàn.
　　　 怪不得　他　的　脸色　 这么　 难看。

(2) A: Lǐ Píng qù Měiguó le.
　　　 李　 平　去　美国　 了。

　　 B: Guàibude hǎojiǔ méi jiàndào tā.
　　　 怪不得　好久　 没　见到　 他。

(3) A: Zhège cài wǒ wàngjì fàng yán le.
　　　 这个　菜　我　忘记　 放　盐　了。

　　 B: Guàibude méi wèidao.
　　　 怪不得　没　味道。

4. (把)舌头伸出来,给我看看(……出去)

(1) Tā bǎ shū cóng bāo li ná chulai.
　　他　把　书　从　包　里　拿　出来。

(2) Bàba cóng fángjiān zǒu chulai.
　　爸爸　从　房间　 走　出来。

(3) Qǐng bǎ zhè fēng xìn jì chuqu.
　　请　把　这　封　信　寄　出去。

(4) Qǐng bǎ háizi dài chuqu wán.
　　请　把　孩子　带　出去　玩。

5. (把)舌头伸出来,给我看看

(1) Nǐ de yǐngjí gěi wǒ kànkan, xíng ma?
　　你　的　影集　给　我　看看，　行　吗?

(2) Gěi bàba kànkan nǐ de chéngjìdān ba.
　　给　爸爸　看看　你　的　成绩单　 吧。

(3) Nǐ de xiàngpí gěi wǒ yòng yíxià.
　　你　的　橡皮　给　我　用　一下。

(4) Xìn nálai gěi wǒ chēng yíxià.
　　信　拿来　给　我　称　一下。

6. 解开上衣,让我听听

(1) Nǐ de yǐngjí ràng wǒ kànkan, xíng ma?
　　你　的　影集　让　我　看看，　行　吗?

(2) Ràng bàba kànkan nǐ de chéngjìdān ba.
　　让　爸爸　看看　你　的　成绩单　 吧。

(3) Ràng dìdi qù mǎi fèn bàozhǐ lai.
　　让　弟弟　去　买　份　报纸　 来。

(4) Lǎoshī ràng xuésheng dú liǎng biàn kèwén.
　　老师　让　学生　 读　两　遍　课文。

☆ 词 语 (Word list) ☆

1.	ménzhěn 门诊	（名）	outpatient service	2.	wàikē 外科	（名）	surgical department

1. ménzhěn 门诊 （名） outpatient service
2. wàikē 外科 （名） surgical department
3. xiǎo'érkē 小儿科 （名） pediatric department
4. fùkē 妇科 （名） department of gynecology
5. chǎnkē 产科 （名） department of obstetrics
6. pífūkē 皮肤科 （名） dermatological department
7. yǎnkē 眼科 （名） department of ophthalmology
8. ěrbíhóukē 耳鼻喉科 （名） ear-nose-throat department
9. yákē 牙科 （名） department of dentistry
10. bìnglìkǎ 病历卡 （名） medical record
11. zhùyuàn 住院 （动） be hospitalized
12. chūyuàn 出院 （动） leave hospital, be discharged from hospital
13. bìngfáng 病房 （名） ward
14. hòuzhěnshì 候诊室 （名） waiting room
15. jízhěn 急诊 （名） emergency treatment
16. jiùhùchē 救护车 （名） ambulance
17. yīshēng 医生 （名） doctor
18. hùshi 护士 （名） nurse
19. xīyī 西医 （名） western medical science
20. zhōngyī 中医 （名） traditional Chinese medical science
21. zhēnjiǔ 针灸 （名） acupuncture and moxibustion
22. tuīná 推拿 （动） massage
23. kànbìng 看病 （动） see a doctor (for a patient); see a patient (for a doctor)
24. bìngrén 病人 （名） patient
25. zhìliáo 治疗 （动） treatment, therapy
26. dòng shǒushù 动 手术 perform an operation; have an operation

☆ 练 习 (Exercises) ☆

一、替换练习 (Substitution exercises)

1. 三天以前开始肚子疼。　　半小时　　　　　　手术
　　　　　　　　　　　　　几分钟　　　　　　检查身体
　　　　　　　　　　　　　三四年　　　　　　有心脏病
　　　　　　　　　　　　　七八年　　　　　　用这种药治疗

2. 就那儿疼。　　　　　　　你按的地方　　　　疼
　　　　　　　　　　　　　在这家医院　　　　看
　　　　　　　　　　　　　吃这种药　　　　　有效 (yǒuxiào/effective)
　　　　　　　　　　　　　是你介绍的那个医生　给我看病

二、选择填空（Select the appropriate phrase to fill in the blanks）

出来　　　　　　下　　　　　　出去

1. 他把书从包里拿_____。

2. 他累了,回到家就躺_____了。

3. 箱子不能放在这里,请拿_____。

4. 把孩子带_____玩吧。

5. 胸口难受,吐_____就好了。

三、读句子（Read the following sentences aloud）

1. 请留下你的地址。

2. 请写下你的电话号码。

3. 他放下钱就走了。

4. 我累极了（lèijí le/extremely tired）,回到家就躺下了。

5. 他在中国住了五年,怪不得汉语说得这么好。

6. 他生病了,怪不得没来上课。

四、会话（Conversation）

医　生：哪里不舒服?

大　卫：发烧、头疼、咳嗽,大概是感冒了。

医　生：量过体温吗?

大　卫：刚才（gāngcái/just now）护士给我量过了,是三十八度二。

医　生：什么时候开始不舒服的?

大　卫：昨天晚上。

医　生：让我看看。还有别的不舒服吗?

大　卫：还喉咙疼。

医　生：问题不大。吃点儿药就会好的。要多喝水、多休息。

大　卫：谢谢。

☆　**练习答案**（Key to the exercises）　☆

二、1. 出来　　2. 下　　3. 出去　　4. 出去　　5. 出来

32　在 医院₂   IN A HOSPITAL ₂

Zài Yīyuàn

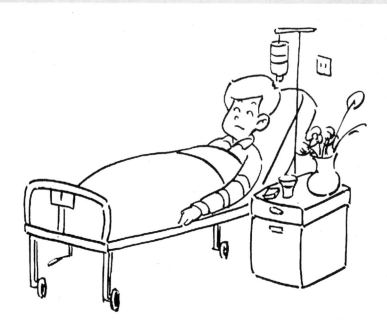

1. （请） 张开 嘴。
（Qǐng） zhāngkāi zuǐ.
Please open your mouth.

2. （请） 吸 气。
（Qǐng） xī qì.
Breathe in, please.

3. （请） 深 呼吸。
（Qǐng） shēn hūxī.
Take a deep breath, please.

4. （你） 要 验 一下 血。
（Nǐ） yào yàn yíxià xiě.
You should have your blood tested.

5. （你） 要 做 个 心电图。
（Nǐ） yào zuò ge xīndiàntú.
You should have an electrocardiogram.

6. （你） 要 拍 片子。
（Nǐ） yào pāi piānzi.
You should take an X-ray.

7. 你 去 X光室， 做 肺部 透视 吧。
Nǐ qù X guāngshì, zuò fèibù tòushì ba.
Please go to the X-ray Room to have your chest X-rayed.

8. 你 要 住院。
Nǐ yào zhùyuàn.
You should be hospitalized.

9.
Nǐ bìxū dòng shǒushù.
你 必须 动 手术。

You need an operation.

10. A: Yīshēng, wǒ déle shénme bìng?
医生，我 得了 什么 病？

Doctor, what's wrong with me?

B: Shì chángwèiyán.
是 肠胃炎。

It's enterogastritis.

A: (Wǒ de bìng) yàojǐn ma?
（我 的 病）要紧 吗？

Is it serious?

B: Bié dānxīn, chīle yào, guò
别 担心，吃了 药，过

There's nothing to worry about. You will be

sì-wǔ tiān jiù huì hǎo de.
四五 天 就 会 好 的。

fine in four or five days after taking this medicine.

Nǐ yǐqián shēngguo zhè zhǒng
你 以前 生过 这 种

Have you had this disease before?

bìng ma?
病 吗？

A: Shēngguo yí cì.
生过 一 次。

Yes, I had it once.

Wǒ yào zhùyì xiē shénme?
我 要 注意 些 什么？

What should I pay attention to?

B: Yào hǎohāor xiūxi, bié tài
要 好好儿 休息，别 太

Have a good rest and don't tire yourself out.

lèi le.
累 了。

Nǐ zuìhǎo xiūxi jǐ tiān.
你 最好注 休息 几 天。

You'd better take it easy for several days.

Yàoshi bú jiànhǎo, nǐ zài
要是 不 见好，你 再

Come back to see me again if you still feel

lái ba.
来 吧。

bad.

☆ 注 释 (Note) ☆

"最好"表示和其他事情比较，这是最佳选择。

"最好" indicates that it is the best choice to compare with the others.

(1) Zhè jiàn shì, zuìhǎo nǐ qīnzì bàn.
这 件 事，最好 你 亲自 办。 It would be best if you handle the matter yourself.

(2) Nǐ zuìhǎo duō hē kāishuǐ.
你 最好 多 喝 开水。 You'd better drink more boiled water.

☆ 句型提示（Sentence pattern references） ☆

1. 你必须动手术。 请参看 332 页句型 85。
2. 你最好休息几天。 请参看 326 页句型 72。
3. 要是不见好,你再来吧。 请参看 388 页句型 210。

☆ 词语用法举例（Examples for usage of the words） ☆

1. （请）张开嘴

（1）请 打开 窗。 （打开：open）
Qǐng dǎkāi chuāng.

（2）请 大家 翻开 课本。 （翻开：open）
Qǐng dàjiā fānkāi kèběn.

（3）把 西瓜 切开, 请 大家 吃 吧。 （切开：cut）
Bǎ xīguā qiēkāi, qǐng dàjiā chī ba.

（4）他 跟 父母 分开 住。 （分开：separately）
Tā gēn fùmǔ fēnkāi zhù.

2. 你要验一下血

（1）从 这儿 乘 公共 汽车 去 人民 广场 要 换 车 吗?
Cóng zhèr chéng gōnggòng qìchē qù Rénmín Guǎngchǎng yào huàn chē ma?

（2）出国 旅行 要 办 什么 手续?
Chūguó lǚxíng yào bàn shénme shǒuxù?

（3）取 邮件 要 有 身份证。 （邮件：mail）
Qǔ yóujiàn yào yǒu shēnfènzhèng.

（4）买 机票 要 带 护照 去。 （护照：passport）
Mǎi jīpiào yào dài hùzhào qu.

3. （我的病）要紧吗

（1）A：听说 他 病 了,要紧 吗?
Tīngshuō tā bìng le, yàojǐn ma?

　　B：不 要紧。
Bú yàojǐn.

（2）A：听说 他 住院 了,要紧 吗?
Tīngshuō tā zhùyuàn le, yàojǐn ma?

　　B：病 得 很 厉害。
Bìng de hěn lìhai.

4. 你以前生过这种病吗?

（1）你 去过 澳大利亚 吗?
Nǐ qùguo Àodàlìyà ma?

Wǒ chīguo Rìběncài.
（2）我 吃过 日本菜。

Wǒ méi kànguo jīngjù.
（3）我 没 看过 京剧。

Tā méi dāngguo jiàoshī.
（4）他 没 当过 教师。

5. 生过一次

Zhè jiàn shì, tā duì wǒ shuōguo liǎng cì.
（1）这 件 事，他 对 我 说过 两 次。

Wǒ qùguo yí cì Déguó.
（2）我 去过 一 次 德国。

Tā dāngguo sān nián jiàoshī.
（3）他 当过 三 年 教师。

Wǒ hǎoxiàng jiànguo tā yí cì.
（4）我 好像 见过 他 一 次。

6. 要是不见好

Wǒ késou de lǎomáobìng yìzhí bú jiànhǎo.
（1）我 咳嗽 的 老毛病 一直 不 见好。（老毛病:old trouble）

Chīle hěn duō yào, kěshì zǒng bú jiànhǎo.
（2）吃了 很 多 药，可是 总 不 见好。

Rúguǒ bú jiànhǎo huàn yì zhǒng yào ba.
（3）如果 不 见好 换 一 种 药 吧。

Tā bú ànshí chīyào, suǒyǐ bìng zǒng bú jiànhǎo.
（4）他 不 按时 吃药，所以 病 总 不 见好。（按时:on time）

☆　词　语（Word list）　☆

tóu yūn
1. 头 晕　　　　dizzy

ěxin
2. 恶心　（形）feel like vomiting

lā dùzi
3. 拉 肚子　　diarrhea

biànmì
4. 便秘　（动）constipation

dīrè
5. 低热　（名）low fever

tán
6. 痰　（名）phlegm

liú bítì
7. 流 鼻涕　　have a runny nose

shīmián
8. 失眠　（动）suffer from insomnia

shuìbuzháo
9. 睡不着　　can not fall asleep

gāoxuèyā
10. 高血压　（名）high blood pressure, hypertension

wèikǒu hǎo hǎo
11. 胃口 不 好　lose one's appetite

áizhèng
12. 癌症　（名）cancer

gǔzhé
13. 骨折　（动）fracture

shòushāng
14. 受伤　（动）be injured, be wounded

211

15. 切伤 qiēshāng
be cut

16. 烫伤 tàngshāng
scald

17. 肿 (动) zhǒng
swell

18. 消肿 xiāo zhǒng
reduce the swelling, cause a swelling to go down

19. 皮肤痒 pífū yǎng
itch on skin

20. 流血 liú xiě
bleed

21. 出冷汗 chū lěnghàn
be in a cold sweat, break out in a cold sweat

22. 全身 (名) quánshēn
whole body, all over the body

23. 没劲儿 (动) méijìnr
feel weak

24. 发炎 (动) fāyán
inflame

25. 打喷嚏 dǎ pēntì
sneeze

26. 打哈欠 dǎ hāqian
yawn

☆ 练 习 (Exercises) ☆

一、读词组 (Read the following word groups aloud)

1. 挂号费   药费   验血费   注射费   住院费
2. 做检查   做手术   做 B 超   做心电图   做 CT
3. 得病   得肺病   得胃病   得关节炎   得癌症
4. 好好休息   好好睡觉   好好吃药   好好学习   好好工作

二、模仿造句 (Write sentences by following the patterns and imitating the example sentences)

1. 动词词组 + 就 + 结果。
   吃了药就会好的。
   有了钱就可以买很多好东西。
   多锻炼就不会生病。

   _____

2. 最好 + 建议 (jiànyì/suggestion)。
   你最好休息几天。
   今天出去你最好带伞。
   这件事最好不要告诉他。

   _____

三、用括号中的词语完成对话 (Complete the following conversations with the words in brackets)

1. A: 医生,我儿子的病要紧吗?
   B: 不要紧,_____。(担心)
   A: _____?(注意)
   B: 让他多休息就可以了。

2. A：我想吃辣豆腐。

　　B：不行,生病的时候要_____。（注意）

3. A：他的病怎么样?

　　B：_____。不用动手术。（要紧）

4. A：这种药怎么样?

　　B：这种药不好。我吃了三天也_____。（见好）

四、会话(Conversation)

郭放：医生,您好。我肚子疼,已经拉了几次了。

医生：什么时候开始的?

郭放：下午就开始了。

医生：那你早上和中午吃了什么不干净的东西没有?

郭放：早上没吃什么。中午是在一个小饭店吃的,可能有问题(wèntí/problem)吧。

医生：吐吗?

郭放：不吐。可是有点儿恶心。

医生：还有什么不舒服?

郭放：还出冷汗。

医生：你先去验一下大便(dàbiàn/stool)吧。

郭放：医生,这是化验(huàyàn/examine, test)单,您看是什么问题?

医生：嗯,是食物中毒(shíwù zhòngdú/food poisoning)。

郭放：要紧吗?

医生：不要紧,你大概吃得不多。不过,你最好留在医院里观察(guānchá/observe)一天。

☆　　练习答案(Key to the exercises)　　☆

三、1. B：不用担心

　　　A：我要注意什么

　　2. B：注意饮食(yǐnshí/diet, food and drink)

　　3. B：不要紧

　　4. B：不见好

33　Zài Yīyuàn　在 医院₃　IN A HOSPITAL ₃

1. A：Lǐ Zhìjiān! Lǐ Zhìjiān!
   李 志坚! 李 志坚!

   Li Zhijian!

   B：Wǒ shì.
   我 是。

   Yes.

   A：Yàopiàn xiǎo de 注1 měi cì
   药片 小 的注1 每 次
   liǎng lì, dà de yí lì.
   两 粒，大 的 一 粒。

   Take two of the small pills each time and one of the big ones.

   B：Xiǎo de liǎng lì, dà de yí
   小 的 两 粒，大 的 一
   lì, duì ma?
   粒，对 吗?

   Two of the small and one of the big, right?

   A：Duì.
   对。

   Right.

   B：Yì tiān chī jǐ cì?
   一 天 吃 几 次?

   How many times a day?

   A：Dà de yì tiān sān cì.
   大 的 一 天 三 次。

   Three times a day for the big pills.

Xiǎo de yì tiān liǎng cì,
小 的 一 天 两 次，   And for the small ones, twice a day, two pills

zǎowǎn gè chī liǎng lì.
早晚 各 吃 两 粒。   in the morning and evening respectively.

   Yàoshuǐ ne?
B：药水 呢？   What about the medicine liquid?

   Yàoshuǐ měi tiān (hē) sì
A：药水 每 天 （喝） 四   Take the liquid four times a day, one measure

cì, měi cì yì gé.
次， 每 次 一 格。   each time.

Zhè shì wàiyòngyào, qiānwàn
这 是 外用药， 千万注2   And this is for external use only. Be sure not

búyào kǒufú.
不要 口服。   to take it orally.

Qǐng fàngzài xiǎohái ná bu
请 放在 小孩 拿 不   Please keep it out of children's reach.

dào de dìfang.
到 的 地方。

   Nǐ zuìjìn dǎguo qīngméisù ma?
2. A：你 最近 打过 青霉素 吗？   Have you had an injection of penicillin recently?

   Méi dǎguo.
B：没 打过。   No, I haven't.

   Yào xiān zuò shìyàn.
A：要 先 做 试验。   Then you should take a test first.

Nǐ dǎ qīngméisù guòmǐn,
你 打 青霉素 过敏，   You are allergic to penicillin.

bù néng dǎ.
不 能 打。   So you can't have a penicillin injection.

   Nà wǒ gāi zěnme bàn?
B：那 我 该 怎么 办？   What should I do then?

   Qǐng yīshēng huàn bié de
A：请 医生 换 别 的   Please ask the doctor to change the prescrip-

yào ba.
药 吧。   tion.

☆ 注 释 (Notes) ☆

1. "形容词 + 的"相当于一个名词。
   "adjective + 的" may be regarded as a noun.

   Wǒ xǐhuan chī tián de.
(1) 我 喜欢 吃 甜 的   I like to eat sweets.

（2）
Yǒu piányi yìdiǎnr de ma?
有 便宜 一点儿 的 吗?　Do you have something cheaper?

2. "千万"是在提醒或叮嘱别人时用的。

"千万"is used when you remind, advise or urge someone else.

（1）
Qiānwàn zǎo diǎnr huílai.
千万 早 点儿 回来。　Be sure to come back early.

（2）
Qiānwàn bié pèng zhège.
千万 别 碰 这个。　Never touch this!

☆　句型提示（Sentence pattern references）　☆

1. 千万不要口服。　　　　　　　　请参看 393 页句型 221。

2. 你最近打过青霉素吗? 没打过。　请参看 310 页句型 37。

3. 你打青霉素过敏,不能打。　　　请参看 337 页句型 95。

☆　词语用法举例（Examples for usage of the words）　☆

1. 药水每天（喝）四次

（1）
Měi rén yào yì wǎn fàn.
每 人 要 一 碗 饭。

（2）
Měi bān xuǎn yí ge dàibiǎo.
每 班 选 一 个 代表。

（3）
Měi bēi fàng yí lì táng.
每 杯 放 一 粒 糖。

（4）
Měi ge jiàoshì fàng yì tái diànshìjī.
每 个 教室 放 一 台 电视机。

2. 千万不要口服

（1）
Qiānwàn yào guānhǎo ménchuāng.
千万 要 关好 门窗。　（关好:close　门窗:door and window）

（2）
Qiānwàn búyào jiǔ hòu kāichē.
千万 不要 酒 后 开车。　（酒后:after drink 开车:drive）

（3）
Qiānwàn bié hēzuì le.
千万 别 喝醉 了。　（喝醉:drunk）

（4）
Qiānwàn bié dài wēixiǎnpǐn shàng chē.
千万 别 带 危险品 上 车。　（危险品:dangerous articles）

☆　词　语（Word list）　☆

xīyào
1. 西药　　（名）western medicine

zhōngyào
2. 中药　　（名）traditional Chinese medicine

3.	chéngyào 成药	（名）	patent medicine；pharmacist-prepared medicine	4.	ruǎngāo/yàogāo 软膏/药膏	（名）	ointment, salve
5.	jiǔjīng 酒精	（名）	alcohol	6.	diǎnjiǔ 碘酒	（名）	tincture of iodine
7.	hóngyàoshuǐ 红药水	（名）	mercurochrome	8.	tú 涂	（动）	apply, spread on
9.	xiāodújì 消毒剂	（名）	disinfectant	10.	kàngshēngsù 抗生素	（名）	antibiotic
11.	ānmiányào 安眠药	（名）	sleeping pill	12.	zhǐké yàoshuǐ 止咳 药水	（名）	cough syrup
13.	tuìrèpiàn 退热片	（名）	antipyretic	14.	zhǐtòngpiàn 止痛片	（名）	pain-killer, analgesic
15.	xiāoyánpiàn 消炎片	（名）	antiphlogistic	16.	yǎnyàoshuǐ 眼药水	（名）	eye drops
17.	āsīpǐlín 阿斯匹林	（名）	aspirin	18.	wéishēngsù 维生素	（名）	vitamin
19.	pútaotáng 葡萄糖	（名）	glucose	20.	tǐwēnjì 体温计	（名）	thermometer
21.	dǎzhēn 打针	（动）	give/have an injection	22.	shūyè/diàozhēn 输液/吊针	（动）	fluid infusion, intravenous drip
23.	yàofāng 药方	（名）	prescription	24.	fāyàochù 发药处	（名）	medicine-taking place

☆ **练 习**（Exercises） ☆

一、读词组（Read the following word groups aloud）

一粒药　　　　　　　　　　　一片（piàn,量词）药

一管（guǎn,量词）药膏　　　　一贴（tiē,量词）中药

一格药水　　　　　　　　　　一瓶药水

开药方（give a prescription）　　换药（change a fresh dressing for a wound）

滴（dī）眼药水（put drops in one's eyes）　涂药膏（apply ointment）

二、选择填空（Select the appropriate phrase to fill in the blanks）

　　　每　　　各

1. 他＿＿＿个月出差一次。

2. 我＿＿＿天锻炼一个小时。

3. ＿＿＿桌＿＿＿准备两瓶红酒吧。

4. ＿＿＿人＿＿＿回答一个问题。

三、回答问题（Answer the following questions）

1. 你在哪家医院看病？这家医院好不好？

2. 你听得懂中国医生的话吗？

3. 你吃过中药吗? 你觉得有效吗?

4. 你对青霉素过敏吗?

5. 你家里准备了什么药?

四、会话（Conversations）

大卫: 这种咳嗽糖浆（tángjiāng/syrup）我以前喝过。

玛丽: 有效吗?

大卫: 很有效,不过味道不太好。

玛丽: 良药苦口（liángyào kǔkǒu/good medicine tastes bitter）嘛。

大卫: 不是苦,是太甜。这个感冒药放在我的口袋里,带到公司去吧。

玛丽: 医生说要好好休息,明天就不要上班了吧。

大卫: 不行,明天要签一个重要（zhòngyào/important）的合同,不能请假。（签合同:qiān hétong/sign a contract）

护士: 你打青霉素过敏吗?

大卫: 以前打过几次,有时候过敏,有时候不过敏。

护士: 先做一下试验吧。

……

护士: 好了。现在不过敏。请到那边准备注射。

☆ **练习答案**（Key to the exercises） ☆

二、1. 每　2. 每　3. 每　各　4. 每　各

34

Diūle Dōngxi
丢了 东西   LOST ARTICLES

Wǒ de shǒujī diū le.
1. A：我 的 手机 丢 了。 My mobile phone is lost.

Shénme shíhou diū de?
B：什么 时候 丢 的? When and where did you lose it?

Zài nǎli diū de?
在 哪里 丢 的?

Gāngcái zài fàndiàn chīfàn,
A：刚才 在 饭店 吃饭， I had dinner in a restaurant and maybe left it

kǒngpà diū zài nàr le.
恐怕 丢 在 那儿 了。 behind there.

Wǒmen huíqu zhǎo yi zhǎo ba.
B：我们 回去 找 一 找 吧。 Let's go back there to look for it.

Wǒ bǎ bāo wàngzài chūzūchē
2. A：我 把 包 忘在 出租车 I've left my bag in the taxi.

shang le.
上 了。

Yí ge xiǎoshí yǐqián chéng
一 个 小时 以前 乘 I took a taxi one hour ago and forgot to take it

219

chūzūchē, xià chē shí wàngjì
出租车，下 车 时 忘记

with me when I got out.

ná le.
拿 了。

Nǐ chéng de shì nǎge gōngsī
B：你 乘 的 是 哪个 公司

Which company did the taxi belong to?

de chē?
的 车?

Dàzhòng (Chūzū Qìchē Gōngsī).
A：大众 （出租 汽车 公司）。

Dazhong Taxi Company.

Bié zháojí, dǎ ge diànhuà
B：别 着急，打 个 电话

Don't worry. Make a call to ask them.

wènwen ba.
问问 吧。

Qǐngwèn, nǐmen jiǎndào shǒutíbāo
3. A：请问， 你们 捡到 手提包

Excuse me. Have you picked up a handbag?

méiyǒu?
没有?

Nǐ de bāo shì shénme
B：你 的 包 是 什么

What does your bag look like?

yàngzi de?
样子 的?

Hēisè de, shàngmian xiězhe
A：黑色 的， 上面 写着

It's black and there are two characters "幸福"

"xìngfú" liǎng ge zì.
"幸福" 两 个 字。

on the bag.

Lǐmian yǒu shénme dōngxi?
B：里面 有 什么 东西?

What is there inside the bag?

Yǒu hùzhào、 qiánbāo shénme
A：有 护照、 钱包 什么

There are my passport, wallet and so on, and

de. Hái yǒu yì běn 《Xiàndài
的。还 有 一 本 《现代

a *Modern English-Chinese Dictionary* as well.

Hànyǔ Cídiǎn》.
汉语 词典》。

Qiánbāo li yǒu duōshao qián?
B：钱包 里 有 多少 钱?

How much money is there in the wallet?

Jì bu qīngchu le dàgài yǒu
A：记 不 清楚注 了,大概 有

I can't remember exactly, maybe about six or

liù-qībǎi kuài ba.
六七百 块 吧。

seven hundred *yuan* .

B：Zhè shì nín de bāo ma?
这 是 您 的 包 吗？　　Is this your bag?

A：Duì, zhè jiù shì wǒ de bāo.
对，这 就 是 我 的 包。　　Yes, this is my bag. Thank you.

Xièxie!
谢谢！

4. A：Qián jǐ tiān zài gōnggòng qìchē
前 几 天 在 公共 汽车　　My wallet was stolen on a bus several days

shang bèi páshǒu tōule qiánbāo.
上 被 扒手 偷了 钱包。　　ago.

B：Nà zhēn dǎoméi a!
那 真 倒霉 啊！　　What bad luck!

☆　注　释（Note）　☆

"记不清楚"也可以说"记不得"、"想不起来"。

"记不清楚"has the same meaning as"记不得"and "想不起来".

(1) Xiǎo shíhou de shìqing, wǒ yìdiǎnr yě jìbude le.
小 时候 的 事情，我 一点儿 也 记不得 了。　I remain no memory of my childhood at all.

(2) Tā de dìzhǐ, wǒ xiǎng bu qǐlái le.
他 的 地址，我 想 不 起来 了。　I cannot remember his address.

☆　句型提示（Sentence pattern references）　☆

1. 里面有什么东西？　　请参看 305 页句型 26。
2. 有护照、钱包什么的。　　请参看 382 页句型 199。
3. 记不清楚了，大概有六七百块吧。　　请参看 345 页句型 115。
4. 前几天在公共汽车上被扒手偷了钱包。　请参看 329 页句型 79。

☆　词语用法举例（Examples for usage of the words）　☆

1. 恐怕丢在那儿了

(1) Tiān zhème àn, kǒngpà yào xià yǔ le.
天 这么 暗，恐怕 要 下 雨 了。

(2) Zhème wǎn, tā kǒngpà bù lái le.
这么 晚，他 恐怕 不 来 了。

(3) Zhè jiàn shì, yì tiān kǒngpà zuò bu wán.
这 件 事，一 天 恐怕 做 不 完。

(4) Nídàyī, liǎngbǎi kuài kǒngpà mǎi bu dào.
呢大衣，两百 块 恐怕 买 不 到。

2. 下车时忘记拿了

(1) Yǒu jiàn shì zuótiān wàngjì gàosu nǐ le.
有 件 事 昨天 忘记 告诉 你 了。

(2) Wǒ wàngjì dài yǔsǎn le.
我 忘记 带 雨伞 了。

(3) Zǎoshang wàngjì tīng tiānqì yùbào le.
早上 忘记 听 天气 预报 了。

(4) Zhè shì túshūguǎn de shū, wǒ wàngjì huán le.
这 是 图书馆 的 书, 我 忘记 还 了。 (还:return)

3. 有护照、钱包什么的

(1) Nǐ shàngjiē mǎi diǎnr shuǐguǒ、diǎnxin shénme de ba.
你 上街 买 点儿 水果、 点心 什么 的 吧。

(2) Bǐhé li yǒu qiānbǐ、yuánzhūbǐ、xiàngpí shénme de.
笔盒 里 有 铅笔、 圆珠笔、 橡皮 什么 的。

(3) Xīngqītiān zài jiā li kànkan zázhì、xiǎoshuō shénme de.
星期天 在 家 里 看看 杂志、 小说 什么 的。

(4) Chōuti li fàngzhe xìn、wénjiàn shénme de.
抽屉 里 放着 信、 文件 什么 的。 (抽屉: drawer)

4. 记不清楚了

(1) Shēnfènzhèng hàomǎ, wǒ jì bu qīngchu.
身份证 号码, 我 记 不 清楚。

(2) Tā shì nǎ nián shēng de, wǒ jì bu qīngchu le.
他 是 哪 年 生 的, 我 记 不 清楚 了。

(3) Wǒ jì bu qīngchu tā de shǒujī hàomǎ.
我 记 不 清楚 他 的 手机 号码。

(4) Wǒ jì bu qīngchu huìyì rìqī.
我 记 不 清楚 会议 日期。

☆ 词 语 (Word list) ☆

1. 找 zhǎo	(动)	look for, seek, try to find	2. 找到 zhǎodào		have found
3. 找不到 zhǎobudào		can not find	4. 失物 招领 shīwù zhāolǐng		notice for lost properties
5. 身份证 shēnfènzhèng	(名)	identification, ID	6. 工作证 gōngzuòzhèng	(名)	employee's card
7. 学生证 xuéshēngzhèng	(名)	student's identity card	8. 居留证 jūliúzhèng	(名)	residence permit
9. 出入证 chūrùzhèng	(名)	pass	10. 眼镜 yǎnjìng	(名)	glasses, spectacles
11. 手表 shǒubiǎo	(名)	watch	12. 手套 shǒutào	(名)	gloves

13.	帽子	（名）	cap, hat	14.	雨伞	（名）	umbrella

_{máozi} above 帽子, _{yǔsǎn} above 雨伞

13. 帽子 （名） cap, hat　　14. 雨伞 （名） umbrella

15. 手绢 （名） handkerchief　　16. 挂失 （动） report the loss

☆ 练 习（Exercises） ☆

一、模仿造句（Write sentences by following the patterns and imitating the example sentences）

1. 我的伞丢在商店了。
　我的手提包丢在饭店里了。
　老师的书忘在我这儿了。

　_____

2. 我在公共汽车上丢了钱包。
　苏菲在西安丢了护照。
　我在地铁里丢了一块手表。

　_____

3. 我忘了预订座位。
　我忘了告诉他明天四点钟开会。
　他出门的时候忘了带钱包。

　_____

4. 手提包上面写着"幸福"两个字。
　纸上写着他的地址。
　那幅画儿上画着一只狗。

　_____

5. 包里有护照、钱包什么的。
　她在家里帮妈妈洗衣服、做饭什么的。
　我买了肉、鱼什么的。

　_____

二、完成对话（Complete the following conversations）

1. A：你还记得上小学时候的事吗？
　 B：_____。

2. A：_____？
　 B：我的伞是蓝色（lánsè/blue）的，上面画着一些红色的花。

3. A：_____？
　 B：我坐的是锦江（Jǐnjiāng）公司的出租车。

4. A：你把包忘在哪儿了？

B：_____。

三、回答问题（Answer the following questions）

1. 在中国你丢过东西吗？丢了什么东西？

2. 丢了东西以后怎么办？

3. 你丢的东西后来找到了吗？

4. 信用卡丢了以后怎么办？

四、会话（Conversation）

玛　丽：今天真高兴，买了这么多东西。

于雪来：玛丽，你买了两套衣服是不是？

玛　丽：是啊，是两套啊。

于雪来：可是现在你手里只有一个袋子。

玛　丽：哎呀（āiyā/oh），还有一个袋子呢？

于雪来：别急，想一想，买了那套衣服以后我们去了咖啡厅……

玛　丽：从咖啡厅出来还有。然后我们进了时装（shízhuāng/fashionable clothes）店……一
　　　　定是忘在那个时装店里了。

于雪来：那我们回去找找吧。

玛　丽：小姐，你还记得我吗？我刚才在这儿买了一条裙子。

售货员：对，是你。你是回来找东西的吧？

玛　丽：那么说，你捡到了？

售货员：你看，这个袋子是你的吗？

玛　丽：是的，是的。里面是一套新买的衣服，蓝色的。

于雪来：刚买的。我想发票也在里面吧，四百四十八块呢。

售货员：没错，里面有一张发票。

玛　丽：谢谢你。

☆　**练习答案**（Key to the exercises）　☆

二、1. B：记得

　　2. A：你的伞是什么样子的

　　3. A：你坐哪个公司的车

　　4. B：忘在公共汽车上了

35　在　百货　商店　IN A DEPARTMENT STORE

Zài　Bǎihuò　Shāngdiàn

1. A：**(请)　给　我　看看　那　件**
　　(Qǐng)　gěi　wǒ　kànkan　nà　jiàn
　　衬衣。
　　chènyī.
　　Please show me that shirt.

B：**您　要　什么　颜色　的?**
　　Nín　yào　shénme　yánsè　de?
　　What color do you like?

A：**(要)　白色　的。**
　　(Yào)　báisè　de.
　　White.

　　这　件　好像　太　长
　　Zhè　jiàn　hǎoxiàng　tài　cháng
　　了，有　短　点儿　的　吗?
　　le,　yǒu　duǎn　diǎnr　de　ma?
　　This one seems too long. Do you have a shorter one?

B：**这　件　怎么样?**
　　Zhè　jiàn　zěnmeyàng?
　　How about this one?

A：**这　件　长短　正好，**
　　Zhè　jiàn　chángduǎn　zhènghǎo,
　　不过注1**艳　了　一点儿。**
　　búguò　yàn　le　yìdiǎnr.
　　The length is OK, but it seems too gaudy.

B：Nàme, zhè jiàn sù de kěyǐ
那么，这 件 素 的 可以
ma?
吗?
Then, how about this plain color one?

Nín zhè niánjì chuān zhèng héshì.
您 这 年纪 穿 正 合适。
It suits your age.

A：Wǒ bù zěnme 注2 xǐhuan zhè
我 不 怎么 注2 喜欢 这
zhǒng yánsè.
种 颜色。
I don't really like the color.

B：Zhè zhǒng yánsè xǐhuan ma?
这 种 颜色 喜欢 吗?
How about this color?

A：Zhè jiàn wǒ hěn xǐhuan,
这 件 我 很 喜欢,
jiù yào zhè jiàn ba.
就 要 这 件 吧。
I like this one very much. I'll take it.

2. A：Zhè shuāng xié, wǒ shìshi
这 双 鞋, 我 试试
kěyǐ ma?
可以 吗?
May I try on this pair of shoes?

B：Kěyǐ, qǐng ba.
可以, 请 吧。
Sure, please.

A：Xiétóu tài zhǎi le.
鞋头 太 窄 了。
The toe cap seems too narrow.

B：Nà jiù shìshi zhè shuāng.
那 就 试试 这 双。
Then try this pair please.

A：Zhè shuāng zhènghǎo.
这 双 正好。
It fits exactly.

Yǒu bié de yàngzi ma?
有 别 的 样子 吗?
Are there other styles?

B：Yǒu, zhè shuāng zěnmeyàng?
有, 这 双 怎么样?
Yes. How about this pair?

A：Zhège yàngzi hěn hǎo.
这个 样子 很 好。
It looks very nice.

C：Zhè shuāng tài guì le, háishi
这 双 太 贵 了, 还是
mǎi nà zhǒng hǎo.
买 那 种 好。
It is too expensive. Better buy that pair.

A：Wǒ fēicháng xǐhuan zhè zhǒng
我 非常 喜欢 这 种
I like this style very much. I shall buy it even

shìyàng, jíshǐ guì yě yào mǎi.
式样，即使 贵 也 要 买。 though it's expensive.

Rúguǒ yǒu zhìliàng wèntí,
B：如果 有 质量 问题， If there are quality problems, we can replace

kěyǐ tuìhuàn.
可以 退换。 it or refund your money.

☆ 注 释 (Notes) ☆

1. "不过"表示转折,比"但是"的转折语气轻一些,常在口语中使用。
"不过"indicates a turn in mood. It is not as strong as "但是" and usually used in spoken language.

Zhège hěn piányi, búguò wǒ bú tài xǐhuan.
(1) 这个 很 便宜， 不过 我 不 太 喜欢。 This one is very cheap, but I don't like it much.

Zhège rén wǒ jiànguo, búguò xiǎngbuqǐ tā de míngzi le.
(2) 这个 人 我 见过， 不过 想不起 他 的 名字 了。 I have met this man before, but I could not remember his name.

2. "不怎么"和"不太"意思差不多。
The meanings of "不怎么" and "不太" are close.

Zhè běn shū bù zěnme hǎo.
(1) 这 本 书 不 怎么 好。 This book is not very good.

Zhège fángjiān bù zěnme liàng.
(2) 这个 房间 不 怎么 亮。 This room is not very bright.

☆ 句型提示 (Sentence pattern references) ☆

1. 有短点儿的吗? 请参看 342 页句型 109。
2. 这件长短正好,不过艳了一点儿。 请参看 342 页句型 108。
3. 这件长短正好,不过艳了一点儿。 请参看 391 页句型 215。
4. 还是买那种好。 请参看 325 页句型 71。
5. 即使贵也要买。 请参看 388 页句型 211。

☆ 词语用法举例 (Examples for usage of the words) ☆

1. 有短点儿的吗
Zhège fángjiān tài xiǎo, yǒu dà diǎnr de ma?
(1) 这个 房间 太 小， 有 大 点儿 的 吗?

Zhè jiàn dàyī tài shòu, yǒu féi diǎnr de ma?
(2) 这 件 大衣 太 瘦， 有 肥 点儿 的 吗?

(3)　_{Zhè zhǒng diǎnxin tài tián. Wǒ yào dàn diǎnr de.}
这　种　点心　太　甜。我　要　淡　点儿　的。

(4)　_{Wǒ xǐhuan qīngdàn diǎnr de cài.}
我　喜欢　清淡　点儿　的　菜。

2. 这件长短正好

(1)　_{Zhè jiàn chènyī féishòu zhènghǎo.}
这　件　衬衣　肥瘦　正好。　（肥瘦：degree of tightness）

(2)　_{Zhè shuāng xié dàxiǎo zhènghǎo.}
这　双　鞋　大小　正好。　（大小：the size）

(3)　_{Zhège cài xiándàn zhènghǎo.}
这个　菜　咸淡　正好。　（咸淡：degree of saltiness）

(4)　_{Zhè jiàn máoyī hòubáo zhènghǎo.}
这　件　毛衣　厚薄　正好。　（厚薄：degree of thickness）

3. 我试试可以吗

(1)　A：_{Nǐ huì qí zìxíngchē ma?}
你　会　骑　自行车　吗？

　　B：_{Hěn jiǔ méi qí le, wǒ shìshi ba.}
很　久　没　骑　了，我　试试　吧。

(2)　A：_{Nǐ néng chī là de ma?}
你　能　吃　辣　的　吗？

　　B：_{Bù néng chī, búguò jīntiān wǒ xiǎng shìshi.}
不　能　吃，不过　今天　我　想　试试。

(3)　_{Zhège cài hěn róngyì zuò de, nǐ lái shìshi ba.}
这个　菜　很　容易　做　的，你　来　试试　吧。

(4)　_{Nǐ shìshi yòng Hànyǔ dǎ diànhuà.}
你　试试　用　汉语　打　电话。

☆　词　语（Word list）　☆

1. _{fúzhuāngdiàn}
服装店　（名）clothing store

2. _{xiédiàn}
鞋店　（名）shoe store

3. _{shòuhuòyuán}
售货员　（名）shop assistant, salesclerk

4. _{gùkè}
顾客　（名）customer

5. _{lǐngzi}
领子　（名）collar

6. _{xiùzi}
袖子　（名）sleeve

7. _{niǔkòu}
钮扣　（名）button

8. _{chǐcun}
尺寸　（名）size

9. _{dàhào}
大号　（形）large-size

10. _{zhōnghào}
中号　（形）middle-size

11. _{xiǎohào}
小号　（形）small-size

12. _{féi}
肥　（形）loose, large

13.	zhǎi/shòu 窄/瘦	（形）	narrow, tight	14.	shēn 深	（形）	dark, deep
15.	qiǎn 浅	（形）	light, pale	16.	hóngsè 红色	（名）	red
17.	fěnhóng 粉红	（形）	pink	18.	lǜsè 绿色	（名）	green
19.	mòlǜ 墨绿	（形）	blackish green	20.	cǎolǜ 草绿	（形）	grass green
21.	lánsè 蓝色	（名）	blue	22.	shēnlán 深蓝	（形）	dark blue
23.	tiānlán 天蓝	（形）	sky blue	24.	hēisè 黑色	（名）	black
25.	báisè 白色	（名）	white	26.	zǐsè 紫色	（名）	purple, violet
27.	huángsè 黄色	（名）	yellow	28.	chásè 茶色	（名）	brown, dark brown
29.	jīnsè 金色	（名）	golden	30.	yínsè 银色	（名）	silvery
31.	huīsè 灰色	（名）	gray	32.	píxié 皮鞋	（名）	leather shoes
33.	gāogēnxié 高跟鞋	（名）	high-heel shoes	34.	liángxié 凉鞋	（名）	sandals
35.	xuēzi 靴子	（名）	boots	36.	tuōxié 拖鞋	（名）	slippers
37.	xiédài 鞋带	（名）	shoelace	38.	xiéyóu 鞋油	（名）	shoe polish, shoe cream
39.	shímáo 时髦	（形）	fashionable	40.	lǐngdài 领带	（名）	tie
41.	guàng 逛	（动）	stroll, ramble, roam	42.	liàozi 料子	（名）	material for making clothes, woolen fabric
43.	páizi 牌子	（名）	brand	44.	gāodàng 高档	（形）	high-grade, superior quality
45.	xiūxiánfú 休闲服	（名）	casual clothes	46.	zhìfú 制服	（名）	uniform
47.	límǐ 厘米	（量）	centimeter	48.	mǐ 米	（量）	meter
49.	chǐ 尺	（名）	scale				

☆　练　习（Exercises）　☆

一、读词语（Read the following word groups aloud）
1. 长短　　　大小　　　厚薄　　　深浅
2. 长度　　　尺寸　　　颜色　　　价格
3. 长短正好　时间正好　咸淡正好　数量（shùliàng/amount）正好

二、模仿造句（Write sentences by following the patterns and imitating the example sentences)

1. 有短点儿的吗？
   有厚点儿的吗？
   有颜色浅点儿的吗？

   _____

2. 您这年纪穿这件正合适。
   这样的天气穿毛衣正合适。
   这个房间两个人住正合适。

   _____

3. 我不怎么喜欢这个样子。
   我不怎么喜欢红色。
   我不怎么看电视。

   _____

三、会话（Conversation）

玛　丽：卡尔，你看，这件格子（gézi/check）上衣怎么样？
卡　尔：挺好看的。
玛　丽：小姐，这是棉布（miánbù/cotton cloth）的吗？
售货员：是的，是全棉的，穿在身上很舒服。
玛　丽：请你拿一件八十厘米的。
售货员：对不起，八十厘米的卖完了。那种样子的有八十厘米的。
玛　丽：可是我不喜欢那样的花纹（huāwén/pattern）。还是这种格子的好。
售货员：这种格子的有八十五厘米的，您要不要？
玛　丽：大了点儿。
售货员：小孩子长（zhǎng/grow up）得快，买大一点儿的没有关系。
玛　丽：说得对，就买这种格子的。
售货员：有黄色、褐色和浅蓝色，您要哪一种？
卡　尔：我要黄色的。

36 Zài Shūdiàn
在 书店　　IN A BOOK STORE

1. A: Qǐngwèn, yǒu wèi wàiguórén
   请问， 有 为 外国人
   biān de Hànyǔ jiàokēshū ma?
   编 的 汉语 教科书 吗?

   Excuse me, do you have Chinese language textbooks for foreigners?

   B: Yǒu, zhè běn 《Wàiguórén Xué
   有， 这 本 《外国人 学
   Hànyǔ》 hěn chàngxiāo.
   汉语》 很 畅销。

   Yes. This *Chinese for Foreigners* is one of the best sellers.

   Nín fānfan ba. Hái fù yǒu
   您 翻翻 吧。还 附 有
   guāngpán.
   光盘。

   Please have a look at it. And there is a CD included.

   A: Hěn shíyòng.
   很 实用。

   It's quite practical.

   B: Shì de, hěn shòu huānyíng de.
   是 的, 很 受 欢迎 的。

   Yes, it is very popular.

   A: Yào yì běn.
   要 一 本。

   I'll take this one.

2. A：
Yǒu guānyú Hànyǔ yǔfǎ de
有 关于 汉语 语法 的

Do you have any books on Chinese grammar?

shū ma?
书 吗?

Wǒ yào Hàn-Yīng duìzhào de.
我 要 汉英 对照 的。

I want a Chinese – English bilingual one.

B：
Tài bù qiǎo le, gāng
太 不 巧 了注，刚

Unfortunately they were just sold out.

màiwán.
卖完。

A：
Tài yíhàn le.
太 遗憾 了。

It's really a pity.

B：
Nín kěyǐ yùdìng.
您 可以 预订。

You can reserve a copy.

Qǐng nín dēngjì yíxià.
请 您 登记 一下。

Please fill out this reservation form.

Shū yí dào, wǒmen jiù huì
书 一 到，我们 就 会

We will inform you as soon as we have the

tōngzhī nín de.
通知 您 的。

book.

3. A：
Zhè běn shū de xiàcè,
这 本 书 的 下册，

Is there a second part of this book?

yǒu ma?
有 吗?

B：
Hái méi chūbǎn.
还 没 出版。

It hasn't been published yet.

A：
Gūjì shénme shíhou cái néng
估计 什么 时候 才 能

When do you think I can get one?

mǎidào?
买到?

B：
Míngnián cái néng chūbǎn.
明年 才 能 出版。

It won't be published until next year.

4. A：
Yǒu Shànghǎi dìtú ma?
有 上海 地图 吗?

Do you have any Shanghai maps?

B：
Duìbuqǐ, màiwán le, nín guò
对不起，卖完 了，您 过

Sorry, they are all sold out. Please come

jǐ tiān zài lái kànkan ba.
几 天 再 来 看看 吧。

back to try in several days.

☆ 注 释(Note) ☆

"不巧"表示没赶上某一时机。

" 不巧 " here means to miss an opportunity.

☆ 句型提示(Sentence pattern references) ☆

1. 有为外国人编的汉语教科书吗？   请参看 359 页句型 148。
2. 有关于汉语语法的书吗？   请参看 363 页句型 155。
3. 您可以预订。   请参看 336 页句型 94。
4. 书一到,我们就会通知您的。   请参看 386 页句型 206。
5. 估计什么时候才能买到？   请参看 340 页句型 102。
6. 估计什么时候才能买到？   请参看 349 页句型 126。
7. 明年才能出版。   请参看 371 页句型 174。

☆ 词语用法举例(Examples for usage of the words) ☆

1. 这本《外国人学汉语》很畅销

    Zuìjìn èrshíjiǔ yīngcùn cǎisè diànshìjī hěn chàngxiāo.
(1) 最近 二十九 英寸 彩色 电视机 很 畅销。 (英寸:inch)

    Zhège páizi de yīfu zài Shànghǎi hěn chàngxiāo.
(2) 这个 牌子 的 衣服 在 上海 很 畅销。

    Wǒmen chǎng de chǎnpǐn chàngxiāo Ōu Měi.
(3) 我们 厂 的 产品 畅销 欧 美。 (欧美:Europe and America)

    Chǎnpǐn néng bu néng chàngxiāo, guānjiàn shì zhìliàng.
(4) 产品 能 不 能 畅销, 关键 是 质量。 (关键:key)

2. 您翻翻吧

    Hǎo jǐ tiān de bàozhǐ dōu méi kàn, xiànzài zhǐ néng fānfan le.
(1) 好 几 天 的 报纸 都 没 看, 现在 只 能 翻翻 了。

    Zhè běn shū wǒ zhǐ fānle yíxià, méi shíjiān kàn.
(2) 这 本 书 我 只 翻了 一下, 没 时间 看。

    Wǎnbào, ràng wǒ fān yi fān zài gěi nǐ.
(3) 晚报, 让 我 翻 一 翻 再 给 你。

    Zhè běn zìdiǎn, wǒ fānle yíxià, biān de búcuò.
(4) 这 本 字典, 我 翻了 一下, 编 得 不错。

3. 太不巧了

    Nǐ Xiānsheng zài jiā ma?
(1) A: 你 先生 在 家 吗？

Tài bù qiǎo le, tā chūchāi qù le.
B：太 不 巧 了，他 出差 去 了。

Gěi wǒ jǐ zhāng xìnzhǐ, hǎo ma?
（2）A：给 我 几 张 信纸，好 吗?

Tài bù qiǎo le, wǒ de yě yòngwán le.
B：太 不 巧 了，我 的 也 用完 了。

Nǐ cóng nàme yuǎn lái, wǒ yòu mǎshàng yào chūchāi, zhēnshi tài bù
（3）你 从 那么 远 来，我 又 马上 要 出差，真是 太 不
qiǎo le.
巧 了。

4. 太遗憾了

Wǒ yǒu liǎng zhāng míngwǎn yīnyuèhuì de piào, yìqǐ qù tīng ba.
（1）A：我 有 两 张 明晚 音乐会 的 票，一起 去 听 吧。

Wǒ míngtiān yào chūchāi, tài yíhàn le.
B：我 明天 要 出差，太 遗憾 了。

Zhè cì méi néng zài Shànghǎi jiànmiàn, tài yíhàn le.
（2）这 次 没 能 在 上海 见面，太 遗憾 了。

Bù néng cānjiā tóngxué jùhuì, tài yíhàn le.
（3）不 能 参加 同学 聚会，太 遗憾 了。 （同学聚会：gathering of school-
mates）

Tài yíhàn le, wǒ méi mǎidào piào.
（4）太 遗憾 了，我 没 买到 票。

5. 估计什么时候才能买到

Zhè cì kǎoshì wǒ méi kǎohǎo, gūjì bù jígé.
（1）这 次 考试 我 没 考好，估计 不 及格。 （及格：pass a test）

Tīngshuō tā bìng le, gūjì bù néng cānjiā yùndònghuì le.
（2）听说 他 病 了，估计 不 能 参加 运动会 了。 （运动会：games,
sports meet）

Wù zhème dà, wǒ gūjì fēijī bù néng qǐfēi.
（3）雾 这么 大，我 估计 飞机 不 能 起飞。

Zhège gōngchéng, gūjì yào liǎng nián cái néng wánchéng.
（4）这个 工程，估计 要 两 年 才 能 完成。

☆ 词 语（Word list） ☆

bàozhǐ
1. 报纸 （名） newspaper

rìbào
2. 日报 （名） daily

wǎnbào
3. 晚报 （名） evening paper

zázhì
4. 杂志 （名） magazine

huàbào
5. 画报 （名） pictorial

xiǎoshuō
6. 小说 （名） novel, fiction

234

7.	shīgē 诗歌	（名）	poem	8.	sǎnwén 散文	（名）	prose
9.	xìjù 戏剧	（名）	drama, play	10.	gùshi 故事	（名）	story, tale
11.	mànhuà 漫画	（名）	cartoon	12.	cānkǎoshū 参考书	（名）	reference book
13.	zīliào 资料	（名）	material	14.	shǒucè 手册	（名）	handbook, manual
15.	kējì 科技	（名）	science and technology	16.	wényì 文艺	（名）	literature and art
17.	zhèngzhì 政治	（名）	politics	18.	jīngjì 经济	（名）	economy
19.	zhéxué 哲学	（名）	philosophy	20.	lìshǐ 历史	（名）	history
21.	fǎlǜ 法律	（名）	law	22.	yīxué 医学	（名）	medicine
23.	yīnyuè 音乐	（名）	music	24.	tǐyù 体育	（名）	sport
25.	dúzhě 读者	（名）	reader	26.	zuòzhě 作者	（名）	author
27.	yìzhě 译者	（名）	translator	28.	biānzhě 编者	（名）	editor; author
29.	jìzhě 记者	（名）	reporter, journalist, correspondent	30.	bàoshè 报社	（名）	newspaper publisher
31.	chūbǎnshè 出版社	（名）	publisher, publishing house	32.	yuèkān 月刊	（名）	monthly
33.	zhōukān 周刊	（名）	weekly	34.	yuánbǎn 原版	（名）	original edition

☆ 练 习 (Exercises) ☆

一、模仿造句（Write sentences by following the patterns and imitating the example sentences）

1. 这是为外国人编的汉语教科书。
   这是为孩子写的故事。
   这是公司为职员准备的茶和咖啡。

   _____

2. 我想买关于汉语语法的书。
   我看过关于中国历史的戏剧。
   他订了很多关于旅游的杂志。

   _____

二、回答问题 (Answer the following questions)

1. 你的汉语词典是哪个出版社出版的？是什么时候出版的？

2. 最近你们国家什么书最畅销？

3. 你常看什么方面（fāngmiàn/field）的书？

4. 你看过中文原版书吗？

三、造句（Sentence-making）

1. 估计

2. 遗憾

3. 登记

四、完成对话（Complete the conversations）

1. A：这套书一共有几册？

　　B：＿＿＿＿＿＿＿＿＿＿＿。

　　A：只买上册可以吗？

　　B：＿＿＿＿＿＿＿＿＿＿＿。

2. A：我到书店的时候，那本书刚卖完。

　　B：＿＿＿＿＿＿＿＿＿＿＿。

3. A：他出差了，不能来和大家见面了。

　　B：＿＿＿＿＿＿＿＿＿＿＿。

4. A：请问，老刘在吗？

　　B：哎呀，＿＿＿＿＿＿＿＿＿＿＿，他刚出去。

五、会话（Conversation）

玛　丽：请问，有关于汉语水平（shuǐpíng/level）考试（HSK）的书吗？

售货员：在那边。有好几种。

玛　丽：老师，您看我买哪一本合适？

老　师：这两本都不错。红色封面（fēngmiàn/front cover）的这本比较深（shēn/difficult, abstruse），白的那本浅（qiǎn/simple, easy）一点儿。你可以看一看。

玛　丽：这本太难了，大部分不懂。还是买那本吧。我还想买关于中国文化（wénhuà/culture）的书。

老　师：玛丽，这本书很好。你看，《中国社会文化礼俗》。

玛　丽：太好了。我买一本。

☆　**练习答案**（Key to the exercises）　☆

四、1. B：三册　可以　2. B：太不巧了　3. B：太遗憾了　4. B：太不巧了

37 游览 上海 SIGHTSEEING IN SHANGHAI

Yóulǎn Shànghǎi

A: Shànghǎi yǒu shénme dìfang hǎowán?
上海 有 什么 地方 好玩?

What interesting places are there in Shanghai?

B: Hǎowán de dìfang hěn duō Yǒu
好玩 的 地方 很 多。 有

There are many interesting places such as the

Wàitān、 Yùyuán、 Rénmín Guǎngchǎng
外滩、 豫园、 人民 广场

Bund, Yuyuan Garden, People's Square and

děngděng.
等等。

so on.

A: Wàitān hé Yùyuán, wǒmen yǐjīng
外滩 和 豫园, 我们 已经

We've been to the Bund and Yuyuan Garden,

qùguo le, Rénmín Guǎngchǎng hái
去过 了, 人民 广场 还

but not to People's Square.

méi qù.
没 去。

C: Tīngshuō Rénmín Guǎngchǎng shì
听说 人民 广场 是

I've heard that People's Square is at the cen-

Shànghǎi Shì de zhōngxīn, shì ma?
上海 市 的 中心, 是 吗?

ter of Shanghai. Is that true?

D: Shì de. Guǎngchǎng de běimian
是 的。 广场 的 北面
yǒu Rénmín Dàshà. Shànghǎi Shì
有 人民 大厦。 上海 市
Rénmín Zhèngfǔ jiù zài lǐmian.
人民 政府 就 在 里面。

Yes. In the north end of the Square is the People's Mansion, where the Shanghai Municipal Hall is also located.

B: Rénmín Dàshà de xībian yǒu
人民 大厦 的 西边 有
yījiǔjiǔbā nián jiànchéng de
一九九八 年 建成 的
Shànghǎi Dàjùyuàn.
上海 大剧院。

To the west of the People's Mansion is the Shanghai Grand Theater, which was completed in 1998.

A: Shànghǎi Bówùguǎn yě zài Rénmín
上海 博物馆 也 在 人民
Guǎngchǎng ma?
广场 吗？

Is the Shanghai Museum also in the People's Square?

B: Shì de, zài guǎngchǎng de
是 的， 在 广场 的
nánmian.
南面。

Yes, in the south of the Square.

A: Qù Rénmín Guǎngchǎng chéng jǐ
去 人民 广场 乘 几
lù chē hǎo?
路 车 好?

Which bus shall we take to People's Square?

B: Qù Rénmín Guǎngchǎng chéng dìtiě
去 人民 广场 乘 地铁
hěn fāngbiàn.
很 方便。

It's very convenient to get to People's Square by subway.

D: Xiūxirì hěn duō rén dàizhe
休息日 很 多 人 带着
xiǎoháir qù guǎngchǎng wán.
小孩儿 去 广场 玩。

Many people take their children to the Square on holidays.

C: Hái yǒu bié de dìfang hǎowán ma?
还 有 别 的 地方 好玩 吗？

Are there other interesting places?

D: Pǔdōng de Dōngfāngmíngzhū
浦东 的 东方明珠
Guǎngbōdiànshìtǎ, yīnggāi qù
广播电视塔， 应该 去
kànkan.
看看。

The Oriental Pearl TV Tower in Pudong is one place you ought to see.

B：Dēngshang nàge tǎ, kěyǐ kàndào
登上 那个 塔，可以 看到
You can get a full view of Shanghai when you

Shànghǎi de quánjǐng.
上海 的 全景。
get to the top of the Tower.

A：Nà jiù fēi qù bùkě le.
那 就 非 去 不可 了。
So, we must go there.

C：Nǐmen néng gěi wǒmen dāng
你们 能 给 我们 当
Would you please be our guide?

dǎoyóu ma?
导游 吗?

D：Dāngrán kěyǐ.
当然 可以。
With pleasure.

C：Nà jiù máfan nǐmen chōukòng péi
那 就 麻烦 你们 抽空 陪
Many thanks. Please arrange a time to

wǒmen qù ba.
我们 去 吧。
accompany us there.

D：Xíng. Wǒmen chéng Shànghǎi
行注。 我们 乘 上海
All right. Let's take the Jinjiang Tour Bus

Jǐnjiāng Guānguāng Bāshì ba.
锦江 观光 巴士 吧。
there.

C：Hǎo de, zài shénme dìfang
好 的，在 什么 地方
OK. Where do we get on the bus?

shàng chē?
上 车?

D：Zài Màomíng Nánlù Huāyuán
在 茂名 南路 花园
At the gate of the Garden Hotel in Maoming

Fàndiàn ménkǒu shàng chē.
饭店 门口 上 车。
Nanlu (South Maoming Rd.)

C：Nǎli néng mǎidào Shànghǎi
哪里 能 买到 上海
Do you know where I can buy a Shanghai

dìtú, nǐ zhīdao ma?
地图，你 知道 吗?
map?

D：Shūdiàn yǒu mài.
书店 有 卖。
You can buy it in book stores.

C：Wǒmen gāng dào Shànghǎi, hái
我们 刚 到 上海，还
We are newcomers and are not familiar with

bú tài rènshi lù.
不 太 认识 路。
Shanghai.

☆　注　释(Note)　☆

"行"表示允许,和"可以"一样。否定式是"不行"。

"行", like "可以", means to give permission. Its negative form is "不行".

(1) A：帮 个 忙, 行 吗?　　Can you give me a hand?
      Bāng ge máng, xíng ma?

    B：行。 说 吧。　　Sure. Just tell me.
      Xíng. Shuō ba.

(2) A：在 这里 抽烟 行 吗?　　Can I smoke here?
      Zài zhèli chōuyān xíng ma?

    B：不行, 不 能 抽。　　No, you can't.
      Bùxíng, bù néng chōu.

☆　句型提示(Sentence pattern references)　☆

1. 浦东的东方明珠广播电视塔,应该去看看。　请参看 338 页句型 98。
2. 哪里能买到上海地图,你知道吗?　请参看 295 页句型 5。

☆　词语用法举例(Examples for usage of the words)　☆

1. 去人民广场乘地铁很方便

  (1) 这里 的 交通 很 方便。
      Zhèli de jiāotōng hěn fāngbiàn.

  (2) 公寓 周围 有 很 多 商店, 买 东西 很 方便。　(周围:around)
      Gōngyù zhōuwéi yǒu hěn duō shāngdiàn, mǎi dōngxi hěn fāngbiàn.

  (3) 地铁 建成 后, 这 一带 的 交通 比 以前 方便 多 了。
      Dìtiě jiànchéng hòu, zhè yídài de jiāotōng bǐ yǐqián fāngbiàn duō le.

  (4) 从 上海 去 苏州 很 方便, 乘 汽车、 火车 都 行。
      Cóng Shànghǎi qù Sūzhōu hěn fāngbiàn, chéng qìchē、 huǒchē dōu xíng.

2. 休息日很多人带着小孩儿去广场玩

  (1) 我 不 认识 路, 你 带 我 去 吧。
      Wǒ bú rènshi lù, nǐ dài wǒ qù ba.

  (2) 我 今天 要 带 孩子 去 看病。
      Wǒ jīntiān yào dài háizi qù kànbìng.

  (3) 下午 会 下 雨, 记住 带 伞。
      Xiàwǔ huì xià yǔ, jìzhù dài sǎn.

  (4) 不准 带 危险品 上 车。
      Bùzhǔn dài wēixiǎnpǐn shàng chē.

3. 还有别的地方好玩吗

(1) Zhèxiē shì wǒ de, bié de dōu shì tā de.
这些 是 我 的，别 的 都 是 他 的。

(2) Shuǐguǒ zhōng, wǒ zuì xǐhuan lí, bié de bú tài xǐhuan.
水果 中，我 最 喜欢 梨，别 的 不 太 喜欢。

(3) Hái yǒu bié de yàngzi ma?
还 有 别 的 样子 吗？

(4) Zhè tào cíqì zuì hǎokàn, bié de bú tài hǎo.
这 套 瓷器 最 好看，别 的 不 太 好。

4. 应该去看看

(1) Dào Bālí yīnggāi qù Āifēi'ěr Tiětǎ wánwan.
到 巴黎 应该 去 埃菲尔 铁塔 玩玩。

(2) Nǐ lái Zhōngguó, yīnggāi chángchang Zhōngguócài.
你 来 中国，应该 尝尝 中国菜。

(3) Zhè běn xiǎoshuō xiě de hěn hǎo, nǐ yīnggāi kànkan.
这 本 小说 写 得 很 好，你 应该 看看。

(4) Xī Hú fēngjǐng hěn měi, yīnggāi qù wánwan.
西 湖 风景 很 美，应该 去 玩玩。

5. 那就非去不可了

(1) Lái Zhōngguó, fēi qù Chángchéng bùkě.
来 中国，非 去 长城 不可。

(2) Qù Rìběn, fēi chī shēngyúpiàn bùkě.
去 日本，非 吃 生鱼片 不可。

(3) Zhè jiàn shì fēi zhèyàng zuò bùkě.
这 件 事 非 这样 做 不可。

(4) Nǐ fēi dàoqiàn bùkě. （道歉：apologize）
你 非 道歉 不可。

6. 你们能给我们当导游吗

(1) Tā yìzhí dāng fānyì.
他 一直 当 翻译。

(2) Xiǎo Míng xīwàng zhǎngdà yǐhòu dāng lǜshī.
小 明 希望 长大 以后 当 律师。

(3) Tā de lǐxiǎng shì dāng yīshēng.
他 的 理想 是 当 医生。

(4) Dāng bàba māma de, zǒng wèi háizi cāoxīn. （操心：worry about）
当 爸爸 妈妈 的，总 为 孩子 操心。

7. 麻烦你们抽空陪我们去吧

Zhège yuè yào chōukòng huí lǎojiā kànkan fùmǔ.
(1) 这个 月 要 抽空 回 老家 看看 父母。

Tā měi tiān chōu yí ge xiǎoshí xuéxí Yīngyǔ.
(2) 他 每 天 抽 一 个 小时 学习 英语。

Jīntiān yào chōu yìdiǎnr shíjiān qù lǐfà.
(3) 今天 要 抽 一点儿 时间 去 理发。

Zuótiān chōukòng qùle yí tàng túshūguǎn.
(4) 昨天 抽空 去了 一 趟 图书馆。 （趟：量词）

☆ 词 语 (Word list) ☆

	chéngshì				nóngcūn		
1.	城市	（名）	city	2.	农村	（名）	countryside, rural area
3.	zhǎnlǎnguǎn 展览馆	（名）	exhibition hall	4.	měishùguǎn 美术馆	（名）	art gallery
5.	tǐyùguǎn 体育馆	（名）	gymnasium	6.	jìniànguǎn 纪念馆	（名）	memorial hall
7.	yīnyuètīng 音乐厅	（名）	concert hall	8.	yóulèchǎng 游乐场	（名）	amusement park
9.	dòngwùyuán 动物园	（名）	zoo	10.	zhíwùyuán 植物园	（名）	botanical garden
11.	ménpiào 门票	（名）	admission ticket	12.	lǎohǔ 老虎	（名）	tiger
13.	shīzi 狮子	（名）	lion	14.	xiàng 象	（名）	elephant
15.	hóuzi 猴子	（名）	monkey	16.	xióngmāo 熊猫	（名）	panda
17.	lù 鹿	（名）	deer	18.	niú 牛	（名）	cattle
19.	mǎ 马	（名）	horse	20.	yáng 羊	（名）	sheep
21.	gǒu 狗	（名）	dog	22.	māo 猫	（名）	cat
23.	niǎo 鸟	（名）	bird	24.	gēzi 鸽子	（名）	pigeon, dove
25.	kǒngquè 孔雀	（名）	peacock	26.	húdié 蝴蝶	（名）	butterfly
27.	shù 树	（名）	tree	28.	zhúzi 竹子	（名）	bamboo
29.	yè 叶	（名）	leaf	30.	huā 花	（名）	flower, blossom
31.	méigui 玫瑰	（名）	rose	32.	méihuā 梅花	（名）	plum blossom
33.	héhuā 荷花	（名）	lotus	34.	mòlì 茉莉	（名）	jasmine
35.	lánhuā 兰花	（名）	orchid	36.	júhuā 菊花	（名）	chrysanthemum

37. 草 ^{cǎo}　　（名）　grass　　　　38. 草坪 ^{cǎopíng}　　（名）　lawn

☆　练　习（Exercises）　☆

一、模仿造句（Write sentences by following the patterns and imitating the example sentences）

1. 上海有很多好玩的地方,有外滩、豫园、人民广场等等。
   他家里有很多中国的东西,有中国字画、中国瓷器等等。
   她能帮妈妈做很多事,洗碗、打扫房间等等。

   _____

2. 你能给我当导游吗?
   你能给我当辅导（fǔdǎo/tutor）老师吗?
   你能给我儿子当武术（wǔshù/martial arts）老师吗?

   _____

3. 哪里能买到上海地图?
   哪里能看到京剧?
   哪里能找到张先生?

   _____

二、用括号中的词语完成对话（Complete the following conversations with the words in brackets）

1. A：你一个人去吗?
   B：不,_____。（陪）

2. A：暑假你带孩子去哪儿?
   B：_____。（带）

3. A：听说图书馆有一个关于西藏（Xīzàng）的展览。
   B：好啊,_____。（抽空）

4. A：经理,李先生请你_____。（抽空）
   B：这两天没空,_____。（再说）

三、回答问题（Answer the following questions）

1. 你们国家的人喜欢到什么地方旅游?
2. 在大城市旅游,你喜欢看什么?
3. 你带孩子去过动物园吗?
4. 你喜欢自己出去旅游还是跟旅行社出去? 为什么?
5. 你的家乡有什么好玩的地方?

四、会话（Conversation）

玛丽：爸爸、妈妈，你们累了吧。

爸爸：不累。

玛丽：今天你们先好好休息一下，明天我陪你们去玩。

妈妈：好啊。你来安排（ānpái/arrange）吧。

爸爸：来之前我看过介绍，听说东方明珠电视塔很漂亮。

玛丽：是的。这是一定要去看看的。电视塔里面还有一个上海城市历史发展陈列（chénliè/exhibition）馆。

爸爸：是博物馆吗？

玛丽：是历史发展陈列馆。

卡尔：妈妈，我也要去。

爸爸：啊，卡尔没去过吗？

玛丽：两个月以前带他去看过。

卡尔：可是我还想去嘛。

妈妈：玛丽，我们的邻居岛村太太去年来中国旅行，带了几块中国的蓝印（lán yìn）花布（huā bù）回去。我很喜欢那种蓝布，你知道哪儿能买到？

玛丽：很多地方都能买到。过两天我陪您去吧。

卡尔：爷爷，野生（yěshēng）动物园也很有意思（yǒu yìsi/interesting），有老虎、狮子、大象等等。

爸爸：野生动物园嘛，就不去了。

☆ **练习答案**（Key to the exercises） ☆

二、1．B：我先生陪我去

2．B：我带他去海边

3．B：我们抽空去看一看

4．A：抽空去一下

B：过几天再说吧

38 旅游
Lǚyóu

TRAVELING

Wǒ yǒu jǐ tiān jiàqī, xiǎng
A：我 有 几 天 假期，想

I have several days holiday and want to go

qù lǚyóu.
去 旅游。

traveling.

Dǎsuan qù nǎli wán?
B：打算 去 哪里 玩?

Where do you plan to go?

Xiànzài hái méi juédìng. Nǐ
A：现在 还 没 决定。你

Haven't decided yet. Where do you

kàn qù nǎli hǎo?
看注1 去 哪里 好?

suggest?

Nǐ qùguo Hángzhōu ma?
B：你 去过 杭州 吗?

Have you ever been to Hangzhou?

Méi qùguo.
A：没 去过。

No, I haven't.

Nàme, qù Hángzhōu ba. Hángzhōu
B：那么，去 杭州 吧。 杭州

If so, go to Hangzhou. The scenery of the

de Xī Hú fēngjǐng hěn měi.
的 西湖 风景 很 美。

West Lake is beautiful.

A: Zhōngguórén cháng shuō: "Shàng
中国人 常 说: "上
yǒu tiāntáng, xià yǒu Sū Háng."
有 天堂, 下 有 苏 杭。"

There is a Chinese saying "Up above there is Paradise, down here there are Suzhou and Hangzhou."

B: Shì de, Sūzhōu、 Hángzhōu díquè
是 的, 苏州、 杭州 的确
shì hǎo dìfang.
是 好 地方。

Yes, Suzhou and Hangzhou are really good places.

A: Nà shì zhíde qù wánwan de.
那 是 值得 去 玩玩 的。

So, it is worth taking a tour there.

Qù Hángzhōu chéng shénme chē
去 杭州 乘 什么 车
zuì hǎo?
最 好?

What is the best way to get to Hangzhou?

B: Chéng huǒchē zuì kuài, yí ge
乘 火车 最 快, 一 个
duō xiǎoshí jiù dào le.
多 小时 就 到 了。

The fastest way is by train. It will take less than two hours to get there.

C: Chéng qìchē yě hěn kuài, cóng
乘 汽车 也 很 快, 从
gāosù gōnglù zǒu, zhǐ yào liǎng
高速 公路 走, 只 要 两
ge xiǎoshí.
个 小时。

Taking a coach is also very fast. It will only take you about two hours if going by the expressway.

A: Chúle Xī Hú yǐwài, hái yǒu shénme
除了 西湖 以外, 还 有 什么
dìfang hǎowán?
地方 好玩?

Are there other scenic spots besides the West Lake?

B: Hǎowán de dìfang kě duō le,
好玩 的 地方 可注2 多 了,
bǐrú Língyǐnsì、 Yuèfēimù、 Liùhétǎ
比如 灵隐寺、 岳飞墓、 六和塔
děngděng.
等等。

There are many, such as Lingyin Temple, Yuefei's Tomb, Liuheta Pagoda and so on.

C: Lìngwài, Hángzhōu jiāoqū yǒu ge
另外, 杭州 郊区 有 个
Lóngjǐngcūn, nàr chūchǎn de lǜchá
龙井村, 那儿 出产 的 绿茶

Besides, there is a Longjing Village in Hangzhou's suburb. The green tea produced there

hěn yǒumíng. Nǐ kěyǐ qù nàli
很 有名。你 可以 去 那里　　is very famous. You should visit there.
kànkan.
看看。

Wǒ tīngshuōguo, nà zhǒng lǜchá
A：我 听说过， 那 种 绿茶　　I've heard that kind of green tea is called
jiào lóngjǐngchá.
叫 龙井茶。　　Longjing Tea.

Nǐ shuō de dìfang dōu zhíde
你 说 的 地方 都 值得　　The places you mentioned are all worth
qù wán.
去 玩。　　going.

Yóulǎn Hángzhōu yào jǐ tiān?
游览 杭州 要 几 天?　　How many days shall I spend in Hangzhou for

sightseeing?

Zhìshǎo yào liǎng tiān, zuì hǎo
B：至少 要 两 天， 最 好　　At least two days, and three days is better.
yǒu sān tiān.
有 三 天。

Nǐ yí ge rén qù ma?
C：你 一 个 人 去 吗?　　Are you going there alone?

Bù, dǎsuan hé nǚpéngyou
A：不， 打算 和 女朋友　　No, I am going there with my girlfriend.
yìqǐ qù.
一起 去。

Shénme shíhou chūfā?
B：什么 时候 出发?　　When are you going?

Gēn nǚpéngyou shāngliang yǐhòu
A：跟 女朋友 商量 以后　　I will make a decision after consulting with my
zài juédìng.
再 决定。　　girlfriend.

☆ 注 释(Notes) ☆

1. 在征求对方的意见时用"你看"，表示自己的意见时用"我看"。
"你看" is used when asking other's opinion and "我看" is used when you give your own opinion.
Wǒ kàn zhè běn shū hěn yǒuqù, nǐ kàn ne?
(1) 我 看 这 本 书 很 有趣， 你 看 呢?
I think that this book is very interesting. What's your opinion?

（2）
Wǒ kàn zhège bīnguǎn búcuò, nǐ kàn ne?
我 看 这个 宾馆 不错, 你 看 呢?
I think this hotel is good. What do you think?

2. "可"跟"很"意思差不多,多用于口语。"可……了"这种格式表示感叹的语气。

"可" has the similar meaning as "很" and is used mostly in spoken language. The pattern of "可……了" expresses a feeling of surprise, excitement, etc.

（1）
Zhōngguócài kě hǎochī le.
中国菜 可 好吃 了。　　The Chinese food is delicious!

（2）
Tā Hànyǔ shuō de kě hǎo le.
他 汉语 说 得 可 好 了。　　His Chinese is excellent!

☆　句型提示（Sentence pattern references）　☆

1. 现在还没决定。	请参看 374 页句型 182。
2. 中国人常说:"上有天堂,下有苏杭。"	请参看 368 页句型 166。
3. 一个多小时就到了。	请参看 373 页句型 180。
4. 只要两个小时。	请参看 369 页句型 170。
5. 你可以去那里看看。	请参看 337 页句型 96。
6. 你说的地方都值得去玩。	请参看 369 页句型 171。

☆　词语用法举例（Examples for usage of the words）　☆

1. 现在还没决定

（1）
Xuéxiào juédìng xià ge yuè shíwǔ hào jǔxíng yùndònghuì.
学校 决定 下 个 月 十五 号 举行 运动会。　（举行: hold）

（2）
Bàba juédìng dào Xiānggǎng gōngzuò.
爸爸 决定 到 香港 工作。

（3）
Wǒ juédìng cānjiā yìbǎi mǐ sàipǎo.
我 决定 参加 一百 米 赛跑。　（一百米赛跑: 100m run）

（4）
Huí guó de rìqī hái méi juédìng.
回 国 的日期 还 没 决定。

（5）
Pài shuí chūchāi, xiànzài hái bù néng juédìng.
派 谁 出差, 现在 还 不 能 决定。　（派: send）

2. 好玩的地方可多了

（1）
Tā de nǚ'ér kě cōngming le.
她 的 女儿 可 聪明 了。

（2）
Tā de érzi kě nénggàn le.
她 的 儿子 可 能干 了。　（能干: capable）

（3）
Zuówǎn de yǎnchū kě jīngcǎi le.
昨晚 的 演出 可 精彩 了。

Nàge rén kě huài le.
(4) 那个 人 可 坏 了。

3. 你说的地方都值得去玩

Dūnhuáng hěn zhíde qù kànkan.
(1) 敦煌 很 值得 去 看看。

Zhè shì mínghuà, huā duōshao qián dōu zhíde.
(2) 这 是 名画, 花 多少 钱 都 值得。

Qù Ōuzhōu huāle hěn duō qián, dànshì hěn zhíde.
(3) 去 欧洲 花了 很 多 钱, 但是 很 值得。

Zhège shǒubiǎo zhìliàng hěn hǎo, guì yě zhíde.
(4) 这个 手表 质量 很 好, 贵 也 值得。

4. 至少要两天

Zhè cì wàichū, zhìshǎo yào dài liǎngqiān kuài qián.
(1) 这 次 外出, 至少 要 带 两千 块 钱。

Zǒule zhìshǎo sìshí fēnzhōng.
(2) 走了 至少 四十 分钟。

Lǐfàdiàn (li) rén hěn duō, zhìshǎo yào děng yí ge xiǎoshí.
(3) 理发店（里）人 很 多, 至少 要 等 一 个 小时。

Jīntiān wǒ zhìshǎo huāle wǔbǎi kuài qián.
(4) 今天 我 至少 花了 五百 块 钱。

5. 跟女朋友商量以后再决定

Wǒ gēn bàba māma shāngliang jiéhūn de shì.
(1) 我 跟 爸爸 妈妈 商量 结婚 的 事。

Wǒ gēn tóngshì shāngliang qiāndìng hétong de shì.
(2) 我 跟 同事 商量 签订 合同 的 事。

Zhè jiàn shì wǒ yào gēn xiānsheng shāngliang.
(3) 这 件 事 我 要 跟 先生 商量。

Guānyú cháhuàhuì de shì, wǒmen shāngliang yíxià ba.
(4) 关于 茶话会 的 事, 我们 商量 一下 吧。

☆ 词 语 (Word list) ☆

jǐngdiǎn
1. 景点 （名） scenic spot

shān
2. 山 （名） mountain, hill

shuǐ
3. 水 （名） water

hé
4. 河 （名） river

hú
5. 湖 （名） lake

hǎi
6. 海 （名） sea

7.	pùbù 瀑布	（名）	waterfall	8.	wēnquán 温泉	（名）	hot spring
9.	sìmiào 寺庙	（名）	temple	10.	tíngzi 亭子	（名）	pavilion
11.	lǚxíngshè 旅行社	（名）	travel agency	12.	dǎoyóutú 导游图	（名）	tourist map
13.	lǚfèi 旅费	（名）	traveling expense	14.	yóukè 游客	（名）	tourist, visitor
15.	chūfā 出发	（动）	set out, start off	16.	jíhé 集合	（动）	gather, assemble
17.	dòuliú qījiān 逗留 期间		period of stay	18.	rìchéngbiǎo 日程表	（名）	time table, schedule
19.	gǎibiàn rìchéng 改变 日程		change the schedule	20.	dàngtiān wǎngfǎn 当天 往返		one-day return trip
21.	tíqián yì tiān 提前 一 天		move up for one day	22.	tuīchí yì tiān 推迟 一 天		postpone for one day
23.	jiàqī 假期	（名）	holiday, vacation	24.	jiàrì 假日	（名）	holiday
25.	fàngjià 放假	（动）	have a holiday	26.	dùjià 度假	（动）	spend holidays
27.	huángjīnzhōu 黄金周	（名）	golden week	28.	tànxiǎn 探险	（动）	make exploration
29.	míngshèng gǔjì 名胜 古迹	（名）	scenic spots and historical sites	30.	wàngjì 旺季	（名）	busy season
31.	dànjì 淡季	（名）	off season				

☆ 练 习（Exercises） ☆

一、模仿造句（Write sentences by following the patterns and imitating the example sentences）

1. 我有很多工作,另外,有朋友要来,所以这星期不能上汉语课了。

   这个饭店的菜又好吃又便宜,另外,服务也很好。

   这个房间又大又亮,另外,从这里还可以看到远处的小山。

   _____

2. 好玩的地方可多了。

   那个节目（jiémù/program）可有意思了。

   他可能干了。

   _____

二、用括号中的词语完成对话（Complete the following conversations with the words in brackets）

1. A：听说四川的东西比较便宜,是真的吗?

   B：_____。（的确）

2. A：这件事大家都知道了，你真的不知道？

   B：我＿＿＿＿＿＿＿＿＿＿。（的确）

3. A：除了中国以外，你还到过哪些国家？

   B：我去过很多国家，＿＿＿＿＿＿＿＿＿＿。（比如）

4. A：听说中国菜有很多种，是吗？

   B：是的。各个地方的菜是不同的，＿＿＿＿＿＿＿＿＿＿。（比如）

5. A：爬山太累了。

   B：可是富士山上的风景很美，＿＿＿＿＿＿＿＿＿＿。（值得）

6. A：那个电影怎么样？

   B：故事太简单，＿＿＿＿＿＿＿＿＿＿。（值得）

三、用画线的词语回答问题（Answer the following questions with the underlined words）

1. 每年春天，美国中学生有多长的假期？

2. 除了上海、杭州以外，你还到过中国的什么地方？

3. 我觉得跟旅行社玩不自由（zìyóu/free），你看呢？

4. 在黄石公园（Huángshí Gōngyuán/Yellowstone National Park）游玩，至少要几天？

5. 如果有十天的假期，你打算去哪里旅行？

6. 今年夏天到什么地方去度假，你决定了吗？

7. 决定比较重要的事的时候，你跟谁商量？

四、会话（Conversation）

大卫：玛丽，下个月有一个星期假期，我想跟你商量一下，我们去哪里玩？

玛丽：你打算回国还是在中国旅行？

大卫：在中国好不好？

玛丽：去西藏（Xīzàng）吧，听说那儿可漂亮呢，天特别（tèbié/exceptionally, particularly）蓝。你看呢？

大卫：好啊。不过，听说那儿交通不太方便，自己去能行吗？

玛丽：汉语老师已经去过了，她说西藏很值得去，交通、住宿都没问题。不过，她说很多人在西藏会头疼。

大卫：如果西藏真的很美，头疼也值得啊。

玛丽：老师说西藏的确很美，是很特别的美。

大卫：我去订机票，下个月三号出发。

☆　**练习答案**（Key to the exercises）　☆

二、1. B：四川的东西的确很便宜　　2. B：的确不知道这件事

   3. B：比如法国、英国、意大利　　4. B：比如北方菜比较咸，四川菜比较辣

   5. B：累也值得　　6. B：不值得看

39 乘 飞机[1]
Chéng Fēijī

TAKING AN AIRPLANE[1]

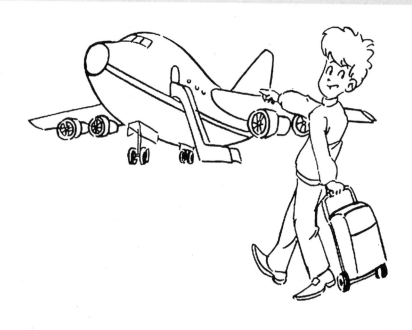

1. A: Wǒ yào mǎi yì zhāng hòutiān
   我 要 买 一 张 后天
   dào Niǔyuē de jīpiào.
   到 纽约 的 机票。

   I want a ticket for New York the day after tomorrow.

   B: Hǎo de. Hòutiān shì wǔ
   好 的。 后天 是 五
   hào. Xiàwǔ liǎng diǎn qǐfēi,
   号。 下午 两 点 起飞,
   kěyǐ ma?
   可以 吗?

   All right. The day after tomorrow is the fifth.
   The departure time is 2pm. Is that OK?

   A: Kěyǐ. Yào láihuípiào. Shíqī
   可以。 要 来回票。 十七
   hào cóng Niǔyuē huílai.
   号 从 纽约 回来。

   OK. I want a return ticket from New York on the 17th.

   B: Yào tóuděngcāng háishi jīngjìcāng?
   要 头等舱 还是 经济舱?

   First class or economy class?

   A: (Wǒ) yào jīngjìcāng.
   (我) 要 经济舱。

   Economy class.

   B: Yào mǎi hángkōng bǎoxiǎn ma?
   要 买 航空 保险 吗?

   Do you want to buy aviation insurance?

A: Yào de.
要 的。
Yes, I do.

2. A: Zài nǎli bàn dēngjī shǒuxù?
在 哪里 办 登机 手续?
Where shall I check in?

B: Nín chéng nǎge hángbān?
您 乘 哪个 航班?
Which flight are you taking?

A: Wǔ'èrsān hángbān.
5 2 3 航班。
Flight 523.

B: Qǐng dào wǔ hào tái bànlǐ.
请 到 五 号 台 办理。
Please go to the Desk 5.

3. A: Wǒ yào bàn dēngjī shǒuxù.
我 要 办 登机 手续。
I would like to check in, please.

B: Qǐng ràng wǒ kànkan nín
请 让 我 看看 您
de hùzhào.
的 护照。
May I see your passport?

A: Wǒ xiǎng yào kào chuāngkǒu
我 想 要 靠 窗口
de zuòwèi, yǒu ma?
的 座位, 有 吗?
I want to have a window seat. Is one available?

B: Yǒu de. Qǐng bǎ yào tuōyùn
有 的。 请 把 要 托运
de xíngli nádào zhèr lai.
的 行李 拿到 这儿 来。
Yes. Please put the baggage you want to check here.

A: Zhè jiàn yào tuōyùn, duōshao
这 件 要 托运, 多少
qián?
钱?
I'd like to have this piece of baggage checked. How much shall I pay for it?

B: Guīdìng miǎnfèi tuōyùn èrshí
规定 免费 托运 二十
gōngjīn xíngli, chāoguò de
公斤 行李, 超过 的
lìngwài fù qián.
另外注 付 钱。
The allowance of checked baggage is 20 kilograms. The weight beyond the allowance will be charged.

4. A: Wǔ'èrsān hángbān cóng nǎr
5 2 3 航班 从 哪儿
shàng fēijī?
上 飞机?
Where do I board Flight 523?

B: Qǐng dào liù hào dēngjīkǒu
请 到 六 号 登机口
Please wait at Gate 6.

děnghòu.
等候。

A：
Fēijī néng ànshí qǐfēi ma?
飞机 能 按时 起飞 吗？

Will our plane take off on time?

B：
Yīnwèi tiānqì de guānxì, yào
因为 天气 的 关系， 要

tuīchí yì xiǎoshí qǐfēi.
推迟 一 小时 起飞。

There will be a delay of one hour due to the weather.

Shénme shíhou néng qǐfēi,
什么 时候 能 起飞,

xiànzài hái bù zhīdao.
现在 还 不 知道。

We are not sure now when the plane will take off.

A：
Shànghǎi dào Niǔyuē yào fēi
上海 到 纽约 要 飞

jǐ ge xiǎoshí?
几 个 小时？

How many hours do we need to get to New York?

B：
Yào shíliù ge xiǎoshí zuǒyòu.
要 十六 个 小时 左右 。

About 16 hours.

☆ 注 释 (Note) ☆

"另外"在这里作副词用，表示上文所说的范围以外。

"另外"is used as an adverb here to indicate that something is beyond the above mentioned scope.

☆ 句型提示 (Sentence pattern references) ☆

1. 请把要托运的行李拿到这儿来。　　请参看 328 页句型 77。
2. 规定免费托运二十公斤行李。　　　请参看 319 页句型 57。
3. 因为天气的关系，要推迟一小时起飞。　请参看 389 页句型 212。

☆ 词语用法举例 (Examples for usage of the words) ☆

1. 要来回票

(1)
Wǒ shàngbān láihuí dōu chéng dìtiě.
我 上班 来回 都 乘 地铁。

(2)
Zǒulù dehuà, yí ge láihuí yào liǎng ge xiǎoshí zuǒyòu.
走路 的话， 一 个 来回 要 两 个 小时 左右。

(3)
Wǒ mǎi láihuípiào, kěyǐ dǎzhé ma?
我 买 来回票， 可以 打折 吗？

(4)
Huǒchēpiào yě kěyǐ mǎi láihuípiào ma?
火车票 也 可以 买 来回票 吗？

2. 在哪里办登机手续

(1) Qǐng dào nàbian bàn rùjìng shǒuxù.
请 到 那边 办 入境 手续。 （入境：enter a country）

(2) Shénme shíhou bàn rùxué shǒuxù?
什么 时候 办 入学 手续?

(3) Qù Xiānggǎng yào bàn shénme shǒuxù?
去 香港 要 办 什么 手续?

(4) Wǒ míngtiān qù lǐngshìguǎn bàn qiānzhèng shǒuxù.
我 明天 去 领事馆 办 签证 手续。

3. 我想要靠窗口的座位

(1) Tā kào qiáng zhànzhe kàn diànshì.
他 靠 墙 站着 看 电视。

(2) Qiánmian wēixiǎn, qǐng kàohòu.
前面 危险, 请 靠后。

(3) Huāpíng fàngdào kào yīnxiǎng de dìfang ba.
花瓶 放到 靠 音响 的 地方 吧。

(4) Qǐng kàoyòu zǒu.
请 靠右 走。

4. 规定免费托运二十公斤行李

(1) Zhè shì xuéxiào de guīdìng.
这 是 学校 的 规定。

(2) Àn guīdìng zhèxiē dōngxi yào shàngshuì.
按 规定 这些 东西 要 上税。 （上税：pay tax）

(3) Àn guīdìng zhèxiē yìránpǐn bù néng dài shàng chē.
按 规定 这些 易燃品 不 能 带 上 车。

(4) Shìzhèngfǔ guīdìng shìzhōngxīn bù néng fàng biānpào.
市政府 规定 市中心 不 能 放 鞭炮。 （放鞭炮：explode firecrackers）

5. 飞机能按时起飞吗

(1) Nǐ yào jìzhù ànshí chīyào.
你 要 记住 按时 吃药。

(2) Yào ànshí qǐchuáng, bié shuì lǎnjiào.
要 按时 起床, 别 睡 懒觉。 （睡懒觉：get up late）

(3) Tā zǒng shì ànshí shàngbān, cóng bù chídào.
他 总 是 按时 上班, 从 不 迟到。

(4) Yīnwèi guā táifēng, bù néng ànshí kāichuán.
因为 刮 台风, 不 能 按时 开船。 （开船：sail）

6. 因为天气的关系,要推迟一小时起飞

(1) Yīnwèi shíjiān guānxì, jīntiān jiù tǎolùn dào zhèr.
因为 时间 关系, 今天 就 讨论 到 这儿。 （讨论：discuss）

(2) 因为 资金 关系, 这个 工程 不 能 按时 开工。 (开工: start)
Yīnwèi zījīn guānxì, zhège gōngchéng bù néng ànshí kāigōng.

(3) 因为 健康 关系, 他 不 能 担任 这个 职务。 (职务:post,position)
Yīnwèi jiànkāng guānxì, tā bù néng dānrèn zhège zhíwù.

(4) 因为 身体 关系, 他 提前 退休 了。
Yīnwèi shēntǐ guānxì, tā tíqián tuìxiū le.

7. 要推迟一小时起飞

(1) 买 不 到 机票, 只好 推迟 两 天 出发 了。
Mǎi bú dào jīpiào, zhǐhǎo tuīchí liǎng tiān chūfā le.

(2) 因为 公司 有 重要 的 事, 休假 只好 推迟。
Yīnwèi gōngsī yǒu zhòngyào de shì, xiūjià zhǐhǎo tuīchí.

(3) 因为 没 准备 好, 会议 推迟 一 天 召开。
Yīnwèi méi zhǔnbèi hǎo, huìyì tuīchí yì tiān zhàokāi.

(4) 因为 下 雨, 运动会 推迟 到 下周 举行。
Yīnwèi xià yǔ, yùndònghuì tuīchí dào xiàzhōu jǔxíng.

☆　词　语(Word list)　☆

1. 售票处 （名） booking office
shòupiàochù

2. 单程票 （名） one-way ticket
dānchéngpiào

3. 双程票 （名） return ticket
shuāngchéngpiào

4. 问讯处 （名） information desk
wènxùnchù

5. 候机 大厅 （名） airport lounge
hòujī dàtīng

6. 登机口 （名） gate
dēngjīkǒu

7. 登机牌 （名） boarding card
dēngjīpái

8. 行李 标签 （名） baggage tag
xíngli biāoqiān

9. 行李车 （名） baggage cart
xínglichē

10. 机场 （名） airport
jīchǎng

11. 安全 检查 （动）security check
ānquán jiǎnchá

12. 降落 （动） land
jiàngluò

13. 送票 上门 deliver tickets to someone/some place
sòngpiào shàngmén

14. 退票 （动） refund for a ticket
tuìpiào

15. 改 日期 change the date
gǎi rìqī

☆　练　习(Exercises)　☆

一、读词组 (Read the following phrases aloud)

1. 来回票　　一个来回　　来回要两个小时　　来回五百公里(gōnglǐ/kilometer)
2. 靠窗口　　靠门的座位　　靠边放　　　　　　靠在墙上
3. 航空公司　航班　　　　航天(space flight)　航海
4. 办手续　　办登机手续　办托运手续　　　　办入学手续

二、用括号中的词语完成句子（Complete the following sentences with the words in brackets）

1. 新书桌放在＿＿＿＿＿＿＿＿＿＿。（靠）

2. 这个包自己拿，那两个箱子＿＿＿＿＿＿＿＿＿。（托运）

3. 因为有雾，所以飞机不能＿＿＿＿＿＿＿＿＿。（按时）

4. 今天下午的会议很重要，请大家＿＿＿＿＿＿＿＿＿。（按时）

5. 飞机上的饮料＿＿＿＿＿＿＿＿＿。（免费）

6. A：行李放到哪儿？B：请＿＿＿＿＿＿＿＿＿。（把）

三、选择填空（Select the appropriate words to fill in the blanks）

规定   等候   超过   起飞   推迟   免费

1. 身高＿＿＿一米二的孩子坐公共汽车要买票。

2. 校车（xiàochē/school bus）＿＿＿接送（jiēsòng/transport）孩子。

3. 候机室里的乘客已经＿＿＿了三个小时了。

4. 从广州＿＿＿的 FM304 航班将在一点二十分降落。

5. 因为他身体不好，这次旅游＿＿＿一个星期。

6. 在飞机上不能打手机，这是民航局的＿＿＿。

四、会话（Conversation）

玛丽：是上海航空公司售票处吗？

职员：是的。您是要订机票吗？

玛丽：是的。你们能送票上门吗？

职员：可以免费送票上门。您要订到哪里的机票？

玛丽：下星期五到拉萨（Lāsà）的票有吗？

职员：没有星期五的，只有星期六早上七点二十八分起飞的，您要吗？

玛丽：要，要三张。多少钱？

职员：一张是两千两百一十元。三张一共……

玛丽：对不起，等一等，小孩子可以半价吗？

职员：多大的孩子？我们公司规定，暑假期间学生票是六折。

玛丽：我的儿子十岁。

职员：那么一共是五千七百四十六元。您的地址？

玛丽：海天花园 2 号 302 室。我一天都在家。

职员：送票员大概在下午三点到您家，可以吗？

玛丽：好的，好的，谢谢。我等着。

职员：还要请您准备好大人的身份证和孩子的学生证。

玛丽：我们是美国人，我们有护照。

职员：那好，就这样。

☆　练习答案（Key to the exercises）　☆

二、1. 靠窗的地方　　2. 要托运　　3. 按时起飞　　4. 按时出席

　　5. 是免费的　　6. B：把行李拿到房间

三、1. 超过　　2. 免费　　3. 等候　　4. 起飞　　5. 推迟　　6. 规定

40 乘 飞机₂ TAKING AN AIRPLANE₂

Chéng Fēijī

1. A: Gè wèi lǚkè, huānyíng chéngzuò
各 位 旅客，欢迎 乘坐

　　Dōngfāng Hángkōng Gōngsī de
　　东方 航空 公司 的

　　bānjī, zhù dàjiā lǚtú
　　班机，祝注 大家 旅途

　　yúkuài.
　　愉快。

Ladies and gentlemen, welcome aboard Oriental Airlines. We wish you all a pleasant journey.

　 B: Bāng ge máng, xíng ma?
　　帮 个 忙，行 吗?

Would you please do me a favor?

　 A: Shénme shì? Qǐng shuō ba.
　　什么 事? 请 说 吧。

Sure. What can I do?

　 B: Qǐng bāng wǒ bǎ xiāngzi
　　请 帮 我 把 箱子

　　fàngdào xínglijià shang.
　　放到 行李架 上。

Please help me to put this suitcase up into the overhead compartment.

2. A: Gè wèi chéngkè, fēijī kuàiyào
各 位 乘客，飞机 快要

Ladies and gentlemen, we are going to take

qǐfēi le, qǐng dàjiā jìhǎo
起飞 了， 请 大家 系好

off soon. Please fasten your seat belts.

ānquándài.
安全带。

Wèile dàjiā de ānquán, qǐng
为了 大家 的 安全， 请

For your own safety, please don't use mobile

búyào shǐyòng shǒujī.
不要 使用 手机。

phones.

Qǐng guānshang nín de shǒujī.
请 关上 您 的 手机。

Please switch off your mobile phones.

Qǐng búyào zài fēijī shang
请 不要 在 飞机 上

And please don't smoke on board.

chōuyān.
抽烟。

Jiùshēngyī fàngzài zuòwèi de
救生衣 放在 座位 的

The life jacket is under your seat.

xiàmian.
下面。

Rúguǒ yǒu shì qǐng àn líng.
如果 有 事 请 按 铃。

If you have any requests, please push the

bell-button.

Fēijī shang miǎnfèi tígōng
3. A: 飞机 上 免费 提供

Free drinks are served on board.

yǐnliào.
饮料。

Nín yào shénme yǐnliào?
您 要 什么 饮料?

What drink do you want?

(Yào) kuàngquánshuǐ.
B: (要) 矿泉水。

Mineral water.

Nín hái yào ma?
A: 您 还 要 吗?

Do you want any more?

Zài yào yì bēi. Xièxie.
B: 再 要 一 杯。 谢谢。

One more cup, please. Thank you.

Wǒ yǒu diǎnr lěng, qǐng gěi
我 有 点儿 冷， 请 给

I feel a bit cold. Please give me a blanket.

wǒ yì tiáo tǎnzi.
我 一 条 毯子。

Hǎo de.
A: 好 的。

All right.

Qǐngwèn, xǐshǒujiān zài nǎr?

C：请问， 洗手间 在 哪儿？　　Excuse me, where is the washroom?

Zài nàbian.

A：在 那边。　　It's over there.

Běn bānjī dàodá Shànghǎi

4. A：本 班机 到达 上海　　Our flight will arrive at Shanghai at 16:50.

de shíjiān shì shíliù diǎn

的 时间 是 十六 点

wǔshí fēn.

五十 分。

Fēijī yǐjīng zhǔnshí zài

飞机 已经 准时 在　　Our plane has landed on time at Pudong Air-

Pǔdōng Jīchǎng jiàngluò.

浦东 机场 降落。　　port.

Qǐng dàjiā děng fēijī tíng-

请 大家 等 飞机 停　　Please don't undo your seat belt until the

wěn hòu zài jiěkāi ānquándài.

稳 后 再 解开 安全带。　　plane comes to a full stop.

Shànghǎi dào le, qǐng dàjiā

上海 到 了，请 大家　　We have arrived at Shanghai. Please get your

dàiqí zìjǐ de xínglǐ zhǔnbèi

带齐 自己 的 行李 准备　　belongings ready to disembark.

xià fēijī.

下 飞机。

☆ 注 释 (Note) ☆

"祝"是表示良好的愿望的词。如果是说话人表示祝愿时，"我"常常省略。
"祝" is a word to express good wishes. When the speaker expresses the wish, the subject "我" is often omitted.

☆ 句型提示 (Sentence pattern references) ☆

1. 飞机快要起飞了。　　请参看 307 页句型 32。
2. 为了大家的安全,请不要使用手机。　　请参看 360 页句型 149。
3. 请关上您的手机。　　请参看 351 页句型 130。
4. 请大家等飞机停稳后再解开安全带。　　请参看 385 页句型 204。

☆ **词语用法举例(Examples for usage of the words)** ☆

1. 祝大家旅途愉快

　Zhù nǐ xīnnián kuàilè!
(1)祝 你 新年 快乐! (快乐:happy)

　Zhù nǐ yílù-píng'ān!
(2)祝 你 一路平安! (一路平安:have a pleasant journey)

　Zhù nǐ gōngzuò shùnlì!
(3)祝 你 工作 顺利! (顺利:successful)

　Zhù nín shēntǐ jiànkāng!
(4)祝 您 身体 健康!

2. 为了大家的安全

　Wèile shēntǐ jiànkāng, tā měi tiān pǎobù.
(1)为了 身体 健康, 他 每 天 跑步。

　Wèile zhàogù shēngbìng de māma, tā qǐngle yí ge xīngqī jià.
(2)为了 照顾 生病 的 妈妈, 她 请了 一 个 星期 假。

　　(照顾:take care of)

　Wèile néng kǎoshang dàxué, tā pīnmìng xuéxí.
(3)为了 能 考上 大学, 他 拼命 学习。 (拼命:try one's utmost)

　Wèile jiànkāng, wǒ juédìng jiè yān.
(4)为了 健康, 我 决定 戒 烟。 (戒烟:give up smoking)

3. 飞机已经准时在浦东机场降落

　Huǒchē zhǔnshí dàodá Shànghǎizhàn.
(1)火车 准时 到达 上海站。

　Huìyì zhǔnshí kāishǐ.
(2)会议 准时 开始。

　Tā zhǔnshí dàole yuēdìng de dìdiǎn.
(3)他 准时 到了 约定 的 地点。 (约定:appoint)

　Yīnwèi yǎnyuán yùdào jiāotōng shìgù, bù néng zhǔnshí kāiyǎn.
(4)因为 演员 遇到 交通 事故, 不 能 准时 开演。

　　(开演:begin performance)

4. 请大家等飞机停稳后再解开安全带

　Děng yéye huílai zài chī fàn.
(1)等 爷爷 回来 再 吃 饭。

　Děng cài shāoshúle zài fàng wèijīng.
(2)等 菜 烧熟了 再 放 味精。

　Děng lǐngle gōngzī zài mǎi ba.
(3)等 领了 工资 再 买 吧。 (领工资:receive the pay)

　Děng yǔ tíngle zài chūqu.
(4)等 雨 停了 再 出去。

☆　词　语（Word list）　☆

1.	jiùshēngyī 救生衣	（名）	life jacket	2.	tàipíngmén 太平门	（名）	exit

1. 救生衣　（名）　life jacket
2. 太平门　（名）　exit
3. 清洁袋 qīngjiédài　（名）　cleaning bag
4. 厕所 cèsuǒ　（名）　washroom, lavatory
5. 正点 zhèngdiǎn　（动）　be on time, be on schedule
6. 晚点 wǎndiǎn　（动）　late, behind schedule
7. 延误 yánwù　（动）　delay
8. 时差 shíchā　（名）　time difference
9. 空姐 kōngjiě　（名）　airline stewardess
10. 乘务员 chéngwùyuán　（名）　aircrew
11. 机长 jīzhǎng　（名）　aircraft commander
12. 飞行员 fēixíngyuán　（名）　pilot
13. 呼吸 困难 hūxī kùnnan　short of breath, breathe with difficulty
14. 气流 qìliú　（名）　airflow, air stream
15. 平稳 píngwěn　（形）　stable, steady
16. 机械 故障 jīxiè gùzhàng　mechanical breakdown, mechanical failure
17. 空运 kōngyùn　（动）　air transport
18. 航班 取消 hángbān qǔxiāo　cancel a flight

☆　练　习（Exercises）　☆

一、读词组（Read the following phrases aloud）

1. 各位旅客　　各位同事　　各个国家　　各个公司
2. 关上手机　　关上电灯　　关上窗子　　关上柜门
3. 乘飞机　　　乘汽车　　　乘海船　　　乘电梯
4. 系好安全带　系好领带　　系好鞋带　　系好绳子（shéngzi/rope, string）
5. 安全带　　　安全帽　　　大家的安全　安全到达

二、模仿造句（Write sentences by following the patterns and imitating the example sentences）

1. 祝大家旅途愉快。
   祝你生日快乐。
   祝大家节日愉快。
   _____

2. 在飞机上请不要抽烟。
   在教室里请不要穿拖鞋。
   在公共场合请不要大声说话。
   _____

三、用括号中的词语完成对话（Complete the following conversations with the words in brackets）

1．A：妈妈，为什么这么早回家？

B：你看天暗了，_____。（要……了）

2．A：你的出国签证办好了，是吗？

B：是啊，我_____。（要……了）

3．A：刘小姐瘦（shòu /thin）了很多。

B：她_____，每天只吃一顿饭。（为了）

4．A：听说美江回国了？

B：是的，她的妈妈生病了，她回国是_____。（为了）

5．A：你一个人能拿这么多东西吗？

B：当然不能，有他_____。（帮）

四、会话（Conversations）

空姐：欢迎乘坐我们的班机。

卡尔：妈妈，我想坐靠窗的座位，行吗？

玛丽：好吧。系上安全带。

机长：各位乘客，对不起，有一位乘客已经办了登机手续，可是还没有登机。为了大家的安全，我们正在检查行李。请大家等一会儿。

玛丽：不会有问题吧。

空姐：不会的。请不用担心。

机长：各位乘客，最后一位乘客已经登机。请大家系好安全带，我们马上就要起飞了。

空姐：如果需要我们的服务，请按服务灯。祝大家旅途愉快。

机长：各位乘客，我们将在十点三十分准时到达拉萨机场。地面温度二十四摄氏度。

空姐：请大家系好安全带，等飞机停稳以后再站起来。

玛丽：好了，到了。

☆ **练习答案**（Key to the exercises） ☆

三、1．B：要下雨了

2．B：要出国了/要走了

3．B：为了减肥（jiǎnféi/reduce weight）

4．B：为了照顾妈妈

5．B：帮我拿/帮忙

41 　*Zhù　Bīnguǎn*　住　宾馆　　　IN A HOTEL

Wǒ　xiǎng　yùdìng　fángjiān.
1. A：我　想　预订　房间。　　I'd like to make a reservation.

Nín　yào　shénme　shíhou　de?
B：您　要　什么　时候　的?　　When do you need it?

Wǔ　yuè　shíliù　hào.　Yào　yí
A：五　月　十六　号。要　一　　On the 16th of May. A double room.
ge　shuāngrén　fángjiān.
个　双人　房间。

Méiyǒu kòng de shuāngrén fángjiān
B：没有　空　的　双人　房间　　We don't have any vacancies of double room.
le,　dānrén　fángjiān　kěyǐ　ma?
了，单人　房间　可以　吗?　　Is a single room acceptable?

Kěyǐ.　Zhù yì tiān duōshao qián?
A：可以。住　一　天　多少　钱?　　OK. How much does it cost for one night?

(Zhù)　yì　tiān　sānbǎi　kuài.
B：(住)　一　天　三百　块。　　300 *yuan* one night.

Wǒ jiào Xú Mín. Wǒ yùdìngle
2. A：我　叫　徐民。我　预订了　　My name is Xu Min. I've reserved a room.

fángjiān.
房间。

B：
Huānyíng guānglín. Nín de
欢迎 光临。您 的

fángjiān shì wǔyāolíng hào.
房间 是 5 1 0 号。

Zhè shì fángjiān yàoshi.
这 是 房间 钥匙。

Welcome. Your room number is 510. Here is your key.

3. A：
Qǐng bāng wǒ·bǎ xíngli ná-
请 帮 我·把 行李 拿

dào fángjiān ba.
到 房间 吧。

Please send my baggage to my room.

B：
Nín de xíngli sònglai le.
您 的 行李 送来 了。

Here is your baggage.

A：
Xièxie, jiù fàngzài zhèr ba.
谢谢， 就 放在 这儿 吧。

Thank you. Just put it here.

B：
Yào xǐ de yīfu qǐng
要 洗 的 衣服 请

fàngdào xǐyīdài li.
放到 洗衣袋 里。

Please put away the clothes you want washed to the cleaning bag.

A：
Shénmen dìfang kěyǐ duìhuàn
什么 地方 可以 兑换

wàibì?
外币？

Where can I exchange money?

B：
Yī lóu yǒu Zhōngguó Yínháng
一 楼 有 中国 银行

de zhīháng.
的 支行。

There's a branch of the Bank of China on the first floor.

Nín hái yǒu bié de shì ma?
您 还 有 别 的 事 吗？

Is there anything else I can do for you?

A：
Qǐng míngtiān zǎoshang liù diǎn
请 明天 早上 六 点

jiàoxǐng wǒ.
叫醒 我。

Please give me a morning call at six o'clock tomorrow morning.

B：
Hǎo de. .Yàoshi yǒu shénme
好 的。要是注 有 什么

shì, qǐng suíshí jiào wǒ.
事， 请 随时 叫 我。

All right. If you need any help, please call me any time.

4. A：
Qǐng jiézhàng.
请 结账。

Check out, please.

Wǔ yuè shíliù hào dào èrshí
B：五 月 十六 号 到 二十　　From the 16th of May to the 20th, you've

hào, yígòng zhùle wǔ tiān.
号，一共 住了 五 天。　　stayed here for five nights.

Qǐng fù yìqiān wǔbǎi kuài.
请 付 一千 五百 块。　　1,500 yuan please.

Xièxie, huānyíng xià cì zài lái.
谢谢，欢迎 下 次 再 来。　　Thank you. See you next time.

☆ 注 释 (Note) ☆

"要是"跟"如果"意思一样,表示假定,常用于口语。

"要是" and "如果" have the same meaning. They express an assumption and are often used in spoken language.

Yàoshi yǒu kòng, wǒ yídìng qù.
(1) 要是 有 空，我 一定 去。　　If I have time, surely I'll go.

Rúguǒ qí chē qù, jiù láidejí.
(2) 如果 骑 车 去，就 来得及。　　You are able to make it if you ride a bicycle.

☆ 句型提示 (Sentence pattern references) ☆

1. 请帮我把行李拿到房间吧。　　请参看 328 页句型 77。
2. 放在这儿吧。　　请参看 349 页句型 124。
3. 要洗的衣服请放到洗衣袋里。　　请参看 349 页句型 125。

☆ 词语用法举例 (Examples for usage of the words) ☆

1. 我想预订房间

Xiànzài kěyǐ yùdìng xià ge yuè de jīpiào ma?
(1) 现在 可以 预订 下 个 月 的 机票 吗?

Wǒ yùdìngle xià ge xīngqīliù wǎnshang yīnyuèhuì de piào.
(2) 我 预订了 下 个 星期六 晚上 音乐会 的 票。

Wǒ yùdìng de shūcài wèi shénme hái méi sònglai?
(3) 我 预订 的 蔬菜 为 什么 还 没 送来?

Zhōumò fàndiàn gùkè duō, bú yùdìng zuòwèi bùxíng.
(4) 周末 饭店 顾客 多，不 预订 座位 不行。

2. 请明天早上六点叫醒我

Xiǎo bǎobao xǐng le.
(1) 小 宝宝 醒 了。

Ānjìng diǎnr, bié chǎoxǐng dìdi.
(2) 安静 点儿，别 吵醒 弟弟。

Zuówǎn bànyè xǐng le, zài yě shuìbuzháo le.
（3）昨晚　半夜　醒　了，再　也　睡不着　了。（半夜：midnight）

Xǐngle jiù qǐchuáng, bié shuì lǎnjiào.
（4）醒了　就　起床，　别　睡　懒觉。

3. 要是有什么事，请随时叫我

Suíshí dōu kěyǐ dǎ yāoyāosì chá diànhuà hàomǎ.
（1）随时　都　可以　打　1 1 4　查　电话　号码。

Dàizhe yǔsǎn ba, suíshí dōu huì xià yǔ de.
（2）带着　雨伞　吧，随时　都　会　下　雨　的。

Bié líkāi hòujīshì, fēijī suíshí huì qǐfēi.
（3）别　离开　候机室，飞机　随时　会　起飞。

Rúguǒ yǒu shénme wèntí, qǐng suíshí gēn wǒ liánxì.
（4）如果　有　什么　问题，请　随时　跟　我　联系。（联系：contact）

☆　词　语（Word list）　☆

1. 住宿 登记 zhùsù dēngjì — check in
2. 服务台 fúwùtái （名）reception desk
3. 大堂 dàtáng （名）lobby
4. 电梯 diàntī （名）elevator
5. 自动 扶梯 zìdòng fútī（名）escalator
6. 楼梯 lóutī （名）stairs
7. 整理 床铺 zhěnglǐ chuángpù — make the bed
8. 打扫 dǎsǎo （动）clean, sweep
9. 设备 shèbèi （名）facilities, equipment
10. 毯子 tǎnzi （名）blanket
11. 洗脸盆 xǐliǎnpén （名）washbowl
12. 洗漱 用具 xǐshù yòngjù（名）utensils for wash and tooth-cleaning
13. 牙刷 yáshuā （名）toothbrush
14. 牙膏 yágāo （名）toothpaste
15. 打火机 dǎhuǒjī （名）lighter
16. 客房 服务员 kèfáng fúwùyuán（名）room attendant
17. 请勿打扰 牌子 qǐngwùdǎrǎo páizi — "no disturbance" sign
18. 空房间 kòngfángjiān （名）vacant room
19. 单人 房间 dānrén fángjiān（名）single room
20. 双人 房间 shuāngrén fángjiān（名）double room
21. 标准房 biāozhǔnfáng （名）standard room
22. （宾馆）客满 （bīnguǎn）kèmǎn — no vacancy

☆　练　习（Exercises）　☆

一、读词组（Read the following word groups aloud）

1. 预订房间　　预订酒席　　电话预订
2. 叫醒我　　把我叫醒　　叫醒服务

3. 随时叫我　　　随时出发　　　随时打电话

4. 双人房间　　　双人床　　　　双层车（shuāngcéngchē/double-decker）

二、用"要是"改写句子（Use "要是" to rewrite the following sentences）

1. 如果明天天气好,我们就去动物园吧。

2. 如果这里不安全,我们就不住在这里。

3. 你再迟到,我就生气了。

三、回答问题（Answer the following questions）

1. 旅行的时候,你喜欢住什么样的旅馆?

2. 在中国你住过宾馆吗?

3. 你觉得中国的宾馆怎么样?

四、会话（Conversation）

职员:欢迎光临。

大卫:我们已经预订了房间。我是大卫·布朗,这是我的护照。

职员:啊,布朗先生、布朗太太,欢迎。你们的房间是 507 号。这间房的朝向很好,从窗口就可以看到山。请在这张表上登记一下。你们准备住几天?

大卫:两天。

职员:好的,这是钥匙。餐厅在一楼,有免费早餐供应（gōngyìng/supply）。

玛丽:这里有叫醒服务吗?

职员:有的,你可以在房间打电话给客房部。

☆　　**练习答案**（Key to the exercises）　　☆

二、1. 要是明天天气好,我们就去动物园吧。

　　2. 要是这里不安全,我们就不住在这里。

　　3. 要是你再迟到,我就生气了。

42 拍照
Pāizhào

TAKING PICTURES

1. A: 这儿 的 景色 太 美 了！
Zhèr de jǐngsè tài měi le!
拍 张 照片儿 吧。
Pāi zhāng zhàopiānr ba.

How beautiful the scenery is! Let's take a picture here.

B: 我 给 你 拍 吧。
Wǒ gěi nǐ pāi ba.

Let me take one for you.

A: 我 想 和 你 合 拍
Wǒ xiǎng hé nǐ hé pāi
一 张，请 别人 按 一
yì zhāng, qǐng biéren àn yí-
下 吧。
xià ba.

I'd like to take one with you. Let's ask someone to take it for us.

B: 麻烦 您，帮 我们 按
Máfan nín, bāng wǒmen àn
一下，可以 吗？
yíxià, kěyǐ ma?

Excuse me, could you take a picture for us?

C: 好 的，只 按 快门 就
Hǎo de, zhǐ àn kuàimén jiù

Sure. I just need to push the shutter button,

269

xíng le, shì ma?
行 了，是 吗？ right?

B：Shì de. Zhànzài zhèr hǎo ma?
是 的。 站在 这儿 好 吗？ Yes. Is this position OK?

C：(Qǐng) kàoyòu yìdiǎnr.
（请） 靠右 一点儿。 Please move a bit to the right.

(Qǐng) liǎng ge rén kàojìn
（请） 两 个 人 靠近 You two get closer, please.

yìdiǎnr.
一点儿。

B：Zhèyàng xíng ma?
这样 行 吗？ Is it all right now?

C：Xíng, hǎo le, wǒ yào
行， 好 了， 我 要 OK. I'll shoot.

zhào le.
照 了。

2. A：Wǒ yào chōng jiāojuǎn.
我 要 冲 胶卷。 I'd like to develop these films.

B：Yào yìn jǐ zhāng?
要 印 几 张？ How many sets do you want to print?

A：Měi zhāng dǐpiàn gè yìn yì
每 张 底片 各 印 一 One print for each negative. And I want this

zhāng. Zhè zhāng dǐpiàn yào
张。 这 张 底片 要 negative enlarged.

fàngdà yì zhāng.
放大 一 张。

B：Fàngdà dào jǐ yīngcùn?
放大 到 几 英寸？ What size do you want the picture enlarged to?

A：Qī yīngcùn.
七 英寸。 Seven inches.

Wǒ jízhe yòng, kuài diǎnr
我 急着 用， 快 点儿 Can you hurry it up? It's badly needed.

kěyǐ ma?
可以 吗？

B：Jīntiān xiàwǔ jiù kěyǐ qǔ.
今天 下午 就 可以 取。 You can get it this afternoon.

A：Xiàwǔ jǐ diǎn kěyǐ qǔ?
下午 几 点 可以 取？ What time can I get it this afternoon?

B：Zuì kuài yě děi xiàwǔ sì diǎn.
最 快 也 得注 下午 四 点。 Four o'clock is the earliest time.

☆ 注 释(Notes) ☆

"得"读"děi",表示"必须"的意思,只用在口语中。否定时说"不用",不说"不得"。

"得" here is pronounced as "děi" and means "必须". It is used only in spoken Chinese. Its negative form is "不用" instead of "不得".

Jīntiān xīngqīliù, kěshì wǒ děi qù gōngsī.
(1) 今天 星期六,可是 我 得 去 公司。 I have to go to the company though it is Saturday today.

Jīntiān xīngqīliù, wǒ búyòng qù gōngsī.
(2) 今天 星期六, 我 不用 去 公司。 It's Saturday today. I don't need to go to the company.

☆ 句型提示(Sentence pattern references) ☆

1. 这儿的景色太美了!   请参看 394 页句型 223。
2. 我给你拍吧。   请参看 321 页句型 60。
3. 放大到几英寸?   请参看 356 页句型 140。

☆ 词语用法举例(Examples for usage of the words) ☆

1. 帮我们按一下,可以吗

Bāng wǒ ná yíxià, xíng ma?
(1) 帮 我 拿 一下, 行 吗?

Qǐng bāng wǒ zhǎo yíxià jīnglǐ.
(2) 请 帮 我 找 一下 经理。

Nǐ shàng jiē dehuà, shùnbiàn bāng wǒ mǎi fèn bàozhǐ.
(3) 你 上 街 的话, 顺便 帮 我 买 份 报纸。

(顺便:conveniently, without extra effort)

Bāng wǒ dào xǐyīdiàn qǔ yīfu, hǎo ma?
(4) 帮 我 到 洗衣店 取 衣服, 好 吗?

2. 只按快门就行了

Zhǐ dài qián jiù xíng le, bié de búyòng dài.
(1) 只 带 钱 就 行 了, 别 的 不用 带。

Zhǐ fàng yán jiù xíng le, bié de búyào fàng.
(2) 只 放 盐 就 行 了, 别 的 不要 放。

Xiànzài qù Guǎngzhōu, zhǐ chuān chènyī jiù xíng le.
(3) 现在 去 广州, 只 穿 衬衣 就 行 了。

Nǐ zhǐ mǎi huā jiù xíng le, bié de wǒ dōu mǎi le.
(4) 你 只 买 花 就 行 了, 别 的 我 都 买 了。

3. 我急着用

(1) Tā bàba shēng zhòng bìng, tā jízhe gǎn huí lǎojiā qu.
他 爸爸 生 重 病, 他 急着 赶 回 老家 去。

(2) Yí dào Bālí, tā jiù jízhe gěi bàba māma dǎ diànhuà.
一 到 巴黎, 他 就 急着 给 爸爸 妈妈 打 电话。

(3) Yǒu jiàn zhòngyào de shì, wǒ jízhe yào gàosu tā.
有 件 重要 的 事, 我 急着 要 告诉 他。

(4) Tāng tài tàng le, bié jízhe hē.
汤 太 烫 了, 别 急着 喝。

4. 最快也得下午四点

(1) Xià zhōu kǎoshì, děi hǎohāor fùxí.
下 周 考试, 得 好好儿 复习。

(2) Zhēn lěng a! Chūqu děi chuān dàyī.
真 冷 啊! 出去 得 穿 大衣。

(3) Nǐ shénme shíhou jiéhūn, děi gàosu wǒ.
你 什么 时候 结婚, 得 告诉 我。

(4) Nǐ fā gāoshāo le, děi qù yīyuàn.
你 发 高烧 了, 得 去 医院。

☆ 词 语 (Word list) ☆

1. 摄影 shèyǐng (动)	take a photograph, shoot a film	2. 拍照 pāizhào (动)	take pictures
3. 相片 xiàngpiàn (名)	picture, photo	4. 影集 yǐngjí (名)	photo album
5. 照相机 zhàoxiàngjī (名)	camera	6. 傻瓜相机 shǎguā xiàngjī (名)	foolproof camera
7. 数码相机 shùmǎ xiàngjī (名)	digital camera	8. 彩色胶卷 cǎisè jiāojuǎn (名)	color film
9. 镜头 jìngtóu (名)	lens	10. 按快门 àn kuàimén	push shutter button, shoot
11. 闪光灯 shǎnguāngdēng (名)	flash	12. 光线 guāngxiàn (名)	light
13. 对好焦距 duìhǎo jiāojù	focus	14. 背景 bèijǐng (名)	background
15. 合影 héyǐng (动/名)	have a group photo taken; group photo	16. 表情 biǎoqíng (名)	expression
17. 半身照 bànshēnzhào (名)	half-length portrait	18. 全身照 quánshēnzhào (名)	full-length portrait
19. 全家福 quánjiāfú (名)	picture of whole family	20. 证件照 zhèngjiànzhào (名)	picture for ID use
21. 摄像机 shèxiàngjī (名)	video camera	22. 镜框 jìngkuàng (名)	frame

☆ 练 习（Exercises） ☆

一、读词组（Read the following word groups aloud）
1. 照片儿　　　拍照　　　　拍照片儿　　　　拍一张照片儿
2. 相片　　　　照相　　　　照一张相　　　　照相机
3. 合影　　　　一张合影　　拍一张合影　　　我跟你拍一张合影
4. 胶卷　　　　一卷儿胶卷　彩色胶卷　　　　黑白胶卷

二、选择填空（Select the appropriate words to fill in the blanks）
　　　靠近　　拍　　冲　　印
1. 这个文件要_____几份？
2. 手表不要放在_____电视机的地方。
3. 我不注意的时候,他给我_____了一张。
4. _____一卷胶卷要多少钱？

三、模仿造句 （Write sentences by following the patterns and imitating the example sentences）
1. 最快也得一天。
　 最少也得五块钱。
　 最早也得后天才能取。

　 _____

2. 照片要放大到几英寸？
　 价钱要提高到一百块。
　 电灯要增加到四盏（zhǎn,量词）。

　 _____

3. 每张底片各印一张。
　 每种点心各尝一块。
　 每种花各买六朵（duǒ,量词）。

　 _____

四、会话（Conversation）
玛丽：卡尔,你站在那块石头（shítou/stone, rock）旁边,妈妈给你拍一张。
卡尔：妈妈,爸爸为什么总是对着空地方拍？
玛丽：你爸爸喜欢拍风景。
大卫：是啊,卡尔,你看,蓝的天、绿的草地,真美啊！
玛丽：我们拍一张合影吧。
大卫：好,那边有一个人,请他帮帮忙。先生,能不能帮我们按一下？
游客：好的,这个就是快门吗？
大卫：是的,按这里就可以了。麻烦您把后面那个庙拍进去。

273

游客：行。如果要拍庙,人只能拍半身。

大卫：可以啊。

游客：准备,笑一笑,一二三。好了。

大卫：谢谢。

☆ 练习答案(Key to the exercises) ☆

二、1. 印　　2. 靠近　　3. 拍　　4. 冲

43 业余 活动
Yèyú Huódòng

SPARETIME ACTIVITIES

1. A：星期六 你 有 什么 安排？
   Xīngqīliù nǐ yǒu shénme ānpái?
   Do you have any arrangements on Saturday?

   B：没 什么 安排。
   Méi shénme ānpái.
   No. I haven't any arrangements.

   A：我们 下午 去 参观 博物馆， 晚上 到 大 剧院 看 话剧， 好 吗？
   Wǒmen xiàwǔ qù cānguān bówùguǎn, wǎnshang dào Dà-jùyuàn kàn huàjù, hǎo ma?
   Let's visit the Museum in the afternoon and go to see a stage play in the Grand Theater in the evening. Is that OK?

   B：那 太 好 了! 你 先 给 我 介绍 一下 吧。
   Nà tài hǎo le! Nǐ xiān gěi wǒ jièshào yíxià ba.
   That's wonderful. Please tell me something about it in advance.

   A：上海 博物馆 是 一九五二 年 开馆 的。是 著名 的
   Shànghǎi Bówùguǎn shì yī jiǔ wǔ'èr nián kāiguǎn de. Shì zhùmíng de
   Shanghai Museum was founded in 1952. It is famous at ancient Chinese art.

275

Zhōngguó gǔdài yìshù bówùguǎn.
中国　古代 艺术 博物馆。

Nà lǐmian yǒu shí ge chénlièguǎn,
那 里面 有 十 个 陈列馆，

There are ten exhibition halls with a collection

guǎncángpǐn dá shí'èr wàn jiàn.
馆藏品　达 十二 万 件。

of more than 120,000 items there.

B：Zhème duō dōngxi, yí ge
这么 多 东西， 一 个

How can we see so many things in one after-

xiàwǔ kàn de wán ma?
下午 看 得 完 吗？

noon?

A：Zhǐhǎo zǒu mǎ kàn huā le.
只好注1 走 马 看 花 了注2。 We will just do our best.

B：Huàjù piào nǐ mǎihǎo le ma?
话剧 票 你 买好 了 吗？ Have you booked the play tickets?

A：Zǎo jiù mǎihǎo le.
早 就 买好 了。 I've bought the tickets already.

B：Xīngqīliù yǎn shénme?
星期六 演 什么？ What's on Saturday evening?

A：Xīngqīliù yǎn de shì 《Léiyǔ》.
星期六 演 的 是 《雷雨》。 The play on Saturday is "Thunderstorm".

B：Shànghǎi Dàjùyuàn shì gāng
上海　大剧院 是 刚

Was the Shanghai Grand Theater completed

jiànchéng de ba?
建成　的 吧？

only a short while ago?

A：Shì de, lǐmian yǒu sān ge
是 的， 里面 有 三 个

Yes. There are three theaters inside the

jùchǎng. Qízhōng dàjùchǎng
剧场。 其中　大剧场

Grand Theater. The big one has 1,800 seats.

yǒu yìqiān bābǎi ge zuòwèi.
有 一千 八百 个 座位。

B：Jǐ diǎn kāichǎng?
几 点 开场？ What time will the play begin?

A：Qī diǎn bàn (kāichǎng).
七 点 半 （开场）。 At half past seven.

B：Wǒ dānxīn tīng bu dǒng.
我 担心 听 不 懂。 I am afraid I won't understand the play.

A：Bié dānxīn, wǒ xiān gěi nǐ
别 担心， 我 先 给 你

Don't worry. I'll tell you the story of the play

jiǎngjiang jùqíng ba.
讲讲　剧情 吧。

in advance.

2. A：Jīntiān de xì kàndǒng le ma?
今天 的 戏 看懂 了 吗？

Did you understand today's play?

B：Yīnwèi yùxiān zhīdao jùqíng,
因为 预先 知道 剧情，

I understood the basic meaning since I knew

jīběnshang kàndǒng le.
基本上 看懂 了。

the story before.

A：Táicí tīng de qīngchu ma?
台词 听 得 清楚 吗？

Could you catch the lines?

B：Yǎnyuán shuō de tài kuài,
演员 说 得 太 快，

The performers spoke too fast so I could not

wǒ méi tīng qīngchu.
我 没 听 清楚。

catch all of them.

A：Chūchǎng de dōu shì míng
出场 的 都 是 名

The actors and actresses that appeared to-

yǎnyuán, nǐ juéde tāmen
演员， 你 觉得 他们

night are all famous. What did you think of

yǎn de zěnmeyàng?
演 得 怎么样？

their performances?

B：Wǒ hěn xīnshǎng nǚzhǔjué
我 很 欣赏 女主角

I particularly admired the performance of the

de yǎnjì.
的 演技。

leading actress.

Nánzhǔjué yǎn de bú tài
男主角 演 得 不 太

But the leading actor was not so good.

hǎo.
好。

☆ 注 释 (Notes) ☆

1. "只好"表示由于条件的限制或情况的变化，没有别的选择。

"只好" indicates the only choice under the certain circumstances or due to the change of the condition.

2. "走马看花"表示粗略地看看，大致了解一下的意思。也可以说"走马观花"。

"走马看花" means to gain a shallow understanding from a fleeting glance. It is also said "走马观花".

☆　句型提示（Sentence pattern references）　☆

1. 这么多东西，一个下午看得完吗?
   台词听得清楚吗?　　　　　　　　请参看 344 页句型 114。
2. 我担心听不懂。　　　　　　　　　请参看 345 页句型 115。
3. 今天的戏看懂了吗?　　　　　　　请参看 346 页句型 116。
4. 我没听清楚。　　　　　　　　　　请参看 346 页句型 117。
5. 演员说得太快，我没听清楚。　　　请参看 343 页句型 112。
6. 男主角演得不太好。　　　　　　　请参看 344 页句型 113。

☆　词语用法举例（Examples for usage of the words）　☆

1. 星期六你有什么安排

   (1) Zhōumò rúguǒ nǐ méi shénme ānpái, wǒ qǐng nǐ kàn jīngjù.
       周末　如果　你　没　什么　安排，我　请　你　看　京剧。

   (2) Shǔjià de huódòng ānpái hǎo le.
       暑假　的　活动　安排　好　了。

   (3) Cháhuàhuì de shì ràng Zhōu Míng ānpái ba.
       茶话会　的　事　让　周　明　安排　吧。

   (4) Dǎoyóu yào ānpái hǎo kèren de chī、hē、zhùsù.
       导游　要　安排　好　客人　的　吃、喝、住宿。

2. 这么多东西

   (1) Zhème duō dōngxi, wǒ yí ge rén chī bu wán.
       这么　多　东西，我　一　个　人　吃　不　完。

   (2) Zhème piányi, duō mǎi diǎnr ba.
       这么　便宜，多　买　点儿　吧。

   (3) zhème hǎochī de shēngyúpiàn, nǐ bù chī, tài yíhàn le.
       这么　好吃的　生鱼片，你　不　吃，太　遗憾　了。　（生鱼片：sashimi）

   (4) Zhème guì de dōngxi, mǎi bu qǐ.
       这么　贵　的　东西，买　不　起。　（买不起：cannot afford）

3. 只好走马看花了

   (1) Méiqìlú huài le, zhǐhǎo chī fāngbiànmiàn le.
       煤气炉　坏　了，只好　吃　方便面　了。　（方便面：instant noodles）

   (2) Jīntiān tíngshuǐ, zhǐhǎo chūqu chī fàn le.
       今天　停水，只好　出去　吃　饭　了。

   (3) Zìxíngchē huài le, zhǐhǎo chéng gōnggòng qìchē le.
       自行车　坏　了，只好　乘　公共　汽车　了。

   (4) Hái yǒu sānshí fēnzhōng jiù kāiyǎn, zhǐhǎo jiào chē qù le.
       还　有　三十　分钟　就　开演，只好　叫　车　去　了。

4. 早就买好了

(1) Fángjiān wǒ zǎo jiù yùdìng le.
房间　我　早　就　预订　了。

(2) Xiānggǎng wǒ zǎo jiù qùguo le.
香港　　我　早　就　去过　了。

(3) Wǒ zǎo jiù tīngshuō tā shēngzhí le.
我　早　就　听说　他　升职　了。（升职：be promoted）

(4) Míngnián de gōngzuò, shèzhǎng zǎo jiù ānpái hǎo le.
明年　的　工作，　社长　早　就　安排　好　了。

5. 别担心

(1) Bú shì shénme dàbìng, bié dānxīn.
不　是　什么　大病，别　担心。

(2) Bié dānxīn, zhǐ shì yìdiǎnr qīngshāng.
别　担心，只　是　一点儿　轻伤。

(3) Wǒ dānxīn míngtiān xià yǔ, bù néng qù.
我　担心　明天　下　雨，不　能　去。

(4) Yí ge rén qù, wǒ dānxīn mílù.
一　个　人　去，我　担心　迷路。

6. 我很欣赏女主角的演技

(1) Tā fēicháng xīnshǎng gǔdiǎn yīnyuè.
他　非常　欣赏　古典　音乐。

(2) Wǒ hěn xīnshǎng jīngjù de wǔdǎ.
我　很　欣赏　京剧　的　武打。（武打：acrobatic fighting）

(3) Jīnglǐ tèbié xīnshǎng tā de cáinéng.
经理　特别　欣赏　他　的　才能。

(4) Xiàozhǎng hěn xīnshǎng Huáng Tāo de kǒucái.
校长　很　欣赏　黄　涛　的　口才。（口才：eloquence）

☆ 词　语（Word list）☆

1.	chūtǔ wénwù 出土 文物	（名）	unearthed artifacts, archaeological finds	2.	gǔdǒng 古董 （名）	antique
3.	yùqì 玉器	（名）	jade	4.	táocí 陶瓷 （名）	pottery
5.	zhēnpǐn 真品	（名）	authentic	6.	fùzhìpǐn 复制品 （名）	replica, reproduction
7.	zhǎnchū 展出	（动）	exhibit, display	8.	xìjù 戏剧 （名）	drama, play
9.	gējù 歌剧	（名）	opera	10.	jīngjù 京剧 （名）	Beijing Opera

11.	xǐjù 喜剧	（名）	comedy	12.	bēijù 悲剧	（名）	tragedy	
13.	yǎnchū 演出	（动）	perform, appear on stage	14.	shàngyǎn 上演	（动）	perform, put on the stage	
15.	dǎoyǎn 导演	（名）	director	16.	juésè 角色	（名）	role, part	
17.	zhǔjué 主角	（名）	leading role	18.	pèijué 配角	（名）	supporting role	
19.	guānzhòng 观众	（名）	audience	20.	gǔzhǎng 鼓掌	（动）	applaud	
21.	xièmù 谢幕	（动）	answer a curtain call	22.	hǎibào 海报	（名）	playbill, poster	
23.	jiémùdān 节目单	（名）	bill, program	24.	zìmù 字幕	（名）	subtitles	

☆　练　习（Exercises）　☆

一、模仿造句（Write sentences by following the patterns and imitating the example sentences）

1. 藏品多达十二万件。

　气温高达三十五度。

　那件晚礼服价钱高达一万块。

　_____

2. 这么多东西一个下午看得完吗？

　这些工作一个星期做得完吗？

　这桶水两天喝得完吗？

　_____

二、选择填空（Select the appropriate words to fill in the blanks）

A　安排　　　参观　　　著名　　　担心　　　预先　　　欣赏　　　基本上

1. 杭州是中国_____的旅游城市。

2. 他还没回来,我_____路上出事。

3. 对不起,我这两天已经有_____了,没有时间跟你去苏州。

4. 时间安排如果有变化,请_____通知我。

5. 去北京的游客都要去_____故宫。

6. 小林又聪明又努力,老板很_____他。

7. 我们学校的留学生_____都是美国人。

B　看得懂　　　　修得好　　　　买得到　　　　修不好
　　打扫得完　　　看得清楚　　　记得住　　　　看不清楚

1. A：墙上的通知你_____吗?
   B：不太难,我都_____。

2. A：这台电视机你一天_____吗?
   B：对不起,一天_____。

3. A：地图上的字你_____吗?
   B：字太小,我_____。

4. A：听说最近飞机票很难买,你_____吗?
   B：提前一个星期,应该_____。

5. A：这个房间你二十分钟_____吗?
   B：本来就挺干净,_____。

6. A：这么多生词你_____吗?
   B：有好几个是已经学过的,我_____。

三、用"动词 + 好"完成句子(Use "verb + 好" to complete the following sentences)

1. 你的自行车放在我这里修,_____了再付钱。
2. 这本书你先看,你_____就给我。
3. 等肉片熟了再放入已经_____的笋片。
4. 没_____作业不可以看电视。

四、会话 (Conversations)

于雪来：玛丽,你这个星期六有安排吗?
玛　丽：本来有。可是大卫要加班,我正在想怎么办。
于雪来：上海美术馆有一个儿童画展览,我想带孩子去,你和卡尔也一起去吧。
玛　丽：好啊。
于雪来：上午看画展,下午去植物园好不好?
玛　丽：你安排得真好。这样吧,我们带一些三明治(sānmíngzhì/sandwich)、饮料什么
　　　　的,到植物园野餐(yěcān/picnic)。
于雪来：那孩子们可就高兴了。

于雪来：你们觉得这个画展好看吗?
郭明明：好看。我最喜欢那幅标题(biāotí/title, headline)叫"小狗生气了"的画,小狗生气
　　　　的样子多可爱(kě'ài/lovely)啊。
玛　丽：我也喜欢那幅,作者才六岁呢,画得那么好。卡尔,你说说。
卡　尔：那幅《小鸟的家》我觉得画得好。
郭明明：我也觉得那幅好。

于雪来：是吗？为什么好呢？那幅画的意思，你看得懂吗？

郭明明：看得懂，说不出来。

于雪来：卡尔，你说。

卡　尔：树都倒(dǎo/fall down, be uprooted)了，那些小鸟没有家了，它们多可怜(kělián/piti-ful)啊。

玛　丽：说得对。

卡　尔：于阿姨，你能帮我一个忙吗？

于雪来：当然可以啊。说吧。

卡　尔：我们学校下个星期有一个活动，要用汉语表演节目。我练习的时候请您听一听。如果有错，帮我纠正(jiūzhèng/correct)一下，好吗？

于雪来：好呀，你现在就给我们表演一下吧。

卡　尔：在这里吗？旁边有不认识的人呢，我说不出来。

玛　丽：别不好意思，来吧，让大家看看。

☆　练习答案(Key to the exercises)　☆

二、A：1. 著名　2. 担心　3. 安排　4. 预先　5. 参观　6. 欣赏　7. 基本上

　　B：1. A：看得懂　　B：看得懂　　　　　2. A：修得好　B：修不好

　　　3. A：看得清楚　B：看不清楚　　　　4. A：买得到　B：买得到

　　　5. A：打扫得完　B：打扫得完　　　　6. A：记得住　B：记得住

三、1. 修好　　2. 看好　　3. 炒好　　4. 做好

44

Xìngqù、Àihào
兴趣、爱好

INTERESTS

Nǐ yǒu shénme àihào?
1. A：你 有 什么 爱好？

What interests do you have?

Wǒ cóngxiǎo jiù xǐhuan yīnyuè.
B：我 从小 就 喜欢 音乐。

I have been fond of music since my childhood.

Yèyú shíjiān nǐ zuò shénme ne?
A：业余 时间 你 做 什么 呢？

What do you do in your spare time?

Wǎnshang yǒushí kànkan diànshì,
B：晚上 有时 看看 电视，

In evenings I sometimes watch TV, and some-

yǒushí kànkan bàozhǐ、 zázhì
有时 看看 报纸、 杂志

times read newspapers, magazines or some-

shénme de.
什么 的。

thing like that.

Xīngqīliù hé xīngqītiān chángcháng
星期六 和 星期天 常常

I often go to the countryside outside the city

qù jiāowài huà huàr.
去 郊外 画 画儿。

for painting on Saturdays and Sundays.

Nǐ huà de hěn hǎo ba?
A：你 画 得 很 好 吧？

You are good at painting, aren't you?

B：Bù zěnme hǎo, yě bú tài chà, yìbān.
不 怎么 好，也 不 太 差[注1]，一般。

Not very good, but not too bad either. Just so-so.

Nǐ xǐhuan huà huàr ma?
你 喜欢 画 画儿 吗？

Do you like drawing pictures?

A：Wǒ yìdiǎnr yě bú huì, búguò xǐhuan kàn měishù zhǎnlǎn.
我 一点儿 也 不 会，不过 喜欢 看 美术 展览。

No, not a bit. But I like visiting art galleries.

B：Nà nǐ de xìngqù shì shénme ne?
那 你 的 兴趣 是 什么 呢？

Then, what hobbies do you have?

A：Wǒ xǐhuan tǐyù, yóuqí ài kàn zúqiú bǐsài.
我 喜欢 体育，尤其 爱 看 足球 比赛。

I like sports, especially watching football matches.

B：Zuótiān de zúqiúsài xiànchǎng zhíbō, nǐ kànle ma?
昨天 的 足球赛 现场 直播，你 看了 吗？

Did you watch yesterday's live football match on TV?

A：Kàn le, shì Zhōngguó nǚduì duì Ruìdiǎn nǚduì de bànjuésài.
看 了，是 中国 女队 对 瑞典 女队 的 半决赛。

Yes. It was the Chinese women's team vs. the Swedish team in the semifinal.

B：Wǒ méi kàn, wǒ duì zúqiú bú tài gǎn xìngqù.
我 没 看，我 对 足球 不 太 感 兴趣。

I didn't watch it. I am not interested in football.

A：Tài yíhàn le, nà chǎng qiúsài jīngcǎi jí le.
太 遗憾 了，那 场 球赛 精彩 极 了。

What a pity! That game was extremely exciting.

B：Tīngshuō Zhōngguóduì (yǐ) wǔ bǐ líng yíng le.
听说 中国队 （以）5 比 0 赢[注2] 了。

I heard the Chinese won five to zero.

2. A：Zhè shì nǎge duì gēn nǎge duì bǐsài?
这 是 哪个 队 跟 哪个 队 比赛？

What teams are in the match?

B：Shì Fǎguóduì duì Déguóduì.
是 法国队 对 德国队。 France vs. Germany.

A：Xiànzài chǎngshang de bǐfēn
现在 场上 的 比分 What's the score now?

shì duōshao?
是 多少?

B：Èr bǐ yī, Fǎguóduì lǐngxiān
2 比 1，法国队 领先 Two to one. The French team has the lead.

yí ge qiú.
一 个 球。

A：Liǎng ge duì de shuǐpíng
两 个 队 的 水平 Both teams have showed great skill.

dōu hěn gāo.
都 很 高。

B：Liǎng ge duì dōu shì shìjiè
两 个 队 都 是 世界 They are both among the world's top teams.

yìliú de qiúduì.
一流 的 球队。

A：Bǐsài jiéshù le. Déguóduì （yǐ）
比赛 结束 了。德国队 （以） The match is over. It's a pity that the German

yì qiú zhī chā 注3 shūgěile
一 球 之 差注3 输给了 team lost to French by one goal only.

Fǎguóduì. Zhēn kěxī!
法国队。 真 可惜!

☆ 注 释（Notes） ☆

1. 这里的"差"是形容词，表示不好。
   "差" is an adjective here. It means "不好".
2. "赢"和"输"多用在口语中。书面语中常用"胜"和"败"。
   "赢" and "输" are often used in spoken Chinese. "胜" and "败" are often used in written Chinese.
3. 这里的"差"是名词，表示事物间的不同。
   "差" is a noun here to indicate the difference.

☆ 句型提示（Sentence pattern references） ☆

1. 我从小就喜欢音乐。 请参看 318 页句型 54。
2. 不怎么好，也不太差，一般。 请参看 366 页句型 162。

3. 昨天的足球赛现场直播,你看了吗? 请参看 309 页句型 36。
4. 我对足球不太感兴趣。 请参看 362 页句型 153。
5. 那场球赛精彩极了。 请参看 395 页句型 225。

☆　**词语用法举例**(Examples for usage of the words)　☆

1. 你有什么爱好

(1) Gè rén yǒu gè rén de àihào.
各 人 有 各 人 的 爱好。

(2) Wǒ de àihào hé yéye de àihào yíyàng.
我 的 爱好 和 爷爷 的 爱好 一样。

(3) Tā cóngxiǎo àihào kēxué.
他 从小 爱好 科学。

(4) Wǒmen dōu àihào hépíng.
我们 都 爱好 和平。

2. 不怎么好,也不太差

(1) Gāng mǎilái jiù huài le, zhìliàng tài chà.
刚 买来 就 坏 了, 质量 太 差。

(2) Zhège rén de pǐndé hěn chà.
这个 人 的 品德 很 差。 (品德:moral character)

(3) Tā bú rènzhēn xuéxí, suǒyǐ jìshù hěn chà.
他 不 认真 学习,所以 技术 很 差。

(4) Zhè zhǒng cháyè hái kěyǐ, bú tài hǎo yě bú tài chà.
这 种 茶叶 还 可以, 不 太 好 也 不 太 差。

3. 尤其爱看足球比赛

(1) Tā de zì xiě de hěn hǎo, yóuqí shì máobǐzì.
他 的 字 写 得 很 好, 尤其 是 毛笔字。

(2) Wǒ xǐhuan kàn xiǎoshuō, yóuqí shì chángpiān xiǎoshuō.
我 喜欢 看 小说, 尤其 是 长篇 小说。

(3) Shūshu xǐhuan tīng yīnyuè, yóuqí ài tīng gǔdiǎn yīnyuè.
叔叔 喜欢 听 音乐, 尤其 爱 听 古典 音乐。

(4) Mǎlù shang chángcháng dǔchē, yóuqí shì shàngxiàbān de shíhou.
马路 上 常常 堵车,尤其 是 上下班 的 时候。

4. 尤其爱看足球比赛

(1) Tā cóngxiǎo ài tán gāngqín.
他 从小 爱 弹 钢琴。

(2) Yéye zuì ài hē pútaojiǔ.
爷爷 最 爱 喝 葡萄酒。

(3) Tàitai ài guàngjiē, wǒ zhǐhǎo fèngpéi.
太太 爱 逛街, 我 只好 奉陪。 (奉陪:keep someone company)

(4)
Nǎinai ài chī yú, bú ài chī ròu.
奶奶 爱 吃 鱼, 不 爱 吃 肉。

5. 我对足球不太感兴趣

(1)
Gēge duì tiānwén hěn gǎn xìngqù.
哥哥 对 天文 很 感 兴趣。

(2)
Jiějie duì shízhuāng hěn gǎn xìngqù.
姐姐 对 时装 很 感 兴趣。

(3)
Bàba duì fángchǎn guǎnggào hěn gǎn xìngqù.
爸爸 对 房产 广告 很 感 兴趣。

(4)
Wǒ duì guàng shāngdiàn bù gǎn xìngqù.
我 对 逛 商店 不 感 兴趣。

6. 那场球赛精彩极了

(1)
Shànghǎi Zájìtuán de yǎnchū jīngcǎi jí le.
上海 杂技团 的 演出 精彩 极 了。 (杂技:acrobatics)

(2)
Zài Shànghǎi Dàjùyuàn yǎnchū de gējù jīngcǎi jí le.
在 上海 大剧院 演出 的 歌剧 精彩 极 了。

(3)
Zhège jùběn xiě de hěn jīngcǎi.
这个 剧本 写 得 很 精彩。 (剧本:script)

(4)
Guānzhòng wèi yǎnyuán de jīngcǎi biǎoyǎn gǔzhǎng.
观众 为 演员 的 精彩 表演 鼓掌。

7. 真可惜

(1)
Tā yīnwèi chā wǔ fēn méi kǎoshang dàxué, zhēn kěxī!
他 因为 差 五 分 没 考上 大学, 真 可惜!

(2)
Nǐ fàngqì zhème hǎo de jīhuì, tài kěxī.
你 放弃 这么 好 的 机会, 太 可惜。 (放弃:give up)

(3)
Hěn xiǎng hé dàjiā yìqǐ lǚxíng, kěxī shēngbìng zhùyuàn le.
很 想 和 大家 一起 旅行, 可惜 生病 住院 了。

(4)
Wǒ hěn xǐhuan nà jiàn dàyī, kěxī qián búgòu.
我 很 喜欢 那 件 大衣, 可惜 钱 不够。

☆ 词 语 (Word list) ☆

1. chàng(gē)
唱(歌) (动) sing

2. tiàowǔ
跳舞 (动) dance

3. gǔdiǎn yīnyuè
古典 音乐 (名) classical music

4. liúxíng gēqǔ
流行 歌曲 (名) pop music

5. tán gāngqín
弹 钢琴 play piano

6. měishù
美术 (名) the fine arts

7. shūfǎ
书法 (名) calligraphy

8. Àolínpǐkè
奥林匹克 (名) Olympic Games

9. guànjūn
冠军　　（名）　champion

10. yàjūn
亚军　　（名）　runner-up, second place

11. dì-sānmíng
第三名　　third place

12. shèng
胜　　（动）　win

13. bài
败　　（动）　lose

14. lánqiú
篮球　　（名）　basketball

15. páiqiú
排球　　（名）　volleyball

16. wǎngqiú
网球　　（名）　tennis

17. bàngqiú
棒球　　（名）　baseball

18. gāo'ěrfūqiú
高尔夫球　（名）　golf

19. yóuyǒng
游泳　　（名/动）　swim

20. guǎngbō
广播　　（名/动）　broadcast

21. píndào
频道　　（名）　channel

22. jiémù
节目　　（名）　program

23. jiāoxiǎng yīnyuèhuì
交响 音乐会（名）　symphony concert

24. héchàng
合唱　　（动）　chorus

25. dúchàng
独唱　　（动）　solo

26. xiànchǎng zhíbō
现场 直播（动）　live broadcast

27. chóngbō
重播　　（动）　rebroadcast

28. jùlèbù
俱乐部　　（名）　club

29. jiànshēnfáng
健身房　　（名）　gym

☆ 练 习(Exercises) ☆

一、用"对……感兴趣"回答问题 (Use "对……感兴趣" to answer the following questions)

1. 你喜欢抽烟吗?

2. 你常常看体育比赛吗?

3. 旅游的时候,山水风景和古代建筑,你更喜欢什么?

4. 你喜欢谈论政治吗?

二、选择填空 (Select the appropriate words to fill in the blanks)

　　赢　　输　　精彩　　遗憾　　直播　　一流　　从小　　可惜

1. 李教授的演讲(yǎnjiǎng/speech, lecture)非常_____。你没去听,真是太_____了。

2. 今天晚上电视台要_____NBA 篮球赛,我一定要看。

3. 我_____就希望能成为一个音乐家。

4. 那场比赛他因为脚痛,_____给了对手。

5. 他是_____的时装设计师。

6. 他的水平比小张高,所以,十次比赛他_____了七次。

7. 哎呀,酒瓶打碎了,这么好的酒,_____了。

三、回答问题（Answer the following questions）

1. 你有什么爱好？业余时间你做什么？

2. 你喜欢古典音乐还是流行音乐？

3. 你看过中国的京剧吗？

四、根据指定内容作一个介绍（Give a brief description on the following subjects）

1. 你们国家圣诞节（Shèngdàn Jié/Christmas）的情况。

2. 你家乡的天气情况。

五、会话（Conversation）

玛　丽：明明画得真不错。

郭明明：老师说我画画儿有进步。

于雪来：卡尔呢？他有什么爱好？

玛　丽：他喜欢踢（tī/play, kick）球，还有游泳。男孩子就是喜欢运动（yùndòng/sports）。

于雪来：玛丽，你喜欢体育运动吗？

玛　丽：我喜欢比较安静的活动，听听音乐、看看小说什么的。你呢，小于？

于雪来：我喜欢看戏。现在很多年轻人对传统艺术不感兴趣，可是我觉得很有意思。

玛　丽：你先生也爱看戏吗？

于雪来：他？他什么爱好都没有。

郭明明：爸爸爱抽烟。

于雪来、玛丽：哈哈。

于雪来：这不是爱好，这是不良嗜好（shìhào/hobby, addiction）。

☆　　练习答案（Key to the exercises）　　☆

二、1. 精彩　遗憾　　2. 直播　　3. 从小　　4. 输
　　5. 一流　　　　　6. 赢　　　7. 可惜

Chinese for Foreigners

外国人学汉语

Practical Sentence Patterns

常用句型

1. 陈述句＋吗？

Be ... ? Do + verb ... ?

Tā shì xuésheng ma?
(1) 他 是 学生 吗？

Is he a student?

Shì de, tā shì xuésheng.
——是 的，他 是 学生。

— Yes, he is a student.

Míngtiān nǐ qù gōngsī ma?
(2) 明天 你 去 公司 吗？

Are you going to the company tomorrow?

Qù.
——去。

— Yes, I am.

Shūjià shang yǒu bàozhǐ ma?
(3) 书架 上 有 报纸 吗？

Is there a newspaper on the bookshelf?

Méiyǒu.
——没有。

— No, there isn't.

Tā xǐhuan yīnyuè ma?
(4) 他 喜欢 音乐 吗？

Does he like music?

Tā bù xǐhuan yīnyuè.
——他 不 喜欢 音乐。

— No, he doesn't.

2. 动词＋了＋没有/吗？

Have + verb（past participle）... ?
Did + verb ... ?

Nǐ fùxíle méiyǒu?
(1) 你 复习了 没有？

Have you reviewed（your lessons）?

Fùxí le.
——复习 了。

— Yes, I have.

Tā qù chūchāile méiyǒu?
(2) 他 去 出差了 没有？

Has he already gone on business?

Hái méi qù.
——还 没 去。

— Not yet.

Tā kǎoshang dàxué le ma?
(3) 他 考上 大学 了 吗？

Has he passed the university entrance exami-

nation?

Kǎoshang le.
——考上 了。

— Yes, he did.

Zǎoshang de diànshì xīnwén,
(4) 早上 的 电视 新闻，

Did you watch the morning news on TV?

nǐ kànle ma?
你 看了 吗？

Méi kàn.
——没 看。

— No, I didn't.

这是询问动作是否完成的格式。

This pattern is used to ask whether an action is completed or not.

293

3. 可以……吗？ ……，可以吗？　　Can/May ... ?

(1) Kěyǐ jìnlai ma?
　　可以 进来 吗？　　　　　May I come in?

　　——Qǐng jìn.
　　——请 进。　　　　　　　— Yes, please.

(2) Kěyǐ kāi chuāng ma?
　　可以 开 窗 吗？　　　　　May I open the window?

　　——Kěyǐ.
　　——可以。　　　　　　　— Yes, please.

(3) Zài zhèli tíngchē, kěyǐ ma?
　　在 这里 停车，可以 吗？　Can I park my car here?

　　——Bùxíng.
　　——不行。　　　　　　　— No, you can't.

(4) Zài zhèli chōuyān, kěyǐ ma?
　　在 这里 抽烟，可以 吗？　Can I smoke here?

　　——Bùxíng.
　　——不行。　　　　　　　— No, you can't.

这是询问对方是否允许自己做某事的格式。

This pattern is used to ask for permission.

4. ……也/都 + 行吗？　　May/Can ... ?

(1) Yòng qiānbǐ xiě yě xíng ma?
　　用 铅笔 写 也 行 吗？　　Is it all right to write with pencil?

　　——Xíng.
　　——行。　　　　　　　　— All right.

(2) Wǎn yìdiǎnr lái yě xíng ma?
　　晚 一点儿 来 也 行 吗？　May I come a little later?

　　——Xíng.
　　——行。　　　　　　　　— OK.

(3) Zhège jiāogěi shuí dōu xíng ma?
　　这个 交给 谁 都 行 吗？　Is it OK to give this to anyone (there)?

　　——Bù, qǐng jiāogěi xiàozhǎng.
　　——不，请 交给 校长。　— No, please give it to the principal.

(4) Zhège fàngzài nǎr dōu xíng ma?
　　这个 放在 哪儿 都 行 吗？May I put it wherever I like?

　　——Bù, yào fàngzài zhuōzi shang.
　　——不，要 放在 桌子 上。— No, put it on the desk.

在有多项选择的情况下，问话人询问自己是否可以选择某一项。

The pattern is used to ask if the questioners could make a choice among several alternatives.

5. 知道……吗？ ……，知道吗？

(1) Nǐ zhīdao shénme shíhou kǎoshì ma?
你 知道 什么 时候 考试 吗？
——（Zhīdao, shì）xià ge xīngqī.
——（知道，是）下 个 星期。

(2) Nǐ zhīdao nǎge fàndiàn hǎo ma?
你 知道 哪个 饭店 好 吗？
——Xīnyǎ Yuècàiguǎn.
——新雅 粤菜馆。

(3) Hànzì yǒu duōshao, nǐ zhīdao ma?
汉字 有 多少， 你 知道 吗？
——Bù zhīdao.
——不 知道。

(4) Zhōngguó guótǔ yǒu duō dà, nǐ zhīdao ma?
中国 国土 有 多 大， 你 知道 吗？
——Bù zhīdao.
——不 知道。

Do you know ... ?

Do you know when the exam will take place?

— Yes, next week.

Do you know which restaurant is good?

— The Xinya Cantonese Restaurant.

Do you know how many Chinese characters are there?

— No, I don't.

Do you know how big the area of China is?

— No, I don't know.

6. 什么？ 什么 + 名词？

(1) Zhè shì shénme?
这 是 什么？
——Zhè shì huā.
——这 是 花。

(2) Nǐ zài zuò shénme?
你 在 做 什么？
——Zài tīng yīnyuè.
——在 听 音乐。

(3) Nǐ jiào shénme míngzi?
你 叫 什么 名字？
——Wǒ jiào Lǐ Xiǎomíng.
——我 叫 李 小明。

(4) Nà běn shì shénme shū?
那 本 是 什么 书？
——Shì xiǎoshuō.
——是 小说。

What? What + noun?

What are they?

— They are flowers.

What are you doing?

— I am listening to the music.

What is your name?

— My name is Li Xiaoming.

What kind of book is that?

— That is a novel.

7. 哪个？　哪些？　哪种？　　　　**Which one?**

Nǎge bēizi shì bàba de?
（1）哪个　杯子　是　爸爸　的？　　Which is dad's cup?

　　　Nàge lánsè de.
　　——那个　蓝色　的。　　　　　　— The blue one.

Nǎxiē qiānbǐ shì dìdi de?
（2）哪些　铅笔　是　弟弟　的？　　Which pencils are my younger brother's?

　　　Zhèxiē shì dìdi de.
　　——这些　是　弟弟　的。　　　　— Those are his.

Nǎ zhǒng píngguǒ zuì tián?
（3）哪　种　苹果　最　甜？　　　Which kind of apple is the sweetest?

　　　Zhè zhǒng.
　　——这　种。　　　　　　　　　— This kind is.

Nǐ xǐhuan nǎ zhǒng yàngzi?
（4）你　喜欢　哪　种　样子？　　Which style do you like?

　　　Nà zhǒng.
　　——那　种。　　　　　　　　　— That one.

8. 哪里？　哪儿？　什么地方？　**Where? What place? Which direction?**
　　哪边？

Shànghǎi Bówùguǎn zài nǎli?
（1）上海　博物馆　在　哪里？　Where is the Shanghai Museum?

　　　Zài Rénmín Guǎngchǎng.
　　——在　人民　广场。　　　　— In People's Square.

Nǐ qù nǎr?
（2）你　去　哪儿？　　　　　　Where are you going?

　　　Qù gōngsī.
　　——去　公司。　　　　　　　— To my company.

Shénme dìfang yǒu dìtú mài?
（3）什么　地方　有　地图　卖？　Where can I buy maps?

　　　Shūdiàn yǒu mài.
　　——书店　有　卖。　　　　　— In bookstores.

Nǎbian shì dōng?
（4）哪边　是　东？　　　　　　Which direction is east?

　　　Nàbian.
　　——那边。　　　　　　　　　— That direction.

9. 什么时候？

When? What time?

(1) Nǐ shénme shíhou qù Běijīng?
你 什么 时候 去 北京？

When are you going to Beijing?

Míngtiān.
——明天。

— Tomorrow.

(2) Tā shénme shíhou bìyè?
他 什么 时候 毕业？

When will he graduate?

Míngnián.
——明年。

— Next year.

(3) Tā shénme shíhou huí guó?
他 什么 时候 回 国？

When will he return to his country?

Xià ge yuè.
——下 个 月。

— Next month.

(4) Bàba shénme shíhou chūchāi?
爸爸 什么 时候 出差？

When will dad go on a business trip?

Xià ge xīngqī.
——下 个 星期。

— Next week.

10. 哪……？ 几……？

What time ... / Which (time)?

(1) Nǐ shì nǎ nián shēng de?
你 是 哪 年 生 的？

Which year were you born in?

Yījiǔliùjiǔ nián shēng de.
——一九六九 年 生 的。

— I was born in 1969.

(2) Xuéxiào jǐ yuè kāixué?
学校 几 月 开学？

Which month will the school term begin in?

Jiǔ yuè.
——九 月。

— In September.

(3) Jīntiān jǐ hào? Xīngqī jǐ?
今天 几 号？ 星期 几？

What date and what day is it today?

Sān hào, xīngqīsān.
——三 号，星期三。

— The third, Wednesday.

(4) Xiànzài jǐ diǎn?
现在 几 点？

What time is it now?

Bā diǎn.
——八 点。

— Eight o'clock.

这里的"哪"、"几"是询问时点。

"哪" and "几" here are used to ask exact time.

11. 几……? — How long/ many (time period)?

（1）你 在 上海 住了 几 年？
Nǐ zài Shànghǎi zhùle jǐ nián?
How long have you been in Shanghai?

——五 年。
Wǔ nián.
— For five years.

（2）一 个 学期 有 几 个 月？
Yí ge xuéqī yǒu jǐ ge yuè?
How many months does a school term have?

——五 个 月。
Wǔ ge yuè.
— Five months.

（3）你 打算 在 这儿 待 几 天？
Nǐ dǎsuan zài zhèr dāi jǐ tiān?
How many days are you going to stay here?

——四 天。
Sì tiān.
— Four days.

（4）一 个 月 有 几 个 星期？
Yí ge yuè yǒu jǐ ge xīngqī?
How many weeks are there in a month?

——四 个 星期。
Sì ge xīngqī.
— Four weeks.

（5）这个 会 要 开 几 个 小时？
Zhège huì yào kāi jǐ ge xiǎoshí?
How many hours will this meeting last?

—— 两 个 小时。
Liǎng ge xiǎoshí.
— Two hours.

这里的"几"是询问时段。
"几" here is used to ask time period.

12. 多少……?　几+量词? — How many/much + measure word?

（1）这 双 鞋 多少 钱？
Zhè shuāng xié duōshao qián?
How much is this pair of shoes?

——一百 八十 块。
Yìbǎi bāshí kuài.
— 180 *yuan*.

（2）礼堂 里 有 多少 学生？
Lǐtáng li yǒu duōshao xuésheng?
How many students are there in the hall?

——两百 多。
Liǎngbǎi duō.
— More than 200.

（3）那里 有 几 个 孩子？
Nàli yǒu jǐ ge háizi?
How many children are there over there?

——六七 个。
Liù-qī ge.
— About six or seven.

（4）你 有 几 本 英语 杂志？
Nǐ yǒu jǐ běn Yīngyǔ zázhì?
How many English magazines do you have?

Yǒu sān běn.
——有 三 本。 — Three.

这是询问数量的格式。估计数量在十以上时用"多少"来提问,估计数量在十以下时用"几 + 量词"提问。

This pattern is used to ask quantity. When the quantity is estimated to be more than ten, use "多少" to make the question, otherwise, use "几 + 量词".

13. 怎么……? 为什么……? Why ... ? What is the matter?

Tā zěnme méi lái?
(1) 他 怎么 没 来? Why didn't he come?

Tā shēngbìng le.
——他 生病 了。 — He is ill.

Nǐ zěnme bú qù lǚyóu?
(2) 你 怎么 不 去 旅游? Why didn't you take a tour?

Wǒ méi kòng.
——我 没 空。 — Because I was busy.

Nǐ wèi shénme chídào?
(3) 你 为 什么 迟到? Why are you late?

Yīnwèi lù shang dǔchē.
——因为 路 上 堵车。 — I was caught in a traffic jam.

Dìdi wèi shénme kū?
(4) 弟弟 为 什么 哭? Why is my younger brother crying?

Yīnwèi kǎoshì bù jígé.
——因为 考试 不 及格。 — He failed the examination.

Zěnme la?
(5) 怎么 啦? What's the matter?

Wǒ yǒu diǎnr bù shūfu.
——我 有 点儿 不 舒服。 — I feel a bit unwell.

Zěnme huí shì?
(6) 怎么 回 事? What's the matter?

Qiánmian chū chēhuò le.
——前面 出 车祸 了。 — There is a traffic accident ahead.

这是询问原因的格式。

This pattern is used to ask reasons.

14. 怎么 + 动词?
How + verb?

Qù Xī'ěrdùn Bīnguǎn zěnme zǒu?
（1）去 希尔顿 宾馆 怎么 走?
How can I get to the Hilton Hotel?

Xiàng yòu guǎi jiù dào le.
——向 右 拐 就 到 了。
— Just turn right, then you'll get there.

Zhè jiàn shì zěnme bàn?
（2）这 件 事 怎么 办?
How should I deal with this?

Nǐ wèn kēzhǎng ba.
——你 问 科长 吧。
— Please ask the boss.

Nǐ shì zěnme lái de?
（3）你 是 怎么 来 的?
How did you come here?

Zǒulai de.
——走来 的。
— On foot.

Gēn tā zěnme liánxì?
（4）跟 他 怎么 联系?
How should I contact him?

Kěyǐ dǎ diànhuà.
——可以 打 电话。
— You may make a phone call.

这是询问动作方式的格式。
This pattern is used to ask the way of doing something.

15. ……怎么样?
How?

Zhè zhǒng bù zěnmeyàng?
（1）这 种 布 怎么样?
How is this cotton cloth?

Yòu piányi yòu hǎokàn.
——又 便宜 又 好看。
— It is cheap and looks nice.

Tā Hànyǔ xué de zěnmeyàng?
（2）他 汉语 学 得 怎么样?
How are his Chinese studies?

Jìnbù hěn kuài.
——进步 很 快。
— He has made great progress.

Nánjīng de tiānqì zěnmeyàng?
（3）南京 的 天气 怎么样?
How is the weather in Nanjing?

Hé Shànghǎi chàbuduō.
——和 上海 差不多。
— Similar to the weather in Shanghai.

Nǐ māma de bìng zěnmeyàng le?
（4）你 妈妈 的 病 怎么样 了?
How is your mother?

Yǐjīng hǎo le.
——已经 好 了。
— She is well again.

这里的"怎么样"是询问人或事物的状况。
"怎么样" here is used to ask the situation of somebody or something.

16. A 不 A?　　A(B) 不 AB?　Be ... ? Do + verb ... ?

(1) Tā shì bu shì xuésheng?
他 是 不 是 学生？

Is he a student?

——Shì de, tā shì xuésheng.
——是 的，他 是 学生。

— Yes, he is a student.

(2) Nǐ dìdi huì bu huì Yīngyǔ?
你 弟弟 会 不 会 英语？

Can your younger brother speak English?

——Bú huì.
——不 会。

— No, he can't.

(3) Hánjià nǐ huí (guó) bu huí guó?
寒假 你 回 (国) 不 回 国？

Are you going back to your country for winter vacation?

——Bù huíqu.
——不 回去。

— No, I am not.

(4) Zhège cài hǎo(chī) bu hǎochī?
这个 菜 好(吃) 不 好吃？

Is this dish delicious?

——Hěn hǎochī.
——很 好吃。

— Yes, it is.

　　这是用肯定形式和否定形式并列构成的疑问句。跟句型 1 的意思一样。A 是动词或形容词。

　　This pattern is used to form an interrogative sentence by putting an affirmative and a negative forms of the predicate side by side. The meaning of this pattern is the same as the Pattern 1. Here "A" is a verb or adjective.

17. A 还是 B?　A or B?

(1) Zhè shì nǐ de háishi tā de?
这 是 你 的 还是 他 的？

Is this yours or his?

——Shì tā de.
——是 他 的。

— It is his.

(2) Nǐ xǐhuan bái de háishi lǜ de?
你 喜欢 白 的 还是 绿 的？

Do you like the white one or the green one?

——Xǐhuan bái de.
——喜欢 白 的。

— I like the white one.

(3) Wǒmen jīntiān qù háishi míngtiān qù?
我们 今天 去还是 明天 去？

Shall we go there today or tomorrow?

——Míngtiān qù ba.
——明天 去 吧。

— Let's go tomorrow.

Zhè jiàn shì, nǐ zuò háishi
(4) 这 件 事, 你 做 还是
tā zuò?
他 做?

Who will do this? You or him?

Wǒ zuò ba.
——我 做 吧。

— Let me do it.

这是选择疑问句。在两种或几种情况中,询问对方的选择。

This pattern is used to form an alternative question. The questioner asks the choice of the other party from two or more alternatives.

18. 名词/代词 + 呢?   Where ... ?

Wǒ de shǒutào ne?
(1) 我 的 手套 呢?

Where are my gloves?

Zài yīguì li.
——在 衣柜 里。

— In the wardrobe.

Chén kēzhǎng ne?
(2) 陈 科长 呢?

Where is Mr. Chen?

Zài bàngōngshì.
——在 办公室。

— In the office.

Jīpiào ne?
(3) 机票 呢?

Where is my air ticket?

Fàngdào shǒutíbāo li le.
——放到 手提包 里 了。

— It's been put into your bag.

Nǐ de háizi ne?
(4) 你 的 孩子 呢?

Where are your kids?

Qù yòu'éryuán le.
——去 幼儿园 了。

— Gone to the kindergarten.

在特定的情况下,询问人或事物在什么地方。这个格式等于"……在什么地方?"

This pattern is used to ask the location of somebody or something under certain circumstances. It's equal to "……在什么地方?"

19. A……, B 呢?   A ... , how/what about B?

Wǒ míngtiān qù Pǔdōng, nǐ ne?
(1) 我 明天 去 浦东, 你 呢?

I am going to Pudong tomorrow, what about you?

Wǒ yě qù.
——我 也 去。

— I'll go there too.

Jīntiān cānguān bówùguǎn,
(2) 今天 参观 博物馆,

(The schedule is) to visit the museum today,

míngtiān ne?
明天 呢？   then what about tomorrow?

     Cānguān měishùguǎn.
——参观 美术馆。   — Visit the art gallery.

     Nǐ xǐhuan chàng gē, tiàowǔ ne?
(3) 你 喜欢 唱 歌，跳舞 呢？   You like singing, how about dancing?

     Yě xǐhuan.
——也 喜欢。   — I like dancing too.

     Jiějie hěn piàoliang, mèimei ne?
(4) 姐姐 很 漂亮， 妹妹 呢？   The elder sister is pretty, how about the

     younger sister?

     Mèimei bú tài piàoliang.
——妹妹 不 太 漂亮。   — Not so pretty.

在特定的情况下，询问人或事物的状况。这个格式等于"A……，B 怎么样？"

The pattern is used to ask the situation of somebody or something under certain circumstances. It's equal to "A……，B 怎么样？"

20. 多 + 形容词？ 有 + 多 + 形容 How + adjective?
词？

     Zhè zuò dàlóu yǒu duō gāo?
(1) 这 座 大楼 有 多 高？   How high is this building?

     Yǒu sānbǎi wǔshí mǐ.
——有 三百 五十 米。   — 350 meters.

     Zhège xiāngzi duō zhòng?
(2) 这个 箱子 多 重？   How heavy is the box?

     Yǒu èrshíwǔ gōngjīn.
——有 二十五 公斤。   — 25 kilograms.

     Zhèr dào jīchǎng duō yuǎn?
(3) 这儿 到 机场 多 远？   How far is it to the airport?

     Zuò chē yào sìshí fēnzhōng.
——坐 车 要 四十 分钟。   — 40 minutes' drive.

     Nǐ de érzi duō dà?
(4) 你 的 儿子 多 大？   How old is your son?

     Jiǔ suì le.
——九 岁 了。   — Nine years old.

这是询问程度、数量的格式。

This pattern is used to ask the degree or the quantity.

21. A 是 B

A + be + B

(1) 他　是　学生。
Tā shì xuésheng.

He is a student.

(2) 这　位　是　校长。
Zhè wèi shì xiàozhǎng.

This is Mr. President.

(3) 这　是　今天　的　报纸。
Zhè shì jīntiān de bàozhǐ.

This is today's newspaper.

(4) 那　是　妈妈　的　房间。
Nà shì māma de fángjiān.

That is my mother's room.

22. A 不是 B

A + be + not + B

(1) 我　不　是　教师。
Wǒ bú shì jiàoshī.

I am not a teacher.

(2) 他　不　是　美国人。
Tā bú shì Měiguórén.

He is not an American.

(3) 这　不　是　我　的　书。
Zhè bú shì wǒ de shū.

This is not my book.

(4) 这　不　是　弟弟　的　本子。
Zhè bú shì dìdi de běnzi.

That is not my younger brother's notebook.

23. 人/物 + 在 + 处所

Somebody/something + place

(1) 爸爸　在　公司　里。
Bàba zài gōngsī li.

My father is at his company.

(2) 妈妈　在　家　里。
Māma zài jiā li.

My mother is at home.

(3) 杂志　在　桌子　上。
Zázhì zài zhuōzi shang.

The magazine is on the desk.

(4) 我　的　伞　在　外面。
Wǒ de sǎn zài wàimian.

My umbrella is outside (this room).

24. 人/物 + 不在 + 处所

Somebody/something + not + place

(1) 哥哥　不　在　学校　里。
Gēge bú zài xuéxiào li.

My elder brother is not in the school.

(2) 弟弟　不　在　院子　里。
Dìdi bú zài yuànzi li.

My younger brother is not in the yard.

(3) 大衣　不　在　床　上。
Dàyī bú zài chuáng shang.

The overcoat is not on the bed.

(4) 鞋子　不　在　椅子　下。
Xiézi bú zài yǐzi xia.

The shoes are not under the chair.

25. 在 + 处所 + 动词

Verb + place

Wǒ zài xuéxiào xuéxí Hànyǔ.
(1) 我 在 学校 学习 汉语。

I am studying Chinese at school.

Tā zài jiàoshì fùxí.
(2) 他 在 教室 复习。

He is reviewing his lessons in the classroom.

Tā zài yīyuàn gōngzuò.
(3) 她 在 医院 工作。

She works at the hospital.

Bàba zài kètīng kàn bàozhǐ.
(4) 爸爸 在 客厅 看 报纸。

My father is reading newspapers in the living room.

26. A + 有 + B

A + have + B

Wǒ yǒu yí ge gēge.
(1) 我 有 一 个 哥哥。

I have an elder brother.·

Tā yǒu zhàoxiàngjī.
(2) 他 有 照相机。

He has a camera.

Jīntiān wǒ yǒu yuēhuì.
(3) 今天 我 有 约会。

I have an appointment today.

Wǒ yǒu shì, bù néng qù.
(4) 我 有 事，不 能 去。

I have something to do. I can't go.

27. A + 没（有）+ B

A + have + not + B

Wǒ méiyǒu mèimei.
(1) 我 没有 妹妹。

I don't have a younger sister.

Dìdi méiyǒu shǒubiǎo.
(2) 弟弟 没有 手表。

My younger brother doesn't have a watch.

Niánqīngrén méiyǒu jīngyàn.
(3) 年轻人 没有 经验。

Young people lack experience.

Wǒ méi qián.
(4) 我 没 钱。

I have no money.

28. 处所 + 有（ + 数量）+ 人/物

There + be（ + numeral – measure word）+ somebody/something + place

Jiàoshì li yǒu shí ge xuésheng.
(1) 教室 里 有 十 个 学生。

There are ten students in the classroom.

Dàshù xia yǒu（yì）zhī gǒu.
(2) 大树 下 有（一）只 狗。

There is a dog under the tree.

Shūbāo li yǒu wénjùhé.
(3) 书包 里 有 文具盒。

There is a stationery box in the schoolbag.

Zhuōzi shang yǒu liǎng ge lí.
(4) 桌子 上 有 两 个 梨。

There are two pears on the table.

29. 处所 + 没有 + 人/物

There + be + not + somebody/something + place

Jiàoshì li méiyǒu jiàoshī.
（1）教室　里　没有　教师。

There are no teachers in the classroom.

Cāochǎng shang méiyǒu xiǎoháir.
（2）操场　　上　没有　小孩儿。

There are no children on the playground.

Fángjiān li méiyǒu diànshìjī.
（3）房间　里　没有　电视机。

There is no TV in the room.

Shūjià shang méiyǒu bàozhǐ.
（4）书架　　上　没有　报纸。

There are no newspaper on the bookshelf.

30. a 经常 + 动词
   b 不常 + 动词

Often/regularly/frequently/always + verb

Hardly/scarcely + verb

Wǒ jīngcháng zǎoshang qī diǎn
（1）我　经常　　早上　七　点
qǐchuáng.
起床。

I usually get up at seven o'clock every day.

Tā cháng qù Hángzhōu.
（2）他　常　去　杭州。

He went to Hangzhou regularly.

Zhèli zuìjìn zǒng guā fēng.
（3）这里　最近　总　刮　风。

It has been windy recently.

Tā měi tiān duànliàn shēntǐ.
（4）他　每　天　锻炼　身体。

He exercises every day.

Tā bù cháng lái zhèli.
（5）他　不　常　来　这里。

He hardly came here.

Zhèli de dōngtiān bù cháng xià xuě.
（6）这里　的　冬天　不　常　下　雪。

There is little snow here in winter.

Tā hěn shǎo chōuyān.
（7）他　很　少　抽烟。

He rarely smokes.

Tā hěn shǎo hē jiǔ.
（8）他　很　少　喝　酒。

He hardly drinks.

　　这个句型中的动词是经常性的动作、行为。在动词的前面要加上表示经常性的词语，如："经常"、"常常"、"常"、"总"、"每天"等。否定时要加上"不常"或"很少"。

　　In this pattern the verb indicates that the action happens frequently. The words like "经常", "常常", "常", "总", "每天" etc. should be added before the verb. In negative sentences, the word "不常" or "很少" should be added.

31. a（将＋）动词　　　　Will + verb
b 不＋动词　　　　　Will + not + verb

（1）Wǒ míngtiān qù Běijīng chūchāi.
我 明天 去 北京 出差。

I will go to Beijing on business tomorrow.

（2）Xià ge yuè jiāng zhàokāi
下 个 月 将 召开

dǒngshìhuì.
董事会。

The meeting of the Board of Directors will be

held next month.

（3）Míngtiān tā bù lái.
明天 他 不 来。

He will not come tomorrow.

（4）Hòutiān bù kāihuì.
后天 不 开会。

There is no meeting the day after tomorrow.

　　"将＋动词"表示将要发生的动作,一般用于书面语中。口语中不必加"将"。b 是 a 的否定形式。

　　"将＋动词" indicates that the action will happen in the future. It is usually used in written language. In spoken Chinese"将" can be omitted. The pattern "b" is the negative form of pattern "a".

32.（就/快＋）要＋动词＋了　　Will + verb + soon

（1）Yào xià yǔ le, kuài huí jiā ba.
要 下 雨 了, 快 回 家 吧。

It is going to rain soon. Let's go home.

（2）Jiù yào kǎoshì le, bú qù
就 要 考试 了, 不 去

lǚxíng le.
旅行 了。

The examination is coming. We should cancel

the trip.

（3）Fēijī jiù yào qǐfēi le,
飞机 就 要 起飞 了,

shàng fēijī ba.
上 飞机 吧。

The airplane will take off soon. Let's go on

board.

（4）Nà kē shù kuài yào dǎo le.
那 棵 树 快 要 倒 了。

That tree will fall over soon.

　　这个格式表示动作马上要发生。
　　This pattern indicates that the action will happen very soon.

33. a（正）在 + 动词（+ 呢）
正 + 动词 + 呢

b 没（+ 在）+ 动词

Be + verb（present participle）

Be + not + verb（present participle）

(1)	Māma zhèngzài xiě xìn. 妈妈 正在 写 信。	Mother is writing a letter.
(2)	Bàba zài kàn shū. 爸爸 在 看 书。	Father is reading a book.
(3)	Tāmen zhèng shàngkè ne. 他们 正 上课 呢。	They are attending a class now.
(4)	Tā zài dǎ wǎngqiú ne. 他 在 打 网球 呢。	He is playing tennis.
(5)	Tā méi zài zuò zuòyè, zài wán ne. 他 没 在 做 作业，在 玩 呢。	He is not doing his homework. He is playing.
(6)	Wǒ méi kàn diànshì, zài dǎsǎo ne. 我 没 看 电视，在 打扫 呢。	I am not watching TV. I am cleaning up.

a 表示动作在进行中。b 是 a 的否定形式。

The pattern "a" indicates that the action is underway. The pattern "b" is the negative form of "a".

34. a 动词 + 着
b 没 + 动词（+ 着）

Be + verb（participle）; Be + condition

Be + not + verb（participle）; Be + not + condition

(1)	Mén guānzhe. 门 关着。	The door is closed.
(2)	Diàndēng kāizhe. 电灯 开着。	The lamp is on.
(3)	Mèimei názhe píngguǒ. 妹妹 拿着 苹果。	My younger sister is holding an apple.
(4)	Mén méi suǒ. 门 没 锁。	The door is not locked.
(5)	Diàndēng méi kāizhe. 电灯 没 开着。	The lamp is not on.
(6)	Diànshìjī méi guān. 电视机 没 关。	The TV hasn't been switched off.

a 表示动作或动作结果的状态在持续。b 是 a 的否定形式。

The pattern "a" indicates the action continues or the result of the action exists. The pattern "b" is the negative form of "a".

35. a 处所 + 动词 + 着（+ 数量）+ 人/物

b 处所 + 没 + 动词 + 人/物

There + be + somebody/something + verb（participle）+ place; Somebody/something + be + place

There + be + not + somebody/something + verb（participle）+ place; Somebody/something + be + not + place

	Qiáng shang guàzhe shìjiè dìtú.	
(1)	墙 上 挂着 世界 地图。	There is a world map hung on the wall.

(1)
Qiáng shang guàzhe shìjiè dìtú.
墙 上 挂着 世界 地图。
There is a world map hung on the wall.

(2)
Hēibǎn shang xiězhe tā de míngzi.
黑板 上 写着 他 的 名字。
His name is written on the blackboard.

(3)
Zhuōzi shang fàngzhe yí ge zhōng.
桌子 上 放着 一 个 钟。
There is a clock on the desk.

(4)
Shāfā shang zuòzhe sān ge rén.
沙发 上 坐着 三 个 人。
Three persons are sitting on the sofa.

(5)
Huāpíng li méi chā huā.
花瓶 里 没 插 花。
There is no flower in the vase.

(6)
Hēibǎn shang méi xiě zì.
黑板 上 没 写 字。
There is no word on the blackboard.

(7)
Zhèli méi xiě jiàqian.
这里 没 写 价钱。
No price is marked here.

(8)
Shāfā shang méi zuò rén.
沙发 上 没 坐 人。
No one is sitting on the sofa.

a 表示在某处某个动作在持续。b 是 a 的否定形式。

The pattern "a" indicates that the action is underway or a condition exists in some place. The pattern "b" is the negative form of "a".

36. a 动词 + 了　动词 + 过 + 了
b 没 + 动词

Verb（past tense）; Have + past participle
Did not + verb; Have + not + past participle

(1)
Bàba liù diǎn chūle mén.
爸爸 六 点 出了 门。
Dad went out at six o'clock.

(2)
Tā zuótiān qùle Tiānjīn.
他 昨天 去了 天津。
He went to Tianjin yesterday.

(3)
Māma shàngwǔ xiěle xìn.
妈妈 上午 写了 信。
Mother wrote a letter in the morning.

(4)
Lǐ Huá qiántiān láile Shànghǎi.
李 华 前天 来了 上海。
Li Hua came to Shanghai the day before yesterday.

Wǒ xǐguo tóu le.
(5) 我 洗过 头 了。

I have had my hair washed.

Wǒ chīguo fàn le.
(6) 我 吃过 饭 了。

I have had my meal.

Zuótiān wǒ méi fùxí.
(7) 昨天 我 没 复习。

I didn't review my lessons yesterday.

Shǔjià tā méi qù lǚxíng.
(8) 暑假 他 没 去 旅行。

He didn't take a tour in the summer vacation.

Xīngqīliù wǒ méi xuéxí.
(9) 星期六 我 没 学习。

I didn't study (last) Saturday.

Zhōngwǔ wǒ méi chī fàn.
(10) 中午 我 没 吃饭。

I didn't have lunch at noon.

a 表示动作已经发生并完成。b 否定动作发生过。

The pattern "a" indicates the action has happened and been completed. The pattern "b" is the negative form of "a".

37. a 动词 + 过   **Have + past participle**
b 没 + 动词 + 过   **Have + not + past participle**

Tā qùguo Yīngguó.
(1) 他 去过 英国。

He has been to England.

Wǒ kànguo zhè běn shū.
(2) 我 看过 这 本 书。

I have read this book.

Dìdi xuéguo Fǎyǔ.
(3) 弟弟 学过 法语。

My younger brother has learnt French.

Wǒ méi kànguo jīngjù.
(4) 我 没 看过 京剧。

I've never seen the Beijing Opera.

Wǒ méi jiànguo nàge rén.
(5) 我 没 见过 那个 人。

I've never seen that man.

Tā méi quēxíguo.
(6) 他 没 缺席过。

He has never been absent.

a 表示曾经发生某种事情。b 表示从来没有发生某种事情。

The pattern "a" indicates that something has happened before. The pattern "b" indicates that something has never happened.

38. 动词 1 + 了 + 动词 2   **Verb 2 + after + verb 1**

Wǒ xiàle kè qù túshūguǎn.
(1) 我 下了 课 去 图书馆。

I'll go to the library after the class.

Wǒ chīle fàn qù kàn diànyǐng.
(2) 我 吃了 饭 去 看 电影。　　I'll go to the cinema after the meal.

Wǒ xiàle bān gēn nǚpéngyou
(3) 我 下了 班 跟 女朋友　　I'll see my girl friend after work.
jiànmiàn.
见面。

Nǐ chīle wǎnfàn lái wǒ de
(4) 你 吃了 晚饭 来 我 的　　Please come to my home after supper.
jiā ba.
家 吧。

假设动作 1 完成后将进行动作 2。

This pattern indicates that action 2 will happen after the completion of the action 1.

39. 动词 1 + 动词 2　　**Verb 1 and then verb 2**

Tā dàishang màozi chūmén le.
(1) 他 戴上 帽子 出门 了。　　He put on a cap, and then went out.

Wǒ cāshang féizào xǐle shǒu.
(2) 我 擦上 肥皂 洗了 手。　　I applied soap, and then washed my hands.

Tā pàole chá hē.
(3) 他 泡了 茶 喝。　　He made tea and drank it.

Wǒ mǎile ge miànbāo chī.
(4) 我 买了 个 面包 吃。　　I bought a bun and ate it.

这个格式表示先后连续的动作。

This pattern indicates that two actions happen successively.

40. 动词 1 + 着 + 动词 2　　**Verb 2 + verb 1（present participle）**

Wǒmen zǒuzhe qù ba.
(1) 我们 走着 去 吧。　　Let's go on foot.

Lǎoshī zhànzhe jiǎngkè.
(2) 老师 站着 讲课。　　The teacher is giving a lesson standing there.

Tā tǎngzhe kàn shū.
(3) 他 躺着 看 书。　　He is reading a book lying there.

Tā dàizhe háizi qù gōngyuán.
(4) 她 带着 孩子 去 公园。　　She went to the park with her child.

这个格式表示两个动作同时进行。动作 1 是动作 2 的方式。

This pattern indicates that two actions are going on simultaneously. The action 1 describes the way of the action 2.

41. 来/去 + 处所 + 动词

Go/Come to somewhere + verb + something

(1)
Ānnà lái Zhōngguó xuéxí Hànyǔ.
安娜 来 中国 学习 汉语。

Anna came to China to study Chinese.

(2)
Lǐ Fāng lái Shànghǎi kāihuì.
李 芳 来 上海 开会。

Li Fang came to Shanghai to take part in a meeting.

(3)
Wǒ qù jiàoshì zuò zuòyè.
我 去 教室 做 作业。

I'll go to the classroom to do my exercises.

(4)
Tā qù péngyou jiā wán le.
他 去 朋友 家 玩 了。

He went to see his friend at home.

这个格式中的动词表示"来"、"去"的目的。

In this pattern the verb expresses the purpose of "来" or "去".

42. 没 + 动词1 + 就 + 动词2 + 了

Did ... （action2） without doing ... （action1）

(1)
Wǒ méi chī zǎofàn jiù shàngbān le.
我 没 吃 早饭 就 上班 了。

I went to work without breakfast.

(2)
Wǒ méi fùxí jiù cānjiā kǎoshì le.
我 没 复习 就 参加 考试 了。

I took the examination without preparation.

(3)
Tā méi qiāo mén jiù jìnlai le.
他 没 敲 门 就 进来 了。

He entered the room without knocking at the door.

(4)
Tā méi xiàbān jiù huílai le.
她 没 下班 就 回来 了。

She came back before the normal time for knocking off.

按常理应该做了第一个动作后再做第二个动作。这个格式表示不按常理,不做第一个动作,直接做第二个动作。

Usually the action 2 shall be done after the action 1. This pattern expresses an unusual order：doing the action 2 without doing the action 1 first.

43．动词1＋动词1　　　Verb（for a little while）

（1）Wǒ qùqu jiù lái.
我 去去 就 来。
I'll go there for a little while, and then come back.

（2）Ràng wǒ kànkan.
让 我 看看。
Let me have a look.

（3）Zhège wèntí wǒ kǎolù kǎolù.
这个 问题 我 考虑 考虑。
I need to think about this problem.

（4）Zhè jiàn shì wǒmen zài tǎolùn tǎolùn.
这 件 事 我们 再 讨论 讨论。
Let's discuss this matter again.

这里的动词重叠表示动作时间短。

The repeat of a verb here implies that the time period of the action is short.

44．动词1＋一＋动词1　　　Verb（for a little while）

（1）Ràng wǒ kàn yi kàn.
让 我 看 一 看。
Let me have a look.

（2）Ràng wǒ tiāo yi tiāo.
让 我 挑 一 挑。
Let me choose.

（3）Wǒ xiǎng dú yi dú zhè běn shū.
我 想 读 一 读 这 本 书。
I want to read this novel.

（4）Zhège wèntí wǒ yào xiǎng yi xiǎng.
这个 问题 我 要 想 一 想。
I need to think about this problem.

相同两个单音节动词中间加"一"表示动作时间短。这个格式跟句型43的意思一样。双音节动词中间不能加"一"，比如，不能说"讨论一讨论"。

When the word "一" is added between two identical single disyllable verbs, it implies that the time period of the action is short. If the verb has two disyllables, ie two Chinese characters, the word "一" can not be used between the verbs. For example, we can't say "讨论一讨论". The meaning of this pattern is the same as that in Pattern 43.

45. 动词 + 一下   **Verb**

(1) Wǒ yòng yíxià diànhuà,
我 用 一下 电话,
kěyǐ ma?
可以 吗?

May I use the phone?

(2) Qǐng bāng wǒ xiū(lǐ) yíxià.
请 帮 我 修(理) 一下。

Please help me to repair it.

(3) Qǐng děng yíxià.
请 等 一下。

Please wait a moment.

(4) Wǒ lái jièshào yíxià.
我 来 介绍 一下。

Let me introduce ...

这里的"一下"表示动作时间短。有时起缓和语气的作用。

Here "一下" indicates that the time period of the action is short. Sometimes it functions to make the tone mild.

46. 动词 1 + 动词 1   **Verb (with ease)**

(1) Wǒ xiǎng qù Sūzhōu wánwan.
我 想 去 苏州 玩玩。

I want to take a tour to Suzhou.

(2) Jīntiān wǒmen bù gōngzuò, qù
今天 我们 不 工作, 去
jiāowài zǒuzou ba.
郊外 走走 吧。

We are off today. Let's go to the outskirts for a walk.

(3) Jīntiān wǒ gēn péngyou hēhe
今天 我 跟 朋友 喝喝
chá, liáoliao tiān, hěn yúkuài.
茶、 聊聊 天, 很 愉快。

I had a nice chat with my friends and drank tea with them today. It was really enjoyable.

(4) Xīngqītiān zài jiā tīngting yīnyuè、
星期天 在 家 听听 音乐、
kànkan diànshì, hěn shūfu.
看看 电视, 很 舒服。

It is enjoyable to listen to music and watch TV at home on Sundays.

这里的动词重叠表示动作很轻松、随意地进行。

The repeat of a verb here indicates the action goes on in a casual way or with ease.

47. 动词1+动词1

Try ...

Wǒ xiǎng chángchang wēishìjì.
（1）我 想 尝尝 威士忌。 May I try some whisky?

Tā xiǎng chángchang Sìchuāncài.
（2）她 想 尝尝 四川菜。 She wants to try the Sichuan cuisine.

Zhè màozi wǒ dàidai, kàn héshì
（3）这 帽子 我 戴戴，看 合适 Let me try on this cap and see if it fits.
bu héshì.
不 合适。

Zhè zhǒng xiāngzào wǒ yòngyong,
（4）这 种 香皂 我 用用， Let me try this toilet soap and see if it's good
kàn hǎo bu hǎo.
看 好 不 好。 or not.

这里的动词重叠表示尝试的意思。

The repeat of a verb here means to have a try.

48. 人/事/物+副词+形容词

Somebody/something + be + adverb + adjective

Zhège jiàoshì hěn dà.
（1）这个 教室 很 大。 This classroom is very big.

Tā hěn piàoliang.
（2）她 很 漂亮。 She is very beautiful.

Chén xiānsheng fēicháng rèqíng.
（3）陈 先生 非常 热情。 Mr. Chen is very warmhearted.

Nà běn shū zhēn yǒuqù.
（4）那 本 书 真 有趣。 That book is quite interesting.

这是形容词当谓语的句型。形容词当谓语时，一般要在它的前面加副词。只有表示比较的时候才可以单独充当谓语。例如：这本书好，那本也不错。

In this pattern the adjective acts as the predicate. When an adjective is used as the predicate, an adverb shall usually be added in front of the adjective. An adjective alone can act as the predicate only in comparison. For example, "这本书好，那本也不错".

49. 人/事/物 + 不 + 形容词

Somebody/something + be + not + adjective

Jīntiān tiānqì bù hǎo.
(1) 今天 天气 不 好。

Today's weather is not good.

Zhège bàngōngshì bú dà.
(2) 这个 办公室 不 大。

This office is not big.

Zhège cài bù hǎochī.
(3) 这个 菜 不 好吃。

This dish is not tasty.

Zhèli de dōngtiān bù lěng.
(4) 这里 的 冬天 不 冷。

The winter here is not cold.

这是句型 48 的否定形式。

This is the negative form of Pattern 48.

50. a A + B + 形容词

B of A + be + adjective

　　 b A + B + 不 + 形容词

B of A + be + not + adjective

Wǒ tóu hěn téng.
(1) 我 头 很 疼。

I have a severe headache.

Tā ěrduo hěn lóng.
(2) 他 耳朵 很 聋。

He is severely deaf.

Nàge sījī fúwù tàidù hěn hǎo.
(3) 那个 司机 服务 态度 很 好。

The service of that driver is good.

Xī Hú jǐngsè hěn yōuměi.
(4) 西 湖 景色 很 优美。

The scenery of Xihu (the West Lake) is beautiful.

Nǎinai xīnqíng bù hǎo.
(5) 奶奶 心情 不 好。

My grandma is in a bad mood.

Zhège xiǎoqū huánjìng bù hǎo.
(6) 这个 小区 环境 不 好。

The environment in this residential area is not good.

这是主谓词组作谓语的句型。B 是 A 的一部分。

In this pattern a subject-predicate phrase acts as the predicate of the sentence. "B" is a part of "A".

51. A 说："……"

Somebody + said, " ... "

(1)
Bàba shuō: "Bù huílai chī
爸爸 说："不 回来 吃
wǎnfàn."
晚饭。"

Dad said, "I will not come back for supper."

(2)
Jīnglǐ shuō: "Xiàwǔ sān diǎn
经理 说："下午 三 点
kāihuì."
开会。"

The manager said, "We will have a meeting at 3 pm."

(3)
Māma shuō: "Míngtiān qù
妈妈 说："明天 去
gōngyuán."
公园。"

My mother said, "Go to the park tomorrow."

(4)
Yīshēng shuō: "Nǐ yào
医生 说："你 要
zhùyuàn."
住院。"

The doctor said, "You need to be hospitalized."

这是直接引用他人说话内容时用的格式。
This is the pattern used for direct speech.

52. 听说…… 据说……

It is said that ... ; They say that ... ; I've heard that ...

(1)
Tīngshuō Hé lǎoshī zhùyuàn le.
听说 何 老师 住院 了。

I've heard that Teacher He has been hospitalized.

(2)
Tīngshuō Zhōu Líng jiéhūn le.
听说 周 玲 结婚 了。

I've heard that Zhou Ling was married.

(3)
Tīngshuō Wǔhàn xiàtiān hěn rè.
听说 武汉 夏天 很 热。

It is said that it is very hot in summer in Wuhan.

(4)
Tīngshuō zhè běn shū hěn hǎo.
听说 这 本 书 很 好。

They say that this book is very good.

(5)
Jùshuō nàli nào shuǐzāi le.
据说 那里 闹 水灾 了。

It is said that there is a flood there.

(6)
Jùshuō tā fùqīn qùshì le.
据说 他 父亲 去世 了。

It is said that his father died.

这是转述传闻时用的格式。
This is the pattern to report hearsay or information.

53. 听 A 说…… 　据 A 说……

I've heard from A that ...; A said that ...

(1)
Tīng Xiǎo Lǐ shuō Xú Wén
听 小 李 说 徐 文
qù Fǎguó le.
去 法国 了。

I've heard from Xiao Li that Xu Wen has gone to France.

(2)
Tīng tā shuō nà bù diànyǐng
听 他 说 那部 电影
hěn yǒuqù.
很 有趣。

I've heard from him that that movie is very interesting.

(3)
Tīng Xiǎo Wáng shuō Lǐ Lì
听 小 王 说 李力
shēngbìng le.
生病 了。

I've heard from Xiao Wang that Li Li is ill.

(4)
Tīng tā shuō Dōngběi hěn lěng.
听 他 说 东北 很 冷。

He said that it was very cold in the Northeast.

(5)
Jù tiānqì yùbào shuō hòutiān
据 天气 预报 说 后天
guā táifēng.
刮 台风。

The forecast said that there would be a typhoon the day after tomorrow.

(6)
Jù bàozhǐ shuō zuìjìn hěn duō
据 报纸 说 最近 很 多
rén gǎnmào.
人 感冒。

The newspaper said that many people had caught a cold recently.

54. A + 喜欢(+ 动词) + B

A + like (+ verb) + B

(1)
Wǒ xǐhuan yīnyuè.
我 喜欢 音乐。

I like music.

(2)
Shūshu xǐhuan tǐyù.
叔叔 喜欢 体育。

My uncle is fond of sports.

(3)
Tā xǐhuan kàn jīngjù.
他 喜欢 看 京剧。

He likes Beijing Opera.

(4)
Mǎlì xǐhuan chī Zhōngguócài.
玛丽 喜欢 吃 中国菜。

Mary likes Chinese food.

55. A + 不喜欢(+ 动词) + B

A + not + like (+ verb) + B

(1)
Mèimei bù xǐhuan huīsè.
妹妹 不 喜欢 灰色。

My younger sister does not like the gray color.

(2)
Wǒ bù xǐhuan tián de.
我 不 喜欢 甜 的。

I don't like sweet food.

(3) Dìdi bù xǐhuan yángwáwa.
弟弟　不　喜欢　洋娃娃。　　My younger brother does not like dolls.

(4) Tā bù xǐhuan hē niúnǎi.
他　不　喜欢　喝　牛奶。　　He does not like milk.

56. A + 决定 + 动词　　　　　A + decide + verb

(1) Wǒ juédìng shí hào huí guó.
我　决定　十　号　回　国。　　I've decided to return to my country on the tenth.

(2) Xuéxiào juédìng xià zhōu kāi
学校　决定　下　周　开
yùndònghuì.
运动会。　　The school has decided to hold the school games next week.

(3) Wǒ juédìng bú qù Sūzhōu le.
我　决定　不　去　苏州　了。　　I decided not to go to Suzhou.

(4) Tā juédìng bù chōuyān le.
他　决定　不　抽烟　了。　　He has decided to give up smoking.

57. (A +) 规定……　　　　(A +) prescribe ...

(1) Guīdìng bùxǔ jiǔ hòu kāichē.
规定　不许　酒　后　开车。　　It is prescribed that driving after drinking alcohol is prohibited.

(2) Guīdìng zài gōnggòng chǎngsuǒ
规定　在　公共　场所
bùxǔ chōuyān.
不许　抽烟。　　It is stipulated that smoking in public places is not allowed.

(3) Xuéxiào guīdìng bā diǎn shàngkè.
学校　规定　八　点　上课。　　The school has made a regulation that classes begin at eight.

(4) Shāngdiàn guīdìng shàngwǔ qī
商店　规定　上午　七
diǎn kāishǐ yíngyè.
点　开始　营业。　　It is a regulation that the shop opens at 7am.

319

58. A + 给 + B + <u>物</u>　　　　A gave B something

(1) Sūn lǎoshī gěile wǒ yì běn zìdiǎn.
孙 老师 给了 我 一 本 字典。　　Mr. Sun gave me a dictionary.

(2) Wǒ gěile Sūn lǎoshī yì zhāng diànyǐngpiào.
我 给了 孙 老师 一 张 电影票。　　I gave Mr. Sun a movie ticket.

(3) Bàba gěile dìdi yí ge wánjù.
爸爸 给了 弟弟 一 个 玩具。　　My father gave my younger brother a toy.

(4) Dìdi gěile bàba yí fù yǎnjìng.
弟弟 给了 爸爸 一 副 眼镜。　　My younger brother gave my father a pair of glasses.

(5) Péngyou gěile wǒ shèngdàn lǐwù.
朋友 给了 我 圣诞 礼物。　　My friend sent me Christmas gifts.

(6) Wǒ gěile péngyou xīnnián lǐwù.
我 给了 朋友 新年 礼物。　　I gave my friend gifts for the New Year.

这里的"给"是动词。这个格式表示 A 给了 B 物品。

The "给" here is a verb. This pattern indicates that "A" gave something to "B".

59. A + 给 + B + 动词 + <u>物</u>　　　　A did something for B

(1) Māma gěi wǒ zuòle hǎochī de.
妈妈 给 我 做了 好吃 的。　　Mama cooked some delicious food for me.

(2) Wǒ gěi māma mǎile yí jiàn máoyī.
我 给 妈妈 买了 一 件 毛衣。　　I bought my mother a sweater.

(3) Tā gěi wǒ mǎile yì shuāng xié.
他 给 我 买了 一 双 鞋。　　He bought a pair of shoes for me.

(4) Gēge gěi wǒ huàle yì fú huàr.
哥哥 给 我 画了 一 幅 画儿。　　My elder brother drew a picture for me.

这里的"给"是介词。这个格式表示 A 为 B 做了某事,使 B 得到了物品。

The "给" here is a preposition. This pattern indicates that "A" did something for "B" and made "B" have something.

60. A + 给 + B + 动词　　　A does something to/for B

(1) Wǒ gěi tā dǎle diànhuà.
我 给 他 打了 电话。　　　I gave him a phone call.

(2) Wǒ gěi māma fāle diànzǐ yóujiàn.
我 给 妈妈 发了 电子 邮件。　　I sent an E – mail to my mother.

(3) Wǒ gěi nǐ jièshào yíxià.
我 给 你 介绍 一下。　　　Let me introduce to you ...

(4) Lǎoshī zhèngzài gěi wǒmen jiǎng
老师 正在 给 我们 讲　　　The teacher is telling us a story.
gùshi.
故事。

这个格式表示 A 向着 B 做某事。B 是 A 发出动作的对方。

This pattern indicates that "A" does something towards "B". "B" is the other party whom "A" does the action towards/for.

61. A + 认为/觉得……　　　A + think/believe that ...

(1) Wǒ rènwéi zuò fēijī hǎo.
我 认为 坐 飞机 好。　　　I think it is better to take a flight.

(2) Wǒ rènwéi zhè shì hǎo shì.
我 认为 这 是 好 事。　　　I believe it is a good thing.

(3) Nǐ juéde Hànyǔ nán ma?
你 觉得 汉语 难 吗?　　　Do you think the Chinese language is difficult?

(4) Wǒ juéde zhèli jiāotōng hěn
我 觉得 这里 交通 很　　　I think that the transport facilities are good
fāngbiàn.
方便。　　　here.

"认为"、"觉得"表示对事物有某种看法或作出某种判断。

"认为" and "觉得" are used to express one's opinion or judgment towards
something.

62. A + 想……　　　A + think/ guess that ...

(1) Wǒ xiǎng tā huì lái de.
我 想 他 会 来 的。　　　I guess he will come.

(2) Wǒ xiǎng tā shì wàiguórén.
我 想 她 是 外国人。　　　I guess she is a foreigner.

(3) Wǒ xiǎng zhège yídìng hěn guì.
我 想 这个 一定 很 贵。　　　I think that it must be expensive.

（4）
Wǒ xiǎng zhè shì lǎoshī de dōngxi.
我　想　这　是　老师　的　东西。　I think that this is the teacher's.

这里的"想"表示估计、猜想。
"想" here means "guess" or "estimate".

63. (A +) 没 + 想到　　　A + never + thought that ...

（1）
Méi xiǎngdào qiūtiān hái zhème rè.
没　想到　秋天　还　这么　热。　I've never thought that it is so hot in autumn.

（2）
Méi xiǎngdào néng zài zhèli jiànmiàn.
没　想到　能　在　这里　见面。　I've never thought that we could meet here.

（3）
Wǒ méi xiǎngdào tā shì lǎoshī
我　没　想到　他　是　老师
de háizi.
的　孩子。
I've never thought that he is the son of our teacher.

（4）
Méi xiǎngdào zhème piányi.
没　想到　这么　便宜。　It is hard to imagine that it is so cheap.

"没想到"表示对已发生的事没有料到。
"没想到" means what has happened has not been expected.

64. A 比 B (+ 还/更) + 形容词　　　A + be + adjective in comparative degree + than B

（1）
Běijīng bǐ Shànghǎi gǔlǎo.
北京　比　上海　古老。
Beijing is older than Shanghai.

（2）
Shànghǎi rénkǒu bǐ Běijīng duō.
上海　人口　比　北京　多。
The population of Shanghai is more than that of Beijing.

（3）
Jīntiān bǐ zuótiān hái lěng.
今天　比　昨天　还　冷。
It is colder today than it was yesterday.

（4）
Zhège bǐ nàge gèng piányi.
这个　比　那个　更　便宜。
This one is cheaper than that one.

（5）
Tā bǐ wǒ gāo sān límǐ.
他　比　我　高　三　厘米。
He is three centimeters taller than I am.

（6）
Zhège bǐ nàge guì shí kuài qián.
这个　比　那个　贵　十　块　钱。
The price of this one is ten *yuan* higher than that one.

如果形容词后面有补语的话,形容词的前面一般不用"还"、"更"。
If there is a complement after the adjective, generally "还"、"更" can't be added in front of the adjective.

65. A 比 B + 形容词 + 得多/多了

A + be + much + adjective in comparative degree + than B

(1) Jīntiān bǐ zuótiān rè de duō.
今天 比 昨天 热 得 多。

It is much hotter today than it was yesterday.

(2) Zhège bǐ nàge piányi de duō.
这个 比 那个 便宜 得 多。

This one is much cheaper than that one.

(3) Zhège fángjiān bǐ nàge liàng de duō.
这个 房间 比 那个 亮 得 多。

This room is much brighter than that room.

(4) Jiǎozi bǐ miànbāo hǎochī duō le.
饺子 比 面包 好吃 多 了。

Dumplings are much more delicious than bread.

这个格式表示 A 跟 B 的差别很大。

This pattern indicates that there is a big difference between "A" and "B".

66. 比起 A(来),B……

To compare with A, B … ; Compared to A, B …

(1) Bǐqǐ miànbāo lái, jiǎozi gèng hǎochī.
比起 面包 来, 饺子 更 好吃。

Dumplings are more delicious compared to bread.

(2) Bǐqǐ Shànghǎi lái, Sūzhōu hěn xiǎo.
比起 上海 来, 苏州 很 小。

Compared to Shanghai, Suzhou is small.

(3) Bǐqǐ yǐqián, xiànzài de shēnghuó hǎo duō le.
比起 以前, 现在 的 生活 好 多 了。

The living standard now is much better to compare with that in the old days.

(4) Bǐqǐ jiāoqū, shìqū de jiāotōng gèng fāngbiàn.
比起 郊区, 市区 的 交通 更 方便。

The transport facilities in urban areas are better as compared with that in suburbs.

67. A 和/跟 B + 一样 + 形容词　　A + be + as + adjective + as B

(1)　Huáihǎi Lù hé Nánjīng Lù
　　淮海 路 和 南京 路
　　yíyàng rènao.
　　一样 热闹。

It is as lively on Huaihai Rd. as on Nanjing Rd.

(2)　Zhào Yǒng hé Lǐ Wěi yíyàng
　　赵 勇 和 李 伟 一样
　　rèqíng.
　　热情。

Mr. Zhao Yong is as warmhearted as Mr. Li Wei.

(3)　Fǎyǔ hé Yīngyǔ yíyàng nán.
　　法语 和 英语 一样 难。

French is as difficult to learn as English.

(4)　Jīntiān gēn zuótiān yíyàng rè.
　　今天 跟 昨天 一样 热。

It is as hot today as it was yesterday.

68. A 没 B (+ 这么/那么) + 形容词　　A + be + not + as + adjective + as B

(1)　Zhèli méi nàli ānjìng.
　　这里 没 那里 安静。

It is not as quiet here as there.

(2)　Mǎ Lì méiyǒu Lín Tāo gāo.
　　马 立 没有 林 涛 高。

Mr. Ma Li is not as tall as Mr. Lin Tao.

(3)　Rìyǔ de fāyīn méiyǒu Hànyǔ
　　日语 的 发音 没有 汉语
　　zhème nán.
　　这么 难。

The Japanese pronunciation is not as difficult as Chinese pronunciation.

(4)　Mántou méiyǒu bāozi nàme
　　馒头 没有 包子 那么
　　hǎochī.
　　好吃。

Steamed bread is not as tasty as steamed stuffed buns.

69. A + 算 + B　　A + be + regarded as/considered B

(1)　Tā shēntǐ suàn jiànkāng.
　　他 身体 算 健康。

His health can be regarded as good.

(2)　Dìdi suàn cōngming.
　　弟弟 算 聪明。

My younger brother may be considered smart.

(3)　Jīnnián de shōucheng suàn
　　今年 的 收成 算
　　búcuò.
　　不错。

The harvest this year is counted as a good one.

（4）
Zhèlǐ de jiāotōng suàn
这里 的 交通 算
fāngbiàn.
方便。

The transport facilities here are regarded as good.

这个句格式表示 A 属于 B 的范围里面。

This pattern indicates that "A" is within the scope of "B".

70. A + 不算 + B

A + be + not + regarded as/considered B

（1）
Jiàqian bú suàn guì.
价钱 不 算 贵。

The price can't be regarded as an expensive one.

（2）
Zhìliàng bú suàn hǎo.
质量 不 算 好。

The quality isn't really good.

（3）
Tā bú suàn pàng.
他 不 算 胖。

He isn't really fat.

（4）
Tā Hànyǔ shuō de bú suàn hǎo.
他 汉语 说 得 不 算 好。

His Chinese can't be regarded as good.

这是句型 69 的否定形式。

This is the negative form of pattern 69.

71. （比起 A）还是 + B + 好

B is better compared with A

（1）
（Bǐqǐ nàge,） háishi mǎi
（比起 那个,） 还是 买
zhège hǎo.
这个 好。

It's better to buy this one (compared to that one).

（2）
（Bǐqǐ qítā jiāotōng gōngjù,）
（比起 其他 交通 工具,）
háishi chéng dìtiě hǎo.
还是 乘 地铁 好。

It's better to take subway (compared to other means of transportation).

（3）
（Bǐqǐ qítā dìfāng,） háishi
（比起 其他 地方,） 还是
jiāxiāng hǎo.
家乡 好。

Nowhere is better than home (to compare with other places).

（4）
（Bǐqǐ nàge,） háishi zhège
（比起 那个,） 还是 这个
bànfǎ hǎo.
办法 好。

This way is preferable (to compare with that way).

这个格式表示经过比较、考虑以后,在 A 和 B 中选择了 B。一般不用说出 A。

This pattern expresses that "B" is the choice after consideration and comparison between "A" and "B". Usually "A" is not mentioned.

72. （比起 A）最好 + B
B is the best choice

Nǐ zuìhǎo chī diǎnr yào.
(1) 你 最好 吃 点儿 药。
You'd better take some medicine.

Nǐ zuìhǎo duō hē diǎnr shuǐ.
(2) 你 最好 多 喝 点儿 水。
You'd better drink more water.

Zuìhǎo yòng Zhōngwén xiě.
(3) 最好 用 中文 写。
It's better to write in Chinese.

Qù Fúzhōu Lù zuìhǎo chéng dìtiě.
(4) 去 福州 路 最好 乘 地铁。
It's the best way to take the subway to Fuzhou Rd.

"B" 是经过比较后的最佳选择。一般 A 不用说出。
"B" is the best choice after consideration. Usually "A" is not mentioned.

73. （与其）A 不如 B
B + rather than A; B + be better than A; Prefer B to A

Yǔqí xiūlǐ, bùrú mǎi xīn de.
(1) 与其 修理，不如 买 新 的。
It's better to buy a new one rather than repair it.

Qiú rén, bùrú zìjǐ gàn.
(2) 求 人，不如 自己 干。
Rather than asking for help, it'd be better to do it by ourselves.

Qù kàn diànyǐng, bùrú zài jiā kàn diànshì.
(3) 去 看 电影，不如 在 家 看 电视。
It's better to watch TV at home rather than going to cinema.

Chéng gōnggòng qìchē, bùrú qí zìxíngchē.
(4) 乘 公共 汽车，不如 骑 自行车。
It is preferable to ride a bicycle than take a bus.

这个句型表示经过比较以后,放弃 A,选择 B。
This pattern means to choose "B" and give up "A" after comparison.

74. 把 A + 动词
Verb + A

Qǐng bǎ nà jiàn jiákè xǐ gānjìng.
(1) 请 把 那 件 夹克 洗 干净。
Please wash that jacket.

Qǐng dàjiā bǎ shū dǎkāi.
(2) 请 大家 把 书 打开。
Open your books, please.

Wǒ bǎ mén suǒshang le.

(3) 我 把 门 锁上 了。　　　　I have locked the door.

Bàba bǎ diàndēng xiūhǎo le.

(4) 爸爸 把 电灯 修好 了。　　My father has fixed the light.

　　"把"后面的 A 是动词的宾语,靠"把"字移到动词的前面。这个格式强调动作的结果,所以动词的后面大多有表示结果的成分。如果不是强调结果,可以不用"把"字。比如例句(1)如果不强调"洗"的结果"干净",可以说成"请洗干净那件夹克"。

　　The "A" after "把" is the object of the verb. The "把" moves "A" to the front of the verb. This pattern emphasizes the result of the action. Usually there are some words after the verb to describe the result. If we don't want to emphasize the result, it isn't necessary to use the word "把". For example, if we don't emphasize that "干净" is the result of "洗" in the first example, we may just say "请洗干净那件夹克".

75. 把 A + 动词 + 成/为 + B　　　Verb（change）A to B

Wǒ bǎ měiyuán huànchéng

(1) 我 把 美元 换成　　　　I changed US dollar to RMB.

rénmínbì.

人民币。

Tā bǎ nà běn xiǎoshuō yìchéng

(2) 他 把 那 本 小说 译成　　He translated that novel into German.

Déyǔ.

德语。

Qǐng bǎ huìyì shíjiān gǎiwéi

(3) 请 把 会议 时间 改为　　Please change the meeting time to 3 pm.

xiàwǔ sān diǎn.

下午 三 点。

Qǐng bǎ zhège fángjiān gǎiwéi

(4) 请 把 这个 房间 改为　　Please convert this room to a reception room.

huìkèshì.

会客室。

　　这是一定要用"把"字的句式。A 是动作的对象,靠"把"字提到动词的前面。动作完成后,A 变成 B。

　　In this pattern "把" is indispensable. "把" moves the object of the action, "A", to the front of the verb. After the completion of the action, "A" is changed to "B".

76. 把 A + 动词 + 做／成 + B

Regard/treat A as B

Wǒ bǎ Xiǎo Wú kànzuò dìdi.
(1) 我 把 小 吴 看做 弟弟。

I regard Xiao Wu as my younger brother.

Wǒmen bǎ zhè běn shū dàngzuò
(2) 我们 把 这 本 书 当做
jiàokēshū.
教科书。

We regard this book as a textbook.

Nǎinai bǎ yìbǎi kuài qián dàngzuò
(3) 奶奶 把 一百 块 钱 当做
shí kuài le.
十 块 了。

My grandmother treated the 100 *yuan* note as

a 10 *yuan* one.

Yǒushí yǒu rén bǎ nàge Rìběnrén
(4) 有时 有 人 把 那个 日本人
dàngchéng Zhōngguórén.
当成 中国人。

Sometimes people mistake Japanese people

for Chinese.

这是一定要用"把"字的句式,A 是动作的对象,靠"把"字提到动词的前面。这个格式表示 A 被认为是 B,或者 A 被作为 B 使用。

This pattern expresses that "A" is regarded as "B", or "A" is treated as "B". In this pattern "把" is indispensable. "把" moves the object of the action, "A", to the front of the verb.

77. 把 A + 动词 + 到 + 处所

Verb + A + place

Nǐ bǎ fànguō nádào chúfáng ba.
(1) 你 把 饭锅 拿到 厨房 吧。

Please take the rice cooker to the kitchen.

Wǒ bǎ shū fàngdào shūjià
(2) 我 把 书 放到 书架
shang le.
上 了。

I put the book on the bookshelf.

Wǒ bǎ xíngli sòngdào nín de
(3) 我 把 行李 送到 您 的
fángjiān le.
房间 了。

I have sent your baggage to your room.

Tā bǎ qián cúndào yínháng le.
(4) 他 把 钱 存到 银行 了。

He deposited money into a bank.

这是一定要用"把"字的句式。A 是动作的对象。动作完成后 A 从某处到达另一处。

In this pattern "把" must be used. "A" is the object of the action. After the completion of the action, "A" is moved from a place to another.

78. 把 A + 动词 + 在 + 处所

Verb + A + place

(1) Wǒ bǎ jīpiào fàngzài nǐ de zhuōzi shang le.
我 把 机票 放在 你 的 桌子 上 了。

I have put the air ticket on your desk.

(2) Tā bǎ huàbào fàngzài shūjià shang le.
他 把 画报 放在 书架 上 了。

He put the pictorial on the bookshelf.

(3) Tā bǎ qiánbāo wàngzài chūzūchē shang le.
他 把 钱包 忘在 出租车 上 了。

He left his wallet in the taxi.

(4) Wǒ bǎ diànhuà hàomǎ xiězài zhǐ shang le.
我 把 电话 号码 写在 纸 上 了。

I wrote down the telephone number on a sheet of paper.

这是一定要用"把"字的句式。A 是动作的对象。动作完成后 A 存在于某处。

In this pattern "把" must be used. "A" is the object of the action. After the completion of the action, "A" is in another place.

79. A 被 B + 动词

A + be + verb（past participle）+ by B

(1) (Wǒ de) liǎn bèi wénzi dīng le.
（我 的）脸 被 蚊子 叮 了。

I was bitten by mosquitoes on my face.

(2) Tā de jiǎo bèi rén cǎi le.
他 的 脚 被 人 踩 了。

His foot was trodden on by someone.

(3) Wǒ bèi bàba mà le.
我 被 爸爸 骂 了。

I was scolded by my father.

(4) Tā bèi piàn le, hěn shēngqì.
他 被 骗 了，很 生气。

He is very angry at being cheated.

(5) Yīfu bèi (yǔ) línshī le.
衣服 被 （雨）淋湿 了。

The clothes were wet from the rain.

这是表示被动的句式。主语 A 是动作的受事者，B 是动作的施事者。有"被"字的句子有时带有不如意、不愉快的色彩。

This is a pattern of passive form. The "A" is the object of the action and the "B" is the subject of the action. In some cases a sentence with the word "被" implies something unpleasant or unsatisfactory.

80. A 得到……

A 受到/很受……

A + receive/win ... ;

A + be + verb（past participle）

（1）
Lǐ Lì jīntiān dédàole xiàozhǎng de biǎoyáng.
李 立 今天 得到了 校长 的 表扬。

Mr. Li Li received praise from the principal today.

（2）
Xú Jié dédào hěn duō rén de xìnrèn.
徐 洁 得到 很 多 人 的 信任。

Miss Xu Jie enjoys the trust of many people.

（3）
Wàiguó kèren shòudàole rèliè de huānyíng.
外国 客人 受到了 热烈 的 欢迎。

The foreigners were given an enthusiastic welcome.

（4）
Liúxíng gēqǔ hěn shòu qīngnián xǐhuan.
流行 歌曲 很 受 青年 喜欢。

Pop songs are very well received by young people.

81. A 让 B + 动词

A + make/allow/let + B + verb

（1）
Māma ràng wǒ zuò jiāwù.
妈妈 让 我 做 家务。

Mamma made me do the housework.

（2）
Lǎoshī ràng Liú Píng huídá wèntí.
老师 让 刘 平 回答 问题。

The teacher asked Liu Ping to answer the question.

（3）
Ràng tā shuō xiàqu.
让 他 说 下去。

Let him go on.

（4）
Ràng Wáng Yǒng qù ba.
让 王 勇 去 吧。

Let Wang Yong go.

（5）
Tā zǒng shì hěn wǎn huí jiā, ràng māma dānxīn.
他 总 是 很 晚 回 家，让 妈妈 担心。

He always comes home very late. It worries his mother.

这个格式表示 A 指使 B 做某事，或者 A 的行为使 B 产生某种状态。

In this pattern "A" makes "B" do something, or the behavior of "A" turns "B" into a certain condition.

82. a 想 + 动词

Want to do something

b 不想 + 动词

Not want to do something

Wǒ xiǎng chī jiǎozi.
(1) 我 想 吃 饺子。
I would like to have dumplings.

Tā xiǎng xué Hányǔ.
(2) 他 想 学 韩语。
He wants to learn Korean.

Sū Líng xiǎng qù Fǎguó.
(3) 苏 玲 想 去 法国。
Su Ling wants to go to France.

Nǐ xiǎng qù dehuà, yě kěyǐ qù.
(4) 你 想 去 的话, 也 可以 去。
If you want, you may go too.

Wǒ gǎnmào le, bù xiǎng chī.
(5) 我 感冒 了, 不 想 吃。
I have a cold, so I don't want to eat.

Wǒ nǎr yě bù xiǎng qù.
(6) 我 哪儿 也 不 想 去。
I don't want to go anywhere.

Tā bù xiǎng kǎo dàxué.
(7) 他 不 想 考 大学。
He doesn't want to take the university entrance examination.

Tā shuí yě bù xiǎng jiàn.
(8) 他 谁 也 不 想 见。
He wants to see no one.

a 表示希望、打算做某事。b 是 a 的否定形式。

In this pattern, "a" expresses a desire for doing something, and "b" is the negative form of "a".

83. 要 + 动词

Want to do something

Wǒ yào kàn nà chū xì.
(1) 我 要 看 那 出 戏。
I want to see that drama.

Tā yǒu huà yào duì nǐ shuō.
(2) 他 有 话 要 对 你 说。
He wants to talk to you.

Shǔjià nǐ yào qù nǎr?
(3) 暑假 你 要 去 哪儿?
Where do you want to go during the summer vacation?

Wǒ bù xiǎng chūqu.
——我 不 想 出去。
— I don't want to go anywhere.

Nǐ yào xǐzǎo ma?
(4) 你 要 洗澡 吗?
Do you want to take a bath?

Xiànzài bù xiǎng xǐ.
——现在 不 想 洗。
— No, not now.

这里的"要 + 动词"表示做某事的意愿, 跟句式 82"想 + 动词"的意思差不多。表示否定时一般不说"不要",而说"不想"。

"要 + 动词" expresses a determination of doing something. The meaning is similar to "想 + 动词" in Pattern 82. In negative form, we usually say "不想", not "不要".

84. a 想要 + 物   **Want something**
b 不想要 + 物   **Not want something**

(1)
Wǒ xiǎng yào yí kuài xīn shǒubiǎo.
我 想 要 一 块 新 手表。
I want a new watch.

(2)
Tā xiǎng yào yì běn zìdiǎn.
他 想 要 一 本 字典。
He wants a dictionary.

(3)
Dìdi xiǎng yào yí liàng qìchē.
弟弟 想 要 一 辆 汽车。
My younger brother wants a car.

(4)
Mèimei xiǎng yào yí jiàn máoyī.
妹妹 想 要 一 件 毛衣。
My younger sister wants a woolen sweater.

(5)
Wǒ bù xiǎng yào zhàoxiàngjī.
我 不 想 要 照相机。
I don't want a camera.

(6)
Tā bù xiǎng yào gāngbǐ.
他 不 想 要 钢笔。
He doesn't want a pen.

(7)
Nǐ bù xiǎng yào xīn dàyī ma?
你 不 想 要 新 大衣 吗?
Don't you want a new coat?

(8)
Wǒ shénme yě bù xiǎng yào.
我 什么 也 不 想 要。
I want nothing.

a 表示希望得到某物。b 是 a 的否定形式。

In this pattern, "a" expresses a desire for something and "b" is the negative form of "a".

85. 要/必须 + 动词   **Must + verb; Have to + verb**

(1)
Wǒ shēngbìng le, yào chīyào.
我 生病 了, 要 吃药。
I am ill and must take medicine.

(2)
Nǐ hòutiān yǐqián yào fù fángzū.
你 后天 以前 要 付 房租。
You have to pay the rent by the day after tomorrow.

(3)
Dào Wàitān yào huànchē.
到 外滩 要 换车。
You have to change buses to get to the Bund.

(4) Qù Xiānggǎng bìxū shìxiān
去 香港 必须 事先
shēnqǐng.
申请。

You must apply for a travel permit before going to Hong Kong.

这个格式表示不可以不做某事。

This pattern indicates that it is impossible not to do something.

86. 不用/不必 + 动词

Not need + verb; Not necessary ...

(1) Jīntiān hěn nuǎnhuo, búyòng
今天 很 暖和, 不用
chuān dàyī.
穿 大衣。

It is quite warm today and there is no need to wear an overcoat.

(2) Jiālèfú lí zhèr hěn jìn,
家乐福 离 这儿 很 近,
búyòng chéng chē.
不用 乘 车。

Carrefour is near here and it isn't necessary to take the bus.

(3) Nǐ qù dehuà, nà wǒ
你 去 的话, 那 我
búbì qù le.
不必 去 了。

It's not necessary for me to go there if you go.

(4) Yào wǒ péi nǐ qù ma?
要 我 陪 你 去 吗?
Búyòng le.
——不用 了。

Do you need me to accompany you there?

— No, it's not necessary.

这个格式表示可以不做某事。

This pattern indicates that it is not necessary to do something.

87. 打算/准备 + 动词

Intend to ... ; Plan to ...

(1) Wǒ dǎsuan hòutiān dòngshēn.
我 打算 后天 动身。

I plan to leave the day after tomorrow.

(2) Nǐ dǎsuan zài Xī'ān dāi jǐ tiān?
你 打算 在 西安 待 几 天?

How many days are you going to stay in Xi'an?

(3) Zhōu Lìwén zhǔnbèi qù Měiguó
周 利文 准备 去 美国
liúxué.
留学。

Mr. Zhou Liwen intends to go to America to study.

(4) Tā zhǔnbèi jìn dàxué xuéxí.
他 准备 进 大学 学习。

He intends to go to university.

88．不＋打算／准备＋动词

Not + intend/want + verb

Wǒ bù dǎsuan jiàn tā.
（1）我　不　打算　见　他。

I don't intend to see him.

Nǐ bù dǎsuan qù lǚxíng ma?
（2）你　不　打算　去　旅行　吗?

Don't you want a tour?

Lǐ Yàn bù zhǔnbèi jiéhūn.
（3）李　艳　不　准备　结婚。

Miss Li Yan has no plan for marriage.

Hé Ān bù zhǔnbèi cānjiā gāokǎo.
（4）何　安　不　准备　参加　高考。

Mr. He An doesn't plan to take part in the

university entrance examination.

89．a 会＋动词
　　b 不会＋动词

Can + verb; Be able to + verb
Can not + verb

Wǒ huì shuō Yīngyǔ.
（1）我　会　说　英语。

I can speak English.

Nǐ huì shuō Fǎyǔ ma?
（2）你　会　说　法语　吗?

Can you speak French?

Tā huì kāi qìchē.
（3）他　会　开　汽车。

He can drive.

Wǒ bú huì yóuyǒng.
（4）我　不　会　游泳。

I can't swim.

Tā bú huì qí zìxíngchē.
（5）她　不　会　骑　自行车。

She can't ride a bicycle.

a 表示经过学习,学得某种本领。b 是 a 的否定形式。

In this pattern, "a" means to have some abilities after study and "b" is the negative form of "a".

90．会＋动词＋了

Be able to do something now;
Can do something now

Jiékè xiànzài huì xiě Hànzì le.
（1）杰克　现在　会　写　汉字　了。

Jack knew how to write Chinese now.

Tā xiànzài huì tán gāngqín le.
（2）她　现在　会　弹　钢琴　了。

She can play piano now.

Dìdi xiànzài huì zǒulù le.
（3）弟弟　现在　会　走路　了。

My younger brother is able to walk now.

Mèimei xiànzài huì shuōhuà le.
（4）妹妹　现在　会　说话　了。

My younger sister is able to speak now.

这个格式表示由原来"不会"变成"会"。

This pattern indicates the change from "不会" to "会".

91. a 会 + 动词(+ 的)
b 不会 + 动词(+ 的)

Will + verb
Will not + verb

(1) Yuànzhǎng huì lái de.
    院长　会　来　的。
The principal will come.

(2) Xīngqītiān gōngyuán huì yǒu
    星期天　公园　会　有
    hěn duō rén de.
    很　多　人　的。
There will be many people in the park on Sundays.

(3) Dìdi kàndào qiǎokèlì huì
    弟弟　看到　巧克力　会
    hěn gāoxìng de.
    很　高兴　的。
My younger brother will be happy when he sees the chocolate.

(4) Tā bú huì tóngyì de.
    他　不　会　同意　的。
He will not agree.

(5) Tā bú huì lái de.
    她　不　会　来　的。
She will not come.

    a 表示肯定某种可能性。"的"在这里是语气词,加强肯定的语气。b 是 a 的否定形式。

    The pattern "a" confirms a possibility. Here "的" is a modal particle used to strengthen the mood. "b" is the negative form of "a".

92. a 能 + 动词
b 不能 + 动词

Can + verb
Can not + verb

(1) Tā néng yòng Yīngyǔ chàng gē.
    他　能　用　英语　唱　歌。
He can sing songs in English.

(2) Mèimei néng zìjǐ chuān yīfu.
    妹妹　能　自己　穿　衣服。
My younger sister can put on her clothes by herself.

(3) Tā yí ge rén néng zuòwán
    她　一　个　人　能　做完
    zhè jiàn shì.
    这　件　事。
She is able to complete this work alone.

(4) Tā yì fēnzhōng néng dǎ
    他　一　分钟　能　打
    yìbǎi wǔshí ge zì.
    一百　五十　个　字。
He is able to type 150 words per minute.

(5)
Wǒ hái bù néng yòng Hànyǔ
我 还 不 能 用 汉语
dǎ diànhuà.
打 电话。

I can't make a phone call in Chinese.

(6)
Dìdi hái bù néng zìjǐ chī fàn.
弟弟 还 不 能 自己 吃 饭。

My younger brother can not feed himself.

这里的"能"强调具有某种能力或者达到某种效率。b 是 a 的否定形式。
Here "能" emphasizes to have some kind of ability or reach a certain level. "b" is the negative form of "a".

93. 能 + 动词 + 了   Could + verb

(1)
Tā bìng hǎo le, néng qǐlai le.
他 病 好 了, 能 起来 了。

He has recovered and could get out of bed.

(2)
Wǒ dòngle shǒushù, néng kànjian
我 动了 手术, 能 看见
dōngxi le.
东西 了。

I can see something now after the operation.

(3)
Ānnà xiànzài néng tīngdǒng
安娜 现在 能 听懂
Hànyǔ le.
汉语 了。

Anna could understand Chinese now.

(4)
Sūshān xiànzài néng xiě hěn
苏珊 现在 能 写 很
duō Hànzì le.
多 汉字 了。

Susan could write many Chinese characters now.

这里的"能"表示恢复某种能力或者达到了原来没有的水平。
Here "能" indicates that some ability has recovered or reached a new level.

94. 能 + 动词   可以 + 动词   Can + verb

(1)
Zhè běn shū míngnián néng chūbǎn.
这 本 书 明年 能 出版。

This book can be published next year.

(2)
Bàba shénme shíhou néng huí jiā?
爸爸 什么 时候 能 回 家?

When can Dad come home?

(3)
Zhū xiānsheng néng cānjiā huìyì
朱 先生 能 参加 会议
ma?
吗?

Can Mr. Zhu participate in the meeting?

Míngtiān wǒ yǒu kòng, kěyǐ lái.
（4）明天　我　有　空，可以　来。　I am free tomorrow and can come.

这里的"能"和"可以"表示客观条件允许做某事。

Here "能" and "可以" indicate that the objective condition permits to do something.

95．不能 + 动词　　　　　　　　Can not + verb

Jiàoshì li bù néng tī zúqiú.
（1）教室　里　不　能　踢　足球。　Playing football is prohibited in classrooms.

Zhèli bù néng chōuyān.
（2）这里　不　能　　抽烟。　　　　No smoking here.

Túshūguǎn de bàozhǐ bù néng
（3）图书馆　的　报纸　不　能　　It is not allowed to take the newspapers out

ná huíqu.
拿　回去。　　　　　　　　　　from the library.

Wǒ méi kòng, bù néng qù.
（4）我　没　空，不　能　去。　I could not go since I am busy.

这里的"不能"表示客观条件不允许做某件事。一般不说"不可以"。

Here "不能" indicates that the objective condition does not permit to do something. Usually we don't say "不可以".

96．可以 + 动词　　　　　　　　Be worth + verb（present participle）；
Should + verb

Shìjì Gōngyuán hěn dà, nǐ
（1）世纪　公园　很　大，你　　　Century Park is very big. It is worth going

kěyǐ qù wánwan.
可以　去　玩玩。　　　　　　there.

Zhōngguó de zhēnsī hěn yǒumíng,
（2）中国　的　真丝　很　有名，　Chinese silk is famous. You should bring

nǐ kěyǐ mǎi xiē dài huíqu.
你可以　买　些　带　回去。　some back.

Zǎoshang nǐ kěyǐ zuòzuo tǐcāo.
（3）早上　你　可以　做做　体操。　You'd better do some exercises in the morning.

Yǒukòng nǐ kěyǐ sànsanbù.
（4）有空　你　可以　散散步。　You should take a walk when you are free.

这里的"可以"表示建议。

Here "可以" expresses a suggestion.

97. 应该 + 动词/形容词　　Should be + adjective; Should + verb

(1) Xīngqītiān xuéxiào li yīnggāi méi rén.
星期天　学校　里　应该　没　人。

There should be no one in the school on Sundays.

(2) Tā hěn yònggōng, yīnggāi kǎo de shàng dàxué.
他　很　用功，　应该　考　得　上　大学。

He studied very hard and should pass the university's entrance examination.

(3) Tā chéng bā diǎn de fēijī, xiànzài yīnggāi dào le.
他　乘　八　点　的　飞机，现在　应该　到　了。

The departure time of his flight was eight o'clock. So he should have arrived by now.

(4) Wǒ zài cài li fàngle wèijīng, wèidao yīnggāi xiān.
我　在　菜　里　放了　味精，味道　应该　鲜。

I've put some special flavoring in the dish, it should be delicious.

这里的"应该"表示说话人估计事情一定是某种情况。

Here "应该" expresses an estimate or judgment of the speaker.

98. a 应该 + 动词/形容词
　　b 不应该 + 动词/形容词

Should/ought to/must + verb/adjective
Should/ought to/must + not + verb/adjective

(1) Zuòle duìbuqǐ biéren de shì, yīnggāi dàoqiàn.
做了　对不起　别人　的　事　应该　道歉。

You ought to make an apology if you did something wrong to someone.

(2) Péngyou zhījiān yīnggāi hùxiāng bāngzhù.
朋友　之间　应该　互相　帮助。

Friends should help each other.

(3) Wǒ bù yīnggāi ràng dìdi yí ge rén qù.
我　不　应该　让　弟弟　一　个　人　去。

I should not have let my younger brother go alone.

(4) Nǐ bù yīnggāi shuōhuǎng.
你　不　应该　说谎。

You should not have lied.

a 表示情理上必须做某事。b 是 a 的否定形式。

The pattern "a" indicates that logically something must be or should be done. "b" is the negative form of "a".

99. 容易 + 动词　好 + 动词

Easy/convenient to do ...

(1) Zhège cài hěn róngyì zuò.
这个 菜 很 容易 做。

It is very easy to cook this dish.

(2) Zhège shēngcí hěn róngyì jì.
这个 生词 很 容易 记。

It is quite easy to remember this word.

(3) Zhè shì hěn róngyì zuò de
这 是 很 容易 做 的
shìqing.
事情。

This work is easily to be done.

(4) Zhè běn zìdiǎn hěn hǎo chá.
这 本 字典 很 好 查。

It's convenient to look a word up in this dictionary.

100. 难 + 动词　不好 + 动词

Difficult to do ...

(1) Zhège zì hěn nán xiě.
这个 字 很 难 写。

It is very difficult to write this word.

(2) Zhège shēngcí hěn nán jì.
这个 生词 很 难 记。

It is very difficult to remember this word.

(3) Zhè jiàn shì hěn nán bàn.
这 件 事 很 难 办。

This work is difficult to do.

(4) Gōngzuò hěn bù hǎo zhǎo.
工作 很 不 好 找。

It is very difficult to get a job.

101. 可能······　也许······

Perhaps/probably/might ...

(1) Tā kěnéng qù bàngōngshì le.
他 可能 去 办公室 了。

He probably went to his office.

(2) Zǒudào nàr kěnéng yào yí
走到 那儿 可能 要 一
ge xiǎoshí.
个 小时。

He might need one hour to get there.

(3) Tā yěxǔ bù néng lái le.
他 也许 不 能 来 了。

Perhaps he is not able to come.

(4) Kōngtiáo yěxǔ huài le.
空调 也许 坏 了。

The air conditioner is probably out of order.

"可能"、"也许"表示推测。

"可能" and "也许" express a guess or inference.

102. 估计…… / Estimate/suppose/guess …

（1）Wǒ gūjì tā huì kǎoshang
我 估计 他 会 考上
dàxué de.
大学 的。

I guess that he will pass the university's entrance examination.

（2）Wǒ gūjì dàjiā huì zànchéng de.
我 估计 大家 会 赞成 的。

I suppose everyone will agree.

（3）Wǒ gūjì xià ge yuè néng
我 估计 下 个 月 能
wánchéng rènwù.
完成 任务。

I estimate that the project can be completed next month.

（4）Wǒ gūjì tā yào dòng shǒushù.
我 估计 他 要 动 手术。

I guess that he probably needs an operation.

"估计"表示根据某些情况,对事物的性质、数量、变化等作出大概的推断。

"估计" means to estimate the quantity, quality and change etc. of something according to certain knowledge the speaker has got.

103. ……吧 / Probably/ perhaps/maybe …

（1）Tā shuìle ba.
他 睡了 吧。

He probably has gone to bed.

（2）Míngtiān huì xià yǔ ba.
明天 会 下 雨 吧。

It will probably rain tomorrow.

（3）Nàge dàgài shì tā érzi ba.
那个 大概 是 她 儿子 吧。

Perhaps that one is her son.

（4）Nà wèi dàgài shì Lǐ jiàoshòu ba?
那 位 大概 是 李 教授 吧?
Dàgài shì ba.
——大概 是 吧。

Is that man Prof. Li?
— Maybe.

这里的"吧"用在句末,表示推测的语气。

Here "吧" is used at the end of the sentence to express a tone of inference.

104. 好像＋动词/形容词 / Seem/be like ＋adjective; It's likely that …

（1）Méiyīng hǎoxiàng bìng le.
梅英 好像 病 了。

Meiying looks ill.

（2）Nà wèi hǎoxiàng shì Yīngguórén.
那 位 好像 是 英国人。

That man looks like an Englishman.

Zhège cài hǎoxiàng hěn hǎochī.
(3) 这 个 菜 好像 很 好吃。 This dish seems tasty.

Zhè jiàn shì wǒ hǎoxiàng
(4) 这 件 事 我 好像 It's likely that I have heard this matter.
tīngshuōguo.
听说过。

105. 像 + 名词/动词 + 似的   Like ...

Nà zhī gǒu xiàng láng shìde.
(1) 那 只 狗 像 狼 似的。 That dog looks like a wolf.

Tā hěn yòuzhì, xiàng xiǎoháir
(2) 他 很 幼稚, 像 小孩儿 He is immature like a child.
shìde.
似的。

Tā de liǎn xiàng píngguǒ shìde.
(3) 他 的 脸 像 苹果 似的。 His face looks like an apple.

Wǒ zhòng jiǎng le, xiàng
(4) 我 中 奖 了, 像 I have the winning number! It seems like a
zuòmèng shìde.
做梦 似的。 dream.

106. 看上去…… 看样子…… 看来……   Seem ... ; Look like ... ; Look as if ...

Kàn shangqu tā hěn lǎoshi.
(1) 看 上去 他 很 老实。 He seems very honest.

Kàn shangqu tā hěn jiànkāng.
(2) 看 上去 他 很 健康。 He looks fine.

Kàn yàngzi tā hěn niánqīng.
(3) 看 样子 他 很 年轻。 He looks young.

Kànlái tā hěn dānxīn.
(4) 看来 他 很 担心。 He seems to be quite worried.

这个格式表示说话人根据客观情况作出估计。

This pattern is used to make a judgment according to the objective condition the speaker has found.

107. 有点儿 + 形容词/动词   A bit; A little; Rather

Tā yǒu diǎnr bù gāoxìng.
(1) 他 有 点儿 不 高兴。 He is a bit unhappy.

(2)
Wǒ tóu yǒu diǎnr téng.
我 头 有 点儿 疼。
I have a little headache.

(3)
Jīntiān yǒu diǎnr lěng.
今天 有 点儿 冷。
It is rather cold today.

(4)
Zhè fángjiān yǒu diǎnr àn.
这 房间 有 点儿 暗。
This room is a little dark.

"有点儿"在这里是副词,表示程度不高,大多用于不如意的事情。

"有点儿" here is an adverb. It indicates a lesser degree and is usually used to describe something unsatisfactory or disappointing.

108. 形容词 + 了 + (一) 点儿　　　A little + too + adjective

(1)
Zhè fángjiān ànle yìdiǎnr.
这 房间 暗了 一点儿。
This room is a bit too dark.

(2)
Zhè jiàn chènyī duǎnle yìdiǎnr.
这 件 衬衣 短了 一点儿。
This shirt is a little too short.

(3)
Zhè shuāng xié dàle diǎnr.
这 双 鞋 大了 点儿。
This pair of shoes is a little too big.

(4)
Jīntiān bǐ zuótiān lěngle diǎnr.
今天 比 昨天 冷了 点儿。
It is a little cooler today than it was yesterday.

这里的"一点儿"是数量词。这个格式表示事物已经稍微超出了一定的标准。

Here "一点儿" is a numeral-measure word. This pattern indicates that something is slightly beyond a certain standard.

109. 形容词 + (一) 点儿　　　A little + adjective in comparative degree

(1)
Wǒ wǎn yìdiǎnr lái, kěyǐ ma?
我 晚 一点儿 来, 可以 吗?
May I come a little later?

(2)
Nǐ zǎo diǎnr huíqu ba.
你 早 点儿 回去 吧。
You'd better go back earlier.

(3)
Yǒu piányi diǎnr de ma?
有 便宜 点儿 的 吗?
Do you have anything cheaper?

(4)
Wǒ yào dà diǎnr de.
我 要 大 点儿 的。
I want one a little bigger.

这里的"一点儿"是数量词。这个格式表示说话人希望稍微超过某个标准一些。

Here "一点儿" is a numeral-measure word. This pattern indicates that the speaker wants something to be slightly beyond the originally set standard.

110. 动词 + (一)点儿(+ 名词)   **Verb + a little/a few/some (+ noun)**

(1) Wǒ mǎile yìdiǎnr xiāngjiāo.
我 买了 一点儿 香蕉。   I've bought some bananas.

(2) Tā huì yìdiǎnr Yīngyǔ.
他 会 一点儿 英语。   He understands a little English.

(3) Wǒ xiǎng zài chī yìdiǎnr.
我 想 再 吃 一点儿。   I'd like to have some more.

(4) Nǐ qù yínháng qǔ diǎnr qián ba.
你 去 银行 取 点儿 钱 吧。   You'd better go to the bank to withdraw some

money.

这里的"一点儿"是数量词,表示数量少。
Here "一点儿" is a numeral-measure word to describe small quantity.

111. 一点儿 + 也 + 不 + 动词/形容词   **Not at all**

(1) Hànyǔ wǒ yìdiǎnr yě bú huì.
汉语 我 一点儿 也 不 会。   I can't speak Chinese at all.

(2) Tā yìdiǎnr yě bù míngbai.
他 一点儿 也 不 明白。   He didn't understand at all.

(3) Tā yìdiǎnr yě bù dānxīn.
他 一点儿 也 不 担心。   He bears no anxiety.

(4) Wǒ yìdiǎnr yě bú lèi.
我 一点儿 也 不 累。   I don't feel tired at all.

"一点儿也不"表示完全否定。
"一点儿也不" expresses a complete denying.

112. 动词 + 得 + 形容词   **Do something + adjective**

(1) Tā měi tiān qǐ de hěn zǎo.
他 每 天 起 得 很 早。   He gets up very early every day.

(2) Wǒ chī de hěn bǎo le.
我 吃 得 很 饱 了。   I have had enough.

(3) Tā chàng de zhēn hǎo.
她 唱 得 真 好。   She sang very well.

(4) Ānnà Hànyǔ shuō de hěn hǎo.
安娜 汉语 说 得 很 好。   Anna speaks Chinese very well.

(5) Tā fángjiān dǎsǎo de hěn gānjìng.
她 房间 打扫 得 很 干净。   She cleaned up her room thoroughly.

Tā xiě Hànzì xiě de búcuò.
(6) 她 写 汉字 写 得 不错。 She writes Chinese characters well.

这个格式表示动作达到的程度、情态。如果动词有宾语的话,宾语要提到动词的前面,或者重复动词。

This pattern indicates the degree or level that the result of the action has reached. When the verb has an object, the object should be moved to the front of the verb or the verb should be repeated after the object.

113. 动词 + 得 + 不 + 形容词 Not do something + adjective

Zhè cì kǎoshì, wǒ kǎo de bù hǎo.
(1) 这 次 考试, 我 考 得 不好。 I didn't do a good job in the test.

Yǔ xià de bú dà.
(2) 雨 下 得 不大。 The rain is not heavy.

Ānnà Hànyǔ shuō de bú tài hǎo.
(3) 安娜 汉语 说 得 不太好。 Anna doesn't speak Chinese very well.

Tā yīfu xǐ de bù gānjìng.
(4) 她 衣服 洗 得 不 干净。 She didn't wash her clothes clean.

这是句型 112 的否定形式。

This pattern is the negative form of the Pattern 112.

114. 动词1 + 得 + 形容词/动词2 Can do something ...

Wǒ tīng de dǒng tā shuō de huà.
(1) 我 听 得 懂 他 说 的 话。 I understood what he said.

Zhè chū xì dàjiā dōu kàn de míngbai.
(2) 这 出 戏 大家 都 看 得 明白。 Everyone could understand this play.

Zhè jiàn shì zhǐyǒu tā shuō de qīngchu.
(3) 这 件 事 只有 他 说 得 清楚。 It is he who can explain it clearly.

Zhè kuài shǒubiǎo xiū de hǎo ma?
(4) 这 块 手表 修 得 好 吗? Can this watch be repaired?

Zhèli　kàn　de　jiàn　dàhǎi.
(5) 这里 看 得 见 大海。　　You can see the sea here.

Zhè zhāng zhuōzi zuò de xià
(6) 这 张 桌子 坐 得 下　　This table can seat eight persons.
bā　ge　rén.
八 个 人。

这个格式表示可能。"听得懂"就是"能听懂"。
This pattern indicates the possibility. "听得懂" means "能听懂".

115. 动词1＋不＋形容词/动词2　　Can not do something ...

Wǒ　tīng　bu　dǒng　tā　de　huà.
(1) 我 听 不 懂 他 的 话。　I couldn't understand what he said.

Zhè shuōmíngshū, wǒ kàn bu
(2) 这 说明书， 我 看 不　I could not understand this manual.
míngbai.
明白。

Zhè jiàn shì wǒ shuō bu
(3) 这 件 事 我 说 不　I can't explain this matter clearly.
qīngchu.
清楚。

Zhè liàng zìxíngchē xiū bu hǎo
(4) 这 辆 自行车 修 不 好　It is impossible to repair this bicycle.
le.
了。

Zhèli kàn bu jiàn Huángpǔ Jiāng.
(5) 这里 看 不 见 黄浦 江。　You can't see the Huangpu River here.

Zhè zhāng shāfā zuò bu xià
(6) 这 张 沙发 坐 不 下　This sofa can't seat four persons.
sì　ge　rén.
四 个 人。

这是句型114的否定形式。"听不懂"就是"不能听懂"。
This pattern is the negative form of the Pattern 114. "听不懂" means "不能听懂".

116. 动词1 + 形容词/动词2　　Verb + object + adjective/adverb

　　　　Zhuōzi wǒ cā gānjìng le.
（1）桌子 我 擦 干净 了。　　　I have swept the table clean.

　　　　Bàngōngshì wǒ shōushi zhěngqí le.
（2）办公室 我 收拾 整齐 了。　I have tidied up the office.

　　　　Qǐng yòng gāngbǐ xiě qīngchu.
（3）请 用 钢笔 写 清楚。　　Please use a pen to write it clearly.

　　　　Wǒ tīngdǒng nǐ de huà le.
（4）我 听懂 你 的 话 了。　I understood your words.

　　这里的形容词或动词2是动作1完成后达到的结果。
　　Here the adjective or verb2 is the result of the action1.

117. 没 + 动词1 + 形容词/动词2　　Did not + verb + object + adjective/adverb

　　　　Zhuōzi nǐ méi cā gānjìng.
（1）桌子 你 没 擦 干净。　　You didn't sweep the desk clean.

　　　　Tā méi shuō qīngchu.
（2）他 没 说 清楚。　　　　He didn't explain it clearly.

　　　　Nǐ de xiédài hái méi jìjǐn.
（3）你 的 鞋带 还 没 系紧。　You didn't tie up your shoelace tightly.

　　　　Nǐ de huà wǒ méi tīngdǒng.
（4）你 的 话 我 没 听懂。　I didn't understand your words.

　　这是句型116的否定形式。表示动作完成后没有达到一定的结果。
　　This pattern is the negative form of the Pattern 116. It indicates that when the action ends it does not reach the expected result.

118. 动词 + 好　　Have + verb (past participle)

　　　　Wǒ bǎihǎo cānjù le.
（1）我 摆好 餐具 了。　　I have laid the table.

　　　　Wǒ guānhǎo chuāng le.
（2）我 关好 窗 了。　　　I have closed the window.

　　　　Tā xiūhǎo diàndēng le.
（3）他 修好 电灯 了。　　He has fixed up the light.

　　　　Tā zuòhǎo wǎnfàn le.
（4）她 做好 晚饭 了。　　She has cooked supper.

　　这个格式表示很好地完成了动作。
　　This pattern indicates that the action has been well completed.

119. 没 + 动词 + 好

Have + not + verb (past participle)

(1) Nǐ de ānquándài méi jìhǎo.
你 的 安全带 没 系好。
You haven't fastened your seatbelt.

(2) Nǐ chènyī de kòuzi méi kòuhǎo.
你 衬衣 的 扣子 没 扣好。
You haven't buttoned up your shirt.

(3) Bàba méi xiūhǎo diàndēng.
爸爸 没 修好 电灯。
Dad hasn't fixed up the light.

(4) Māma hái méi zuòhǎo wǎnfàn.
妈妈 还 没 做好 晚饭。
Mama hasn't prepared supper yet.

这是句型118的否定形式。表示动作没有圆满地全部完成。

This pattern is the negative form of the Pattern 118. It indicates that the action has not been well completed.

120. 动词 + 光/完

Used up; Run out

(1) Jīntiān de piào yǐjīng màiguāng le.
今天 的 票 已经 卖光 了。
Today's tickets are all sold out.

(2) Zhège yuè de qián wǒ yǐjīng
这个 月 的 钱 我 已经
huāguāng le.
花光 了。
I have spent all my salary for this month.

(3) Jiā li de píngguǒ dōu chīwán le.
家 里 的 苹果 都 吃完 了。
All the apples at home have been eaten up.

(4) Wǒ de běnzi yòngwán le.
我 的 本子 用完 了。
My notebooks are all used up.

这个格式表示动作完成后,作为宾语的物品没有了。

This pattern indicates that as the result of an action, the things which are the object of the verb are all gone.

121. 没 + 动词 + 光/完

Not + used up; Not + run out

(1) Cǎoméi hái yǒu, zuótiān méi
草莓 还 有, 昨天 没
chīguāng.
吃光。
There are some strawberries left. They were not all eaten up yesterday.

(2) Jīntiān de bàozhǐ méi màiguāng.
今天 的 报纸 没 卖光。
Today's newspapers are not sold out.

Zhè shì méi huāwán de qián.
(3) 这 是 没 花完 的 钱。   This is the remaining money.

Miànbāo méi chīwán, búyòng mǎi.
(4) 面包 没 吃完, 不用 买。   The bread hasn't been eaten up. You don't

need to buy more.

这是句型 120 的否定形式。表示动作完成后,作为宾语的物品还有剩余。

This pattern is the negative form of the Pattern 120. It indicates that when the action is completed, the things which are the object of the verb are in surplus.

122. 动词 + 完   Have + finished/completed ...

Wǒ zuòwán zuòyè le.
(1) 我 做完 作业 了。   I have finished my exercises.

Tā xǐwán yīfu le.
(2) 她 洗完 衣服 了。   She has completed washing the clothes.

Māma xiěwán xìn le.
(3) 妈妈 写完 信 了。   Mama finished her letter.

Bàba kànwán bàozhǐ le.
(4) 爸爸 看完 报纸 了。   Dad has finished reading the newspaper.

这个格式强调事情完结。

This pattern emphasizes the completion of the action.

123. 没 + 动词 + 完   Have + not + finished/completed ...

Děng yíxià, huìyì hái méi
(1) 等 一下, 会议 还 没   Wait a moment please, the meeting isn't

kāiwán.
开完。   over.

Tā hái méi huàwán zhuāng.
(2) 她 还 没 化完 妆。   She has not finished putting on her making – up.

Tā méi zuòwán shì jiù zǒu le.
(3) 他 没 做完 事 就 走 了。   He has gone without finishing the work.

Tā méi dúwán dàxué jiù
(4) 她 没 读完 大学 就   She was married before she completed her

jiéhūn le.
结婚 了。   university study.

这是句型 122 的否定形式。

This pattern is the negative form of the Pattern 122.

124. 动词 + 在 + 处所

Be + in/on ... + place

Tā zuòzài shāfā shang.
(1) 他 坐在 沙发 上。

He is sitting on the sofa.

Shū fàngzài shūjià shang.
(2) 书 放在 书架 上。

The book is put on the bookshelf.

Qián cúnzài yínháng li.
(3) 钱 存在 银行 里。

The money is deposited in the bank.

Yīfu fàngzài yīguì li.
(4) 衣服 放在 衣柜 里。

The clothes are put up in the wardrobe.

这个格式表示人或事物在动作完成以后停留在某处。

This pattern indicates someone/something's location after the action.

125. 动词 + 到 + 处所

Verb + to + place

Zázhì qǐng fàngdào shūjià shang.
(1) 杂志 请 放到 书架 上。

Please put the magazine on the bookshelf.

Jìdào Měiguó de xìn yào
(2) 寄到 美国 的 信 要
shí tiān.
十 天。

You need ten days to send a letter to the US.

Huídào Àomén, wǒ mǎshàng
(3) 回到 澳门，我 马上
gěi nǐ fā diànzǐ yóujiàn.
给 你 发 电子 邮件。

I will give you an e-mail after I return to Macao.

Nín de xíngli yǐjīng sòngdào
(4) 您 的 行李 已经 送到
fángjiān le.
房间 了。

Your luggage has been sent to your room.

这个格式表示人或物随动作移动到某个处所。

This pattern indicates that someone moves to or something is moved to some place with the action.

126. 动词 + 到

Have + verb（past participle）

Tā shōudào māma jìlai de
(1) 他 收到 妈妈 寄来 的
bāoguǒ.
包裹。

He has received a parcel from his mother.

    Wǒ   zhōngyú kàndàole Chángchéng.
（2）我   终于   看到了   长城。   I have seen the Great Wall at last!

    Diūle de qiánbāo zhǎodào le.
（3）丢了 的 钱包   找到   了。   The lost wallet has been found.

    Wǒ mǎidàole héshēn de chènyī.
（4）我 买到了 合身 的 衬衣。   I have bought a shirt which fit me well.

这个格式表示动作达到目的或者有了结果。

This pattern indicates that the action has achieved its goal or got a result.

127. 没 + 动词 + 到　　　Have + not + verb (past participle)

    Jīntiān méi jiàndào Lǐ Píng.
（1）今天 没 见到 李 平。   I haven't seen Li Ping today.

    Wǒ méi tīngdào shénme shēngyīn.
（2）我 没 听到 什么   声音。   I haven't heard any sound.

    Tā hái méi zhǎodào gōngzuò.
（3）他 还 没 找到 工作。   He hasn't got a job yet.

    Wǒ méi mǎidào nà běn cídiǎn.
（4）我 没 买到 那 本 词典。   I haven't found that dictionary.

这是句型 126 的否定形式。

This pattern is the negative form of Pattern 126.

128. 动词 + 数量词　　　Do something ... times

    Wǒ dúle sān biàn kèwén.
（1）我 读了 三 遍 课文。   I have read the text three times.

    Wǒ qùle liǎng cì Hángzhōu.
（2）我 去了 两 次 杭州。   I have been to Hangzhou twice.

    Tā zhǎoguo nǐ jǐ huí nǐ dōu
（3）他 找过 你 几 回，你 都   He has come to see you several times, but

    bú zài.
    不 在。   you were not in.

    Tā měi tiān yào shuā sān
（4）她 每 天 要 刷 三   She brushes her teeth three times a day.

    cì yá.
    次 牙。

这个格式表示动作进行的次数。

This pattern indicates the times of the action.

129. 动词 + 时间

Verb + for ... (time)

Wǒ xuéle sān nián.
(1) 我 学了 三 年。
I've studied for three years.

Wǒ xuéle sān nián (de) Hànyǔ.
(2) 我 学了 三 年（的）汉语。
I've studied Chinese for three years.

Wǒ xué Hànyǔ xuéle sān nián.
(3) 我 学 汉语 学了 三 年。
I've studied Chinese for three years.

Wǒ zuòle liǎng ge xiǎoshí.
(4) 我 坐了 两 个 小时。
I've sat here for two hours.

Wǒ zuòle liǎng ge xiǎoshí (de) chē.
(5) 我 坐了 两 个 小时（的）车。
I've been on the bus for two hours.

Wǒ zuò chē zuòle liǎng ge xiǎoshí.
(6) 我 坐 车 坐了 两 个 小时。
I've been on the bus for two hours.

Wǒ děngle Lǐ Míng bàn ge xiǎoshí.
(7) 我 等了 李 明 半 个 小时。
I've waited for Li Ming for half an hour.

Wǒ zhǎole tā yì tiān le.
(8) 我 找了 他 一 天 了。
I've been looking for him all day.

这个格式表示动作或状态持续的时间。有如下表示方法：① 动词 + 时间；②动词 + 时间（ + 的）+ 宾语；③ 动词 + 宾语 + 动词 + 时间；④ 动词 + 人 + 时间。

This pattern indicates the time that an action or a state has lasted. There are four forms for this pattern：①动词 + 时间 ②动词 + 时间（ + 的）+ 宾语 ③动词 + 宾语 + 动词 + 时间 ④动词 + 人 + 时间.

130. 动词 + 上

Verb

Qǐng zài hétong shang qiānshang
(1) 请 在 合同 上 签上
míngzi.
名字。
Please sign your name on the contract.

Wǒ dàishang yǎnjìng cái kàn
(2) 我 戴上 眼镜 才 看
de jiàn.
得 见。
I can't see it until I wear my glasses.

Tā chuānshang xiézi chūmén le.
(3) 他 穿上 鞋子 出门 了。
He put on his shoes and then went out.

Qǐng bǎ mén guānshang.
(4) 请 把 门 关上。
Please lock the door.

这个格式表示通过动作，某一事物附加在某个地方。有时表示动作完成后产生合拢的结果。

This pattern indicates that after the action something is added somewhere. Sometimes it indicates that the action may make things join together.

131．动词＋下　　Verb

（1）同学们， 请 坐下。
Tóngxuémen, qǐng zuòxia.

Everyone, sit down please.

（2）前面 的 车 忽然 停下 了。
Qiánmian de chē hūrán tíngxia le.

The car in front of us stopped suddenly.

（3）他 留下了 家庭 地址。
Tā liúxiale jiātíng dìzhǐ.

He left his home address.

（4）他 摘下了 眼镜。
Tā zhāixiale yǎnjìng.

He took off his glasses.

这个格式表示：①人或事物随动作由高处移向低处；②动作完成后产生的结果固定下来；③动作完成后作为宾语的人或事物脱离原来的位置。

This pattern indicates：①Someone or something moves with the action from a higher place down to a lower place ②The result of the action turns fixed ③Someone or something which is the object of the verb leaves the previous place after the action.

132．动词＋来　　Verb + back

（1）他 拿来了 今天 的 报纸。
Tā nálaile jīntiān de bàozhǐ.

He brought today's newspaper back.

（2）您 的 行李 送来 了。
Nín de xíngli sònglai le.

Your baggage has been sent here.

（3）他 买来了 一 束 鲜花。
Tā mǎilaile yí shù xiānhuā.

He brought back a bunch of flowers.

（4）窗 外 传来了 鞭炮声。
Chuāng wài chuánlaile biānpàoshēng.

The sound of firecrackers comes in through the window.

这个格式表示动作向着说话人进行。

This pattern indicates that the action goes on in the direction towards the speaker.

133. 动词/形容词 + 起来

Start to + verb; Verb + up

(1) Yǔ xià qilai le.
雨 下 起来 了。

It is starting to rain.

(2) Wǒ pàng qilai le.
我 胖 起来 了。

I am getting fat.

(3) Dàjiā zhàn qilai le.
大家 站 起来 了。

Everyone stood up.

(4) Nǐ bǎ tānzài zhuōzi shang de
你 把 摊在 桌子 上 的
shū shōu qilai ba.
书 收 起来 吧。

You'd better tidy up the books strewn on the desk.

这个格式表示:① 动作或状态开始并继续下去;② 人或事物随动作由低处移向高处;③ 人或事物在动作完成后聚拢。

This pattern indicates：①The action starts and goes on ②Someone or something moves with the action from a lower place up to a higher place ③Persons or things join together after the action.

134. 动词 + 下来

Verb + down

(1) Shùyè diào xialai le.
树叶 掉 下来 了。

The leaves fell from the trees.

(2) Shuǐ cóng yuǎnfāng liú xialai.
水 从 远方 流 下来。

The water flows from afar.

(3) Nǐ cóng èrshí lóu zǒu xialai,
你 从 二十 楼 走 下来,
lèi ma?
累 吗?

Are you tired after walking down from the 20th floor?

(4) Zhè shì gǔdài chuán xialai
这 是 古代 传 下来
de shénhuà.
的 神话。

This is a myth handed down from ancient times.

这个格式表示人或事物由高处向低处、由远处向近处朝说话人移动。有时表示由过去继续到现在。

This pattern indicates that someone or something moves from a higher place down to a lower place or towards the speaker from a distant place. Sometimes it indicates the action continues from the past till now.

135. 动词 + 回来　　　　　Verb + back（ + place）

动词 + 回 + <u>处所</u> + 来

Bàba cóng gōngsī zǒu huílai le.
（1）爸爸 从 公司 走 回来 了。　　　Dad walked back from his company.

Diūle de qiánbāo wǒ zhǎo
（2）丢了 的 钱包 我 找　　　　　I have found the wallet I lost.

huílai le.
回来 了。

Nǐ bǎ wǎn náhuí chúfáng lai
（3）你 把 碗 拿回 厨房 来　　　Bring back the bowls to the kitchen.

ba.
吧。

Wǒ bǎ háizi cóng yòu'éryuán
（4）我 把 孩子 从 幼儿园　　　I've brought the child home from the kinder-

jiēhuí jiā lai le.
接回 家 来 了。　　　　　　garten.

这个格式表示人或事物随动作从别处回到原处。

This pattern indicates that someone or something comes back to the original place with the action.

136. 动词 + 去　　　　　　Verb + towards

Mèimei xiàng māma pǎoqu.
（1）妹妹 向 妈妈 跑去。　　　My younger sister is running towards Mama.

Qìchē wǎng jīchǎng kāiqu.
（2）汽车 往 机场 开去。　　　The car is driving to the airport.

Fēijī xiàng dōng fēiqu.
（3）飞机 向 东 飞去。　　　The airplane is flying to the east.

Xiàozhǎng de zázhì sòngqu le.
（4）校长 的 杂志 送去 了。　　　The principal's magazines have been sent to

him.

这个格式表示人或物随动作离开说话人所在地。

This pattern indicates that someone or something departs from the speaker's place with the action.

137. 动词 + 下去

Verb + downwards; Continue to + verb

(1) 电梯 坏了，他 走 下去 了。
Diàntī huàile, tā zǒu xiaqu le.

The elevator is out of order. He has walked down.

(2) 河水 从 这儿 向 远方 流 下去。
Héshuǐ cóng zhèr xiàng yuǎnfāng liú xiaqu.

The river flows from here to a distant place.

(3) 虽然 下 雨 了， 运动会 还是 要 进行 下去。
Suīrán xià yǔ le, yùndònghuì háishi yào jìnxíng xiaqu.

Although it's raining, the sport games are going on.

(4) 想 学好 外语，一定 要 坚持 下去。
Xiǎng xuéhǎo wàiyǔ, yídìng yào jiānchí xiaqu.

If you want to master a foreign language you must stick to it.

这个格式表示人或事物随动作由高处向低处、由近处向远处离开说话人所在地。有时表示动作继续进行。

This pattern indicates that someone or something moves from a higher place down to a lower place or from a nearby place to a distant place departing the speaker with the action. Sometimes it indicates that the action continues.

138. 动词 + 回去
动词 + 回 + 处所 + 去

Return + place; Verb + back

(1) 他 家 很 近，他 走 回去 了。
Tā jiā hěn jìn, tā zǒu huiqu le.

His home is near here, so he has walked back.

(2) 借 老师 的 词典 还 回去 了。
Jiè lǎoshī de cídiǎn huán huiqu le.

The dictionary borrowed from the teacher has been returned.

(3) 他 走回 家 去 了。
Tā zǒuhuí jiā qu le.

He has walked home.

(4) 杰克 飞回 美国 去 了。
Jiékè fēihuí Měiguó qu le.

Jack flew back to the United States.

这个格式表示人或事物从别处回原处。动作是往离开说话人所在地的方向进行的。

This pattern indicates that someone or something comes back to the original place with the action. The action happens in the direction of departing from the speaker.

139. 从 + 起点

Come from ... ; From ...

(1) Tā shì cóng Àodàlìyà lái de.
他 是 从 澳大利亚 来 的。
He came from Australia.

(2) Cóng gébì jiàoshì chuánlai yīnyuèshēng.
从 隔壁 教室 传来 音乐声。
The music comes from the next classroom.

(3) Zhè shì cóng túshūguǎn jièlai de.
这 是 从 图书馆 借来 的。
This book is borrowed from the library.

(4) Shǔjià cóng míngtiān kāishǐ.
暑假 从 明天 开始。
The summer vacation will begin tomorrow.

140. 到 + 终点

Reach ... ; Get to ... ; End at ...

(1) Hánjià dào hòutiān jiéshù.
寒假 到 后天 结束。
The winter vacation will end the day after tomorrow.

(2) Shàngwǔ dào shí'èr diǎn xiàkè.
上午 到 十二 点 下课。
The morning classes will be over at 12 am.

(3) Xiànzài xuédào dì-wǔ kè.
现在 学到 第五 课。
We are studying Lesson 5 now.

(4) Dào Chūn Jié hái yǒu yí ge xīngqī.
到 春 节 还 有 一 个 星期。
Spring Festival is one week from now.

141. 从 + 起点 + 到 + 终点

From ... to ...

(1) Qǐng cóng tóu dào wěi dú yí biàn.
请 从 头 到 尾 读 一 遍。
Please read it from the beginning to the end.

(2) Cóng zhèr dào jīchǎng yuǎn ma?
从 这儿 到 机场 远 吗?
Is it far from here to the airport?

(3) Gōnggòng qìchē cóng zǎo dào wǎn dōu jǐmǎnle rén.
公共 汽车 从 早 到 晚 都 挤满了 人。
The buses are packed from morning till night.

(4) Wǒ cóng bā diǎn dào shí'èr diǎn yìzhí gōngzuò.
我 从 八 点 到 十二 点 一直 工作。
I was working from eight to twelve o'clock.

142. A 离 B

From ... ; ... away

Zhèli lí jīchǎng yuǎn ma?
(1) 这里 离 机场 远 吗?

Is it far from the airport?

(Xiànzài) lí tiān hēi hái yǒu
(2) (现在) 离 天 黑 还 有
liǎng ge xiǎoshí.
两 个 小时。

There are two hours before it gets dark.

(Xiànzài) lí xīnnián hái yǒu
(3) (现在) 离 新年 还 有
yí ge yuè.
一 个 月。

The New Year is one month away.

(Xiànzài) lí kāiyǎn hái yǒu
(4) (现在) 离 开演 还 有
bàn ge xiǎoshí.
半 个 小时。

The show will begin in half an hour.

143. 作为 + 名词

As + noun

Wáng Zhìxióng zuòwéi xuésheng
(1) 王 志雄 作为 学生
dàibiǎo fāle yán.
代表 发了 言。

Mr. Wang Zhixiong made a speech as a representative of the students.

Zuòwéi yì zhǒng àihào, wǒ
(2) 作为 一 种 爱好，我
zài jíyóu.
在 集邮。

I am enjoying stamp collecting as a hobby.

Zuòwéi yīshēng yīnggāi zhèyàng zuò.
(3) 作为 医生 应该 这样 做。

It is what I should do as a doctor.

Zuòwéi fùmǔ zǒng wèi háizi
(4) 作为 父母 总 为 孩子
cāoxīn.
操心。

Parents always worry about their children.

这里的"作为 + 名词"是就人的某种身份或事物的某种性质来说。

Here "作为 + 名词" means having the character or function of somebody/something.

144. 趁……   While

(1) Chèn rè chī ba.
趁 热 吃 吧。   Eat it while it's hot.

(2) Chèn tiān hái méi hēi, kuài
趁 天 还 没 黑， 快   Go home while it isn't dark.
huí jiā ba.
回 家 吧。

(3) Chèn bàba hái méi qù shàngbān,
趁 爸爸 还 没 去 上班，   Talk to your father before he goes to work.
duì tā shuō ba.
对 他 说 吧。

(4) Chèn shāngdiàn hái méi guānmén,
趁 商店 还 没 关门，   The shop hasn't closed yet. Go to buy it.
kuài qù mǎi ba.
快 去 买 吧。

"趁……"表示利用某一条件或机会。

"趁……" means to take advantage of the opportunity or situation.

145. 每次 + 动词1 + 都 + 动词2   **Every time + verb1 ... , verb2;**
                                          When + verb1 ... , always + verb2

每当 + 动词1 + 都 + 动词2   **Every time + verb1 ... , verb2;**
                                          When + verb1 ... , always + verb2

(1) Wǒ měi cì qù Nánjīng Lù,
我 每 次 去 南京 路，   Every time I go to Nanjing Rd., I go to the
dōu dào shūdiàn kànkan.
都 到 书店 看看。   bookstore.

(2) Wǒ měi cì qù Pǔdōng dōu
我 每 次 去 浦东 都   I visit my friend every time I go to Pudong.
dào péngyou nàli.
到 朋友 那里。

(3) Měi dāng kàndào zhèxiē zhàopiàn
每 当 看到 这些 照片   These pictures always remind me of my child-
wǒ dōu xiǎngqǐ xiǎoshíhou.
我 都 想起 小时候。   hood.

(4) Měi dāng shōudào māma de
每 当 收到 妈妈 的   I am always very happy when I get a letter
xìn, wǒ dōu hěn gāoxìng.
信，我 都 很 高兴。   from my mother.

这个格式表示第一个动作进行的时候,第二个动作一定进行。

This pattern indicates that while the first action is in progress the second action is sure to happen.

146. 按照/按/照……＋动词　　Verb + as ... ; Verb + according to ...

Nǐ ànzhào māma shuō de zuò ba.
（1）你 按照 妈妈 说 的 做 吧。　　Do as your mother said.

Wǒ yào zhào lǎoshī shuō de
（2）我 要 照 老师 说 的　　I will study hard as the teacher said.
nàyàng nǔlì xuéxí.
那样 努力 学习。

Àn yùdìng de rìqī kāi
（3）按 预定 的 日期 开　　The tea party will be held as scheduled.
cháhuàhuì.
茶话会。

Qǐng ànzhào yuányàng shōushi hǎo.
（4）请 按照 原样 收拾 好。　　Please put things in order in the same old way.

147. 为＋原因（＋而）＋动词　　To do something for ... (reason) ; To be ... for ... (reason)

Tā wèi xuéfèi búgòu ér fāchóu.
（1）他 为 学费 不够 而 发愁。　　He is worried about his tuition.

Wǒ wèi māma shēntǐ bù hǎo
（2）我 为 妈妈 身体 不 好　　I worry about my mother's health.
dānxīn.
担心。

Wǒ wèi érzi de chénggōng
（3）我 为 儿子 的 成功　　I am proud of my son's success.
zìháo.
自豪。

Wǒ wèi jiàndào lǎopéngyou
（4）我 为 见到 老朋友　　I am glad to have met my old friend.
gāoxìng.
高兴。

148. A 为 B＋动词　　A + do something for B

Tā wèi értóng xiě xiǎoshuō.
（1）他 为 儿童 写 小说。　　He is writing a novel for children.

Zhè shì wèi chéngrén biān de
（2）这 是 为 成人 编 的　　These are the textbooks for adults.
jiàokēshū.
教科书。

(3)
Māma　wèi　kèren　zhǔnbèile
妈妈　为　客人　准备了

hěn　duō　hǎochī　de.
很　多　好吃　的。

Mama has prepared a lot of delicious food for the guests.

(4)
Wǒ　wèi　bàba　xiūlǐle　zìxíngchē.
我　为　爸爸　修理了　自行车。

I fixed the bicycle for my father.

A 是动作发出者。B 是动作受益者。

"A" is the party to carry out the action and "B" is the party which benefits from the action.

149. 为（了）＋目的＋动词　　　Verb + for/to ... (purpose)

(1)
Wèile　dàjiā　de　jiànkāng　gānbēi!
为了　大家　的　健康　干杯!

Let's drink a toast to everyone's health!

(2)
Tā　wèile　qù　Rìběn　zhèngzài
他　为了　去　日本　正在

xué　Rìyǔ.
学　日语。

He is learning Japanese for going to Japan.

(3)
Tā　wèile　gōngzuò　xué　diànnǎo
她　为了　工作　学　电脑

cāozuò.
操作。

She is studying computers for her work.

(4)
Wǒ　wèi　gēn　péngyou　jiànmiàn,
我　为　跟　朋友　见面,

míngtiān　qù　Sūzhōu.
明天　去　苏州。

I am going to Zuzhou tomorrow to meet a friend.

150. 向/往＋方向　　　To/for ... (direction/place)

(1)
Nǐ　yìzhí　xiàng　qián　zǒu　ba.
你　一直　向　前　走　吧。

You should go straight ahead.

(2)
Xiàng　yòu　guǎi　jiù　dào　le.
向　右　拐　就　到　了。

Turn right, and then you will be there.

(3)
Zhè　huǒchē　wǎng　Běijīng　kāi　ma?
这　火车　往　北京　开　吗?

Is this train for Beijing?

(4)
Qìchē　zhèng　wǎng　Pǔdōng　kāiqu.
汽车　正　往　浦东　开去。

The car is heading for Pudong.

151. A 向 B + 动词

A + verb + from B

(1) Wǒ xiàng lǎoshī jièle yì běn xiǎoshuō.
我 向 老师 借了一本 小说。

I borrowed a novel from my teacher.

(2) Dìdi xiàng māma yàole liǎng kuài qiǎokèlì.
弟弟 向 妈妈 要了 两 块 巧克力。

My younger brother got two chocolate bars from Mama.

(3) Xūyào shénme nǐ kěyǐ xiàng tā jiè.
需要 什么 你 可以 向 他 借。

You may borrow from him if you need something.

(4) Wǒ xiàng Mǎlì xué Yīngyǔ.
我 向 玛丽 学 英语。

I am learning English from Mary.

B 是跟动作有关的对方。这个格式与句型 158 的意思大致相同。

"B" is the other party related to the action. The meaning of this pattern is close to that of the Pattern 158.

152. A 对 B + 说……

A + tell/talk/say + (to) B

(1) Lǎoshī duì xuésheng shuō:
老师 对 学生 说:
"Gēn wǒ dú."
"跟 我 读。"

The teacher said to the students,"Read after me".

(2) Yǒu jiàn shì xiǎng duì xiàozhǎng shuō.
有 件 事 想 对 校长 说。

I have something to talk about with the principal.

(3) Nǐ yuànyì dehuà jiù duì tā shuō ba.
你 愿意 的话 就 对 他 说 吧。

Talk to him if you want.

(4) Zhè jiàn shì bié duì tā shuō.
这 件 事 别 对 他 说。

Don't tell him about this.

B 是 A 说话的对象。

"B" is the person whom "A" addresses to.

153. A 对 B + 态度

A + attitude + B

(1)
Tā duì wǒ fēicháng guānxīn.
他 对 我 非常 关心。

He is very concerned about me.

(2)
Tā duì wǒmen zhàogù de hěn zhōudào.
他 对 我们 照顾 得 很 周到。

He took good care of us.

(3)
Nǐ duì gǔwán gǎn xìngqù ma?
你 对 古玩 感 兴趣 吗?

Are you interested in antiques?

(4)
Wǒ duì zhège jìhuà yǒu yìjiàn.
我 对 这个 计划 有 意见。

I have a different opinion on this plan.

这个格式表示 A 对 B 有某种看法或采取某种行动。

This pattern indicates that "A" has certain opinion towards "B" or takes certain action to "B".

154. 对 + 人/物 + 来说

For somebody/something ...

(1)
Duì xiǎoxuéshēng lái shuō, zhège wèntí tài nán le.
对 小学生 来 说, 这个 问题 太 难 了。

This question is too difficult for pupils to answer.

(2)
Duì tā lái shuō, zhè shì zuì hǎo de lǐwù.
对 他 来 说, 这 是 最 好 的 礼物。

This is the best gift for him.

(3)
Duì wàiguórén lái shuō, Hànyǔ zuì nán de shì shēngdiào.
对 外国人 来 说, 汉语 最 难 的 是 声调。

The tones of Chinese are the most difficult thing for foreigners to learn.

(4)
Duì shēngwù lái shuō, kōngqì hé shuǐ zuì zhòngyào.
对 生物 来 说, 空气 和 水 最 重要。

Air and water are essential for all living things.

这个格式表示从某人、某事的角度去看,得出某个结论。

This pattern indicates that a conclusion is drawn from somebody's point of view or from something's angle.

155. 关于……

Concerning/regarding ... ; About ...

(1) Guānyú zhège wèntí, yào
关于 这个 问题，要
shuōmíng yíxià.
说明 一下。

I should give an explanation about this matter.

(2) Guānyú kǎo dàxué de shì, yào
关于 考 大学 的 事，要
hǎohāor kǎolǜ.
好好儿 考虑。

You should carefully consider the matter regarding going to university.

(3) Tā zài xiě guānyú Zhōngguó
他 在 写 关于 中国
fēngsú de shū.
风俗 的 书。

He is writing a book on Chinese customs.

(4) Tāmen zài tánlùn guānyú jiàoyù
他们 在 谈论 关于 教育
de gè zhǒng wèntí.
的 各 种 问题。

They are talking about problems concerning education.

156. 除了……以外

Besides ... ; Except ...

(1) Chúle Měiguó yǐwài, tā hái
除了 美国 以外，他 还
qùguo Yīngguó.
去过 英国。

He has been to Britain besides the United States.

(2) Chúle Hànyǔ yǐwài, tā hái xué
除了 汉语 以外，他 还 学
Yīngyǔ.
英语。

He is studying English besides Chinese.

(3) Chúle tā yǐwài, dàjiā dōu
除了 他 以外，大家 都
zànchéng.
赞成。

Everyone agreed except him.

(4) Chúle Mǎlì yǐwài, wǒ méiyǒu
除了 玛丽 以外，我 没有
bié de wàiguó péngyou.
别 的 外国 朋友。

I haven't any foreign friends, except Mary.

157. A 和/跟 B

A and B

(1) Wǒ mǎile píngguǒ hé lí.
我 买了 苹果 和 梨。

I've bought apples and pears.

Bàba gēn māma sànbù qù le.
(2) 爸爸　跟　妈妈　散步　去　了。　　　Dad and Mama went for a walk.

Xiǎo Chén hé Xiǎo Wáng
(3) 小　陈　和　小　王　　　　　　Xiao Chen and Xiao Wang got married.
jiéhūn le.
结婚　了。

Zuótiān yéye qùle Nánjīng Lù
(4) 昨天　爷爷　去了　南京　路　　　My grandpa went to Nanjing Rd. and Huihai
hé Huáihǎi Lù.
和　淮海　路。　　　　　　　　Rd. yesterday.

"和"、"跟"是连词,表示 A、B 是并列的关系。

"和"、"跟" are conjunctions. They indicate that "A" and "B" exist side by side or simultaneously.

158. A 跟 B + 动词　　　　　A + verb + from/to B

Wǒ gēn Ānnī xuéxí Yīngyǔ.
(1) 我　跟　安妮　学习　英语。　　　I am learning English from Annie.

Tā gēn Xiǎo Zhōu jièle yìbǎi
(2) 他　跟　小　周　借了　一百　　He borrowed 100 *yuan* from Xiao Zhou.
kuài qián.
块　钱。

Wǒ gēn tā shuōle nà jiàn shì.
(3) 我　跟　他　说了　那　件　事。　I've told him that story.

Dìdi gēn māma yàole wǔshí
(4) 弟弟　跟　妈妈　要了　五十　　My younger brother got 50 *yuan* from my
kuài qián.
块　钱。　　　　　　　　　　mother.

Wǒ gēn Hú Jiān liánxì le.
(5) 我　跟　胡　坚　联系　了。　　I've contacted Hu Jian already.

这里的"跟"是介词,指示与动作有关的对方。与句型 151 中的"向"意思大致相同。强调动作方向时多用"向",其他情况时多用"跟"。

Here "跟" is a preposition and indicates the other party related to the action. The meaning of "跟" is close to the meaning of "向" in the Pattern 151. "向" is more often used when the direction of the action is emphasized, otherwise ,"跟" is quite often used.

159. A 和/跟 B······   A + compare with B

(1) Tā de shēngāo hé bàba yíyàng.
他 的 身高 和 爸爸 一样。

His height is the same as his father's.

(2) Tā huà de xióngmāo gēn zhēn de yíyàng.
他 画 的 熊猫 跟 真 的 一样。

The panda he drew looks like a live one.

(3) Tā zhǎng de gēn Xīfāngrén chàbuduō.
他 长 得 跟 西方人 差不多。

He looks like a westerner.

(4) Shànghǎi de tiānqì gēn Běijīng (de tiānqì) bù tóng.
上海 的 天气 跟 北京 (的 天气) 不 同。

The weather in Shanghai is quite different from that in Bejing.

这里的"和"、"跟"是介词,引进比较的对象 B。

Here "和" and "跟" are prepositions. They introduce the compared object, "B".

160. 太 + 形容词/动词   Too + adjective

(1) Zhè jiàn chènyī tài cháng le.
这 件 衬衣 太 长 了。

This shirt is too long.

(2) Zhège tài guì, wǒ bù xiǎng mǎi.
这个 太 贵,我 不 想 买。

This one is too expensive. I will not buy it.

(3) Zhège cài tài là le.
这个 菜 太 辣 了。

This dish is too spicy.

(4) Qǐng bié jiǎn tài duǎn.
请 别 剪 太 短。

Please don't cut it too short.

(5) Nín tài kuājiǎng le.
您 太 夸奖 了。

You flatter me.

这里的"太"是副词,表示程度过头。

Here "太" is an adverb. It indicates that the degree is beyond allowed or desirable.

161. 不太 + 形容词/动词

Not very + adjective/adverb

Zhège cài bú tài hǎochī.
(1) 这个 菜 不 太 好吃。

This dish is not very tasty.

Zhège zhìliàng bú tài hǎo.
(2) 这个 质量 不 太 好。

The quality of this one is not very good.

Wǒ bú tài shúxi Shànghǎi de
(3) 我 不 太 熟悉 上海 的

I am not very familiar with the roads in Shang-

dàolù.
道路。

hai.

Zài kǒuyǔ zhōng, zhège cír
(4) 在 口语 中, 这个 词儿

This word isn't used very often in spoken lan-

bú tài yòng.
不 太 用。

guage.

"不太"减弱了否定的程度,"不太好吃"比"不好吃"程度轻,语气比较婉转。

"不太" is used to soften the tone of negation. "不太好吃" is in a lower degree and is milder compared with "不好吃".

162. 不怎么 + 形容词/动词

Not very + adjective/adverb

Zhè xīguā bù zěnme tián.
(1) 这 西瓜 不 怎么 甜。

This watermelon is not very sweet.

Wǒ bù zěnme xǐhuan chī
(2) 我 不 怎么 喜欢 吃

I don't like western food very much.

xīcān.
西餐。

Nǎinai bù zěnme pàng.
(3) 奶奶 不 怎么 胖。

Grandma is not very fat.

Mèimei bù zěnme yònggōng.
(4) 妹妹 不 怎么 用功。

My younger sister doesn't study very hard.

这个格式跟句型 161 的意思大致相同。

The meaning of this pattern is similar to that of the Pattern 161.

163. 很/挺 + 形容词/动词

Very + adjective/adverb

Zhè běn shū hěn yǒu yìsi.
(1) 这 本 书 很 有 意思。

This book is very interesting.

Tā tǐng piàoliang.
(2) 她 挺 漂亮。

She is very beautiful.

（3）
Wǒ　hěn　xiǎng　jiā.
我　很　想　家。
I am terribly homesick.

（4）
Dìdi　hái　méi　huí jiā, māma　hěn
弟弟　还　没　回 家，妈妈　很
dānxīn.
担心。
My younger brother hasn't come home yet.

My mother is worried about him very much.

"很"、"挺"表示程度高。
"很"and"挺" indicate a high degree.

164. 非常＋形容词/动词　　　Very/extremely + adjective/adverb

（1）
Jīnmào　Dàshà　fēicháng　gāo.
金茂　大厦　非常　高。
The Jinmao Building is very high.

（2）
Néng　rènshi　nǐ　fēicháng　gāoxìng.
能　认识　你　非常　高兴。
I am very happy to know you.

（3）
Tā　fùqīn　qùshì　le,　tā
他　父亲　去世　了，他
fēicháng　shāngxīn.
非常　伤心。
He is awfully sad about his father's death.

（4）
Tā　fēicháng　shēngqì.
他　非常　生气。
He is terribly angry.

"非常"表示程度极高。
"非常" indicates a very high degree.

165. 有时……　　　Sometimes ...

（1）
Zuìjìn　de　tiānqì　yǒushí　lěng,
最近　的　天气　有时　冷，
yǒushí　rè.
有时　热。
The weather is sometimes cold and some-

times hot.

（2）
Zhèli　yǒushí　xià　xuě.
这里　有时　下　雪。
It snows here sometimes.

（3）
Wǒ　yǒushí　yòng　Hànyǔ　shuōhuà.
我　有时　用　汉语　说话。
Sometimes I speak Chinese.

（4）
Bàba　yǒushí　bù　huílai　chī fàn.
爸爸　有时　不　回来　吃 饭。
Sometimes dad doesn't come back for meals.

166. 常（常）······　　　Frequently/often ...

(1) Bàba chángcháng chūchāi.
爸爸　常常　出差。　　My father travels on business frequently.

(2) Wǒ dōngtiān cháng gǎnmào.
我　冬天　常　感冒。　　I often catch a cold in the winter.

(3) Zhèli de chūntiān cháng xià yǔ.
这里 的 春天　常　下 雨。　　There are many rainy days in spring here.

(4) Tā chángcháng quēxí.
他　常常　缺席。　　He is often absent.

167. 先 + 动词······　　　**First + verb**

(1) Wǒmen xiān fùxí yíxià.
我们　先　复习 一下。　　First, let's review the lessons.

(2) Wǒ xiān jièshào yíxià.
我 先 介绍 一下。　　First, please allow me to introduce ....

(3) Nǐ xiān qù ba.
你 先 去 吧。　　You go first.

(4) Tā bù shūfu, xiān huíqu le.
他 不 舒服，先 回去 了。　　He felt sick and went back home already.

168. 再 + 动词······　　　**Verb + again/repeatedly**

(1) Qǐng zài dú yí biàn.
请 再 读 一 遍。　　Please read it once more.

(2) Zài gěi wǒ yì bēi ba.
再 给 我 一 杯 吧。　　Please give me one more cup.

(3) Wǒ bǎo le, bù néng zài
我 饱 了，不 能 再　　I am quite full and can't eat any more.
chī le.
吃 了。

(4) Míngtiān wǒ zài lái.
明天　我 再 来。　　I will come again tomorrow.

这里的"再"表示动作重复或继续。多指未进行的动作。

Here "再" indicates that the action will continue or will be repeated. It mostly refers to the action that still hasn't happened.

169. 又 + 动词　　Verb + again/repeatedly

Wǒ yòu dúle yí biàn.
(1) 我 又 读了 一 遍。　I read it again.

Tā yòu hēle liǎng bēi jiǔ.
(2) 他 又 喝了 两 杯 酒。　He drank two more cups of wine.

Xiǎo Zhōu yòu qùle yí cì Xīzàng.
(3) 小 周 又 去了 一 次 西藏。　Xiao Zhou went to Tibet again.

Tā yòu hēzuì le.
(4) 他 又 喝醉 了。　He is drunk again.

这里的"又"表示动作已经重复进行了。
Here "又" indicates that the action has been repeated.

170. 只 + 动词　　Verb + only/just

Lǐtáng li zhǐ yǒu yǐzi.
(1) 礼堂 里 只 有 椅子。　There are only chairs in the hall.

Wǒ zhǐ mǎi zhège.
(2) 我 只 买 这个。　I will only buy this one.

Zhège bān zhǐ yǒu yí ge Rìběn xuésheng.
(3) 这个 班 只 有 一 个 日本 学生。　There is only one Japanese student in this class.

Wǒ zhǐ xuéguo yìdiǎnr Yīngyǔ, bù néng dāng fānyì.
(4) 我 只 学过 一点儿 英语，不 能 当 翻译。　I know just a little English. I can't work as an interpreter.

"只"表示仅限于某一范围。
"只" indicates that the scope is limited.

171. 都 + 动词/形容词　　Verb + all

Tāmen dōu shì xuésheng.
(1) 他们 都 是 学生。　All of them are students.

Zhèxiē shū dōu shì túshūguǎn de.
(2) 这些 书 都 是 图书馆 的。　All these books are from the library.

Zuòyè wǒ dōu zuòhǎo le.
(3) 作业 我 都 做好 了。　I've finished all the exercises.

Zhèxiē chènyī dōu hěn piàoliang.
(4) 这些 衬衣 都 很 漂亮。　These shirts are all beautiful.

"都"表示包括全部。
"都" means whole or all.

172. 才 + 动词

Nǐ zěnme cái lái jiù zǒu?
(1) 你 怎么 才 来 就 走？

Wǒ cái dào Běijīng, hái méi
(2) 我 才 到 北京，还 没
gēn Wáng Píng liánxì shang.
跟 王 平 联系 上。

Tā cái xià fēijī, ràng tā
(3) 他 才 下 飞机，让 他
xiūxi yíxià ba.
休息 一下 吧。

Wǒ cái kāishǐ xué Hànyǔ, hái
(4) 我 才 开始 学 汉语，还
tīng bu dǒng.
听 不 懂。

Just; Just now

Why are you leaving now? You just came in.

I just came to Beijing and haven't contacted Wang Ping yet.

He got off the plane just now, let him have a rest.

I just started to learn Chinese, so I can't understand.

这里的"才"表示动作在不久前发生。

Here "才" indicates that the action happened not long ago.

173. 时间 + 才 + 动词

Zuówǎn wǒ shí'èr diǎn cái shuì.
(1) 昨晚 我 十二 点 才 睡。

Huìyì qī diǎn cái jiéshù, wǒ
(2) 会议 七 点 才 结束，我
èjí le.
饿极 了。

Tiānqì yùbào shuō dàyǔ yào
(3) 天气 预报 说 大雨 要
wǎnshang cái tíng.
晚上 才 停。

Yuándìng èr hào chūfā, jiéguǒ
(4) 原定 二 号 出发，结果
sān hào cái zǒu.
三 号 才 走。

Did not + verb + until ... (time)

I didn't go to bed until 12 pm last night.

The meeting didn't end until seven. I was very hungry.

The forecast said that the heavy rain would not stop until evening.

(He) didn't leave on the second as planned, but left on the third.

这里的"才"强调动作发生或结束得晚。这个格式跟句型 179 的意思相反。

Here "才" emphasizes that the action started or ended very late. The meaning of this pattern is contrary to that of the Pattern 179.

174. 数量/时间 + 才 + 结果

Did not + verb + until ... (time/quantity)

Wǒ dúle wǔ biàn cái jìzhù.
(1) 我 读了 五 遍 才 记住。

I couldn't remember it until I read it five times.

Wǒ jiǎngle sān biàn, tā cái míngbai.
(2) 我 讲了 三 遍，他 才 明白。

He didn't understand until I explained for three times.

Nà běn shū jiǔ yuè cái néng chūbǎn.
(3) 那 本 书 九 月 才 能 出版。

That book can't be published until September.

Jìdào Měiguó de xìn yào shí tiān cái dào.
(4) 寄到 美国 的 信 要 十 天 才 到。

A letter to US needs ten days to get there.

这里的"才"强调结果出现的条件是数量多、历时长或时间晚。与句型 180 的意思相反。

Here "才" emphasizes that the result appears only when the time is late or the time period is very long or the action has been taken for many times. The meaning of this pattern is contrary to that of the Pattern 180.

175. 条件 + 才 + 结果

Did not + verb + until ... ; Only if ...

Rènzhēn xuéxí cái huì yǒu jìnbù.
(1) 认真 学习 才 会 有 进步。

Progress can be made only if you study hard.

Zhèyàng zuò cái néng jiějué wèntí.
(2) 这样 做 才 能 解决 问题。

The problem can be solved only if you act this way.

Déle bìng cái zhīdao jiànkāng de kěguì.
(3) 得了 病 才 知道 健康 的 可贵。

People don't realize that being in good health is so valuable until they get ill.

Wǒ tīngle nǐ de huà cái fàngxīn.
(4) 我 听了 你 的 话 才 放心。

I could not set my mind at rest until I heard from you.

176. 才 + 数量   Only ...

(1) 他 才 十 岁, 已经 很
　　 Tā cái shí suì, yǐjīng hěn
　　 懂事 了。
　　 dǒngshì le.

Though he is only ten years old, he is considerate.

(2) 这 次 考试, 我 才 得了
　　 Zhè cì kǎoshì, wǒ cái déle
　　 六十 分。
　　 liùshí fēn.

I just got 60 in this examination.

(3) 这 双 鞋 很 便宜, 才
　　 Zhè shuāng xié hěn piányi, cái
　　 一百 块。
　　 yìbǎi kuài.

This pair of shoes is quite cheap, only 100 yuan.

(4) 这个 公司 开办 时 才
　　 Zhège gōngsī kāibàn shí cái
　　 有 五十 个 人。
　　 yǒu wǔshí ge rén.

It had a staff of only 50 members when this company started its business.

这里的"才"表示数量少、程度低。
Here "才" expresses low in degree or less in quantity.

177. 就 + 动词/形容词   Soon; Immediately

(1) 我 就 来。
　　 Wǒ jiù lái.

I'll go right away.

(2) 饭 就 好 了。
　　 Fàn jiù hǎo le.

The meal will be ready in a minute.

(3) 请 等 一下, 会议 就
　　 Qǐng děng yíxià, huìyì jiù
　　 结束 了。
　　 jiéshù le.

Please wait a minute. The meeting will be over soon.

(4) 运动会 就 开始 了。
　　 Yùndònghuì jiù kāishǐ le.

The sport games will begin right now.

这里的"就"表示动作或事情将在很短的时间内发生。
Here "就" indicates that the action or something will happen in very short time.

178. 动词1 + 就 + 动词2

Verb 2 + right after + verb 1

Wǒ zuòwán shì jiù huí jiā.
（1）我 做完 事 就 回 家。

I will go home right after I finish my work.

Nǐ zuòwán zuòyè jiù shuìjiào
（2）你 做完 作业 就 睡觉
ba.
吧。

Go to bed right after you complete your home-

work.

Tā zuòxia jiù kàn diànshì.
（3）他 坐下 就 看 电视。

He watched TV right after sitting down.

Tā tǎngxia jiù shuìzháo le.
（4）他 躺下 就 睡着 了。

He fell asleep immediately after he lay down.

这个格式表示动作1完成后动作2马上开始。
This pattern indicates that the action 2 starts immediately after action1 ends.

179. 时间 + 就 + 动词

As early as ... ; Already ...

Tā bù shūfu, bā diǎn jiù
（1）他 不 舒服，八 点 就
shuì le.
睡 了。

He felt ill and went to bed as early as eight

o'clock.

Huìyì sān diǎn jiù jiéshù, chéng
（3）会议 三 点 就 结束，乘
wǔ diǎn de fēijī, láidejí.
五 点 的 飞机，来得及。

The meeting will end at 3 pm, and there is still

enough time to catch the flight at 5 pm.

Dàyǔ zuówǎn bànyè jiù tíng le.
（3）大雨 昨晚 半夜 就 停 了。

The heavy rain stopped at midnight yesterday.

Tā shíbā suì jiù gōngzuò le.
（4）他 十八 岁 就 工作 了。

He took his first job as early as 18 years old.

这个格式强调动作发生或结束得早。跟句型173的意思相反。
This pattern emphasizes that the action started or ended early. The meaning of this pattern is contrary to that of the Pattern 173.

180. 数量/时间 + 就 + 动词

Right after ... ; Only ...

Wǒ dúle yí biàn jiù jìzhù le.
（1）我 读了 一 遍 就 记住 了。

I remembered it after I read it only once.

Wǒ jiǎngle yí cì tā jiù
（2）我 讲了 一 次 他 就
míngbai le.
明白 了。

He understood right after I told him.

(3)　Nà běn shū zhège yuèdǐ jiù
那　本　书　这个　月底　就　　　That book will be published as early as the end
néng chūbǎn le.
能　出版　了。　　　　　　　　　of this month.

(4)　Qù Sūzhōu kāichē yí ge xiǎoshí
去　苏州　开车　一　个　小时　　　It's only a one hour drive to get to Suzhou.
jiù dào le.
就　到　了。

这里的"就"强调结果出现的条件是数量少、历时短或时间早。这个格式与句型174 的意思相反。

Here "就" emphasizes that the result appears when the time is still early or the time period is short or the action is taken for only a few times. The meaning of this pattern is contrary to that of the Pattern 174.

181．就 + 动词 + 宾语　　　　Only/just + Verb

(1)　Wǒ jiù mǎi zhèxiē.
我　就　买　这些。　　　　　　I will just buy these.

(2)　Wǒ jiù mǎi zhè zhǒng chē.
我　就　买　这　种　车。　　　I will buy this kind of car.

(3)　Xiànzài bàngōngshì jiù shèng
现在　办公室　就　剩　　　　　I am the only one who remains in the office.
wǒ yí ge rén.
我　一　个　人。

这里的"就"表示动作只在宾语的范围内进行。这个格式与句型170 的意思相似。

Here "就" indicates that the action is only within the scope of the object of the sentence. The meaning of this pattern is similar to that of the Pattern 170.

182．还……　　　　　　　　Still …

(1)　Wǒ hái zài lǎo dìfang zhù.
我　还　在　老　地方　住。　　　I still live in the same old place.

(2)　Tā hái zài Xīnhuá Yīyuàn gōngzuò.
他　还　在　新华　医院　工作。　He still works at Xinhua Hospital.

(3)　Zhè jiàn dàyī chuānle sān nián,
这　件　大衣　穿了　三　年，　　This overcoat still looks new though it has
hái hěn xīn.
还　很　新。　　　　　　　　　been used for three years.

(4)　Wǒ yǐjīng qīshí suì le, hái
她　已经　七十　岁　了，还　　　She is still in good health at the age of 70.

hěn　jiànkāng.
很　　健康。

这里的"还"表示动作或状态在持续,没有变化或者变化很小。

Here "还" indicates that the action or state continues, remains unchanged or changes only a little.

183. 还……

Even/still more, In addition; As well; Also

Jīntiān bǐ zuótiān hái lěng.
(1) 今天 比 昨天 还 冷。

It is even colder today than yesterday.

Nà běn shū hái yào sān ge
(2) 那 本 书 还 要 三 个
yuè cái néng chūbǎn.
月 才 能 出版。

The publication of that book still needs another three months.

Tā chúle Yīngyǔ, hái huì Fǎyǔ.
(3) 他 除了 英语, 还 会 法语。

Besides English he can speak French as well.

(Chúle zhèxiē,) nín hái yào
(4) (除了 这些,) 您 还 要
shénme?
什么?

What do you want in addition to this?

这里的"还"表示程度、数量的增加或范围的扩大。

Here "还" indicates the increase of degree, quantity or scope.

184. 还……

Fairly ... ; Passably ...

Yéye de shēntǐ hái hǎo.
(1) 爷爷 的 身体 还 好。

Grandpa is in fairly good health.

Zhèli de jiāotōng hái fāngbiàn.
(2) 这里 的 交通 还 方便。

The transportation facilities here are fairly good.

Zhège cài de wèidao hái búcuò.
(3) 这个 菜 的 味道 还 不错。

This dish is fairly tasty.

Zhè běn xiǎoshuō hái kěyǐ.
(4) 这 本 小说 还 可以。

This novel is presentable.

这里的"还"表示事物的程度勉强过得去。

Here "还" expresses a passable situation.

185. 还……呢

Even ...

(1) Tā Zhōngwén hěn hǎo, hái
他 中文 很 好，还
dāngguo fānyì ne.
当过 翻译 呢。

His Chinese is very good. He even worked as an interpreter.

(2) Tā de shūfǎ zuòpǐn hái zhǎnlǎn-
他 的 书法 作品 还 展览
guo ne.
过 呢。

His calligraphy works have even been on display.

(3) Tā de huàr hái déguo yī
他 的 画儿 还 得过 一
děng jiǎng ne.
等 奖 呢。

His painting has even been awarded the first prize.

(4) Tā chàng de hěn hǎo, hái
他 唱 得 很 好，还
dēngtái biǎoyǎnguo ne.
登台 表演过 呢。

He sings very well and has even performed on stage.

这里的"还……呢"表示赞叹的语气。
Here "还……呢" expresses a tone of praise.

186. 还……呢

... yet; Still ...

(1) Wǒ xiànzài bù néng shuì, zhège
我 现在 不 能 睡，这个
bàogào hái méi xiěwán ne.
报告 还 没 写完 呢。

I can't go to bed now. I haven't finished the report yet.

(2) Xiànzài bù néng zǒu, hái méi
现在 不 能 走，还 没
dào xiàbān shíjiān ne.
到 下班 时间 呢。

We can't go now. It isn't the time to knock off.

(3) Nǐ bié wán le, xià xīngqī hái
你 别 玩 了，下 星期 还
yào kǎoshì ne.
要 考试 呢。

Don't fool around. You have an examination next week.

(4) Zài zuò yíhuìr ba, hái zǎo ne.
再 坐 一会儿 吧，还 早 呢。
Stay a little longer please. It's still early.

这里的"还……呢"是在提醒对方或说明某件事的时候用的。
Here "还……呢" is used in situations of reminding someone or explaining something.

187. 果然······ As expected; Really; Sure enough

(1) 果然 如此。
Guǒrán rúcǐ.

It happened just as expected.

(2) 我 想 他 会 同意 的，
Wǒ xiǎng tā huì tóngyì de,
果然 他 同意·了。
guǒrán tā tóngyì le.

I thought he would agree, and he did agree as expected.

(3) 我 想 他 会 来 的，
Wǒ xiǎng tā huì lái de,
果然 他 来 了。
guǒrán tā lái le.

I thought he would come, and sure enough he did.

(4) 他 上午 说 要 下 雪，
Tā shàngwǔ shuō yào xià xuě,
果然 下午 下 雪，了。
guǒrán xiàwǔ xià xuě, le.

He said in the morning that it would snow, and sure enough it did in the afternoon.

"果然"表示事实跟所估计的相符。

"果然" expresses that what happened confirms to what was expected.

188. 千万(要) + 动词 Be sure to + verb; Must + verb
千万 + 别 + 动词 Be sure not to + verb, Must not + verb

(1) 你 千万 要 注意 安全。
Nǐ qiānwàn yào zhùyì ānquán.

Be sure to pay attention to your safety.

(2) 你 千万 早 点儿 回 家。
Nǐ qiānwàn zǎo diǎnr huí jiā.

Be sure to come back home early.

(3) 到时 你 千万 要 来。
Dàoshí nǐ qiānwàn yào lái.

Be sure to come then.

(4) 你 千万 要 坚持 到底。
Nǐ qiānwàn yào jiānchí dàodǐ.

You must stick it out.

(5) 食物 坏 了，千万 别 吃。
Shíwù huài le, qiānwàn bié chī.

Be sure not to eat rotten food.

(6) 这 件 事 你 千万 别 对 他 说。
Zhè jiàn shì nǐ qiānwàn bié duì tā shuō.

You must not tell him about this.

这里的"千万"是副词,表示恳切的叮咛。

Here "千万" is an adverb. It expresses earnest persuasion.

189 一定 + 动词/形容词

Surely ... ; Must be ...

(1) Tā xià ge yuè yídìng huí guó.
他 下 个 月 一定 回 国。

He will surely return to China next month.

(2) Tā hěn yònggōng, yídìng kǎo
他 很 用功, 一定 考
de hǎo.
得 好。

He has studied very hard and will certainly pass the examination.

(3) Tā chuān de dōu shì míngpái,
他 穿 的 都 是 名牌,
yídìng hěn yǒu qián.
一定 很 有 钱。

All his clothes are the best brands. He must be very rich.

(4) Tā tiāntiān duànliàn, shēntǐ yídìng
他 天天 锻炼, 身体 一定
hěn hǎo.
很 好。

He does physical exercises every day. Surely he is in good health.

这里的"一定"表示必然、确实无疑。

Here "一定" means certainly or unquestionably.

190. 一定 + 动词

Certainly ... ; Must ...

(1) Wǒ yídìng bāng nǐ (de) máng.
我 一定 帮 你 (的) 忙。

I will certainly help you.

(2) Yǐhòu wǒ yídìng nǔlì xuéxí.
以后 我 一定 努力 学习。

From now on, I will study hard.

(3) Yǐhòu wǒ yídìng bù sāhuǎng.
以后 我 一定 不 撒谎。

I swear I will not lie again from now on.

(4) Nǐ míngtiān yídìng lái a!
你 明天 一定 来 啊!

Be sure to come tomorrow.

这里的"一定"表示说话人对做某事意志坚决,或者坚决要求别人做某事。

Here "一定" expresses that the speaker is determined to do something or insist someone do something.

191. 不一定

Might not ... ; Not always ...

(1) Yǒumíng de shípǐn bù yídìng
有名 的 食品 不 一定
hǎochī.
好吃。

Famous foods are not always tasty.

Shū shang shuō de bù yídìng
(2) 书 上 说 的 不 一定 What the books said might not be all correct.
duì.
对。

Tā míngtiān bù yídìng néng lái.
(3) 他 明天 不 一定 能 来。 He might not come tomorrow.

Shíyàn bù yídìng néng chénggōng.
(4) 实验 不 一定 能 成功。 The experiment might not succeed.

"不一定"表示根据估计,不能确认某一个结论。

"不一定" indicates that some conclusion could not be drawn according to sheer estimation.

192. 幸亏/幸好……   **Fortunately ...**

Xià yǔ le, xìngkuī wǒ dàile sǎn.
(1) 下 雨 了,幸亏 我 带了 伞。 It is raining now. Fortunately I have my umbrella with me.

Wǒ mílù le, xìngkuī dàile dìtú.
(2) 我 迷路 了,幸亏 带了 地图。 I am lost. Fortunately I have taken a map with me.

Wǒ fāshāo le, xìnghǎo jīntiān
(3) 我 发烧 了, 幸好 今天 I have a fever. Fortunately I am not on duty
búyòng shàngbān.
不用 上班。 today.

Wǒ qiánbāo diū le, xìnghǎo
(4) 我 钱包 丢 了, 幸好 My wallet is lost. Luckily there was only a
méi duōshao qián.
没 多少 钱。 little money in it.

"幸亏"、"幸好"表示由于偶然有某种有利因素,避免了某种不好的事情。

"幸亏" and "幸好" indicate that a bad or unhappy thing is avoided by chance.

193. ……了。   **Already (past participle) ...**

Tā zuótiān qù Běijīng le.
(1) 他 昨天 去 北京 了。 He already went to Beijing yesterday.

Māma shàngwǔ xiě xìn le.
(2) 妈妈 上午 写 信 了。 Mama wrote a letter this morning.

(3)
Jiāng Tāo qiántiān lái Shànghǎi
江 涛 前天 来 上海
le.
了。

Jiang Tao came to Shanghai the day before yesterday.

(4)
Wǒ chīle fàn le.
我 吃了 饭 了。

I have had my meal already.

这里的"了"放在句末,表示肯定的语气,肯定某件事已经发生。

When "了" is put at the end of a sentence, it expresses an affirmative tone. It confirms that something has already happened.

194. 都……了　　Already ...

(1)
Dōu shí'èr diǎn le, tā hái
都 十二 点 了,他 还
méi shuì.
没 睡。

It is already 12 o'clock, but he hasn't gone to bed yet.

(2)
Tiān dōu hēi le, kuài huí jiā ba.
天 都 黑 了, 快 回 家 吧。

It is dark already, let's go home.

(3)
Cài dōu liáng le, kuài chī ba.
菜 都 凉 了, 快 吃 吧。

The dishes will become cold. Eat them quickly!

(4)
Wǒ dōu sānshí suì le, hái
我 都 三十 岁 了, 还
méiyǒu nǚpéngyou.
没有 女朋友。

I am 30 now, yet I still haven't had a girl-friend.

这里的"都"是"已经"的意思。
Here "都" means "已经".

195. 动词/形容词/名词 + 了　　Already ...

(1)
Mèimei zhǎnggāo le.
妹妹 长高 了。

My younger sister has grown taller.

(2)
Tiān qíng le.
天 晴 了。

The weather has turned fine.

(3)
Qiūtiān le, hái zhème rè.
秋天 了, 还 这么 热。

It is autumn now, but still so hot.

(4)
Xiànzài yǐjīng jiǔ diǎn le.
现在 已经 九 点 了。

It is already nine o'clock now.

这里的"了"表示肯定事态出现了变化。
Here "了" is used to confirm a change.

196. 越来越……

| | More and more ... |

(1) Yǔ yuèláiyuè dà le.
雨 越来越 大 了。

The rain is getting heavier and heavier.

(2) Tiānqì yuèláiyuè rè le.
天气 越来越 热 了。

The weather is getting warmer and warmer.

(3) Wǒ yuèláiyuè xǐhuan yīnyuè le.
我 越来越 喜欢 音乐 了。

I love music more and more.

(4) Wǒ dùzi yuèláiyuè téng le.
我 肚子 越来越 疼 了。

My stomachache is getting more and more severe.

"越来越"表示程度随时间的推移而变化。

"越来越……" expresses that the degree changes with time.

197. 是 + A + 动词 + 的(+ 宾语)

It was ... that ...

(1) Hú Ān shì qiántiān qù de.
胡 安 是 前天 去 的。

It was the day before yesterday that Mr. Hu An left.

(2) Sūn Píng shì qùnián qù de
孙 平 是 去年 去 的
Měiguó.
美国。

It was last year that Mr. Sun Ping went to the United States.

(3) Tā shì qíchē lái de.
他 是 骑车 来 的。

He came here by bicycle.

(4) Tā shì chéng chuán qù de Rìběn.
他 是 乘 船 去 的 日本。

He went to Japan by ship.

(5) Tā shì zài Yīngguó xué de
他 是 在 英国 学 的
Yīngyǔ.
英语。

It was in Britain that he studied English.

A 是动作的时间、地点或方式。需要说明过去的动作发生的时间、地点或者方式的时候可用这个格式。

This pattern can be used to emphasize the time, place or way of the action that happened in the past. Here "A" represents the time, place or way of the action.

198. ……等（等）　　　　　... and so on；... etc.

（1）Jiāyòng diànqì bāokuò diànshìjī、
家用　电器　包括　电视机、
wēibōlú、　diànbīngxiāng　děngděng.
微波炉、　电冰箱　　等等。

Home appliances include TVs, microwave ovens, refrigerators, etc.

（2）Xiǎoxué de kèchéng yǒu Yǔwén、
小学　的　课程　有　语文、
Shùxué、　Yīngyǔ　děngděng.
数学、　英语　等等。

The courses in primary schools are Chinese, Maths, English, etc.

（3）Běn xiào yǒu Měiguó、　Yīngguó
本　校　有　美国、　英国
děng guójiā de xuésheng.
等　国家　的　学生。

There are students from the US, the UK and so on in our school.

（4）Míngtiān Chángchūn、　Shěnyáng
明天　长春、　沈阳
děng dì jiāng xià dàxuě.
等　地　将　下　大雪。

Tomorrow there will be heavy snow in cities such as Changchun, Shenyang, etc.

　　"等（等）"用在两个或几个并列词语的后面，代表省略的部分，表示列举末尽。多用于书面语。

　　"等（等）" is used after two or more words which stand side by side. It indicates that more words are omitted and represents these omitted words. "等（等）" is usually used in written language.

199. ……什么的　　　　　... and so on；... etc.；Something else

（1）Hē diǎnr kāfēi shénme de ba.
喝　点儿　咖啡　什么　的　吧。

Please have coffee or something else.

（2）Tā xǐhuan dú xiǎoshuō、　shīgē
他　喜欢　读　小说、　诗歌
shénme de.
什么　的。

He likes to read novels, poems and so on.

（3）Wǒ mǎile xiāngjiāo、　pútao
我　买了　香蕉、　葡萄
shénme de.
什么　的。

I've bought bananas, grapes and some other fruits.

（4）Shǒutíbāo li yǒu qiánbāo、
手提包　里　有　钱包、
shēnfènzhèng　shénme de.
身份证　　什么　的。

There is a wallet, ID etc. in my handbag.

　　"什么的"跟句型198的"等"意思相同，多用于口语。

　　The meaning of "什么的" is the same as that of Pattern 198. It is usually used in spoken language.

200. （一）边 + 动词 1 +
（一）边 + 动词 2

Verb 2 + while verb 1 ; Verb 1 and verb 2

Tā yìbiān zǒu yìbiān sīkǎo.
(1) 他 一边 走 一边 思考。　He is thinking while walking.

Mèimei biān tán qín biān chàng gē.
(2) 妹妹 边 弹琴 边 唱 歌。　My younger sister is singing while playing the

piano.

Dīng Lì biān gōngzuò biān xuéxí.
(3) 丁 丽 边 工作 边 学习。　Ms. Ding Li has her job, and meanwhile she

keeps studying.

Dàjiā biān hē chá biān shuōhuà.
(4) 大家 边 喝 茶 边 说话。　All of us drank tea and chatted to each other.

这个格式表示两个以上的动作同时进行。

This pattern indicates that two or more actions are going on at the same time.

201. 又……又……

... and ... ; ... as well

Yòu xià yǔ yòu guā fēng.
(1) 又 下 雨 又 刮 风。　It is raining and blowing.

Tā yòu chōuyān yòu hē jiǔ.
(2) 他 又 抽烟 又 喝 酒。　He smokes and drinks as well.

Zhège yòu piányi yòu hǎo.
(3) 这个 又 便宜 又 好。　This one is cheap and good in quality as well.

Zhège fángjiān yòu dà yòu
(4) 这个 房间 又 大 又　This room is bright and big.
míngliàng.
明亮。

这个格式表示几种情况或状态同时存在。

This pattern indicates that two or more states or situations exist at the same time.

202. 不但/不仅 + A + 而且 + B
不但/不仅 + A，B + 也

Not only A, but also B

(1) Tā búdàn cōngming érqiě
她 不但 聪明 而且
yònggōng.
用功。

She is not only clever, but also hard working.

(2) Tā bùjǐn xuéxí chéngjì hǎo,
他 不仅 学习 成绩 好，
érqiě rénpǐn yě hǎo.
而且 人品 也 好。

He is not only good at studies, but also a person of integrity.

(3) Lóngjǐngchá búdàn zài guónèi, zài
龙井茶 不但 在 国内， 在
guówài yě hěn yǒumíng.
国外 也 很 有名。

Longjing Tea is famous not only domestically but also internationally.

(4) Zhège cài búdàn hǎochī,
这个 菜 不但 好吃，
yánsè yě hěn hǎokàn.
颜色 也 很 好看。

This dish not only tastes delicious, but also looks nice.

这个格式表示肯定 A 的同时,进一步肯定 B。
This pattern confirms "A" and "B" as well.

203. (先 +)动词1 + 再 + 动词2

Verb 1 + before + verb 2; Verb 1 first, and then + verb 2

(1) Wǒ xiǎng xiān xǐzǎo zài chī
我 想 先 洗澡 再 吃
fàn.
饭。

I'd like to take a shower first, and then have the meal.

(2) Nǐ yīnggāi xiān zuò zuòyè zài
你 应该 先 做 作业 再
kàn diànshì.
看 电视。

You should finish your homework first before you watch TV.

(3) Wǒ xiān qù yínháng zài qù
我 先 去 银行 再 去
gōngsī.
公司。

First I'll go to the bank, and then I'll go to the company.

(4) Wǒmen hē bēi kāfēi zài
我们 喝 杯 咖啡 再
kāishǐ gōngzuò ba.
开始 工作 吧。

Let's have a cup of coffee before starting to work.

204. (等)……再 + 动词　　Verb + after ... , Verb + until ...

(1) Xiànzài méi kòng, dào qiūtiān
现在 没 空, 到 秋天
zài qù ba.
再 去 吧。

I am busy and can't go now. Let's wait till autumn.

(2) Děng yǔ tíngle zài chūqu.
等 雨 停了 再 出去。

Let's stay here until the rain stops.

(3) Děng lǐngle gōngzī zài mǎi
等 领了 工资 再 买
ba.
吧。

Let's buy it after we get the payment.

(4) Děng rén qíle zài kāihuì.
等 人 齐了 再 开会。

The meeting will not start until everyone is here.

这个格式表示动作要等某种情况出现以后才进行。

This pattern indicates that the action should be delayed until some condition appears.

205. 再……就 + 结果　　If ... , then ...

(1) Nǐ zài chī zhème duō, jiù
你 再 吃 这么 多, 就
huì chéng dàpàngzi le.
会 成 大胖子 了。

If you keep eating so much, then you will become fat.

(2) Nǐ zài zhèyàng huā qián,
你 再 这样 花 钱,
yuèdǐ jiù méi fàn chī le.
月底 就 没 饭 吃 了。

If you spend your money this way, then you might not afford your meals at the end of this month.

(3) Wǒ zài bù zǒu jiù láibují le.
我 再 不 走 就 来不及 了。

I'll be late if I don't leave now.

(4) Nǐ zài bù qǐchuáng jiù yào
你 再 不 起床 就 要
chídào le.
迟到 了。

You will be late if you don't get up now.

这个格式表示如果某种情况继续下去就会出现某种结果。

This pattern indicates that a certain result will appear if the present condition continues.

206. 一……就……　As soon as ... ; Right after ... ; Once ...

(1) Yí dào chūntiān, huā jiù kāi.
一 到 春天, 花 就 开。

The flowers will blossom as soon as the spring comes.

(2) Zhège hěn jiǎndān, wǒ yí kàn jiù míngbai.
这个 很 简单, 我 一 看 就 明白。

It was quite simple. I understood it at a glance.

(3) Tā hěn cōngming, yì xué jiù huì.
他 很 聪明, 一 学 就 会。

He is very smart. He can master something as soon as he learns it.

(4) Dōngběi yí dào dōngtiān jiù xià xuě.
东北 一 到 冬天 就 下 雪。

In the Northeast it will snow once the winter comes.

这个格式表示两件事紧接着发生。
This pattern indicates that one thing happens right after the other.

207. 只要 + 必要条件 + 就 + 结果　If only; As long as ...

(1) Zhǐyào bú xià dàyǔ, wǒ jiù qù.
只要 不 下 大雨, 我 就 去。

I'll go as long as it doesn't rain heavily.

(2) Zhǐyào nǔlì jiù huì chénggōng.
只要 努力 就 会 成功。

As long as you try hard, you will succeed.

(3) Zhǐyào dǎ ge diànhuà, tā jiù huì sònglai.
只要 打 个 电话, 他 就 会 送来。

He will send it here as long as you give him a call.

(4) Zhǐyào jiānchí, jiù néng zǒudào zhōngdiǎn.
只要 坚持, 就 能 走到 终点。

You can get to the end as long as you stick it out.

这个格式表示产生某种结果的必要条件。
This pattern indicates the essential condition for a certain result.

208. 只有 + 唯一条件 + 才 + 结果

Only ...

(1)
Zhǐyǒu tuánjié cái yǒu lìliàng.
只有 团结 才 有 力量。

Only from unity comes strength.

(2)
Zhǐyǒu duō dú、 duō tīng cái
只有 多 读、多 听 才
néng xuéhǎo wàiyǔ.
能 学好 外语。

Only by reading and listening more can you master a foreign language.

(3)
Zhǐyǒu zài jǐnjí de qíngkuàng
只有 在 紧急 的 情况
xià, cái kěyǐ kāi zhège mén.
下，才 可以 开 这个 门。

You should open this door only in an emergency.

(4)
Zhǐyǒu kāidāo, cái néng zhìhǎo
只有 开刀，才 能 治好
tā de bìng.
他 的 病。

His illness can be cured only by an operation.

这个格式表示产生某种结果的唯一条件。

This pattern indicates the only condition for a certain result.

209. 不管 + A + 都 + B

No matter how/what/where ...

(1)
Bùguǎn duō máng, dōu yào
不管 多 忙， 都 要
duànliàn shēntǐ.
锻炼 身体。

No matter how busy you are, you should keep doing physical exercises.

(2)
Bùguǎn yùdào shénme kùnnan,
不管 遇到 什么 困难，
wǒmen dōu bú pà.
我们 都 不 怕。

No matter what difficulty we face, we will not fear.

(3)
Bùguǎn xià bu xià yǔ, wǒ dōu
不管 下 不 下 雨，我 都
chūxí.
出席。

No matter if it rains or not, I'll be present.

(4)
Bùguǎn nǐ qù bu qù, wǒ dōu qù.
不管 你 去 不 去，我 都 去。

No matter if you go or not, I'll go.

A 代表所有情况，B 是结论。这个格式表示在任何情况下，结论都不改变。"不管"常用于口语。书面语中常用"不论（búlùn）""无论（wúlùn）"。

This pattern indicates that under no circumstances will the results change. Here "A" represents all the circumstances and "B" is the result. "不管" is usually used in spoken language and "不论" and "无论" are usually used in written language.

210. (如果/要是 +) A (的话), 就 + B   If A, then B; In case A, then B

(1) 如果 下 雨 的话， 我 就
　　Rúguǒ xià yǔ dehuà, wǒ jiù
　　不 去。
　　bú qù.

In case of rain, I will not go.

(2) 如果 下 雨 我 就 不 去。
　　Rúguǒ xià yǔ wǒ jiù bú qù.

In case of rain, I will not go.

(3) 下 雨 的话， 我 就 不 去。
　　Xià yǔ dehuà, wǒ jiù bú qù.

In case of rain, I will not go.

(4) 下 雨， 我 就 不 去。
　　Xià yǔ, wǒ jiù bú qù.

In case of rain, I will not go.

(5) 如果 天气 好， 就 可以
　　Rúguǒ tiānqì hǎo, jiù kěyǐ
　　看到 月亮。
　　kàndào yuèliang.

If it is clear, you can see the moon.

(6) 要是 骑车 去 就 来得及。
　　Yàoshi qíchē qù jiù láidejí.

You can make it if you go by bicycle.

(7) 价钱 便宜 的话， 我 就
　　Jiàqian piányi dehuà, wǒ jiù
　　多 买 一点儿。
　　duō mǎi yìdiǎnr.

I will buy more if the price is low.

(8) 有 事 就 打 电话 来。
　　Yǒu shì jiù dǎ diànhuà lai.

Call me if you need anything.

　　A 是假设的情况，B 是结论。有时"如果"、"要是"和"的话"可以省略。

　　Here "A" is an assumption and "B" is the result. Sometimes "如果", "要是" and "的话" can be omitted.

211. 即使/就是 + A + 也 + B   Even if ... ; Even ...

(1) 即使 天气 不 好， 我 也 去。
　　Jíshǐ tiānqì bù hǎo, wǒ yě qù.

Even if it rains, I'll go.

(2) 即使 贵， 我 也 要 买。
　　Jíshǐ guì, wǒ yě yào mǎi.

Even if it is expensive, I am going to buy it.

(3) 就是 冷， 我 也 不 在乎。
　　Jiùshì lěng, wǒ yě bú zàihu.

I don't care even if it is cold.

(4) 你 就是 晚 点儿 来 也
　　Nǐ jiùshì wǎn diǎnr lái yě
　　没 关系。
　　méi guānxi.

It doesn't matter even if you come late.

　　A 是假设的情况，B 是结论。这个格式表示 B 不受 A 的影响。

　　Here "A" is an assumption and "B" is the result. This pattern indicates that "B" will not be affected by "A".

212. 因为 + 原因 + 所以 + 结果

Because ... ; So ...

(1) 因为 西瓜 甜，所以 我
　　Yīnwèi xīguā tián, suǒyǐ wǒ
喜欢 吃。
xǐhuan chī.

I like watermelon because it is sweet.

(2) 因为 下 雨 所以 整天
　　Yīnwèi xià yǔ suǒyǐ zhěngtiān
在 家。
zài jiā.

I stayed home all day because of the heavy rain.

(3) 因为 钱 不 够，所以 我
　　Yīnwèi qián bú gòu, suǒyǐ wǒ
没 买。
méi mǎi.

Since I didn't take enough money with me, I didn't buy it.

(4) 李 明 发烧，所以 回 家
　　Lǐ Míng fāshāo, suǒyǐ huí jiā
了。
le.

Li Ming has a fever, so he has returned home already.

(5) 我 感冒 了，所以 请假 了。
　　Wǒ gǎnmào le, suǒyǐ qǐngjià le.

I had caught a cold, so I asked for sick leave.

(6) 因为 天气 好，大家 都
　　Yīnwèi tiānqì hǎo, dàjiā dōu
出去 了。
chūqu le.

Everyone has gone out since the weather is so fine.

(7) 弟弟 因为 睡懒觉，
　　Dìdi yīnwèi shuìlǎnjiào,
迟到 了。
chídào le.

My younger brother got up late, so he was late for school.

这个格式表示因果关系,与句型 214 的意思相同,多用于口语。有时在"因为"、"所以"中,可以省略其中的一个。

This pattern expresses causality and is usually used in spoken language. Its meaning is the same as that of Pattern 214. Sometimes either "因为" or "所以" can be omitted.

213. 结果 + 是 + 因为 + 原因

Because ... ; For ... (reason)

(1) 我 昨天 没 去 是 因为
　　Wǒ zuótiān méi qù shì yīnwèi
有 急事。
yǒu jíshì.

I didn't go there yesterday because of something urgent.

(2)
Wǒ chídào shì yīnwèi lù shang
我 迟到 是 因为 路 上
dǔchē.
堵车。

I am late because of a traffic jam.

(3)
Tā bù gōngzuò shì yīnwèi
他 不 工作 是 因为
shēntǐ bù hǎo.
身体 不 好。

He doesn't take a job due to his poor health.

(4)
Dìdi méi kǎoshang dàxué shì
弟弟 没 考上 大学 是
yīnwèi bù nǔlì.
因为 不 努力。

My younger brother didn't pass the college entrance examination because he didn't study hard.

这个格式是在需要说明或解释事情发生的原因的时候用的。
This pattern is used to explain why something happened.

214. 由于 + 原因 (+ 所以) + 结果

Because … ; For … (reason)

(1)
Yóuyú shíjiān guānxì, huìyì jiù
由于 时间 关系，会议 就
kāidào zhèli ba.
开到 这里 吧。

Since time is limited, we have to close our meeting now.

(2)
Yóuyú tiānqì guānxì, fēijī yào
由于 天气 关系，飞机 要
tuīchí yì xiǎoshí qǐfēi.
推迟 一 小时 起飞。

The departure time of our flight will be postponed for one hour owing to the bad weather.

(3)
Yóuyú bù liǎojiě qíngkuàng, wǒ
由于 不 了解 情况， 我
zànshí bù fābiǎo yìjiàn.
暂时 不 发表 意见。

Since I don't know the whole situation, I can't give you my opinion for the moment.

(4)
Yóuyú jīngfèi búgòu, zhè jiàn
由于 经费 不够，这 件
shì bàn bu chéng le.
事 办 不 成 了。

The project has to be abandoned for lack of funds.

这个格式跟句型212的意思相同，多用于书面或公众场合。
The meaning of this pattern is similar to that of Pattern 212. It is mostly used in written language or in public speeches.

215. （虽然＋）A＋但是/可是/不过 ＋B   Although ... ; However ...

(1)
Zhèli suīrán mǎi dōngxi fāngbiàn,
这里 虽然 买 东西 方便，
dànshì hěn chǎonào.
但是 很 吵闹。

Although it is convenient for shopping here, it's quite noisy.

(2)
Suīrán wǒ hěn xǐhuan, dànshì
虽然 我 很 喜欢， 但是
mǎibuqǐ.
买不起。

I can't afford it though I like it.

(3)
Yǐjīng qiūtiān le, kěshì hái
已经 秋天 了， 可是 还
zhème rè.
这么 热。

It is autumn already. However it is still so hot.

(4)
Yánsè bú tài hǎo, búguò
颜色 不 太 好， 不过
yàngzi búcuò.
样子 不错。

The style is good, though the color is not too good.

　　这个格式表示前后的转折关系。先承认A是事实,然后强调B。A跟B的意思是对立的。"不过"表示转折的程度比"但是"、"可是"轻,多用于口语。

This pattern expresses a turn in meaning. It confirms "A" first, and then puts emphasis on "B". "A" and "B" have opposite meanings. For the degree of turning, "不过" is less emphatic than "但是" and "可是", and mostly used in spoken language.

216. 请……   Please ...

(1)
Qǐng zuò!
请 坐!

Sit down, please.

(2)
Qǐng gēn wǒ dú.
请 跟 我 读。

Please read after me.

(3)
Qǐng yòng Hànyǔ shuō.
请 用 汉语 说。

Please speak in Chinese.

(4)
Qǐng míngtiān zǎo diǎnr lái.
请 明天 早 点儿 来。

Please come early tomorrow.

(5)
Qǐng dǎkāi chuāng.
请 打开 窗。

Please open the window.

　　"请"是希望对方做某事时用的尊敬、礼貌用语。句子的主语和被请的对方一般省略。比如"请坐"的意思是"我请您坐"。

　　"请" is a word used to politely ask the other party to do something. The subject of the sentence and the other party are usually omitted. For example，"请坐" means "我请您坐".

217.（因为＋）原因＋请……　　Since/for … , please …

(1) Hěn rè, qǐng kāi chuāng.
很 热，请 开 窗。　　It is hot, please open the window.

(2) Hěn lěng, qǐng kāi kōngtiáo.
很 冷，请 开 空调。　　It is very cold, please turn on the air conditioner.

(3) Zhèli hěn àn, qǐng xiǎoxīn.
这里 很 暗，请 小心。　　Be careful. It's dark.

(4) Zhèli wēixiǎn, qǐng zǒukāi!
这里 危险，请 走开!　　It is dangerous here. Please leave.

(5) Yīnwèi dǔchē chídào le, qǐng yuánliàng.
因为 堵车 迟到 了，请 原谅。　　I am late due to a traffic jam. Please forgive me.

218. ……吧。　　(Imperative sentence)

(1) Zuò ba.
坐 吧。　　Sit down, please.

(2) Nǐ qù ba.
你 去 吧。　　You may go now.

(3) Nǐ míngtiān zǎo diǎnr lái ba.
你 明天 早 点儿 来 吧。　　Come here early tomorrow morning.

(4) Nǐ hǎohāor xiǎngxiang ba.
你 好好儿 想想 吧。　　Think it over, please.

　　"吧"在这里是希望对方做某事。在对方是同辈、下一辈或关系密切的人时使用。

　　Here "吧" expresses that the speaker wishes the other party to do something. It is used when the other party is a person in the same generation, lower generation or is a close friend of the speaker.

219. ……吧。 **Should ...**

(1)
Nánjīng Lù Bùxíngjiē hěn rènao,
南京 路 步行街 很 热闹，
nǐ qù zǒuzou ba.
你 去 走走 吧。

Nanjing Rd. is quite bustling. You should take a stroll there.

(2)
Zhè běn shū búcuò, nǐ fānfan
这 本 书 不错，你 翻翻
ba.
吧。

This book is really good. You should take a look.

(3)
Nín fàngxīn ba.
您 放心 吧。

Be at ease!

(4)
Nǐ kuài huí jiā ba.
你 快 回 家 吧。

It's time for you to go home.

这里的"吧"表示向对方建议或者催促对方的语气。

Here "吧" indicates that the speaker suggests or urges the other party to do something.

220. ……吧。 **Let ...**

(1)
Wǒ lái bāng nín ná ba.
我 来 帮 您 拿 吧。

Let me help you carry it.

(2)
Wǒ lái máidān ba.
我 来 埋单 吧。

It's my treat.

(3)
Wǒmen zǒu ba.
我们 走 吧。

Let's go.

(4)
Wǒmen qù Ōuzhōu lǚxíng ba.
我们 去 欧洲 旅行 吧。

Let's take a tour to Europe.

这里的"吧"表示说话人希望做某事。有跟对方商量的语气。

Here "吧" indicates that the speaker wishes to do something and consults with the other party.

221. （请）别/不要…… **Do not ... , please.**

(1)
Qǐng bié zài jiàoshì chōuyān.
请 别 在 教室 抽烟。

No smoking in the classroom, please.

(2)
Qǐng bié jiǎn tài duǎn.
请 别 剪 太 短。

Don't cut it too short, please.

(3)
Xiànzài kāishǐ bié shuōhuà.
现在 开始 别 说话。

Don't talk from now on.

(4) Nín bú yào shēngqì.
您 不 要 生气。　　　　Don't be angry.

这个格式是在对方还没做某事时,加以禁止或劝阻。跟句型 222 的意思略有不同。

This pattern is used when you intend to forbid or dissuade the other party from doing something before it really happens. The meaning of this pattern has fine difference to the meaning of Pattern 222.

222. 别/不要……了　　　　Do not ... ; Stop ...

(1) Nǐ bié zài jiàoshì chōuyān le.
你 别 在 教室 抽烟 了。　Stop smoking in the classroom, please.

(2) Yào kǎoshì le, nǐ bú yào
要 考试 了, 你 不 要
wán le.
玩 了。　　　　　　The examination is coming, don't fool around.

(3) Xiànzài kāishǐ bié shuōhuà le.
现在 开始 别 说话 了。　Stop talking from now on.

(4) Xià yǔ le, nǐ bié zǒu le.
下 雨 了, 你 别 走 了。　It is raining now, please stay here.

这个格式是在对方正在做或正想做某事时,加以禁止或劝阻。跟句型 221 的意思略有不同。

This pattern is used when you intend to stop the other party from doing something when he/she is in the process of doing it or about to do it. The meaning of this pattern has fine difference to the meaning of Pattern 221.

223. 太……了!　　　　How/what ... !

(1) Zhè bù diànyǐng tài yǒu yìsi
这 部 电影 太 有 意思
le!
了!　　　　　　　　What a wonderful movie it was!

(2) Zhè chǎng qiúsài tài jīngcǎi le!
这 场 球赛 太 精彩 了!　What an exciting game it was!

(3) Yǎnyuán de fúzhuāng tài
演员 的 服装 太
piàoliang le!
漂亮 了!　　　　　　How beautiful the costumes of the performers

were!

Tā chàng de tài hǎo le!
(4) 他 唱 得 太 好 了!   What wonderful songs he sang!

这是表示赞美、惊叹时用的句型。句末用感叹号(!)。
This pattern is used to expresses admiration and exclamation. Usually an exclamation mark " ! " is used at the end of the sentence.

224. 多(么)/真……啊!　　How/what … !

Zhèli de fēngjǐng duō měi a!
(1) 这里 的 风景 多 美 啊!   How beautiful the scenery is!

Nà zhī xióngmāo duōme kě'ài
(2) 那 只 熊猫 多么 可爱   What a lovely panda!
　　a!
　　啊!

Zhèli zhēn ānjìng a!
(3) 这里 真 安静 啊!   How quiet it is here!

Jīntiān zhēn liángkuai a!
(4) 今天 真 凉快 啊!   How cool it is today!

这个格式跟句型223的意思相同。
The meaning of this pattern is the same as that of Pattern 223.

225. 形容词/动词 + 极/死 + 了!　　How/what …; Extremely …

Tiānqì hǎojí le!
(1) 天气 好极 了!   What a lovely day it is!

Zhège bànfǎ hǎojí le!
(2) 这个 办法 好极 了!   What a good method it is!

Zuìjìn wǒ mángjí le!
(3) 最近 我 忙极 了!   I have been extremely busy lately.

Wǒ gànle yì tiān, lèisǐ le!
(4) 我 干了 一 天, 累死 了!   I am dead tired after a whole day's work.

Tā duì wǒ sāhuǎng, wǒ qìsǐ le!
(5) 他 对 我 撒谎, 我 气死 了!   I am enraged by his lying to me.

Tā zhòngjiǎng le, gāoxìng sǐ le!
(6) 他 中奖 了, 高兴 死 了!   He is extremely exciting for winning a lottery.

这是表示感叹的格式。这里的"极"和"死"表示程度达到最高点。
This pattern expresses exclamation. Here "极" and "死" indicate the highest degree.

Chinese for Foreigners

外国人学汉语

Reading Column
阅读专栏

1 春节
Chūn Jié
THE SPRING FESTIVAL

Chūn Jié shì Zhōngguó nónglì de xīnnián. Chūn Jié shì chūntiān kāishǐ de yìsi.
春节 是 中国 农历 的 新年。 春节 是 春天 开始 的 意思。

Chūn Jié qián, jiājiā-hùhù dōu mángzhe dàsǎochú、 mǎi niánhuò. Zài wàidì
春节 前, 家家户户(1) 都 忙着 大扫除(2)、 买 年货(3)。 在 外地

gōngzuò de rén dōu jǐnliàng gǎnhuí jiāli guònián. Chūn Jié de qiányìtiān jiào chúxī, yě
工作 的 人 都 尽量 赶回 家里 过年(4)。 春节 的 前一天 叫 除夕, 也

jiào dàniányè. Dàniányè quánjiā rén tuánjù zài yìqǐ, gāogāo-xìngxìng de chī niányèfàn.
叫 大年夜(5)。 大年夜 全家 人 团聚(6) 在 一起, 高高兴兴 地 吃 年夜饭。

Xiànzài yě yǒu rén dào fàndiàn chī niányèfàn. Niányèfàn yòu jiào tuányuánfàn. Niányèfàn
现在 也 有 人 到 饭店 吃 年夜饭。 年夜饭 又 叫 团圆(7)饭。 年夜饭

shì yì nián zhōng zuì fēngshèng de yí dùn jiāyàn. Zài hěn duō měiwèi jiāyáo
是 一 年 中 最 丰盛(8) 的 一 顿 家宴。 在 很 多 美味 佳肴(9)

zhōng yídìngyǒu yì pán yú. Zhè jiào "niánniányǒuyú". Yīnwèi "yú" hé "yú" tóngyīn,
中 一定有 一 盘 鱼。 这 叫 "年年有余(10)"。 因为 "鱼" 和 "余" 同音,

"niánniányǒuyú" jiù shì xīwàng láinián shēnghuó fùyù de yìsi. Chīwán niányèfàn,
"年年有余(10)" 就 是 希望 来年(11) 生活 富裕(12) 的 意思。 吃完 年夜饭,

quánjiā rén yìbiān liáotiān yìbiān děngzhe xīnnián de dàolái. Zhè jiào "shǒusuì".
全家 人 一边 聊天 一边 等着 新年 的 到来。 这 叫 "守岁"。

Xīnnián yí dào, wúlùn zài chéngshì háishi xiāngcūn, dōu xiǎngqǐ biānpàoshēng, yǒu-
新年 一 到, 无论 在 城市 还是 乡村, 都 响起(13) 鞭炮声, 有

de chéngshì hái fàng yànhuǒ, shǐ jiérì de tiānkōng gèngjiā měilì. Dànshì wèile
的 城市 还 放 焰火(14), 使 节日 的 天空 更加 美丽。 但是 为了

jiǎnshǎo wūrǎn hé yìwài shìgù, xiànzài yǒude chéngshì jìnzhǐ fàng biānpào le.
减少(15) 污染(16) 和 意外 事故, 现在 有的 城市 禁止 放 鞭炮 了。

Xīnnián li, dàrén yào gěi xiǎohái yāsuìqián. Guònián de shíhou zuì gāoxìng de
新年 里, 大人 要 给 小孩 压岁钱(17)。 过年 的 时候 最 高兴 的

shì xiǎoháizi, yīnwèi guò xīnnián yǒu hěn duō hǎochī de, yòu yǒu xīn yīfu chuān,
是 小孩子, 因为 过 新年 有 很 多 好吃 的, 又 有 新 衣服 穿,

yòu néng nádào yāsuìqián.
又 能 拿到 压岁钱。

Xīnnián de dì-yī tiān jiào "niánchūyī". Cóng
新年 的 第一 天 叫 "年初一"。 从

niánchūyī dào niánchūwǔ, dàjiā chuāndài zhěngqí,
年初一 到 年初五, 大家 穿戴 整齐(18),

dào qīnqi péngyou jiā bàinián. Dàjiā jiànmiàn de
到 亲戚 朋友 家 拜年(19)。 大家 见面 的

shíhou dōu shuō "gōngxǐ! gōngxǐ!" huò "xīnnián hǎo!"
时候 都 说 "恭喜! 恭喜!" 或 "新年 好!"

Chūn Jié shì Zhōngguórén zuì lóngzhòng de
春节 是 中国人 最 隆重(20) 的

jiérì.
节日。

☆ 词 语 ☆

1. 家家户户 jiājiā-hùhù （名） every family
2. 大扫除 dàsǎochú （动） general cleaning
3. 年货 niánhuò （名） special purchases for the Spring Festival
4. 过年 guònián （动） celebrate the Spring Festival
5. 大年夜 dàniányè （名） lunar New Year's Eve
6. 团聚 tuánjù （动） reunite
7. 团圆 tuányuán （动） reunite
8. 丰盛 fēngshèng （形） sumptuous
9. 美味佳肴 měiwèi jiāyáo delicious food
10. 余 yú （动） surplus
11. 来年 láinián （名） next year
12. 富裕 fùyù （形） rich
13. 响起 xiǎngqi sound
14. 放焰火 fàng yànhuǒ set off fireworks
15. 减少 jiǎnshǎo （动） reduce
16. 污染 wūrǎn （动） pollute
17. 压岁钱 yāsuìqián （名） money given to children as a lunar New Year gift
18. 穿戴整齐 chuāndài zhěngqí dress formally
19. 拜年 bàinián （动） pay a New Year call
20. 隆重 lóngzhòng （形） grand, important

2 端午节

THE DRAGON BOAT FESTIVAL

Nónglì wǔ yuè chūwǔ shì Duānwǔ Jié. Zhè shì jìniàn Qū Yuán de jiérì. Qū
农历 五 月 初五 是 端午 节。 这 是 纪念 屈 原 的 节日。 屈

Yuán shì liǎngqiān nián qián Chǔguó de guānyuán, yě shì zhùmíng de shīrén. Tā
原 是 两千 年 前 楚国 的 官员(1), 也 是 著名 的 诗人。 他

hěn rè'ài zìjǐ de guójiā, tíchū liánhé bié de xiǎo guó dǐkàng Qínguó. Dànshì
很 热爱(2) 自己 的 国家, 提出 联合(3) 别 的 小 国 抵抗(4) 秦国。 但是

guójūn tīngle xiǎorén de chányán, bú xìnrèn tā, bǎ tā gǎnchule guódū. Hòulái
国君(5) 听了 小人(6) 的 谗言(7), 不 信任(8) 他, 把 他 赶出(9) 了 国都(10)。 后来

guódū bèi Qínguó gōngpò le. Qū Yuán hěn shāngxīn, jiù tóu Mìluó Jiāng zìshā
国都 被 秦国 攻破(11) 了。 屈 原 很 伤心(12), 就 投(13) 汨罗 江 自杀(14)

le. Chǔguó de bǎixìng huázhe chuán yán jiāng dǎlāo Qū Yuán de shītǐ.
了。 楚国 的 百姓(15) 划(16) 着 船 沿(17) 江 打捞(18) 屈 原 的 尸体(19)。

Yǒude rén yòng ruòyè bāozhe mǐfàn rēngjìn jiāng li jìdiàn tā. Hòulái mànman
有的 人 用 箬叶(20) 包(21)着 米饭 扔进(22) 江 里 祭奠(23) 他。 后来 慢慢

de xíngchéngle xísú, Duānwǔ Jié zhè tiān jǔxíng lóngzhōu bǐsài, yòng ruòyè bāo
地 形成了 习俗(24), 端午 节 这 天 举行(25) 龙舟 比赛, 用 箬叶 包

zòngzi chī.
粽子(26) 吃。

Zòngzi de cáiliào zhǔyào shì nuòmǐ, yòng ruòyè bāozhe, zài yòng xiàn
粽子 的 材料(27) 主要 是 糯米(28), 用 箬叶 包着, 再 用 线(29)

zājǐn. Yǒude zài nuòmǐ zhōng jiā ròu, wèidao xián, jiào "ròuzòng". Yǒude jiā
扎紧(30)。 有的 在 糯米 中 加(31) 肉, 味道 咸, 叫 "肉粽"。 有的 加

hóngdòu huò dòushā, jiào "hóngdòuzòng". Yǒude shénme yě bù jiā, jiào "báizòng",
红豆(32) 或 豆沙(33), 叫 "红豆粽"。 有的 什么 也 不 加, 叫 "白粽",

chī de shíhou zhàn táng. Xiànzài bùjǐn Duānwǔ Jié chī zòngzi, érqiě píngshí
吃 的 时候 蘸(34) 糖。 现在 不仅 端午 节 吃 粽子, 而且 平时(35)

shāngdiàn li yě yǒu zòngzi mài.
商店 里 也 有 粽子 卖。

☆　词　语　☆

1.	guānyuán 官员	（名）	official	2.	rè'ài 热爱	（动）	love
3.	liánhé 联合	（动）	unite	4.	dǐkàng 抵抗	（动）	resist
5.	guójūn 国君	（名）	king	6.	xiǎorén 小人	（名）	a mean man, a base person
7.	chányán 谗言	（名）	slander, calumniation	8.	xìnrèn 信任	（动）	trust
9.	gǎnchu 赶出		expel, drive away	10.	guódū 国都	（名）	capital
11.	gōngpò 攻破	（动）	make a breakthrough	12.	shāngxīn 伤心	（形）	heartbroken
13.	tóu(jiāng) 投（江）	（动）	drown oneself in a river	14.	zìshā 自杀	（动）	commit suicide
15.	bǎixìng 百姓	（名）	common people	16.	huá 划	（动）	row
17.	yán 沿	（介）	along	18.	dǎlāo 打捞	（动）	get out of the water
19.	shītǐ 尸体	（名）	body, corpse	20.	ruòyè 箬叶	（名）	leaves of bamboo or reed
21.	bāo 包	（动）	wrap	22.	rēngjìn 扔进		throw something into
23.	jìdiàn 祭奠	（动）	hold a memorial ceremony for	24.	xísú 习俗	（名）	custom
25.	jǔxíng 举行	（动）	hold (a meeting, ceremony, etc.)	26.	zòngzi 粽子	（名）	*zongzi* (a pyramid shaped dumpling)
27.	cáiliào 材料	（名）	material	28.	nuòmǐ 糯米	（名）	glutinous rice
29.	xiàn 线	（名）	string, thread	30.	zājǐn 扎紧		tie
31.	jiā 加	（动）	add	32.	hóngdòu 红豆	（名）	red bean
33.	dòushā 豆沙	（名）	bean paste	34.	zhàn 蘸	（动）	dip in
35.	píngshí 平时	（名）	ordinarily				

3

Zhōngqiū Jié
中秋 节

THE MID – AUTUMN FESTIVAL

Nónglì bā yuè shíwǔ rì shì Zhōngqiū Jié. Ànzhào Zhōngguó de nónglì, qī、bā、jiǔ
农历 八 月 十五 日 是 中秋 节。 按照 中国 的 农历, 七、八、九

yuè shì qiūjì, bā yuè shíwǔ zhènghǎo zài qiūjì de zhōngjiān, suǒyǐ jiào Zhōngqiū Jié.
月 是 秋季, 八 月 十五 正好 在 秋季 的 中间, 所以 叫 中秋 节。

Zhōngqiū Jié shǎngyuè shì Zhōngguó rénmín de yí ge chuántǒng xísú. Zhōngqiū Jié de
中秋 节 赏月(1) 是 中国 人民 的 一 个 传统(2) 习俗。 中秋 节 的

wǎnshang, quánjiā rén zuòzài yìqǐ, yìbiān chī yuèbing、 huāshēng、 yùnǎi、 shuǐguǒ,
晚上, 全家 人 坐在 一起, 一边 吃 月饼(3)、 花生、 芋艿(4)、 水果,

yìbiān shǎngyuè. Zhè shíhou qiūgāo-qìshuǎng, yuèliang yòu dà yòu yuán yòu liàng.
一边 赏月。 这 时候 秋高气爽(5), 月亮 又 大 又 圆(6) 又 亮(7)。

Rénmen chángcháng huì xiǎngqi Cháng'é bèn yuè de gùshi, hǎoxiàng kàndào yuèliang
人们 常常 会 想起(8) 嫦娥 奔 月 的 故事, 好像 看到 月亮

shang de Guǎnghángōng, kàndào Cháng'é zài guìshù xiàmian bàozhe xiǎo báitù
上 的 广寒宫, 看到 嫦娥 在 桂树(9) 下面 抱(10)着 小 白兔(11)

zhèng wàngzhe rénjiān ne.
正 望(12)着 人间 呢。

Yuèbing shì Zhōngqiū Jié bìbùkěshǎo de shípǐn. Yuèbing zhǔyào yǒu liǎng zhǒng:
月饼 是 中秋 节 必不可少(13) 的 食品。 月饼 主要(14) 有 两 种:

yì zhǒng shì guǎngshì, yánsè bǐjiào shēn; yì zhǒng shì sūshì, yánsè bǐjiào qiǎn.
一 种 是 广式(15), 颜色 比较 深; 一 种 是 苏式, 颜色 比较 浅。

Yuèbing de xiànr yǒu gè shì gè yàng de, bǐrú guǎngshì de yǒu yēróng、
月饼 的 馅儿(16) 有 各式各样 的, 比如(17) 广式 的 有 椰(18)蓉(19)、

liánróng、 dòushā、 huǒtuǐ、 xiándànhuáng děngděng. Sūshì de xiǎnròu yuèbing hěn yǒumíng.
莲(20)蓉、 豆沙、 火腿、 咸蛋黄(21) 等等。 苏式 的 鲜肉 月饼 很 有名。

Yuèbing shì yuán de, hé tiānshang
月饼 是 圆 的, 和 天上

de yuèliang yíyàng, xiàngzhēng
的 月亮 一样, 象征(22)

tuányuán.
团圆。

Zhōngqiū Jié shì tuányuán de
中秋 节 是 团圆 的

jiérì.
节日。

☆　词　语　☆

1. shǎngyuè
赏月　　enjoy a beautiful full moon

2. chuántǒng
传统　（形）traditional

3. yuèbing
月饼　（名）moon cake

4. yùnǎi
芋艿　（名）taro

5. qiūgāo-qìshuǎng
秋高气爽　"autumn high and air brisk"—— clear sky and crisp air in autumn

6. yuán
圆　（形）round, full（for moon）

7. liàng
亮　（形）bright

8. xiǎngqi
想起　remember, call to mind

9. guìshù
桂树　（名）osmanthus

10. bào
抱　（动）carry in arms

11. báitù
白兔　（名）white rabbit

12. wàng
望　（动）look at

13. bìbùkěshǎo
必不可少　absolutely necessary, indispensable

14. zhǔyào
主要　（形）mainly

15. shì
式　（名）style

16. xiànr
馅儿　（名）stuffing

17. bǐrú
比如　（动）for example

18. yē
椰　（名）coconut

19. róng
蓉　（名）mashed fruit or seeds

20. lián
莲　（名）lotus, lotus seed

21. xiándànhuáng
咸蛋黄　（名）yolk of salted egg

22. xiàngzhēng
象征　（动）symbolize

4 嫦娥 奔月 (1) CHANG'E FLEW TO THE MOON

Cháng'é Bèn Yuè

很 久 以前(2)，天上 有 十 个 太阳。人们 热 得 受不了。有 一
个 叫 羿 的 人，射(3) 下来 九 个 太阳。人间 的 天气 好多 了。羿
成了 英雄。他 有 个 美丽 的 妻子，叫 嫦娥。

有 一 天，羿 照 镜子 的 时候，发现(4) 自己 有了 白 头发，很 苦恼(5)。
他 听说 住在 昆仑 山 上 的 西王母 有 仙药(6)。于是 他 经历(7) 了
千辛万苦(8) 来到 昆仑 山，找到 西王母。

西王母 知道 他 是 射 日 英雄，就 给了 他 一 粒 药，说："这 粒
药 只 吃 一半 就 能 长生不老(9)。" 羿 想：我 和 嫦娥 一 人 吃
一半，那么 我们 两 人 都 不 会 死 了。羿 回到 家 里 高高兴兴
地 把 这 件 事 告诉 嫦娥，然后(10) 他 把 药 给 嫦娥，让 她 先
咬(11) 一半。可是 嫦娥 不 小心(12) 把 药 全 吞 下去(13) 了。突然(14)，她 的
身体 变 得 轻飘飘(15) 的，从 窗口 飞(16) 了 出去。她 的 小 白兔
向 上 一 跳(17)，咬住了 她 的 裙子，也 一起 飞 向 天空。她们 飞
呀，飞 呀，一直 飞到 月亮 上。从此(18) 嫦娥 就 住在 广寒宫
里。小 白兔 陪伴(19) 着 她。天气
晴朗(20) 的 晚上，人们 会 看到
在 广寒宫 前面 的 桂树 下，
嫦娥 抱着 小 白兔 正 深情(21)
地 望着 人间。

405

☆　词　语　☆

1. bèn yuè
奔　月　　　　　　fly to the moon

2. hěn jiǔ yǐqián
很　久　以前　　a long time ago

3. shè
射　　　　（动）　shoot

4. fāxiàn
发现　　（动）　find

5. kǔnǎo
苦恼　　（形）　worried, vexed

6. xiānyào
仙药　　（名）　magic drug

7. jīnglì
经历　　（动）　undergo

8. qiānxīn-wànkǔ
千辛万苦　　unnumerable hard-ships

9. chángshēng-bùlǎo
长生不老　　perpetual rejuvenation

10. ránhòu
然后　　（连）　then

11. yǎo
咬　　　（动）　bite

12. bù xiǎoxīn
不　小心　　inattentively

13. tūn xiaqu
吞　下去　　swallow down

14. tūrán
突然　　（副）　suddenly

15. qīngpiāopiāo
轻飘飘　（形）　light

16. fēi
飞　　　（动）　fly

17. tiào
跳　　　（动）　jump

18. cóngcǐ
从此　　（副）　since then

19. péibàn
陪伴　　（动）　accompany

20. qínglǎng
晴朗　　（形）　clear

21. shēnqíng
深情　　（形）　with deep feeling, affectionately

5 说谎(1) 的 孩子 THE CHILD WHO LIED

Shuōhuǎng de Háizi

Wáng Xiǎo'èr gǎnzhe yángqún shàng shāngāng. Tā juéde wúliáo, jiù xiàng shān
王 小二 赶(2)着 羊群(3) 上 山冈(4)。 他 觉得 无聊(5)，就 向 山

xia dàhǎn: "Láng lái le! Láng lái le!"
下 大喊(6)："狼 来 了! 狼 来 了!"

Cūn li de rén tīngjian le, jímáng názhe gùnzi pǎoshang shān lai. Dànshì
村 里 的 人 听见 了， 急忙(7) 拿着 棍子(8) 跑(9)上 山 来。 但是

shān shang gēnběn méiyǒu láng.
山 上 根本(10) 没有 狼。

Jǐ tiān yǐhòu, Wáng Xiǎo'èr yòu dàjiào: "Láng lái le!" Rénmen yòu pǎoshang
几 天 以后， 王 小二 又 大叫："狼 来 了!" 人们 又 跑上

shān lai. Tāmen yòu shàngdàng le.
山 来。 他们 又 上当(11) 了。

Hòulái yǒu yì tiān, láng zhēn de lái le.
后来 有 一 天， 狼 真 的 来 了。

Wáng Xiǎo'èr xià de pīnmìng jiàohǎn: "Láng lái
王 小二 吓(12) 得 拼命(13) 叫喊："狼 来

le! Jiùmìng! Jiùmìng!" Kěshì cūn li de rén shuí
了! 救命(14)! 救命!" 可是 村 里 的 人 谁

yě bù lǐcǎi tā le.
也 不 理睬(15) 他 了。

☆ 词 语 ☆

1.	shuōhuǎng 说谎	(动)	lie	2.	gǎn 赶	(动)	tend (a herd)
3.	yángqún 羊群	(名)	a flock of sheep	4.	shāngāng 山冈	(名)	hill
5.	wúliáo 无聊	(形)	bored	6.	dàhǎn 大喊	(动)	cry out
7.	jímáng 急忙	(副)	in a hurry	8.	gùnzi 棍子	(名)	rod, stick
9.	pǎo 跑	(动)	run	10.	gēnběn 根本	(副)	at all
11.	shàngdàng 上当	(动)	be fooled	12.	xià 吓	(动)	scare
13.	pīnmìng 拼命	(副)	with all one's might	14.	jiùmìng 救命	(动)	Help!
15.	bù lǐcǎi 不 理睬		pay no attention				

6 一 把 筷子 A BUNCH OF CHOPSTICKS

Yì Bǎ Kuàizi

Yì jiā rénjiā yǒu jǐ ge háizi. Xiōngdì jǐ ge yí jiànmiàn jiù chǎojià. Yǒu yì
一 家 人家(1) 有 几 个 孩子。 兄弟 几 个 一 见面 就 吵架(2)。 有 一
tiān, bàba nálai yì bǎ kuàizi shuō: "Nǐmen shìshi zhéduàn tā." Kěshì xiōngdì jǐ ge
天, 爸爸 拿来 一 把 筷子 说: "你们 试试 折(3)断(4) 它。" 可是 兄弟 几 个
shuí yě zhé bu duàn. Bàba bǎ kuàizi
谁 也 折 不 断。 爸爸 把 筷子
chāisǎn, měi rén gěi yì gēn, shuō:
拆散(5), 每 人 给 一 根(6), 说:
"Nǐmen zài shìshi." Zhè cì tāmen yì zhé
"你们 再 试试。" 这 次 他们 一 折
kuàizi jiù duàn le. Bàba shuō: "Yì gēn
筷子 就 断 了。 爸爸 说: "一 根
kuàizi róngyì zhéduàn, dànshì yì bǎ kuàizi
筷子 容易 折断, 但是 一 把 筷子
jiù hěn nán zhéduàn. Nǐmen yǐhòu búyào
就 很 难 折断。 你们 以后 不要
chǎojià le. Tuánjié qilai cái yǒu lìliàng."
吵架 了。 团结(7) 起来 才 有 力量(8)。"

☆ 词 语 ☆

	rénjiā				chǎojià	
1.	人家	（名）family		2.	吵架	（动）quarrel
	zhé				duàn	
3.	折	（动）break, fracture		4.	断	（动）break
	chāisǎn				gēn	
5.	拆散	（动）break apart, disassemble		6.	根	（量）piece
	tuánjié				lìliàng	
7.	团结	（动）unite		8.	力量	（名）strength, force

7

Zìxiāng-máodùn
自相矛盾
CONTRADICT ONESELF

Yǒu yí ge mài máo hé dùn de rén, zài shìchǎng shang bǎikāi tā de tānzi.
有 一个 卖 矛(1) 和 盾(2) 的 人，在 市场 上 摆开(3) 他 的 摊子(4)。

Kěshì kàn de rén duō, mǎi de rén shǎo. Yúshì tā náqi yí kuài dùnpái shuō: "Zhè
可是 看 的 人 多，买 的 人 少。于是(5) 他 拿起 一 块 盾牌 说："这

dùnpái kě jiāngù le, shénme ruìlì de wǔqì dōu bù néng chuōchuān tā." Guòle
盾牌 可 坚固(6) 了，什么 锐利(7) 的 武器(8) 都 不 能 戳穿(9) 它。" 过了

yíhuìr, tā yòu náqi yì zhī máo shuō: "Zhè shì wǒ jīngxīn zhìzuò de máo,
一会儿，他 又 拿起 一 支(10) 矛 说："这 是 我 精心(11) 制作(12) 的 矛，

shénme dùn dōu dǎngbuzhù tā."
什么 盾 都 挡不住(13) 它。"

Wéiguān de rén zhōng, yǒu yí ge rén shuō: "Rúguǒ yòng nǐ de máo chuō nǐ de
围观(14) 的 人 中，有 一 个 人 说："如果 用 你 的 矛 戳 你 的

dùn, jiéguǒ huì zěnmeyàng ne?"
盾，结果(15) 会 怎么样 呢?"

Mài máo hé dùn de rén yíxiàzi liǎn hóng le, shénme huà yě shuō bù chūlai.
卖 矛 和 盾 的 人 一下子(16) 脸 红 了，什么 话 也 说 不 出来。

Hòulái rénmen yòng "zìxiāng-máodùn" bǐyù yǔyán、xíngdòng qiánhòu zìxiāng
后来 人们 用 "自相矛盾" 比喻(17) 语言、行动 前后 自相

dǐchù.
抵触(18)。

☆　词　语　☆

1. máo
矛　　　（名）　spear, lance

2. dùn(pái)
盾(牌)　　（名）　shield

3. bǎikāi
摆开　　　（动）　set up

4. tānzi
摊子　　　（名）　stall

5. yúshì
于是　　　（连）　so

6. jiāngù
坚固　　　（形）　sturdy, strong

7. ruìlì
锐利　　　（形）　sharp

8. wǔqì
武器　　　（名）　weapon

9. chuōchuān
戳穿　　　（动）　pierce

10. zhī
支　　　（量）　piece

11. jīngxīn
精心　　　（形）　meticulous or elaborate

12. zhìzuò
制作　　　（动）　make, manufacture

13. dǎngbuzhù
挡不住　　　can not resist, can not shield

14. wéiguān
围观　　　（动）　surround and watch

15. jiéguǒ
结果　　　（连）　result

16. yíxiàzi
一下子　　　（副）　all of a sudden

17. bǐyù
比喻　　　（动）　metaphor

18. dǐchù
抵触　　　（动）　contradict

8 守(1) 株(2) 待(3) 兔

Shǒuzhū-dàitù

STAND BY A STUMP WAITING FOR MORE HARES TO COME

Gǔ shíhou yǒu yí ge nóngfū, yǒu yì tiān tā zhèngzài dì li gànhuór. Tūrán
古 时候 有 一 个 农夫(4)，有 一 天 他 正在 地(5) 里 干活儿(6)。 突然

yì zhī yětù cuānle chūlai, zhuàngzài dìbiān de shùgēn shang, sǐle. Nóngfū jímáng
一 只 野(7)兔 蹿(8)了 出来， 撞(9)在 地边 的 树根(10) 上， 死了。 农夫 急忙

rēngxia nóngjù, pǎodào shù xià jiǎnqi nà zhī yětù. Tā bú zài gànhuór le. Názhe
扔下 农具(11)， 跑到 树 下 捡起(12) 那 只 野兔。 他 不 再 干活儿 了。拿着

yětù huíle jiā. Nà tiān wǎnshang tā měiměi de
野兔 回了 家。 那 天 晚上 他 美美(13) 地

chīle yí dùn.
吃了 一 顿。

Cóngcǐ yǐhòu, tā měi tiān zuòzài dàshù pángbiān,
从此 以后， 他 每 天 坐在 大树 旁边，

xīwàng zài yǒu tùzi cuān chulai. Tā děng a, děng
希望 再 有 兔子 蹿 出来。 他 等 啊， 等

a, kěshì zài yě méiyǒu kàndào tùzi. Tā de dì li
啊， 可是 再 也 没有 看到 兔子。 他 的 地 里

zhǎngmǎnle yěcǎo.
长满了 野草。

☆ 词 语 ☆

1. 守 shǒu （动） stand by
2. 株 zhū （名） trunk, stump
3. 待 dài （动） wait
4. 农夫 nóngfū （名） peasant, farmer
5. 地 dì （名） fields
6. 干活儿 gànhuór work
7. 野 yě （形） wild
8. 蹿 cuān （动） leap
9. 撞 zhuàng （动） hit
10. 树根 shùgēn （名） stump
11. 农具 nóngjù （名） farming tools
12. 捡起 jiǎnqi pick up
13. 美美 měiměi （副） with great satisfaction

9

Huàshé-tiānzú
画蛇(1) 添(2) 足(3)

DRAW A SNAKE AND ADD FEET TO IT

Gǔ shíhou yǒu yí ge rén, zài bàijì zǔxiān yǐhòu, xiǎng bǎ yí dà bēi jiǔ
古 时候 有 一 个 人， 在 拜祭(4) 祖先(5) 以后， 想 把 一 大 杯 酒

shǎnggěi bàn shì de rén hē.
赏(6)给 办 事 的 人 喝。

Yǒu yí ge bàn shì de rén shuō: "Yì bēi jiǔ jǐ ge rén hē bú guòyǐn.
有 一 个 办 事 的 人 说： "一 杯 酒 几 个 人 喝 不 过瘾(7)。

Zhèyàng ba, wǒmen jǐ ge rén gè huà yì tiáo shé. Shuí xiān huàhǎo shuí jiù hē
这样 吧， 我们 几 个 人 各 画 一 条 蛇。 谁 先 画好 谁 就 喝

zhè bēi jiǔ." Dàjiā dōu zànchéng zhège bànfǎ. Yúshì gè rén jiù mǎshàng dòngshǒu.
这 杯 酒。" 大家 都 赞成(8) 这个 办法。 于是 各 人 就 马上 动手(9)。

Yǒu yí ge rén xiān huàhǎo le. Tā náqi nà bēi
有 一 个 人 先 画好 了。 他 拿起 那 杯

jiǔ, zhèng xiǎng hē, zhè shí tā déyì de xiǎng:
酒， 正 想 喝， 这 时 他 得意(10)地 想：

wǒ zài gěi shé tiānshang jiǎo. Dāng tā huà shéjiǎo
我 再 给 蛇 添上 脚。 当 他 画 蛇脚

de shíhou, lìng yí ge rén yě huàhǎole shé, duóguo
的 时候， 另 一 个 人 也 画好了 蛇， 夺(11)过

nà bēi jiǔ shuō: "Nǐ huà de bú shì shé, zhè bēi
那 杯 酒 说： "你 画 的 不 是 蛇， 这 杯

jiǔ gāi wǒ hē."
酒 该 我 喝。"

☆ 词 语 ☆

1. 蛇 shé	（名）	snake	2. 添 tiān	（动）	add
3. 足 zú	（名）	foot	4. 拜祭 bàijì	（动）	hold a memorial ceremony for
5. 祖先 zǔxiān	（名）	ancestors	6. 赏 shǎng	（动）	reward
7. 过瘾 guòyǐn	（形）	enjoy oneself to the full	8. 赞成 zànchéng	（动）	agree
9. 动手 dòngshǒu	（动）	start to work	10. 得意 déyì	（形）	proud
11. 夺 duó	（动）	seize			

10

Tiěchǔ-chéngzhēn
铁杵(1) 成针(2)

GRIND AN IRON
ROD INTO A NEEDLE

Tángcháo yǒu ge dà shīrén jiào Lǐ Bái. Tā xiǎo shíhou hěn tānwán, bù
唐朝 有 个 大 诗人 叫 李 白。他 小 时候 很 贪玩(3)，不

zhuānxīn xuéxí. Yǒu yì tiān, tā diūxia shūběn pǎodào xiǎoxī biān wán. Tā kànjian
专心(4) 学习。有 一 天，他 丢下(5) 书本 跑到 小溪(6) 边 玩。他 看见

yí ge lǎopópo názhe yì gēn tiěbàng zài shítou shang mó. Lǐ Bái juéde hěn
一 个 老婆婆(7) 拿着 一 根 铁棒(8) 在 石头 上 磨(9)。李 白 觉得 很

qíguài, zǒushang qián wèn: "Lǎopópo, nín zài gàn shénme ya?"
奇怪(10)，走上 前 问："老婆婆，您 在 干 什么 呀？"

Lǎopópo yìbiān bùtíng de mó yìbiān huídá shuō: "Wǒ yào bǎ tiěbàng móchéng
老婆婆 一边 不停 地(11) 磨 一边 回答 说："我 要 把 铁棒 磨成

yì gēn zhēn."
一 根 针。"

Lǐ Bái chījīng de shuō: "Zhè yào módào shénme shíhou?"
李 白 吃惊(12) 地 说："这 要 磨到 什么 时候？"

Lǎopópo xiàozhe shuō: "Zhǐyào wǒ tiāntiān mó, zǒng huì yǒu chénggōng de yì tiān."
老婆婆 笑着 说："只要 我 天天 磨，总 会 有 成功 的 一 天。"

Lǐ Bái tīngle yǐhòu, bú zài wán le. Tā mǎshàng bēnhuí jiā, náqi shūběn,
李 白 听了 以后，不 再 玩 了。他 马上 奔(13)回 家，拿起 书本，

yònggōng de xuéxí.
用功 地 学习。

☆ 词 语 ☆

1. 杵 chǔ	（名）	rod	
2. 针 zhēn	（名）	needle	
3. 贪玩 tānwán		be too fond of playing	
4. 专心 zhuānxīn	（形）	whole-hearted, attentive	
5. 丢下 diūxia	（动）	put aside	
6. 小溪 xiǎoxī	（名）	brook	
7. 老婆婆 lǎopópo	（名）	old woman	
8. 棒 bàng	（名）	rod, stick, bar	
9. 磨 mó	（动）	grind	
10. 奇怪 qíguài	（形）	strange	
11. 不停地 bùtíng de		continuously	
12. 吃惊 chījīng	（动）	be shocked, be surprised	
13. 奔 bēn	（动）	run	

11 练字 的 秘诀(1)

Liànzì de Mìjué

THE SECRET OF PRACTICING CALLIGRAPHY

Jìncháo shūfǎ dàjiā Wáng Xīzhī yǒu yí ge érzi jiào Wáng Xiànzhī. Wáng Xiànzhī yě
晋朝 书法(2) 大家(3) 王 羲之 有 一 个 儿子 叫 王 献之。 王 献之 也

xǐhuan shūfǎ, xīwàng zìjǐ yě chéngwéi xiàng fùqīn nàyàng de shūfǎjiā.
喜欢 书法, 希望 自己 也 成为(4) 像(5) 父亲 那样 的 书法家。

Yǒu yì tiān, tā wèn mǔqīn: "Liànzì yǒu shénme mìjué?"
有 一 天, 他 问 母亲: "练字 有 什么 秘诀?"

Tā mǔqīn mōzhe tā de tóu shuō: "Yǒu de, nǐ gēn wǒ lái." Ránhòu lāqi Xiànzhī
他 母亲 摸(6)着 他 的 头 说: "有 的, 你 跟 我 来。" 然后 拉起(7) 献之

de xiǎo shǒu zǒudào hòuyuàn. Xiànzhī kànjian hòuyuàn páilièzhe shíbā ge shuǐgāng, gāng li
的 小 手 走到 后院(8)。 献之 看见 后院 排列着 十八 个 水缸(9), 缸 里

chéngmǎn yǔshuǐ. Mǔqīn zhǐzhe nàxiē gāng shuō: "Liànzì de mìjué jiù zài zhè shíbā ge
盛满(10) 雨水。 母亲 指(11)着 那些 缸 说: "练字 的 秘诀 就 在 这 十八 个

shuǐgāng li." Xiànzhī gǎndào hěn qíguài. Zhè shí mǔqīn hěn rènzhēn de shuō: "Rúguǒ nǐ
水缸 里。" 献之 感到(12) 很 奇怪。 这 时 母亲 很 认真(13) 地 说: "如果 你

měi tiān yòng gāng zhōng de shuǐ mó mò liànzì, děng nǐ bǎ zhè shíbā gāng shuǐ yòngwán,
每 天 用 缸 中 的 水 磨 墨 练字, 等 你 把 这 十八 缸 水 用完,

jiù zhīdao xiězì de mìjué le."
就 知道 写字 的 秘诀 了。"

Xiànzhī dītóu xiǎngle yíhuìr, zhōngyú míngbai le. Cóng zhè yǐhòu tā měi tiān
献之 低头(14) 想了 一会儿, 终于(15) 明白 了。 从 这 以后 他 每 天

qínfèn de xuéxí, yòngxīn de liànzì. Shuǐgāng li de shuǐ yuèláiyuè shǎo, tā de zì xiě de
勤奋(16) 地 学习, 用心(17) 地 练字。 水缸 里 的 水 越来越 少, 他 的 字 写 得

yuèláiyuè hǎo le. Hòulái Wáng Xiànzhī yě chéngle yí wèi yǒumíng de shūfǎjiā.
越来越 好 了。 后来 王 献之 也 成了 一 位 有名 的 书法家。

☆ 词 语 ☆

1. 秘诀 mìjué	（名）	secret	
2. 书法 shūfǎ	（名）	calligraphy	
3. 大家 dàjiā	（名）	great master	
4. 成为 chéngwéi	（动）	become	
5. 像 xiàng	（动）	be like	
6. 摸 mō	（动）	stroke, feel	
7. 拉起 lāqi		hold (hand)	
8. 后院 hòuyuàn	（名）	backyard	
9. 水缸 shuǐgāng	（名）	vat	
10. 盛满 chéngmǎn		fill	
11. 指 zhǐ	（动）	point	
12. 感到 gǎndào	（动）	feel	
13. 认真 rènzhēn	（形）	serious, earnest	
14. 低头 dītóu	（动）	hang or bow one's head	
15. 终于 zhōngyú	（副）	finally	
16. 勤奋 qínfèn	（形）	diligent, hardworking	
17. 用心 yòngxīn	（形）	diligent, attentive	

12 砸(1)缸救人(2)
Zá Gāng Jiù Rén

SMASH THE VAT TO RESCUE A CHILD

Sīmǎ Guāng shì Sòngcháo de lìshǐxuéjiā. Tā xiǎo shíhou chángcháng hé xiǎopéngyǒu yìqǐ
司马 光 是 宋朝 的 历史学家。他 小 时候 常常 和 小朋友 一起

wán. Yǒu yì tiān zhuōmícáng de shíhou, yí ge xiǎopéngyǒu bù xiǎoxīn diàodào dà shuǐgāng
玩。 有 一 天 捉迷藏(3) 的 时候, 一 个 小朋友 不 小心 掉到(4) 大 水缸

li qu le. Qítā de xiǎopéngyǒu dōu huāng le, yǒude jiào, yǒude kū, yǒude wǎng wài
里 去 了。其他(5) 的 小朋友 都 慌(6) 了, 有的 叫, 有的 哭, 有的 往 外

pǎo. Zhè shí Sīmǎ Guāng méiyǒu huāng, tā zhèndìng de cóng dì shang bānqi yí kuài dà
跑。 这 时 司马 光 没有 慌, 他 镇定(7) 地 从 地 上 搬起(8) 一 块 大

shítou, shuāngshǒu jǔqi shǐjìnr zá nàge gāng. Shuǐgāng bèi shítou zápò le. Gāng li
石头, 双手(9) 举起(10) 使劲儿(11) 砸 那个 缸。 水缸 被 石头 砸破 了。 缸 里

de shuǐ cóng pòdòng zhōng liú chulai le. Zài gāng li de xiǎopéngyǒu déjiù le. Zhè shí
的 水 从 破洞(12) 中 流 出来 了。在 缸 里 的 小朋友 得救(13) 了。这 时

dàrénmen yě pǎolai le. Dàjiā dōu chēngzàn Sīmǎ Guāng. Yǒu rén shuō: "Zhè háizi zhēn
大人们 也 跑来 了。大家 都 称赞(14) 司马 光。 有 人 说:"这 孩子 真

jīling." Yǒu rén shuō: "Zhè háizi dǎnzi dà." Yǒu rén shuō: "Zhè háizi lìqi dà."
机灵(15)。" 有 人 说:" 这 孩子 胆子 大(16)。" 有 人 说:"这 孩子 力气(17) 大。"

Nàge déjiù de háizi de bàba māma duì Sīmǎ Guāng gèng shì gǎnjī bú jìn.
那个 得救 的 孩子 的 爸爸 妈妈 对 司马 光 更 是 感激 不 尽(18)。

☆ 词 语 ☆

1. zá
砸 （动） smash

2. jiù rén
救 人 rescue someone

3. zhuōmícáng
捉迷藏 play hide and seek

4. diàodào
掉到 fall into

5. qítā
其他 （代） other

6. huāng
慌 （形） in panic

7. zhèndìng
镇定 （形） calm

8. bānqi
搬起 lift

9. shuāngshǒu
双手 （名） both bands

10. jǔqi
举起 lift up

11. shǐjìnr
使劲儿 （动） use all strength

12. dòng
洞 （名） hole

13. déjiù
得救 （动） be saved

14. chēngzàn
称赞 （动） praise

15. jīling
机灵 （形） smart

16. dǎnzi dà
胆子 大 bold

17. lìqi
力气 （名） strength

18. gǎnjī bú jìn
感激 不 尽 be deeply grateful

13 Míyǔ 谜语 RIDDLES

1. 　一个红脸老公公，
　　晴天站在天空中。
　　下雨刮风不见面，
　　傍晚回到西山中。

☆ 词 语 ☆

qíngtiān 晴天	（名）	fine day
guā(fēng) 刮（风）	（动）	(of wind) blow
bàngwǎn 傍晚	（名）	dusk

提示: 自然现象

2. 　有时落在山腰，
　　有时挂在树梢。
　　有时像个圆盘，
　　有时像只香蕉。

☆ 词 语 ☆

shānyāo 山腰	（名）	halfway up the mountain
shùshāo 树梢	（名）	tree-top

提示: 自然现象

3.　千条线,万条线,
　　落到河里看不见。

☆　**词　语**　☆

xiàn
线　　　　　　（名）　　　　thread

提示:自然现象

4.　像糖不甜,
　　像盐不咸。
　　冬天满天飞,
　　夏天看不见。

☆　**词　语**　☆

mǎntiānfēi
满天飞　　　　　　　　flutter in the air

提示:自然现象

5.　上边有毛,
　　下边有毛,
　　中间有颗黑葡萄。

☆　**词　语**　☆

kē
颗　　　　　（量）　　　（a measure word）

提示:身体的一部分

6.　左边有一片,
　　右边有一片,
　　永远不相见。

☆　词　语　☆

piàn
片　　　　　（量）　　a flat and thin piece
yǒngyuǎn
永远　　　　（副）　　forever

提示：身体的一部分

7.　小小一把伞，
　　长在树林中，
　　要是撑开来，
　　再也收不拢。

☆　词　语　☆

chēngkāi
撑开　　　　　　　　open, unfurl
shōubulǒng
收不拢　　　　　　　can't take down（an umbrella）

提示：蔬菜

8.　紫树开紫花，
　　紫花结紫瓜，
　　紫瓜肚里有芝麻。

☆　词　语　☆

jiē
结　　　　　（动）　　bear
zhīma
芝麻　　　　（名）　　sesame seed

提示：蔬菜

谜底（Answer）：
1.太阳 2.月亮 3.雨 4.雪 5.眼睛 6.耳朵 7.蘑菇 8.茄子